The Obama Presidency

SUNY series on the Presidency: Contemporary Issues

John Kenneth White, editor

The Obama Presidency
A Preliminary Assessment

Edited by

Robert P. Watson
Jack Covarrubias
Tom Lansford
Douglas M. Brattebo

Cover photo of President Obama courtesy of iStockphoto.

Published by State University of New York Press, Albany

For information, contact State University of New York Press, Albany, NY
www.sunypress.edu

Production by Diane Ganeles
Marketing by Anne M. Valentine

Library of Congress Cataloging-in-Publication Data

The Obama presidency : a preliminary assessment / edited by Robert P.
    Watson ... [et al.].
        p. cm. — (SUNY series on the presidency: contemporary issues)
    Includes bibliographical references and index.
    ISBN 978-1-4384-4329-4 (hardcover : alk. paper)
    ISBN 978-1-4384-4328-7 (pbk.: alk. paper)
        1. United States—Politics and government—2009–   2. Obama, Barack.
I. Watson, Robert P., 1962–

    E907.O225 2012
    973.932092—dc23   2011037744

10 9 8 7 6 5 4 3 2 1

Contents

VII   Conclusion

Illustrations

Figures

Tables

Preface

Barack Obama's presidency is a pivotal one by any historical standard. It came at a time of dramatic political change in the United States and amidst a bewildering array of domestic and foreign policy crises, not the least of which were two wars he inherited from his predecessor and the worst economic conditions—record deficits, massive debt, and a deep recession—since the Great Depression that greeted him as he was sworn into office. At the same time, the tone of political discourse has been defined by hyper-partisanship and incivility. Although the United States has experienced its share of political paranoia, fear mongering, and partisan bickering, rarely has it been more emotionally charged than during the Obama years. Indeed, from the moment of Obama's inauguration, Republicans in Congress stood united in opposition to the lion's share of the president's proposals while the social media (Facebook, Twitter, YouTube, etc.), as well as countless bloggers, radio talkers, and cable television shows, were filled with relentless attacks against everything, including substantive opposition to his policies to wildly irresponsible assaults on his wife, place of birth, patriotism, and religious beliefs.

Concurrent with these challenges is the fact that Barack Obama was the first African American elected to the U.S. presidency, which adds another layer of intrigue and its own symbolic and very real challenges. But this occurrence is an event to be celebrated and considered in any analysis. Not only is the nation at a crossroads on account of this racial milestone but Obama is the highest profile American politician to come of age politically amidst revolutionary innovations in communication and information systems that are changing the nature of political campaigns and governance. While reaching and mobilizing young voters and generating new online sources of funding, the Obama presidential campaign wrote the textbook on how to employ these new technologies. Armed with his personal Blackberry and posting tweets on Twitter and video on YouTube, the president has both embraced and benefited from the Internet.

Not surprisingly, then, both Obama and his decisions have generated a lot of interest by the press, the public, and scholars. Indeed, presidents are typically the focus of a number of scholarly books and popular biographies. These usually take a few years from the end of an administration to complete, as a full rendering of a president's legacy is contingent on the ultimate outcome of his policies and decisions, and, more practically, must wait until his papers are released to the public. Although a full assessment of any presidency takes many years and a president's legacy must stand the test of time, it is beneficial to begin the conversation and assessment during his presidency. To that end, this book offers one of the first, comprehensive examinations of Barack Obama, his decisions and policies, and his presidency and administration.

In late November 2010, a scholarly conference was co-convened by the editors of this text and organized by Tom Lansford and Jack Covarrubias. Held at the University of Southern Mississippi's campus in Long Beach, it was attended by a few dozen scholars of the American presidency from throughout the United States and a few other countries. Over the course of two days, a few dozen papers were presented, roundtable discussions held, and keynotes delivered on a variety of topics pertaining to the Obama presidency. Rigorous but civil debate and an open exchange of ideas and points of analysis marked these academic sessions and continued over adult beverages and a bonfire cookout on the beautiful Gulf Coast! Over the next few months the editors and participants continued their work on the Obama presidency, fine-tuning the presentations, papers, and major points of discussion. The result was this book.

One of the objectives of this project was to produce a scholarly but highly readable book, one suitable for the professional historian and political scientist, but one that is accessible to a general audience and useful for undergraduate and graduate students. As such, the chapters are relatively short and written in a lively narrative. Another objective was to cover an array of topics that we felt defined the first two years of the Obama presidency and would continue to shape his legacy. As such, with shorter chapters we were able to cover more ground.

One of the benefits of this book is the quality of contributors. They constitute an array of dedicated scholars from such disciplines as political science, history, communication, international relations, sociology, American studies, and theology, and reflect an equally wide array of perspectives concerning Barack Obama. We wish to thank the contributors for their work on both the conference and this book and believe they were instrumental in helping us produce an objective, readable, and concise yet thorough assessment of the Obama presidency at midpoint.

We would also like to acknowledge our families and thank them for their patience during the time it took to produce this book. So, to our families—Claudia, Alessandro, and Isabella; Tracy and Savannah; Gina, Ella, and Kate; and Shannon and Freida— thank you for your continued support. Thank you also to Michael Rinella, Diane Ganeles, Anne Valentine, and the staff of SUNY Press, it was a pleasure to work with you on this book.

It will be many years before Barack Obama's legacy is fully written and we may never come to a point of agreement on his standing among presidents. However, this book is dedicated to those efforts. We hope that readers find it helpful as they both digest and weigh in on the debate surrounding Barack Obama, and that scholars find the book to be a valuable resource in determining an initial assessment of the Obama presidency.

I

Introduction

Chapter 1

Rating Presidents and Assessing Obama

Robert P. Watson

The Rating Game

Evaluating presidents is a challenging and controversial endeavor. Yet, everyone with an opinion seems to get in on the action—whether it is a group of scholars working on a book, a public opinion approval poll taken by the media, a panel of commentators on a television talk show, or a group of co-workers huddled around the office water cooler. Indeed, in America there is a natural inclination to rate and rank all things, whether it is a poll of college football's "top 25," a list of the top-grossing movies of the week, or David Letterman's comedic "top 10" list on television. With the American president being the most visible world leader and a daily focus of countless media outlets and online sources, it is perhaps unavoidable to ask the question, "How is the president doing" and to compare him to his predecessors.

Today, there are numerous opinion polls conducted by polling organizations, universities, and major media outlets examining the president's approval and disapproval numbers, major policies and speeches, and his handling of the issue of the day, and they are taken on a daily basis. As such, the public is saturated with regular assessments of the American president. However, these public polls are limited in what they offer history in terms of a president's legacy and rating. For example, C-SPAN, Gallup, and other organizations have polled the American public and asked them to

3

list their favorite presidents or the greatest presidents. Although these polls are interesting and helpful, they are also suspect. For example, recent such polls have listed John F. Kennedy ahead of George Washington and Abraham Lincoln and Ronald Reagan ahead of Theodore Roosevelt and Franklin D. Roosevelt, results no serious scholar of the American presidency would support. At the same time, one recent poll revealed that 13 percent of the public listed Bill Clinton as the top president, whereas 20 percent of the respondents felt Clinton was the worst president. It is, of course, unlikely that any president could be considered as both the best *and* worst president concurrently, and such results tend to point to the role that time plays in the ratings because the most recent three or four presidents are typically those listed at the top *and* bottom of the public's ratings (C-SPAN 2011).

Such ratings also point to the need to have professional historians and scholars of the American presidency weigh in on presidential performance. And this has been the case. Countless scholarly books and articles are produced every year on the topic and there is growing interest among both scholars and the public in presidential ratings.

History

Perhaps the first systematic and scholarly effort to rate and rank the presidents was in 1948 when noted historian, Arthur Schlesinger, surveyed a group of fifty-five of the nation's leading historians.

In his poll, Schlesinger asked the scholars to place the presidents into categories such as "great," "near great," and so on, all the way to "failure" (Schlesinger 1948). The results were published in *Life* magazine. Ever since this poll, there has been a good deal of interest in such ratings by the general public. Recognizing the fact that new information comes to light that changes how we see the presidents and their decisions, Schlesinger conducted a second poll in 1962. This time, he surveyed seventy-five leading historians (Schlesinger 1962). The results were again available to the wider public, as they were published in the *New York Times Magazine*. When John F. Kennedy, who was in office at the time of the poll, expressed strong interest in the poll (and also took satisfaction in the fact that his predecessor, Dwight Eisenhower, was not rated very highly), the popularity of the rankings, which are listed in Table 1.1, was given a boost (Schlesinger 2003).

Table 1.1. Early Ranking Polls of the Presidents

1948 Schlesinger Poll	1962 Schlesinger Poll
GREAT	GREAT
1. Lincoln	1. Lincoln
2. Washington	2. Washington
3. F. D. Roosevelt	3. F. D. Roosevelt
4. Wilson	4. Wilson
5. Jefferson	5. Jefferson
6. Jackson	6. Jackson
NEAR GREAT	NEAR GREAT
7. T. Roosevelt	7. T. Roosevelt
8. Cleveland	8. Polk
9. J. Adams	9. Truman
10. Polk	10. J. Adams
11. J.Q. Adams	11. Cleveland
AVERAGE	AVERAGE
12. Monroe	12. Madison
13. Hayes	13. J. Q. Adams
14. Madison	14. Hayes
15. Van Buren	15. McKinley
16. Taft	16. Taft
17. Arthur	17. Van Buren
18. McKinley	18. Monroe
19. A. Johnson	19. Hoover
20. Hoover	20. B. Harrison
21. B. Harrison	21. Arthur
22. Tyler	22. Eisenhower
23. Coolidge	23. A. Johnson
BELOW AVERAGE	BELOW AVERAGE
24. Fillmore	24. Taylor
25. Taylor	25. Tyler
26. Buchanan	26. Fillmore
27. Pierce	27. Coolidge
28. Grant	28. Pierce
FAILURE	FAILURE
29. Harding	29. Buchanan
	30. Grant
	31. Harding

Over the ensuing years, the rating polls grew to be something of a "cottage industry," in that they were conducted every few years, several scholars and organizations participated in the ranking polls, and they generated much interest by scholars and the public, and likely the presidents themselves (Pederson and McLaurin 1987). In the past twenty-five years there have been several efforts to rank the presidents (C-SPAN 2000; Murray and Blessing 1994), including a well-known poll in 1996 by Schlesinger's son, the two-time recipient of the Pulitzer Prize and former Kennedy aide, Arthur Schlesinger Jr. (Schlesinger 1996). This poll was also released in the *New York Times Magazine*. Like the presidential polls, these more recent efforts survey professional historians and political scientists with expertise on the American presidency, however, the more recent polls generally employ larger numbers of respondents (Table 1.2).

The popularity of these presidential rankings has even translated to polls on the first ladies. The Siena Research Institute at Siena College in New York not only conducts periodic polls on the presidents, but also has conducted two ranking polls on the first ladies. Like the presidential rating polls, these rankings also survey leading scholars of the presidency, and ask respondents to either rank their subjects from best to worst or place them into categories similar to those used by Schlesinger—"Great" to "Failure" (Watson 2000). This includes two polls by Robert Watson, who surveyed a few dozen historians and political scientists who had published scholarly works on the first ladies (Watson 1999, 2003).

Although it is far too early to place either Obama or his immediate predecessor in the rankings, the Siena Research Institute asked more than two-hundred scholars of the presidency to do just that in 2010. The poll offered a very preliminary estimate of Obama's presidency relative to that of other presidents. Unlike George W. Bush, Obama came out on solid ground (Table 1.3, page 8).

Challenges and Debates

Efforts to rate or rank the presidents typically do not include the post-presidential years. Although some presidents have continued their public service after leaving the White House, such as John Quincy Adams and Andrew Johnson, who were elected to the U.S. House and U.S. Senate, respectively, and William Howard Taft, who took a seat on the U.S. Supreme Court, this service is not factored in to the assessments. Likewise, some former presidents have dis-

Table 1.2. Well-Known Recent Polls

1982 Murray–Blessing Poll	1996 Schlesinger, Jr. Poll	2000 C-SPAN Historian Poll
GREAT	GREAT	1. Lincoln
1. Lincoln	1. Lincoln	2. Washington
2. F. D. Roosevelt	2 F. D. Roosevelt	3. F. D. Roosevelt
3. Washington	3. Washington	4. Jefferson
4. T. Roosevelt		5. Truman
	NEAR GREAT	6. Wilson
NEAR GREAT	4. Jefferson	7. Jefferson
5. T. Roosevelt	5. Jackson	8. Kennedy
6. Wilson	6. T. Roosevelt	9. Eisenhower
7. Jackson	7. Wilson	10. L.B. Johnson
8. Truman	8. Truman	11. Reagan
	9. Polk	12. Polk
ABOVE AVERAGE		13. Jackson
9. J. Adams	HIGH AVERAGE	14. Monroe
10. LB. Johnson	10. Eisenhower	15. McKinley
11. Eisenhower	11. J. Adams	16. J. Adams
12. Polk	12. Kennedy	17. Cleveland
13. Kennedy	13. Cleveland	18. Madsion
14. Madison	14. L.B. Johnson	19. J.Q. Adams
15. Monroe	15. Monroe	20. Bush
16. J.Q. Adams	16. McKinley	21. Clinton
17. Cleveland		22. Carter
	LOW AVERAGE	23. Ford
AVERAGE	17. Madison	24. Taft
18. McKinley	18. J.Q. Adams	25. Nixon
19. Taft	19. B. Harrison	26. Hayes
20. Van Buren	20. Clinton	27. Coolidge
21. Hoover	21. Van Buren	28. Taylor
22. Hayes	22. Taft	29. Garfield
23. Arthur	23. Hayes	30. Van Buren
24. Ford	24. Bush	31. B. Harrison
25. Carter	25. Reagan	32. Arthur
26. B. Harrison	26. Arthur	33. Grant
	27. Carter	34. Hoover
BELOW AVERAGE	28. Ford	35. Fillmore
27. Taylor		36. Tyler
28. Tyler	BELOW AVERAGE	37. W.H. Harrison
29. Fillmore	29. Taylor	38. Harding
30. Coolidge	30. Coolidge	39. Pierce
31. Pierce	31. Fillmore	40. A. Johnson
	32. Tyler	41. Buchanan
FAILURE		
32. A. Johnson	FAILURE	
33. Buchanan	33. Pierce	
34. Nixon	34. Grant	
35. Grant	35. Hoover	
36. Harding	36. Nixon	
	37. A. Johnson	
	38. Buchanan	
	39. Harding	

Table 1.3. 2010 Siena Research Institute Poll (with a Ranking of Obama)

1. F. D. Roosevelt
2. T. Roosevelt
3. Lincoln
4. Washington
5. Jefferson
6. Madison
7. Monroe
8. Wilson
9. Truman
10. Eisenhower
11. Kennedy
12. Polk
13. Clinton
14. Jackson
15. Obama
16. L.B. Johnson
17. J. Adams
19. Reagan
20. J.Q. Adams
21. Cleveland
22. McKinley
23. G.H.W. Bush
24. Van Buren
25. Taft
26. Arthur
27. Grant
28. Garfield
29. Ford
30. Coolidge
31. Nixon
32. Hayes
33. Carter
34. Taylor
35. B. Harrison
36. W.H. Harrison
37. Hoover
38. Tyler
39. Fillmore
40. G.W. Bush
41. Pierce
42. Harding
43. Buchanan
44. A. Johnson

tinguished themselves in other ways that ended up improving their public image. This includes Richard Nixon, Jimmy Carter, and Bill Clinton. However, even if such service helps to offset the impact of Watergate, the 444-day Iranian hostage crisis, or the Monica Lewinsky scandal, respectively, the post-presidential years are not factored in to the ratings.

One of the inherent challenges of assessing presidents is that there is but a small "N" to study. At the time of this assessment of Barack Obama, only forty-three men have served in forty-four presidencies (Cleveland was both the twenty-second and twenty-fourth president), and there is much variation among the presidents. It is exceedingly difficult to compare presidents across time, as the challenges facing John Adams and the nature of the office itself were quite dissimilar to those facing Barack Obama.

One of the sources used by scholars to assess presidents is the president's own writings. Fortunately, all presidents serving from Herbert Hoover onward have presidential libraries. Administered by the National Archives and Records Administration (NARA), these libraries house the president's papers. These papers are made available to scholars and the public a few years after the president leaves office, in compliance with the 1978 Presidential Records Act. So too are there numerous edited and published collections of presidential papers and some of the presidents have written memoirs. Sadly, some of the great presidents, such as Abraham Lincoln and Franklin D. Roosevelt, did not survive their terms and history has thus been denied their memoirs. Other presidents chose not to pen accounts of their time in office, while still others wrestled with imperfect and selective memories. But, there are excellent and insightful memoirs, such as those by Harry S. Truman. At the same time, presidents have worried about their standing in history. Several, most notably Thomas Jefferson, Theodore Roosevelt, Richard M. Nixon, and Bill Clinton, have been quite conscious of how their legacies might be understood and shaped over time, whereas Ronald Reagan's supporters continue to actively promote his legacy (Pierson, 1997).

As to be expected, there is much disagreement about how to attempt to assess, much less rank, presidents. Although Schlesinger and his son favored asking scholars to place the presidents into categories such as "great," "near great," and so on, other polls have asked respondents to simply list the presidents chronologically from best to worst, whereas still others have used categories such as the ability to communicate and foreign policy accomplishments and had the respondents rate each president according to the category. As such, some of the aforementioned polls have approached the endeavor by using "holistic" ratings, whereby scholars simply try to offer an overall assessment of the president rather than do so based on narrow facets of the presidency, seen as a "mechanistic" criteria (Schlesinger Jr. 2003). These types of polls consider an array of issues and components of the presidency, including the ability to communicate effectively; the ability to compromise; relations with Congress; party leadership; handling of the economy; foreign policy accomplishments; domestic accomplishments; court appointments; and integrity, to name a few (SRI 2010).

Typically only leading scholars participate in the polls and they are usually professional historians and political scientists with expertise in the presidency. As to the number of scholars polled, the range varies from thirty-two to seventy-five, however, the Siena Research Institute poll surveyed 238 and the Murray–Blessing poll employed a whopping seventeen-page instrument and polled 953 scholars (Murray and Blessing 1982; SRI 2010). There remain questions not about how many or which scholars should participate in the enterprise of assessing presidents, but about which presidents can be ranked. For example, many of the polls fail to include William Henry Harrison (who served only thirty days) and James Garfield (who was assassinated during his first year in office), on account of their abbreviated presidencies (Pious 2003). The same might even be said of Zachary Taylor, who passed away midway into his second year in office.

Another challenge of assessing presidents is to be free from bias. Of the ranking polls, some critics have suggested a "Harvard yard bias" (Bailey 1967). These criticisms maintain that the professors who rate presidents are liberals with a natural preference for activist presidents (Felzenberg 1997, 2003). To counter this alleged bias, some conservative groups such as the Intercollegiate Studies Institute (ISI) have "stacked" polls with conservative pollsters. The ISI ranking polled thirty-eight conservative scholars and, not surprisingly, found that Democratic presidents fared far worse than in other polls, with Clinton and Lyndon B. Johnson even listed as "failures" (Pierson 1997). However, scholar Tim Blessing (2003) argues that bias is not an issue in most scholarly polls. He points to the poor presidencies of such Republicans as Warren G. Harding, Calvin Coolidge, and Herbert Hoover, who served consecutive terms and the scandalous presidencies of other Republicans including Ulysses Grant and Richard Nixon, as accounting for the reason why Republicans tend to be rated slightly lower than Democrats. Yet, the scholarly ranking polls have been fair in placing weak Democratic presidents—James Buchanan, John Tyler, and Franklin Pierce—toward the bottom of the polls, while such Republicans as Theodore Roosevelt and Abraham Lincoln are nearly always in the top five spots.

Criticisms of the ratings have also centered on concerns of "maleness" (Burns 1973, 1984). The celebrated scholar, James MacGregor Burns, noted that men assessed presidents, from male perspectives, and according to male traits. Matters such as war and other "force" issues have been made priorities. The old question of whether the "times makes the man" (or, it might be said, whether the man makes the times) is pertinent here. Teddy Roosevelt, for instance, even worried whether his presidency would be seen as achieving greatness because he believed he did not have the requisite war or crisis to allow him to transcend to such lofty status. However, Roosevelt ended up commanding his times and transforming the office and nation.

One final challenge of assessing presidents is the matter of when to rate them. There are convenient milestones in a presidency—the end of the "first 100 days" and the midterm election—which compel scholars and the public to examine a president's progress. But, such assessments—including this book—are only initial examinations, as it often takes years to get a full appreciation for a presidential legacy. Consider the cases of Harry Truman and Dwight Eisenhower, both of whom landed in unimpressive positions in the polls during the initial years after their presidencies. Although Truman's difficult decisions regarding the rebuilding of Europe, desegregation of the military, the establishment of the state of Israel, the firing of Gen. Douglas MacArthur, and more were often panned during his presidency, today they are hailed as among the most courageous and proper decisions in presidential history. Truman is consistently rated today as one of the country's best presidents and Eisenhower's standing has risen dramatically.

Indeed, there is much movement in the polls over time. A president's standing is not fixed; rather, it varies as new information comes to light, additional documents are available to scholars, and as we look back at history from the vantage point of time (and with closer to 20-20 vision). NARA releases presidential papers through the presidential libraries it administers, but it often takes ten or more years before all the documents are available. At the same time, in 1999 Washington scholars took advantage of the

bicentennial of the great general's passing to reassess his standing. The "Father of His Country" had slipped a position or two in
some of the polls, and traveling museum exhibits, academic conferences, and numerous publications during the bicentennial celebration restated the case for Washington. Likewise, the year 2009
marked the bicentennial of Lincoln's birth, and Lincoln scholars
celebrated with a variety of bicentennial programs and festivities,
as well as the opportunity to reexamine the great emancipator's
legacy (Watson, Pederson, and Williams 2010).

As such, there is the need not only for frequent re-evaluations
in the years after a president leaves office, but initial assessments
and guidelines to be offered during a president's time in office.

Assessing Presidents and Assessing Obama

A subfield of presidency studies has emerged devoted to assessing
presidential performance. A variety of mechanisms exists to assist
in such assessments, including the number of vetoes sustained,
the quality of judicial and executive appointments, the state of the
economy, the number and quality of bills and treaties signed, a
president's ability to deliver on his campaign pledges, and so on.
So too do scholars employ a wide array of frameworks in examining presidential performance: Constitutional, legislative-based,
quantitative, public opinion, and so on.

The assessment in the chapters to follow employs a wide
array of perspectives. Stephen J. Wayne, a leading voice in presidency studies, provides a list of the perspectives used by scholars
to assess presidents (Wayne 2003). Such approaches appear in this
book and include the following: presidential use of power (Neustadt 1980, 1991); leadership style (Burns 1973, 1984; Greenstein
1988, 2000); democratic leadership (Burns 1973, 1984); political
leadership (Milkis and Nelson 2007); effectiveness in modeling contemporary beliefs about leadership (Edwards and Wayne 2009);
how well presidents overcame the paradoxes inherent within the
challenging office (Cronin and Genovese 2009); the historic and
cyclical periods in which presidents serve (Skowronek 2011); and
the rhetorical style used by presidents and their ability to motivate
people (Kernell 2006).

One of the main approaches suggested by Wayne and other
scholars is to assess presidents according to character-based leadership qualities (Barber 1992; Renshon 1975). It has often been

said that, in the presidency, character is king (Shogun 1999). Character transcends personality insofar as presidents like Kennedy and Reagan benefited from their charm and likeability, but were made of something more. But it is an altogether more challenging task to try and define character and examine its impact in the White House. For instance, would the fact that George H. W. Bush went back on his pledge, "Read my lips, no new taxes" be a betrayal and character flaw or would it be better understood as being flexible in the face of the realities of the situation? Nor is character simply a matter of being ethical. Jimmy Carter and Calvin Coolidge were ethical individuals but neither one is rated highly by scholars or has been said to have been made of the "right stuff" for presidential greatness. On the other hand, FDR could be coldly calculating and disingenuous but he is rated as one of the nation's greatest presidents and is sometimes held up as the standard by which all presidents in modern times are judged.

Indeed, character transcends a lack of scandal or a penchant for honesty. Yet, many presidents, such as Nixon, have been ruined by scandal. Others such as Clinton and Reagan had their legacies blemished by scandal, but ended their presidencies quite popular. Scholars are still deciding on the proper impact of the Lewinsky and Iran-Contra scandals on the Clinton and Reagan legacies, just as the debate continues over Johnson's impressive legislative record (that included the Civil Rights Act in 1964 and Medicare in 1965) versus the Vietnam War and Clinton's budget surpluses and economic growth versus the lies surrounding the affair with his intern, Monica Lewinsky. Marital infidelity has not harmed other presidents, just as being slave owners has not denied Washington and Jefferson from their lofty rankings. To be sure, not all scandals are created equal; a case in point is the nature of the differences between the scandals associated with President Nixon— which were crimes of *commission*—and the scandals of President Grant—which were crimes of *omission*. At the midpoint of his presidency, President Obama managed to avoid a serious scandal or ethical brouhaha. Careful analysis is needed of the nature and extent of his character—that is to say, his judgment, disposition, worldview, and personal style (Barber 1992; Renshon 1975).

Momentous Presidency

The size, scope, and roles of the federal government have grown under Obama's presidency, largely in response to the extraordinary array of domestic, fiscal, and international challenges he faced upon assuming the office. However, the course of action taken by the president also reflects his philosophical views and personal experiences. But, even before Obama, the office can safely be said to scarcely resemble the office held by Washington, Lincoln, or even the Roosevelts. Despite the limitations imposed on the presidency by the cautious Framers, the office has grown to become the most dominant force in the American political system. The evolution and growth of the office have been in response to crises and changes in society, as well as presidential character and viewpoints. This continues to be the case under Obama who, like so many of his predecessors, used the "bully pulpit" and an enlarged reading of the powers discussed in Article II of the Constitution.

So too has Obama faced impossibly high expectations from the public and the legacy of the "imperial presidency" described by Schlesinger, whereby the sheer array of interest groups, rising expectations, and both the array and complexity of challenges pose nearly insurmountable obstacles for the president (Schlesinger Jr. 2004). As President Carter admitted, "When things go bad you get entirely too much blame. And I have to admit that when things go good, you get entirely too much credit" (Hodgson 1980: 25). The inherent paradoxes of the presidency seem to be more challenging than ever. As Cronin and Genovese (1998/2009) noted, the public has impossible and unrealistic expectations, wanting the president to address every problem while distrusting the centralized power necessary to do so; the clamor for nonpartisan and bipartisan approaches is more prevalent than ever while society struggles with the most bitter partisanship and venomous political tone in decades; and the "damned if you do, damned if you don't" aspect of the Oval Office is more pronounce than ever. At the same time, Obama was confronted with challenges on par to the Great Depression faced by FDR, the Cuban Missile Crisis faced by Kennedy, the social upheaval faced by Johnson and Nixon, and the threat of terrorism faced by George W. Bush.

It is difficult to evaluate a president at midterm. So much remains in his administration and often the first two years are dramatically different than the next two years, just as first terms are often different than second terms. Such was the case with Reagan, Clinton, and George W. Bush. Scholars have not yet had the advantage of reading the Obama papers or the benefits of hindsight. Accordingly, this evaluation does not pretend to be the definitive word. Far from it; years will pass before a conclusive account can be forwarded. However, this book does offer a relatively comprehensive account of numerous significant policy issues faced by Obama, a dispassionate historical examination of the events surrounding the Obama presidency, and a preliminary assessment of the major facets of his presidency, character, and administration.

Washington and Lincoln continue to loom large in the pantheon of the presidency, just as all modern presidents continue to serve—and struggle—with the shadow of FDR about them. As the yardsticks by which all presidents are measured, many have fallen short, just as there have been successes and failures in the history of the office. It is hard to say where Obama will end up in the presidential ratings, but the bar has been set high and the moment in history that faced him has been among the most challenging ever.

Works Cited

Bailey, Thomas. *Presidential Greatness*. Palo Alto, CA: Stanford University Press, 1967.

Barber, James David. *The Presidential Character: Predicting Performance in the White House*, 4th ed. Englewood Cliffs, NJ: Prentice Hall, 1992.

Blessing, Tim H. "Presidents and Significance: Partisanship as a Source of Perceived Greatness." *White House Studies*. Vol. 3, No. 1 (2003).

Burns, James MacGregor. *Presidential Government: The Crucible of Leadership*, 2nd ed. Boston: Houghton-Mifflin, 1973.

————. *The Power to Lead: The Crisis of the American Presidency*. New York: Simon & Schuster, 1984.

C-SPAN. "Survey of Presidential Leadership: How did the Presidents Rate?" (21 Feb. 2000). http://www.americanpresidents.org/survey/.

C-SPAN Historians Presidential Leadership Survey. 2011 and 2009. http://legacy.c-span.org/presidentialsurvey/presidential-leadership-survey.aspx.

Cronin, Thomas E. and Michael A. Genovese. *The Paradoxes of the American Presidency*. New York: Oxford University Press, 2009 (new edition from 1998).

Edwards, George C. III and Stephen J. Wayne. *Presidential Leadership: Politics and Policy Making*, 8th ed. Belmont, CA: Wadsworth, 2009.

Felzenberg, Alvin. "There You Go Again: Liberal Historians and the New York Times Deny Ronald Reagan His Due." *Policy Review* (March–April 1997).

————. "Partisan Biases in Presidential Ratings: Ulysses, Woodrow, and Calvin, 'We Hardly Knew Ye'." *White House Studies*, Vol. 3, No. 1 (2003).

Greenstein, Fred I. *Leadership in the Modern Presidency.* Cambridge, MA: Harvard University Press, 1988.

————. *The Presidential Difference: Leadership Style from FDR to Clinton.* New York: Free Press, 2000.

Hodgson, Godfrey. *All Things to All Men: The False Promise of the Modern American Presidency.* New York: Simon & Schuster, 1980.

Kernell, Samuel. *Going Public: New Strategies of Presidential Leadership,* 4th ed. Washington, DC: CQ Press, 2006.

Milkis, Sidney M. and Michael Nelson. *The American Presidency: Origins and Development, 1776–2007,* 5th ed. Washington, DC: CQ Press, 2007.

Murray, Robert K. and Tim H. Blessing. *Greatness in the White House: Rating the Presidents.* University Park: Pennsylvania State University Press, 1994.

Neustadt, Richard. *The Politics of Leadership from FDR to Carter.* John Wiley & Sons, 1980.

Pederson, William and Ann McLaurin. *The Rating Game in American Politics.* New York: Irvington, 1987.

————. *Presidential Power and the Modern Presidency: The Politics of Leadership from Roosevelt to Reagan.* New York: Free Press, 1991.

Pierson, James. "Historians and the Reagan legacy." *The Weekly Standard.* (29 Sept. 1997), 22–24.

Pious, Richard M. "Reflections of a Presidency Rater." *White House Studies.* Vol. 3, No 1 (2003).

Renshon, Stanley Allen. *Psychological Analysis and Presidential Personality: The Case of Richard Nixon.* Hoboken, NJ: Atcom, 1975.

Schlesinger, Arthur M. "Historians rate the U.S. Presidents." *Life Magazine.* (1 Nov. 1948), 65–66, 73–74.

————. "Our presidents: A rating by 75 historians." *New York Times Magazine.* (29 July 1962), 12–13, 40–41, 43.

Schlesinger, Jr., Arthur M. "The ultimate approval rating." *New York Times Magazine.* (15 Dec. 1996), 46–47.

————. "Commentary." *White House Studies,* Vol. 3, No. 1 (2003), 75–77.

————.*The Imperial Presidency.* Mariner Books, 2004 (reprint from 1974).

Shogun, Robert. *The Double-Edged Sword: How Character Makes and Ruins Presidents; from Washington to Clinton.* Boulder, CO.: Westview Press, 1999.

Siena Research Institute. "Siena Poll: American Presidents." 2010. http://www.siena.edu/pages/179.asp?item=2566.

Skowronek, Stephen. *Presidential Leadership in Political Time: Reprise and Reappraisal.* Lawrence: University Press of Kansas, 2011.

Watson, Robert P. "Ranking the Presidential Spouses." *The Social Science Journal,* Vol. 36, No. 1 (1999), 117–136.

————. *The Presidents' Wives: Reassessing the Office of First Lady.* Boulder, CO: Lynne Rienner Publishers, 2000, see pages 171–198.

————. "Ranking the First Ladies: Polling Elites to Evaluate Performance." *PRG Report* (Presidency Research Group of the American Political Science Association), Vol. 26, No. 1 (Fall 2003), 15–22.

————., William D. Pederson, and Frank J. Williams. *Lincoln's Enduring Legacy*. Lanham, MD: Lexington Books, 2010.

Wayne, Stephen J. "Evaluating the President: The Public's Perspective through the Prism of Pollsters." *White House Studies*. Vol. 3, No. 1 (2003), 35–40.

II

Character and Identity

Chapter 2

Rhetoric and Image

Casey Malone Maugh

The "A" Word

On June 8, 2010, in an interview with the *Today Show's* Matt
Lauer, President Barack Obama uttered a word so lewd that it
spun media pundits into a frenzy, made American mothers cover
their children's ears, and inspired 28,000 Internet headlines. What
Obama said was the word "ass." The "A" word, in this context,
was not censored by the Federal Communications Commission,
suggesting that the president's language may not have been as
"unpresidential" as Becky Quick, host of CNBC's *Squawk Box*, and
countless other media commentators deemed it to be (Bedard 2010).
However, the "A" word certainly created a kerfuffle discussed around
the globe. Coinciding with the debate over the appropriateness of
a curse word—used in reference to the perpetrators of the BP oil
spill—another debate sprung forth. This one was occasioned by
the *Drudge Report*, which posted a headline stating, "Obama Goes
Street" (Martel 2010).

Mark Halperin, a senior political analyst for *Time*, criticized
Drudge for racial overtones in his report. Both the Drudge headline
and Halperin commentary were picked up by Bill O'Reilly later
that same evening on his Fox News show, *The O'Reilly Factor*.
Ultimately, the nation found Drudge's racialized language the
source of much more debate than the profane language used by
the president on a morning talk show. The controversy shifted
from the use of the "A" word, to the implications of a presidential
image mediated through race.

21

This chapter analyzes Barack Obama's rhetorical image throughout the 2008 presidential campaign cycle and during his first two years in the nation's highest office with respect to mediated portrayals of race. During this time, Obama's image has been both hyper-racialized and completely deracinated. This rhetorical analysis seeks to uncover discursive themes found in media texts that focus primarily on Obama's race. This chapter is an expansion of the work begun by Anthony Sparks (2009) in which he defines historical tropes used to define black men in America. Through an analysis of popular media (magazine, Internet, television, newspaper, and blog entries), this study reveals three major themes, all of which challenge one another and confront the complexities of racial politics in twenty-first-century America. The emergent themes question varying aspects of Obama's public personae. First, tropes of black men (the Brute, the Dandy, and the Magic Negro) are explored as a way of articulating the mediated personae of Barack Obama, as well as the implications of the various myths on popular culture. Then, using the three tropes as a means to identify the strategies used by the media to engage and critique Obama, this chapter explores the faces of Obama, both through the critique that he was "too black" to be electable and through the questioning of Obama's blackness based on critiques that he was not black enough to be the first African American president. Finally, this chapter concludes with a discussion of what it means to elect a black president, the effects of such an election on the mythos of the black man and the implications of post-racial politics on the nation.

The Making of a Presidential Image

Presidential image making is serious business. Keith V. Erickson (2008) argues that "presidents enact a variety of fictive personae (personal and public) in order to heighten their authority and to avoid imposed characterizations" (361). From a mediated perspective, Barack Obama's presidential image construction relies on his being identified as a person of color. Although Obama and his staff have gone to great lengths to minimize race as a factor, the media emphasizes race as a way of vetting him rhetorically, linguistically, and ideologically. This chapter relies on the rhetoric of the media, rather than presidential rhetoric, because although Obama and his administration tend to maintain a neutral position on race, the media consistently uses race to praise or critique the the first African American president. This study examines the rhetoric that lies within popular American media responsible for reinforcing and (re)constructing the racial narratives found within its culture.

Images representing black men in America historically rely on two tropes relating to the minstrel shows of the nineteenth century, the Brute and the Dandy. According to Robert Entman and Andrew Rojecki (2001), the brute figure in minstrelsy typically depicted African American men as animalistic, hyper-sexualized, irresponsible, and criminalized. The Dandy figure, although seemingly more benign, actually reinforced the notion that black men should not be trusted by mimicking white dress and speech and spending time attending social events. Anthony Sparks (2009) argues that the Dandy figure, "helped posit into the soil of America's popular culture the notion of Black humanity as oxymoronic and embed an idea of inescapable Black subjugation and inequality alongside a distrust of the actions and public language of Black men" (28). Both stereotypes are derivative of larger social commentary concerning African American men and their station in society. Although both of these tropes have been layered on Obama at different times throughout his candidacy for and election to the presidency, I argue there exists a third, equally powerful trope that captures mediated representations of Obama, the Magic Negro.

David Ehrenstein (2008) argues that Obama embodies the "Magic Negro" mythical character. The Magic Negro, according to Ehrenstein is a figure of postmodern folk culture created to assuage white guilt over the ills of slavery and segregation by offering a comic-book hero who is unthreatening, despite being black. Obama, in particular, reifies the myth of the Magical Negro with his genial tone, warm voice, and humble presence. Ehrenstein (2008) notes that, "like a comic-book superhero, Obama is there to help; out of the sheer goodness of heart we need not know or understand. For as with all Magic Negroes, the less real he seems, the more desirable he becomes." This trope emerges throughout media discourse as a means of capturing Obama's effect on the electorate during the 2008 cycle, which suggests that the Magic Negro metaphor works as a means of reinforcing the complexities of racial politics in America today. The remainder of this chapter demonstrates the ways in which each of these three tropes have been exploited in mainstream American media, the implications of each trope and discuss the resulting complexities of race in American politics in the twenty-first century.

Is Obama Too Black?

Following Obama's announcement that he would run for president in 2007, the primary concern became his electability based on his being African American. Despite his being the biracial child of a white mother and grandparents who served as his primary caretakers, Obama's African father's heritage colored him enough to make race a major conversation piece. Initially, any dark-skinned candidate would raise concerns over his electability. After all, he followed Jesse Jackson and Al Sharpton, who had been polarizing African American candidates in the past. However, Obama seemed to offer something different.

The Brute trope in American history relies on character identification that highlights "blackness." The Brute trope emphasizes darkened skin and over-drawn facial features (lips, nose, and ears). During his campaign in 2007 and 2008, news stories attempted to capture the notion of blackness, as it related to Obamas' skin color and appearance by emphasizing that the "one-drop rule" still applies. Obama confirmed this idea at the beginning of his campaign, by saying, "if you look African-American, you're treated as an African-American" (Tapper and Hinman 2007). In America, appearing black has historically deemed you so and conferred on the actor all of the qualities associated with the Brute: aggression, hyper-sexuality, and an athletic prowess to name a few.

As questions concerning Obama's race emerged and his identity as the black Brute was reinforced, Rev. Jeremiah Wright's inflammatory remarks on the state of race in America hit the airwaves. A recording of one of Rev. Wright's sermons where he said, "God damn America for treating its citizens as less than human, God damn America as long as she tries to act like she is God and she is supreme. The United States government has failed the vast majority of her citizens of African descent" hit the media circuit (Curry 2008). Not only did Wright's sermons posit a radical position on race, his rhetoric also suggested that 9/11 attacks resulted from America's own provocation. As a result of these comments, Obama's twenty-year relationship with Rev. Wright, Obama's pastor at Chicago's Trinity Church of Christ, came under fire. Even more damning was the fact that Michelle and Barack Obama had been married by Wright, their two children were baptized in his church and Obama cited Wright as a major influence in his faith. As Wright's polarizing sermons became public, Obama's identity as a black man was strongly reinforced; his being "too black" emerged as an electability issue, even after Obama stated "I don't think my church is actually particularly controversial." He said Rev. Wright "is like an old uncle who says things I don't always agree with" (Ross and El-Buri 2008). Despite Obama's distancing rhetoric the media questioned whether Obama believed the same truths that Wright espoused. Wright certainly epitomized the Brute mentality; his rhetoric was in keeping with that of the inflammatory, hot-tempered, irresponsible Brute of the minstrelsy. Because of Obama's close relationship with Wright, he too was in danger of being perceived as a radical zealot. Although Obama responded with a speech that, aside from his 2004 keynote address at the Democratic National Convention, was his most rhetorically sophisticated address, the relationship between the Obama family and Rev. Wright created public scrutiny.

During the 2008 election cycle, Obama's campaign avoided conversations about race. They spent time articulating Obama's experiences in terms of qualifications for the position, experiences, and philosophies of the presidency. Marcus Marbry (2008) noted, "Mr. Obama's campaign so de-emphasized race that for the most of the 17-month nomination contest much of the news media became obsessed with the question of whether he was 'black enough' to win black votes." Much of the rhetoric of race came from media commentary and other political figures who questioned the role of African American men in politics, such as Geraldine Ferraro. Ferraro, a supporter of Obama's oppositional candidate in the primary elections, Hillary Clinton, stated that "If Obama was a white man, he would not be in this position. And if he was a woman of any color, he would not be in this position. He happens to be very lucky to be who he is" (Seelye and Bosman 2008). Ferraro's implication that Obama's success was due to his race and gender, seemed to be echoed in the news headlines, *The Blackness of Barack Obama, Is Obama the End of Black Politics?, Where Whites Draw the Line* and *He's not Black.*

Barack Obama's nomination as the Democratic Party's candidate for the 2008 race suggested that Obama was at the very least, not "too black" for the electorate. Questions of racial authenticity, especially of Obama being "too black" fell off dramatically after Obama's election. However, in summer 2009, African American scholar Henry Louis Gates Jr. was arrested in front of his own home for "disorderly conduct" by a white police officer. Obama found himself at the center of the scandal when he called the officers' actions "stupid." Obama's insertion into the conversation reignited previously quieted conversations about Obama the Brute. Obama came under incredible criticism for his calling the arresting officer's actions "stupid" and subsequently called both Gates and the officer to the White House for a "beer summit" in which Obama facilitated a media opportunity to salvage the racially charged responses to the crisis. This immediately brought race to the fore and reminded the American public that race was not far from their collective consciousness even after electing a "black" president.

Once again, the American public was reminded that Obama, in fact, is black. His brief, thoughtless comments about the white police officer reignited the Brute trope of the Wright controversy and found Obama focusing far too much on the plight of African-Americans rather than remaining quiet on issues of race, as he had done so well in the interim. The discomfort surrounding the Gates incident and the ensuing "Beer Summit" captured the temporarily dormant racial tensions underlying culture in America. Outside of touchstone moments, Obama and his administration have done little to directly address race both during the campaign and since his election.

Damned if You Do, Damned if You Don't

Although Obama faced criticism that he might be "too black" to be the president of the United States, he failed to truly embody the Brute persona just defined. In fact, it is challenging to make the case that he does much to identify with the African American experience in many ways. Most often, Obama has been accused of not being "black enough." Na-Teisha Coates (2007), in an article in *Time,* captured the trouble well by stating, "this is a double-edged sword. As much as his biracial identity has helped Obama build a sizable following in Middle America, it's also opened a gap for others to question his authenticity as a black man" (Coates 2007). Obama's adherence to the Dandy trope has provided an opportunity for the media to question his authenticity as a black man. Historically, the Dandy emphasizes relationships with white people as a way to appeal to a broader audience by speaking as white people do, dressing white, and spending the majority of his time attending social events. Much of the critique haunting Obama relied on the Dandy mythos to do its work. In the media, two major issues emerged relating to the ongoing accusations that Obama is not "black enough." The first of these critiques was Obama's perceived failure to target issues that primarily affect the African American community. The second major problem Obama faces as the first African American president is his rhetorical strategy to remain calm and supress any articualtion of true emotion, especially that of anger.

The Black Issue(s)

Although reports circulated about Obama's authenticity as an African American, other presidential candidates added credence to the suggestion that Obama was not "black enough." During the 2008 campaign, oppositional candidates, such as Ralph Nader, Hillary Clinton, and Joe Biden, targeted Obama's decision to remain largely silent on historically black issues. Hillary and Bill Clinton were accused of race bating by suggesting that they held the power of the African American vote and the working class vote. Hillary Clinton continually constructed a divide in the media between her relationship with the disenfranchised black population and accused Obama of elitism.

Biden, during his brief run for the presidency, made a major political faux pas, which ultimately led to his leaving the race. On the day he joined the race for the 2008 Democratic presidential nomination he was asked his opinion of Barack Obama. He replied, "I mean, you got the first mainstream African American who is articulate and bright and clean and a nice-looking guy. I mean, that's a storybook, man" (Thai & Barrett 2007). Biden's comments further added to the Dandy narrative being constructed in the media. His comments exploded on the Internet and on major media outlets. The use of the words "articulate" and "clean" suggested that Obama indeed was the epitome of the Dandy.

Ralph Nader, rather than covertly questioning Obama's "blackness" as the Clintons had, directly accused the Obama campaign of ignoring "black issues" by comparing Obama's rhetoric to that of Jesse Jackson. According to Nader, Obama failed to be black enough to be electable because he tried to "talk white" and appeal to "white guilt." Nader stated:

> the number one thing that a black American politician aspiring to the presidency should be [*sic*] is to candidly describe the plight of the poor, especially in the inner cities and the rural areas, and have a very detailed platform about how the poor is going to be defended by the law, is going to be protected by the law, and is going to be liberated by the law. (Sprengelmeyer 2008)

Nader's comments demonstrated a pervasive critique from not only those to the left of Obama, but also from the major African American leadership.

During the 2008 campaign, the Revs. Jesse Jackson and Al Sharpton, on multiple occasions, questioned Obama's ability to be "black enough" to represent the plight of black America. Jackson accused Obama of "acting like he's white" and Sharpton, in multiple interviews, communicated his dissatisfaction with Obama's campaign strategy, stating, "Just because you're our color doesn't make you our kind" (Elder 2008). Although both Jackson and Sharpton supported the Obama campaign, they insisted that Obama failed to communicate about issues related to African Americans in meaningful ways, further emphasizing the Dandy trope.

The Angry Black Man Persona

The second major critique leveled at Obama was highlighted in the wake of the BP oil disaster in summer 2010. This critique pertained to his temperament and reaction to the explosion of the Deepwater Horizon vessel, in which millions of gallons of oil went gushing into the Gulf of Mexico. Prior to the Gulf oil disaster, media pundits often latched on to Obama's cool, calm-under-pressure approach as a positive quality, especially during the campaign. His response to the Jeremiah Wright debacle and comments made by fellow presidential candidates were examples of Obama remaining level-headed in the face of serious critique of his authenticity and character. On all accounts, Obama carefully articulated his position of disappointment with the thoughtless nature of the comments and then used them as an opportunity to advance his political neutrality on issues of race. After the oil disaster, the media cried out for a different approach; they wanted the "angry black man" to emerge.

On his late-night talk show, Bill Maher called on the president to embody the Brute persona; he stated, "I thought when we elected a black president, we were going to get a black president. You know, this [BP oil spill] is where I want a real black president. I want him in a meeting with the BP CEOs, you know, where he lifts up his shirt so you can see the gun in his pants. That's—(in black man voice) 'we've got a motherfu**ing problem here?' Shoot somebody in the foot" (Rachel 2010). Conservative columnist Kathleen Parker (2008) argued that Obama does not show the kind of emotion that Americans expect to see from their first black president. D. K. Jamaal (2009) wrote in the examiner that "Obama is the Presidential equivalent of Rodney Dangerfield. He gets no respect . . . because he is a wimp."

As noted in the opening paragraph of this chapter, in June 2010, Obama tried to overcome the perception that he was "too weak" or "too nice" to the BP oil officials by appearing on a nationally syndicated morning talk show and saying, "I don't sit around just talking to experts because this is a college seminar, we talk to these folks because they potentially have the best answers—so I know whose ass to kick." Although Obama's language seemed unpredictable and maybe unpresidential, the conversation that developed out of his use of the "A word" once again became focused on race.

Matt Drudge's headline called Obama's language "street" and *GOP USA* called Obama "gangsta." Other major media outlets released headlines stating that Obama "sullied" the office of the presidency with his language and that he "lost his cool." Immediately Mark Halperin, *Time* magazine's senior political analyst replied that Drudge was purposefully trying to use racial overtones to frame Obama's rhetoric. He stated, "He cannot get angry and be an effective communicator as an African-American. So Matt Drudge takes the Matt Lauer quote, and he casts it as 'Obama Goes Street.' And it includes this photo of an angry-looking Barack Obama. I think it's all pretty clear—it's pretty clear to all of us what's going on there" (Hadro 2010). The media on the left cried foul and argued, as Halperin had, that many of the headlines were racializing Obama's comments. Conservative Fox News host, Bill O'Reilly rejected Halperin's claims that Matt Drudge intended to invoke race by using such rhetoric. O'Reilly seemed not to see where Drudge could have injected racial sentiment in that headline, although he acknowledged that the "going street" slang was used in "African-American precincts." "The only thing black" about this story, O'Reilly asserted, "is the oil in the Gulf." Halperin appeared on O'Reilly's program that same evening and was asked, "You think Matt Drudge wrote a headline, not because it was cool or in, but because Matt Drudge wanted to provoke a racial stereotype?" Short answer from Halperin: Yes, but "it plays on multiple levels" (Martel 2010).

The underwhelming BP oil disaster response was not Obama's only failure to demonstrate his presidential strength. During a national address to the joint houses of Congress in 2009, Rep. Joe Wilson, a Republican from South Carolina, shouted out "you lie" during a pause in Obama's speech. Obama responded with composed silence, followed with "that's not true" and continued his speech as planned. In the days following the outburst by Wilson, Obama said little and Wilson apologized publicly for his "lack of civility" but not for the sentiment behind the outburst (Scherer 2009). On the surface, things seemed to have been smoothed over with Wilson's apology; in an interview the following day, the president said that he accepted Wilson's quick and unequivocal apology. Had Obama responded with anger or outrage, he may have been viewed as overly sensitive or passionate; instead, reinforcing the Dandy mythos, he remained cool under pressure and all but ignored the public critique. The Brute and the Dandy tropes capture some of the mediated view of the president, but they fail to properly account for many other ways in which the public has framed Obama.

The Magical Negro Creates a Post-Racial America

On November 4, 2008, Barack Obama was elected to serve the United States as its forty-fourth president. Throughout the election cycle, the media spent countless pages contemplating the electabililty of an African American man to the presidency. And, inspired by his decisive election over John McCain, media pundits fell over themselves to provide a rational answer for his win. Much of the discourse following Obama's election specualted about the notion that America had moved into a post-racial era. Ushered in by Obama's victory, the nation held the hope that race had once, and for all, been eliminated as a factor in U.S. politics.

As evidenced by the media attacks discussed earlier and rhetorical framing of the president as both a Brute and a Dandy, post-racial America might exist within the Magical Negro. The trope of the Magic Negro serves as a third perspective on the ways America continues to view a black men in political positions. Obama has fallen into the Brute–Dandy binary and Anthony

Sparks (2009) articulates the limitations and consequences of such a move:

> it would seem that the dominant myth of black men as innately and overly aggressive—the minstrel brute—stands in contradiction to the common political "Is he tough enough to lead?" charge. . . . The fact, then, that this charge did and still does appear to have some traction against Obama suggests there exists another, more subversive trope about Black men, one that suggests that the question of toughness in this case was really a more subtle way of questioning Obama's knowledge, inherent intelligence, and basic competence to lead. (35)

The Magic Negro offers a trope that might respond to Sparks' recognition that the Brute–Dandy binary fails to capture Obama's struggle. David Ehrenstein's (2007) claims that during the election Obama was doing something other than simply running for president. He notes, "it's clear that Obama also is running for an equally important unelected office, in the province of the popular imagination—the Magic Negro." He goes on to state that the Magic Negro is "there to assuage white 'guilt' (i.e., the minimal discomfort they feel over the role of slavery and racial segregation in American history), while replacing stereotypes of a dangerous, highly sexualized black man with a benign figure for whom interracial sexual congress holds no interest." The Magic Negro is a comic-book superhero who can resolve all issues in a rational and calm manner. The Magic Negro trope uses an unthreatening rhetoric, refuses to stoop to name calling, and is approachable but not in the way the Dandy presents. Obama's presence throughout the campaign and first years of the presidency provide evidence of this Magic Negro. The Obama campaign intentionally attempted to steer clear of racialized politics. During the 2008 campaign, Obama's handlers set out to erase any sense of race from the voting equation. Gwen Ifill (2009) in *The Breakthrough*, noted that, "[i]n narrowing the differences between Obama and the majority-white nation he was appealing to, the campaign simply set out to erase race as a negative. This was no accident. The formula counted on white voters to be comforted by this approach, and for black voters to be willing to look the other way" (56).

The result of this Magic Negro narrative is the suggestion that somehow Obama's election in 2008 is evidence of a post-racial

America. The Magic Negro provides the façade of a post-racial America. If the Magic Negro persona is embodied in Obama, then America must be post-racial. Daniel Schorr (2008) argued that Obama began to signal an era of post-racial politics when he told a story of a woman who used to work on the segregationist, Strom Thurmon's campaign, came to work for his South Carolina headquarters. Schorr argues that "the post-racial era, as embodied by Obama, is the era where civil rights veterans of the past century are consigned to history and Americans begin to make race-free judgments on who should lead them." White voters can vote for Obama without any sense of disloyalty nor belief that race would automatically preclude an African American man from serving as president. The Magic Negro transcends race.

Although some news outlets clamoured over Obama's perceived blackneess or lack of authenticity, others praised Obama's neutrality on issues of race, claiming that America was ready to move past race. Howard Fineman (2008) wrote that "Obama was making a statement: that his candidacy would be the exclamation point at the end of our four-century long argument over the role of African-Americans in our society. . . . we would finally cease seeing each other through color-coded eyes." Furthermore, Jesse Jackson's son, Jesse Jackson Jr. became co-chairman of Obama's campaign and after Jackson Sr.'s public attacks on Obama, he expressed disappointment with his father. Matt Bai (2008) noted of the divide between the older and younger Jacksons, "This newly emerging class of black politicians . . . seek a broader political brief. Comfortable inside the establishement, bred at universities rather than seminaries, they are just as likely to see themselves as ambassadors *to* the black communities as they are to see themselves as spokesmen for it." The younger black politicians, see the potential for racial transendence, which is precisely why the Magic Negro mythos is so easily enacted.

The three emergent themes explicated in this chapter suggest that we live in anything but a post-race America. The tropes of Brute, Dandy, and the Magic Negro each show little tolerance for the complexities of a human character running for or serving in political office. Throughout the campaign and the first two years of his presidency, Obama's camp attempted to minimize race as an issue of consequence to the office. Christine Temple (2010) argues that "the term (post-racial) and its variations refer to an assumption that African-Americans have finally achieved racial equality, but inherent in this vision of racial equality is an expectation that African-Americans should not seek to be culturally distinct, practicing a way of life with values and worldviews that differ from mainstream" (46).

In America, race complicates the political landscape by placing an automatic marker of historical oppression and racism in front of a candidate who happens to be black in America. This occurs even if that candidate's ancestors were not enslaved in the United States in centuries past. This occurs even if that candidate's mother is white, and he was raised in a predominately white environment. If the United States were a post-racial society, then we would not spend hours writing about how race influences his polling numbers or his electability ratings. In fact, a Canadian reporter quite astutely observed, "one of the things that Obama's candidacy may achieve, is to confirm, not the irrelevance of race as a political issue, but the incoherence of it—the maddening, irresolvable undefinability of it" (Coyne 2007). To this end, the definitional tropes explicated in this essay demonstrate the complexity of race, the inadequacy of tropes to capture an individual's rise to power, and the plea for further exploration of how race operates in American politics.

Works Cited

Arana, M. "He's not black." *The Washington Post* (30 November 2008). http://www.washingtonpost.com/wp-dyn/content/article/2008/11/28/AR2008112802219.html.

Bai, M. "Is Obama the end of black politics?" *The New York Times* (10 August 2008). http://www.nytimes.com/2008/08/10/magazine/10politics-t.html.

Bedard, P. "CNBC host says Obama sullied office with 'ass to kick' line." *U.S. News Politics—Washington Whispers* (8 June 2010). http://politics.usnews.com/news/washington-whispers/articles/2010/06/08/cnbc-host-says-obama-sullied-office-with-ass-to-kick-line.html.

Coates, T.-N. P. "Is Obama black enough?" *Time.com* (1 February 2007). http://www.time.com/time/nation/article/0,8599,1584736,00.html.

Coyne, A. "The blackness of Barack Obama." *Canada.com* (14 February 2007). http://www.canada.com/nationalpost/columnists/story.html?id=a34c64ab-f275-45a2-bfb9-d799ccda8252.

Curry, G. E. "What Rev. Jeremiah Wright really said." *Final Call* (20 April 2008). http://www.finalcall.com/artman/publish/article_4596.shtml.

Ehrenstein, D. "Obama the 'Magic Negro.'" *The Los Angeles Time* (6 May 2008). http://www.latimes.com/news/opinion/commentary/la-oe-ehrenstein19mar19,0,3391015.story.

Elder, L. "Sharpton, Jackson dilemma." *The Washington Post* (12 January 2008). http://www.washingtontimes.com/news/2008/jan/12/sharpton-jackson-dilemma/?page=1.

Entman, R. and A. Rojecki. *The Black Image in the White Mind: Media and Race in America.* Chicago: The University of Chicago Press, 2001

Frank, D. A., and M. L. McPhail. "Barack Obama's Address at the 2004 Democratic National Convention: Compromise, Consilience, and the (Im)Possibility of Racial Reconciliation." *Rhetoric & Public Affairs,* Vol. 8, No. 4 (2005), 571–594.

Hadro, M. "MSNBC's 'Morning Joe' panel: Drudge headline racially-tinged." *Newsbusters* (8 June 2010). http://www.newsbusters.org/blogs/matt-hadro/2010/06/08/msnbc-s-morning-joe-panel-drudge-headline-racially-tinged.

Ifill, G. *The Breakthrough: Politics and Race in the Age of Obama.* New York: Anchor Books, 2009

Jamaal, D. K. "Ooooh! President Obama's response to Joe Wilson has right-wing shaking in fear (or not)." *The Examiner* (10 September 2009). http://www.examiner.com/post-partisan-in-national/ooooh-president-obama-s-response-to-joe-wilson-has-right-wing-shaking-fear-or-not.

Katz, C. 2008. "McCain campaign is cynical, not racist, says Obama." *The New York Daily News* (2 August 2008). http://www.nydaily-news.com/news/politics/2008/08/02/2008-08-02_mccain_campaign_is_cynical_not_racist_sa.html.

Marbry, M. "Color test: Where whites draw the line." *The New York Times* (8 June 2008). http://www.nytimes.com/2008/06/08/weekin review/08mabry.html.

Martel, F. "Bill O'Reilly can't see how Drudge's 'Obama goes street' headline is racist." *Mediate* (Online, 9 June 2010). http://www.mediaite.com/online/bill-oreilly-doesnt-see-how-drudges-obama-goes-street-headline-could-be-racist/.

Rachel, A. "Obama ain't black enough for Bill Maher." *Big Hollywood* (2 June 2010). http://bighollywood.breitbart.com/arachel/2010/06/02/obama-aint-black-enough-for-bill-maher/.

Ross, B., and El-Buri, R. "Obama's pastor: God damn America, U.S. to blame for 9/11." *ABC News* (13 March 2008). http://abcnews.go.com/Blotter/DemocraticDebate/story?id=4443788&page=1.

Scherer, M. "'You lie!': Representative Wilson's oOutburst." *Time* (10 September 2009). http://www.time.com/time/politics/article/0,8599,1921455,00.html.

Seelye, K. Q., and Bosman, J. "Ferraro's Obama remarks become talk of campaign. *New York Times* (12 March 2008). http://www.nytimes.com/2008/03/12/us/politics/12campaign.html.

Sparks, A. "Minstrel Politics or 'He Speaks too Well:' Rhetoric, Race, and Resistance in the 2008 Presidential Campaign." *Argumentation and Advocacy.* Vol. 46 (2009), 21–38,

Sprengelmeyer, M. "Nader: Obama trying to 'talk white.'" *The Rocky Mountain News* (25 June 2008). http://www.rockymountainnews.com/news/2008/jun/25/nader-critical-of-obama-for-trying-to-talk-white/.

Tapper, J., and Hinman, K. "Obama takes hits, keeps on campaigning." *ABC News* (11 February 2007). http://abcnews.go.com/WNT/Politics/story?id=2867210&page=1.

Temple, C. N. "Communicating Race and Culture in the Twenty-First Century: Discourse and the Post-Racial/Post-Cultural Challenge." *Journal of Multicultural Discourses.* Vol. 5, No. 1 (2010) 45–63.

Thai, X., and Barrett, T. "Biden's description of Obama draws scrutiny." *CNN* (31 January 2007). http://articles.cnn.com/2007-01-31/politics/biden.obama_1_braun-and-al-sharpton-african-american-presidential-candidates-delaware-democrat?_s=PM:POLITICS.

Chapter 3

Obama's Lincoln

Image to Ideology

William D. Pederson

Introduction

Most individuals have personal heroes, perhaps an individual who
was president of the United States. For example, the presidents
themselves had heroes, some of whom were other presidents.
Theodore Roosevelt always claimed that Abraham Lincoln was his
personal hero. As such, when confronted with challenges, Roosevelt
tried to emulate what he thought the Great Emancipator might
have done. Woodrow Wilson, later in his life, adopted Lincoln as
his favorite president despite the stark contrasts between the two
on the matter of promoting civil rights for blacks. Barack Obama
claims Lincoln, Mahatma Gandhi, and Martin Luther King Jr. as
his heroes (Mendell 2007). But among Obama's moral triumvirate,
only Lincoln was an elected political leader. This chapter examines
Obama's interest in Lincoln and maintains that, of Obama's three
heroes, the Great Emancipator exerts a profound influence on him
due to Lincoln's approach to politics as well as the psychological
similarity between the two presidents.

To explore these arguments, this chapter is divided into four
sections: 1) a review of Lincolnesque traces in Obama's political
life; 2) the possible psychological ties between Obama and Lincoln;
3) the suggestion that Obama's identification with the Great
Emancipator is so strong that Lincoln's approach to politics may

be seen in Obama's mode of reasoning; and 4) some tentative conclusions regarding what this might mean for the future.

Obama Meets Lincoln

It is unclear when Obama first learned about the Great Emancipator. During his education at an elite private school in Hawaii he surely encountered Lincoln (Percoco 2008). Perhaps his introduction came through his well-educated African father who surely would have known about the Great Emancipator and the related issue of African countries struggling to end years of colonialism (Assensoh and Alex-Assensoh 2004). Obama may even have been exposed to Lincoln during his early years in Indonesia because of that country's independence from the Dutch was inspired by a leader who claimed admiration for the Great Emancipator.

Whenever Obama was introduced to Lincoln the historical figure, that acquaintance undoubtedly was amplified during Obama's move to the continental United States for college. California, the state where Obama started college, is saturated with tributes to the sixteenth American president from Disneyland to the Lincoln Shrine in Redlands, California. The Lincoln Shrine and the College of the Redlands in California have strong ties to Lincoln. The Lincoln Fellowship at Redlands holds an annual Lincoln lecture on its campus. Moreover, in his classroom in nearby Occidental College in Los Angeles, Obama encountered Lincoln in a political science course (Kloppenberg 2010).

After such early experiences with Lincoln, Obama literally entered the "Land of Lincoln" when he moved to Illinois after graduating from Columbia University. After serving as a community organizer in Chicago, Obama became an attorney and then served in the Illinois legislature, which marks a similar path toward the White House as Lincoln more than a century earlier. Obama sought election to the U.S. Senate, a seat Lincoln, too, had been unsuccessful in obtaining. Obama, like Lincoln, displayed an innate ability with words during his early political and professional careers. Tall and lanky, Obama even shared physical similarities, except for skin color, with the democratic hero he professed to admire. With a shared sense of self-depreciating humor, both even joked about their protruding ears.

Enormous physical energy, perhaps even relentless ambition like the Great Emancipator's ambition that "knew no rest," fueled

Obama. Obama also experienced political defeat in pursuing elected office in Illinois, just as had Lincoln. And, during the nation's five-year bicentennial observation of Lincoln's birth, Obama, too, became a successful "dark horse" presidential candidate. Obama announced his candidacy in Springfield, Illinois, the town where Lincoln had practiced law for seventeen years prior to his success as a "dark horse" candidate for the presidency. The identification of the first successful African American presidential candidate with Lincoln's legacy was so apparent that the popular culture of the nation he was about to lead, if not the world, transformed him into "Abraham Obama" (Goede 2009).

That blended image was reinforced at his inauguration with a train ride into Washington, D.C., reminiscent of Lincoln's arrival in the nation's capital, and the selection of the Lincoln Memorial as a venue for some of his pre-inaugural festivities and Lincoln's Bible for his swearing-in ceremony. Regardless of the image projected as a result of these choices, which became media fodder, Obama may be tied to Lincoln on more fundamental levels through psychological similarities.

Psychological Outsiders

Even before the weight of the Civil War descended on his presidential shoulders, Lincoln was typically described as frequently depressed or at least melancholic. In contrast, Obama's nature is seemingly upbeat. These opposite characterizations of their moods aside, they are almost certainly alike in psychological marginality. A difficult term to define, it may be conceptualized as a mental condition found among individuals on the move ("on the make" in the parlance of emerging America), who are cutting old ties and seeking to become part of a new group that they aspire to join. Even if they join the aspiration group, they seldom feel they really fit in; they never feel completely "at home" in the new group. Mentally, these individuals dwell in an emotional limbo, caught in the pull between two spheres of competing influence for their allegiance—on one hand, their origins, and on the other, their desired destination (Berlin 1980). These psychological outsiders exhibit common characteristics. They tend to have and exhibit unusual energy and restlessness. In the vernacular, they appear to "have ants in their pants." Driven by ambition to prove themselves, they are often "joiners" seeking to gain acceptance from those in their aspiration group. Marginality tends to manifest itself in extreme behavior.

There are several standard ways that psychologically marginal individuals react to the discomfort of outsidedness: 1) over conforming to the new group they seek to join; 2) rebelling or using violence; and 3) exhibiting creative behavior. Psychologists tend to see the first two options as negative resolutions while the third is a "positive" resolution of one's marginality.

Examples of over conforming and using violence are numerous among political leaders. Corsican-born Napoleon tried to become more French than the French; Austrian-born Hitler tried to be more German than the Germans; and Georgia-born Stalin tried to become a new brand of Russian. Demagogues often find comfort in ideology and use violence to purge those who oppose them.

Foreign born and illegitimate, Alexander Hamilton was the most marginal of the framers of the U.S. Constitution. Due to height alone, James Madison was the shortest of the framers who came up with a creative new way to handle power. Similarly, B. R. Ambedkar, an "Untouchable" from India's caste system, wrote its constitution at the same time he formed an intellectual bond with Abraham Lincoln and a dislike of Mohandas Gandhi.

Irish statesman Eamon De Valera (1882–1975) made a successful transition from rebel to long-time leader of the Irish Free State and subsequently the Republic of Ireland. He was born outside Ireland and had a Spanish surname. Ireland's neutrality in both world wars cast a cloud over the loyalty of Irish Americans. Irish American Joseph McCarthy resolved his marginality negatively by accusing nearly everyone else of communist subversion. Ironically, it took until 1960 before a Catholic Irish American was elected president with the dubious assistance in Chicago from the last Irish American political machine.

Three common triggers of marginality involve deviations from the norm on physical, social, and intellectual dimensions. Physical "outsiderness" could be any variation from the group norm including a deformity or perceived handicapping condition, height or weight, race or ethnicity (or even accent), or intellectual capacity. Most often marginality is discussed in relation to social class—an individual trying to "rise in society" from a lower to higher status. Even if the individual seeking the change has managed to climb to higher economic rungs, he or she will never feel he or she truly belongs in the new surroundings. This phenomenon is apparent in the *nouveau riche*, as depicted in F. Scott Fitzgerald's *The Great Gatsby*, an example of art imitating life.

It is often suggested that the middle class is the most marginal social class because members often fear slipping into the lower class at the same time they strain to advance up the social ladder. Such pursuit of upward mobility is the American birthright. In terms of intellectual marginality, someone who lacks formal schooling or received an inferior education may feel shame or inadequacy when dealing with better-educated individuals.

A classic twentieth-century case was Lyndon B. Johnson, whose obscure Texas alma mater—a school that was not even accredited at the time of his college graduation—was a source of embarrassment and motivation. The unusually tall LBJ ended up working in Washington with John F. Kennedy's Harvard gang, which mocked not only LBJ's drawl but also his questionable education (Barber 1982).

Lincoln's Marginality

It is possible for an individual to be marginal on more than one dimension. Abraham Lincoln, America's most marginal president, exemplifies this. He was marginal on all three dimensions—physical, social, and intellectual. He was too tall, too skinny, and too ugly to go unnoticed. If not exactly ugly his appearance, by all accounts, was at least described as unusual. Lincoln was especially marginal from a social standpoint. Born in the American South, he was reared on the country's rugged frontier—on the nation's geographic fringe, a metaphor far beyond the bounds of proper society.

Lincoln "married up," a typical move for a socially marginal male. Lincoln wed a true Southern belle. Even though Mary Todd, who was as ambitious as her husband beneath her polished exterior, did her best to brush the frontier dust off her husband and mold him into a gentleman. But, the traditional Northeast power establishment looked at Lincoln askance and viewed him as a frontier hick or worse. Driven by ambition to improve his lot—as a frontiersman he would "pull himself up by his bootstraps"—Lincoln rejected his father's example of making a living with his back and opted instead to work with his brain. He became a lawyer and then a politician.

Despite having less than one year of formal schooling, Lincoln's insatiable appetite for learning, coupled with his ambition, drove him to become an autodidact and very successful lawyer, a career he used as his springboard to politics, just as Obama did much later. Politics has often been a traditional route for ambitious individuals lacking social and intellectual pedigrees, and for such marginalized individuals as Lincoln.

Obama's Marginality

If Obama is not as marginal as Lincoln, to the discerning eye he is not far behind. Obama is slender and lanky like Lincoln, but not to the extreme. However, his race is different from any of his presidential predecessors, which has been and remains, sadly, a major factor in American politics and professional life. Yet, like Lincoln, Obama showed the ability to use self-deprecating humor. Not only was Obama the nation's first black president but his social marginality included his status as America's first biracial president. The son of a white American mother from Kansas and an African father from Kenya, Obama's biracial and binational ancestry are further accentuated by his very name, Barack Hussein Obama.

Moreover, it is clear from reading Obama's books that he exhibits the extraordinary energy and restlessness that mark the marginal:

> In me, one of those flaws had proven to be a chronic restlessness. . . . Whether politics encourages that trait or simply attracts those who possess it is unclear. Someone once said that every man is either trying to live up to his father's expectations or make up for his father's mistakes, and I suppose that may explain my particular malady as well as anything else. (Obama 2006: 2–3)

Obama may not consciously understand that marginality is associated with his self-described "malady" of restlessness or that it is yet another trait he shares with his hero, Lincoln. Lincoln was born in a border state outside the heartland of the nation with which he identified. In Obama's case, he was born and reared in Hawaii—and briefly in Indonesia, far outside the continental mainland and halfway around the globe from the traditional base of American power in the northeast United States.

Comparisons of Marginality

It is fairly clear that both Lincoln and Obama were able to resolve their marginality positively through not only an incredible work ethic and intellect but also through the arena of law and politics, the two great passions of both men. Most presidents have been lawyers. But the most active and flexible among America's lawyer-presidents, whether they had formal legal education like Obama (who graduated from Harvard Law School) or had just "read law" like Lincoln, soon left their law practices to pursue political careers. Interestingly, the lawyers who practice law the longest before becoming president, typically end up among the most passive of the presidents (Green and Pederson 1989). The perfect illustration of this truism is William Howard Taft. Taft traded the political world for a judge's more structured legal environment. America's largest president in terms of girth, Taft is the only president to leave the White House and later don the robe as the chief justice of the Supreme Court. Like other marginals who never positively resolve their marginality, these more passive and flexible presidents, in essence, over conform to the prevailing social/political/economic system. Their behavior constitutes a distinct contrast to the more creative and innovative behavior of those who positively resolve their marginality like Lincoln and Obama (Pederson and Williams 2001).

Lincoln, however, is atypical among the active and flexible presidents, for he practiced the law for nearly two decades but he also first ran for political office even before he became a lawyer, much earlier than any other of America's future lawyer-presidents. His political ambition was clear. Lincoln enjoyed the venue of politics as one that would allow him to use his considerable innate intellectual ability to address political issues. Undeterred by losing his first electoral campaign for a seat in the Illinois state legislature, Lincoln ran for the same seat two years later and won it. After that victory, he spent the rest of his life either seeking or serving in public office (Hofstadter 1948).

Obama's transition from community organizer to Harvard Law School and back to the Land of Lincoln to both teach law at the University of Chicago and engage in community activism and local politics suggests the same type of ambitious route that Lincoln took. Both ultimately sought to fulfill themselves in politics. Obama's marriage to an African American lawyer from Chicago further solidified his identity with the black community and his African American heritage. In a remarkably short time he was serving in the Illinois legislature, as did Lincoln. Once Lincoln resolved his "identity crisis," he rose quickly to a leadership position within his party, and Obama's path was similar. Obama would lose one state legislative election, but ran for the U.S.

Senate and was elected, unlike Lincoln who lost his bid for the same Senate seat. There are notable similarities in their rise in politics. Once each came to the decision to seek personal fulfillment in the political arena rather than through the practice of law, each used the law merely as his vehicle on the road to politics and quickly accomplished his political goals.

The legal-to-political transition as well as the positive resolution of their marginalities was facilitated by the emotional support that each ambitious man received from their marriage family rather than his birth family, and to a degree from their extended families. Lincoln's lifelong episodes of melancholy—perhaps even bipolar in today's terminology (Shenk 2005)—stemmed in part from the early loss of his natural mother and an aloof and unemotional father who failed to understand him. Fortunately, Lincoln's stepmother compensated in large measure for his loss and he came to refer to her as his "angel mother." Similarly, Obama's talented and warm maternal grandparents helped fill the void created by his absentee African father. Obama's grandmother was available for him when his mother was preoccupied as she struggled with her graduate education and fieldwork in Indonesia. In addition to emotional support from his grandmother, Obama's maternal grandparents' income provided the boy a loosely middle-class upbringing and the privilege of attending one of the best private schools in Hawaii. Obama was somewhat emotionally secure despite a tumultuous upbringing.

Still, it was Lincoln's marriage to the affluent, sophisticated, social, and political Mary Todd, and his experience as a father of four boys that helped allay his marginality and serve his emotional needs. The same can be said of Obama, who, in Michelle Robinson and his two daughters, found the social and emotional comforts of a nuclear family.

Obama's family security and geographic remoteness in Hawaii and Indonesia, places where his skin tone was unique but unremarkable, shielded him in many ways from prejudice that he may have experienced in the contiguous United States. It should also be noted that Martin Luther King Jr., Obama's twentieth-century American hero who grew up in the Deep South decades before Obama, was also somewhat shielded from the overt racial segregation faced by most blacks of the era because of his middle-class environment in urban Atlanta, Georgia. Other common ground between Obama and King is that they emerged from families who had high expectations for their children and they expressed virtually no resentment toward American whites compared to many other prominent black leaders. In fact, King and Obama shared admiration for the "self-made" Abraham Lincoln, an identified personal hero of both men (Mendell 2007).

Apart from upholding the democratic electoral process in 1864, while the bloody Civil War raged in a divided nation, Lincoln's marginality propelled him to craft a creative yet rational solution to the intertwined issues of slavery and secession. Rather than siding with the abolitionists or the planters prior to the Civil War, Lincoln initially sought only to stop the spread of that "peculiar institution" that had been protected in the U.S. Constitution. After the South seceded from the Union, Lincoln used the Declaration of Independence to expand the parameters of the Constitution by first issuing the Emancipation Proclamation and then encouraging the Congress to ratify the Thirteenth Amendment to permanently prohibit slavery. Moreover, he reached back to classical magnanimity to justify restoration of the Southern states to the Union as quickly as possible after the war (Arnhart 1983). History records that, in pursuit of sorely needed national healing, Lincoln granted the second highest number of amnesties in American history (Pederson 1989).

Through the Emancipation Proclamation and clemency, coupled with the landmark pieces of legislation that he had signed in 1862 even as war raged—the Land Grant College Act, the Homestead Act, and the Pacific Railway Act—Lincoln was establishing social and economic pillars to expand the nation transformed by the Great Emancipator.

Obama Echoing Lincoln's Leadership

Lincoln drew emotional support from his "angel mother" and the close friends he made throughout his life; he liked people who responded in the same fashion, even though he was guarded and shrewd with his political maneuvers. Obama, like Lincoln, successfully resolved his marginality through the political arena using the law as a means to that end, and also made many friends and exhibited a shrewd and guarded approach to politics. Moreover, the transition of the ambitious ("ants in his pants") Obama from a community organizer to political leader is similar to the Great Emancipator's juggling of his new law practice with "riding circuit" for a good part of the year. At a personal level, Obama had observed his mother's lifetime example of showing concern for others while pursuing her doctoral work.

Obama's marriage to an African American lawyer from Chicago who had once been his boss suggests Lincoln's upwardly mobile marriage to Mary Todd, who hailed at the pinnacle of Kentucky gentry. In a remarkably brief time after starting his political career, Obama was serving in the Illinois legislature, like Lincoln before him, and losing only a single state legislative race. Also like Lincoln, Obama ran for a seat in the U.S. Senate. Unlike Lincoln, however, Obama won his election to the Senate. Still, their rise in politics is quite similar. Both exhibited intense ambition—in Lincoln's case leading to the observation that he was "the little engine that knew no rest"—within the political arena. Both found fulfillment in working on public policy issues as both had successfully resolved their psychological issues. Each found his niche in the political world and was able to aptly handle the demands of his career through sheer enjoyment of it.

Obama's "dark horse" triumph over much more established candidates in his presidential race stunned political analysts just as Lincoln's had. The Great Emancipator's leading opponent was the New York senator William Seward; Obama's was the New York senator Hillary Rodham Clinton. To those who see modern American politics only in terms of special group politics, Obama's triumph stunned African Americans, feminists, and others. For the first time, voters were offered a presidential candidate with African American heritage who, unlike Jesse Jackson or Al Sharpton, was not defined solely by his work on behalf of the black community, and one who was seen as a viable (electable) candidate. Nor did Obama make race the central issue of his campaign. He made an appeal to a broader constituency rather than to a single faction in the Democratic Party.

During the general election, Obama's persona continued a transformation from a majority candidate into a latter-day Abraham Lincoln. It was a metamorphosis depicted literally by modern artists in their fusion of the iconic image of the bearded Lincoln melding with Obama's facial features (Goede 2009). Instead of focusing on African American issues that would polarize voters, Obama suggested changing American foreign policy from that associated with "the ugly American" approach and, like Lincoln, sought common ground, unity, and a shared vision for America's future.

To the subsequent surprise of many, Obama was actually echoing the leadership modality of his hero, Abraham Lincoln. The campaign's meshing with the national bicentennial observance of Lincoln's birth reinforced the image and legacy of the Great Emancipator to such an extent that it masked the fact that Obama was employing Lincoln's "golden mean" ideology in public policy issues. Both stressed reason and moderation; once they were in office, critics on both extremes were flabbergasted or blinded by their own self-righteousness. In a classical Aristotelian tradition, both Lincoln and Obama believed that compromise was a basic fundamental of constitutional democracy.

Both men served during challenging times and times of war. As commanders-in-chief, they both lacked military experience (Lincoln served for a month in the Blackhawk Indian conflict). Obviously, the American Civil War during Lincoln's presidency was the greatest political division in the nation's history. In the short run, the sixteenth president's approach satisfied neither the Southern planters nor the Northern abolitionists. He initially favored applying the "golden mean" approach to slavery, too. Since the Constitution of the United States had been written by the Framers to protect slavery, Lincoln believed that the Old South had a legal right to retain it, although he expected that "the peculiar institution" would disappear eventually as the soil's ability to produce cotton as a profitable crop diminished. At the same time, he refused to sanction the spread of slavery into territories from which new states could be created.

After the crisis of secession, when trigger-happy firebrands began the Civil War at Fort Sumter, Lincoln faced the issue of incompetent Union generals. By the time Ulysses S. Grant, another marginal figure in American history, successfully emerged, Lincoln had transformed the war into one that would finally end slavery, especially after his proposed voluntary "colonization" and compensated emancipation schemes had failed. He did this while saying that his "policy was to have no policy" (Donald 1995). Military victory on the battlefield created the political environment that permitted him to become the Great Emancipator. A pragmatic frontier attorney, throughout his life, Lincoln consistently favored reason over emotion and moderation over extremism when dealing with public policy issues.

If Lincoln inherited a two-headed monster of secession and Civil War, Obama inherited not just a double war in Iraq and Afghanistan, but also a domestic economy in free fall. Most economists believed that the nation was doomed to a second Great Depression unless the federal government intervened immediately. Faced with those enormous challenges, Obama's Lincoln traits kicked in. Obama acted decisively but while seeking common ground. He did not impose further deregulation or nationalize banks as extremists on the right and left, respectively, favored. Instead, he backed a large fiscal stimulus bill and greater Wall Street regulation. As might have been predicted, the "golden mean" actions satisfied neither conservative nor liberal extremists. Nor did the general public, who were experiencing personal economic distress, embrace Obama's actions. Both presidents seemed to favor long-term policies over short-term political successes.

The Gulf oil spill catastrophe of 2010 would have been justification for a demagogue to attack a foreign corporation, but Obama reacted characteristically with a measured approach. Lincoln also dealt with foreign powers with an even and steady hand, rather than resorting to political gamesmanship over European interests in the South's cotton trade and the outcome of the Civil War. In the aftermath of the oil spill and prolonged attempt to stop the flow of oil into the Gulf of Mexico, there was public outrage over Obama's handling of the oil spill, which was fanned by the 24/7 news media and Obama's many political opportunists. The reactions were much like those that had followed Obama's support of taxpayer "bail-out" loans to Wall Street and the auto industry when the country learned of outrageous bonuses paid to executive of the very firms that had caused the economic meltdown, concurrent with average Americans struggling to survive financially. At least in regard to the BP oil spill crisis, Obama's moderation seems to have yielded more effective results than a crusade against the evils of Big Business.

Apart from the economic crisis and against the advice of many political operatives, Obama, like Lincoln, was willing to tackle a fundamental issue facing the nation. He was willing to risk his presidency over the issue of national health care reform. Taking his cue from Lincoln again, Obama allowed Congress to grapple with the issue until the time was finally ripe to resolve it. Although it turned out to be a prolonged and largely partisan debate, Obama ultimately achieved a "first" for the nation. Realizing that he did not have a mandate for a "single-payer" option but rejecting a totally volunteer plan, Obama agreed to a "golden mean" compromise. Both presidents sought bold action but political moderation in the face of overwhelming domestic and foreign policy challenges, a myriad of powerful special interests, and vigorous opposition from countless political opponents.

Obama ended active American combat in Iraq, but after a long and exhaustive review process, he agreed to another year of expanded military involvement in Afghanistan. However, the commander in chief put the military on notice of a timetable for them to produce results. Both courses of action seemed to please no one. Conservatives pushed for stronger action; liberals argued for quick withdrawal. Once again, Obama took a moderate middle course that satisfied neither extreme in the short term, echoes of Lincoln's handling of the Civil War.

Conclusion

In summary, one might conclude that Obama's identification with Lincoln was not a mere campaign ploy but that Obama genuinely looks to Lincoln as his presidential "North Star." The Great Emancipator guides him in an active and moderate approach to public policy. Rather than follow the example of some of their presidential predecessors and just muddle through or do nothing, both Lincoln and Obama were willing to take a moral stance on the largest issues facing the nation. In the short run, the off-year election in 1862 was a setback for the Republicans and Lincoln but in the long run, the wisdom of Lincoln's policies was confirmed on the battlefield.

The 2010 off-year election was similarly a setback for the Democrats and Obama, but immediately thereafter, despite the advice of pundits on the left and on the right during the lame duck session of Congress, Obama compromised to secure unexpected positive accomplishments. He *has* established a consistent record by which he can be judged and scholars may very well continue to evoke Lincoln as a basis for exploring Obama's political psyche.

Works Cited

Arnhart, L. "Statesmanship as Magnanimity: Classical, Christian and Modern. *Polity.* Vol. 16, No. 2 (1983), 263–283.

Assensoh, A. and Alex-Assensoh, Y. "Abraham Lincoln and the Third World in the 21st Century." *Abraham Lincoln Abroad.* Vol. 13, No. 1, (2004), 3–5.

Barber, James David. *Presidential Character.* Englewood Cliffs, NJ: Prentice-Hall, 1982.

Berlin, I. *Against the Current*. New York: Viking, 1980.

Donald, David Herbert. *Lincoln*. New York: Simon and Schuster, 1995.

Goede, D. *Abraham Obama: A Guerrilla Tour Through Art and Politics*. San Francisco: Last Gasp, 2009.

Hofstadter, Richard. *American Political Tradition*. New York: Alfred Knopf, 1948.

Kloppenberg, J. *Reading Obama*. Princeton, NJ: Princeton University Press, 2010.

Mendell, D. *Obama. From Promise to Power*. New York: Amistad, 2007.

Obama, Barack. *Audacity of Hope*. New York: Three River Press, 2006.

Pederson, William D. *The "Barberian" Presidency*. New York: Peter Lang, 1989.

Pederson, William D. and Williams, Frank. "America's presidential triumvirate: Quantitative measures of character." Eds. E. Fishman, William Pederson, and Mark Rozell. *George Washington. Foundations of Presidential Leadership and Character*. Westport, CT: Praeger, 2001, 143–161.

Percoco, J. "Hawaii's aloha to the 16th president." *Washington Times* (27 Nov. 2008).

Shenk, J. W. *Lincoln's Melancholy*. Boston: Houghton Mifflin, 2005.

Chapter 4

The Optimist and the Realist

R. Ward Holder

Barack Obama's Pragmatic Use of Reinhold Nieburh's Thought

In 2007, a tired Barack Obama said to the somewhat disinterested David Brooks, "Reinhold Niebuhr is one of my favorite philosophers" (Brooks 2007). Given the aggressive charges made against Obama by opponents on the political right, this was a somewhat unexpected comment. As far as history goes, the most recent president to attempt so explicitly to shoulder Niebuhr's mantle was Jimmy Carter, whose presidency many wish to avoid as a model for their own. As far as "favorite philosophers" are concerned, the comment also evoked the much-hyped comment by George W. Bush that Jesus was his favorite philosopher. The interplay of these metaphysical models has driven commentators to their keyboards, while analysts have suggested a wide variety of interpretations and implications of the comment regarding Obama's presidency (Brooks 2009; CNN 2010; Judis 2009; Julian 2010; Smith 2008). For instance, did the remark signal Obama's support for the working class against the heartless captains of industry? Or, did it suggest Obama's support for interventionist military policies?

However, there is another way to examine the comment. Is Barack Obama truly a Niebuhrian or does Niebuhr's thought represent a pragmatic choice, another tool in a toolbox that is occasionally used, but just as often set aside for others? The difference between these positions is significant. If Obama actually is influenced in a deep theoretical manner by Niebuhr, then reading Niebuhr's thought gives insight into how Obama might proceed in a variety of situations. On the other hand, if Obama uses Niebuhr as a pragmatist, this will give a very different lesson about the relationship, and about Obama. The difference signals two very different kinds of leaders. Is Obama an idealist, or a pragmatist?

It is argued in this chapter that, while it might have made sense for Obama to develop into a Niebuhrian thinker about a variety of topics, Obama's use of Niebuhr is far more limited than that. Obama's basic anthropology—his conception of what it means to be human—remains too optimistic, and denies both the paradoxical and ironic elements of Niebuhr's conception of both the nature of humanity and the fundamental destiny of the human race. Furthermore, Obama is quite confident about the ability of well-intentioned people to direct the course of history to a good, if not perfect, conclusion. The differences between both men's anthropological and historical approaches are stark, and reveal theoretical chasms that lie between their thought-worlds. This can be demonstrated by a consideration of what I call the Niebuhr periphery and center. Contrary to the insights of many political theorists, the center of Niebuhr's thought is not in his analysis of the political problems between and within nations and empires. For Niebuhr, that was peripheral to his central concern as a pastor to apply the insights of Christian doctrine to the human condition. However, we will see that Obama's thought frequently coincides with Niebuhr's in the periphery, but infrequently in its center.

Reinhold Niebuhr—The Periphery

Much of what Reinhold Niebuhr is known for today belongs to the periphery of his thought. By periphery, I mean the applications of his insights in particular circumstances, as opposed to the center, his foundational commitments and perceptions. That seems overly confident, but the evidence demonstrates that in fact, somewhat ahistorically, Niebuhr's key and central ideas are not those that are most well known today. This can be revealed through a quick overview of two of Niebuhr's points that are considered by analysts—Niebuhr's considerations of economic power and his doctrine of the pragmatic use of force.

Considerations of Economic Power[1]

The contemporary consideration of Niebuhr's thought is absolutely tied to modern or postmodern ideas about the accumulation and use of power. For Niebuhr, the accumulation of power represented a moral challenge to the community. We see this early on in Niebuhr's career, in his consideration of economic realities. He attacked Henry Ford, not simply for making enormous sums of money, but for the manner in which that power was unfettered by other considerations. Niebuhr wrote, "History ought to have taught us that the man who holds power is never as benevolent as he imagines himself to be" (Niebuhr 1926a: 1355). Furthermore, he saw that the churches in America were impacted by this idealization of wealth. He proclaimed that the interests of the Protestant churches in America were aligned with those of the middle class, and only a change toward a prophetic stance could save the church's claim to be the bearer of the gospel (Niebuhr 1922). Niebuhr was suspicious of the accumulation and monopolization of power, and wrote extensively upon this theme in his early career (Niebuhr, 1922, 1926a, 1926b, 1928, 1929, 1931, 1932a).

We see modern analysts caught up in this issue.[2] John Cooper and Dean Brackley's exchange about Niebuhr and Jacques Maritain concentrates on issues of economic reality and power—are unions falling in membership because the underlying issues for the labor movement have been addressed, or because the effectiveness of unions has been reduced (Cooper and Brackley 1988)? Lynn D. Nelson's use of Niebuhr in his consideration of the workings of advanced market nations is sophisticated, but concentrates as well on this level on the effects of Niebuhr's conceptions, rather than their roots (Nelson, 1988).[3] In both cases, contemporary analysts concentrate their efforts on the impact of Niebuhr's concepts of

---

1. Although the use of Niebuhr after 9/11 has concentrated on his consideration of Christian realist approaches to war, that present context should not blind observers to the wider horizon that analysts of Niebuhr addressed.

2. However, a more Niebuhrian approach is outlined by Andrew Finstuen, in his "This American Mess: Where is Reinhold Niebuhr When We Need Him?" *Christian Century* December 1, 2009, 11–12.

3. At times, however, Nelson's sophistication devolves into a recognition that Niebuhr is working with a different anthropology than his own, but one that can be dismissed because economic anthropology does not work the way that Niebuhr describes it (60S).

power and how it works in societies, rather than excavating how those concepts reflect far more basic theories about human nature.[4]

Obama's early presidency clearly echoed this kind of concern. Although economists and sociologists can debate the health care legislation at great length as to whether it was a coverage bill or a cost-containment bill, the president's rhetoric around the issue of health care provides a clear window into the manner in which he sought to rein in economic power. In his remarks the morning after the House passed the health care legislation, Obama said,

> Tonight, after nearly 100 years of talk and frustration, after decades of trying, and a year of sustained effort and debate, the United States Congress finally declared that America's workers and America's families and America's small businesses deserve the security of knowing that here, in this country, neither illness nor accident should endanger the dreams they've worked a lifetime to achieve. . . . We pushed back on the undue influence of special interests. We didn't give in to mistrust or to cynicism or to fear. Instead, we proved that we are still a people capable of doing big things and tackling our biggest challenges. We proved that this government—a government of the people and by the people—still works for the people (Obama 2010a).

This model of concern for the abilities of the less powerful to achieve health care tied to the economic benefit for larger institutions, both businesses and communities, was also the tone Obama took in his campaign rhetoric around the health care issue during the presidential campaign (Obama 2007).

This same stylistic model informed Obama's discussion of financial regulation. The passage of a financial regulatory bill in July 2010 brought out more of Obama's rhetoric that saw the necessity of government protecting consumers from abuse of powers that were deemed "too big to fail." He said "Unscrupulous lenders locked consumers into complex loans with hidden costs. Firms like AIG placed massive, risky bets with borrowed money.

---

4. A different approach is taken by Yamin (2009). The argument can be made that Alicia Ely Yamin's approach is quite Niebuhrian, or at least walks a parallel path. However, it is not clear at all that Obama made this approach his own.

And while the rules left abuse and excess unchecked, they left taxpayers on the hook if a big bank or financial institution ever failed" (Obama 2010b). The model seems Niebuhrian—the government must intervene to stop the irresponsible centers of economic power from gross exploitation of the weak. At first glance, Obama follows the ideals of Niebuhr.

Pragmatic Use of Force

Niebuhr wrote as early as 1932 of the necessity of nations using coercion for the establishment of justice. In his *Moral Man and Immoral Society: A Study in Ethics and Politics*, he wrote, "All social cooperation on a scale larger than the most intimate social group requires a measure of coercion" (Niebuhr 1932a: 3). He could write about the necessity of force in the pursuit or establishment of domestic harmony, and was just as clear-eyed as he considered the necessity of the use of coercive power in international relations. While the 1932 publication of *Moral Man and Immoral Society* may well have set the "conceptual basis" for Niebuhr's mature positions on the use of force and relinquishment of pacifism, it would take him years to state those positions with stark clarity (Bullert 2002: 275). But he did, with his publication of "Must We Do Nothing?" in 1932 (Niebuhr 1932b), with his article for *Christian Century* in December 1940 (Niebuhr 1940), and his call to repeal the Neutrality Act, published only weeks before the attack on Pearl Harbor (Niebuhr 1941). Niebuhr would go on to give far greater consideration to this topic in later writings, most notably *The Nature and Destiny of Man, The Children of Light and the Children of Darkness: A Vindication of Democracy and a Critique of its Traditional Defense,* and *The Irony of American History.*[5] His opinions on this matter would be so clear that one of his greatest opponents would attack him frequently for his positions against Christian pacifism.

Given the applicability of Niebuhr's thought to the post-9/11 world, this area of his thought has received perhaps the greatest sustained analytical attention. The editorial that opened the first 2010 edition of *America* proclaimed that Obama's embrace

---

5. Published in 1941/1943, 1944, and 1952. These were definitely NOT his final words on the matter, but simply demonstrate that he came back to this topic frequently.

of Niebuhr was a "Marching into the Past" (*America* 2010). In late 2009, John Judis wrote on Obama and Niebuhr, although the majority of the article was a quotation of an article by Mac McCorkle. Although McCorkle's analysis is worthy of consideration, it never penetrates past the surface—examining Obama to see where his policies will go, and how the Christian realist theologian should not be considered the darling of the left (Judis 2009). Other analysts have flocked to consider the "Niebuhrian cast" to Obama's Nobel Peace Prize acceptance speech, including David Gibson (2009) in *Politics Daily*, Fred Kaplan (2009) in *Slate.com*, and Ronald Osborn (2010) in *First Things*. Even Joseph Loconte's (2010) diatribe against Obama's opportunistic use of Niebuhr concentrated on outcomes, rather than causes.

Obama has paralleled Niebuhr's concerned acceptance of the pragmatic use of force in his own commitments and declarations. A point that often gets missed in the examination of the Nobel acceptance speech is that Obama was willing to prosecute the war in Afghanistan far more vigorously than other Democratic leaders (Baker 2009; Cordesman 2010). Furthermore, in that speech, Obama famously said, "We must begin by acknowledging the hard truth that we will not eradicate violent conflict in our lifetimes. There will be times when nations—acting individually or in concert—will find the use of force not only necessary but morally justified" (Obama 2009). Although Obama never mentioned Niebuhr in this speech, choosing instead to cite Martin Luther King Jr., Gandhi, and John F. Kennedy, his remarks were quickly and widely analyzed as having a Niebuhrian tone.[6] Again, the echoes of Niebuhr seemed to ring from the president's words.

But did they? The point is not that analysts should not have examined the foundations of Obama's thought, and compared it with Niebuhr's work. Rather, the issue is that in the excitement to look at effects, many theorists have neglected to scrutinize causes. Put another way, if Obama and Niebuhr end up in the same place for different fundamental commitments, is that sameness accidental, rather than substantial? If we wish to be less harsh, we might ask, what "kind" of Niebuhrian is Obama? To see that clearly, we must examine Niebuhr's core commitments.

---

6. I have yet to see a published analysis that notes Niebuhr's influence on King, and the possible manner in which that relationship might have mediated Niebuhr to Obama.

Reinhold Niebuhr—The Center

Although Niebuhr is widely known for his insights into political groups and how they function, that was not central to his thought, but rather an articulated implication from the more central pillars of his philosophy or theology. This is true for at least two reasons. The first I have outlined above—many contemporary analysts have concentrated their efforts on the fruits of Niebuhr's writing on political and ethical matters, thus somewhat obscuring the roots of the Niebuhrian "tree." Second, Niebuhr presented his thought in an ad-hoc manner that masked some of its coherence. The anthropological and historical doctrines that lie at the center of his thought, and that appear clearly in his works published in the 1940s and 1950s, do exist in his early writings, but are fragmentary and inchoately presented.[7] But the center of Niebuhr's thought so dominates the implications that it must be examined.[8]

Niebuhr's Anthropology

Almost all theologians who examine Niebuhr will grant that his doctrine of anthropology, the nature of humanity, stands at the center of his thought. Although Niebuhr saw that humanity was created good, he also noted that the creation itself limited humanity—humanity experiences a "finite, dependent and contingent existence," that was not evil because of that finitude (Niebuhr 1941: 167). However, humanity does not experience this dependent and contingent character as acceptable, and seeks to deny it. Humanity's uneasiness with its own nature results in anxiety, because it is impossible finally to escape the human predicament and become immortal or infinite (Niebuhr 1943: 204). Humanity is both finite and transcendent, this dual character being both the source of creativity and uniqueness, and also the source of sin. Niebuhr wrote:

> The fact that man can transcend himself in infinite regression and cannot find the end of life except in God is the mark of his creativity and uniqueness; closely related to

---

7. See for instance the brief sense of anthropology and history Niebuhr gives in his *Leaves from the Notebook of a Tamed Cynic* (1929).

8. Even those who have disagreed with Niebuhr have frequently done so on this basis. See Plaskow (1980); and Valerie Saiving (1960).

this capacity is his inclination to transmute his partial
and finite self and his partial and finite values into the
infinite good. Therein lies his sin (Niebuhr 1941: 122).

The source of human creativity and transcendence was also
the source of human religious rebellion and the source of radical
injustice (Niebuhr 1941: 179). Finally, this sin presents itself as
pride that shows its character as the pride of power, knowledge,
and virtue (Niebuhr 1941: 188–203). Niebuhr considered this biblical doctrine of man to be empirically demonstrable, although he did
not argue for its truth on that basis. Furthermore, Niebuhr saw
that the various popular modern conceptions of humanity shared
the same flaw—the acceptance of the easy conscience. This was
all the more remarkable because moderns even used contradictory
arguments to arrive at the same conclusion. "The most surprising aspect of the modern man's good conscience is that he asserts
and justifies it in terms of the most varied and even contradictory
metaphysical theories and social philosophies" (Niebuhr 1941: 91).
He believed that this tendency toward the easy conscience stopped
serious reflection on the impact of human nature on ethical, political, and economic structures.

Niebuhr's Doctrine of History

Niebuhr proclaimed the importance of human history, while denying the possibility of humans ever really controlling it. Both of
these poles were critical components of his thought. Niebuhr
believed that humans were involved in, but also transcended history imperfectly. This ability to transcend the flux of nature gave
humanity the capacity to make history (Niebuhr 1943: 1). Humans
live in a paradoxical space, continually bound by natural necessity but never prevented from transcendence. Humans live to die.
No matter what else happens to us, we will grow old, sicken, and
die. But even in the midst of death and dying, humans see the
future, work for better ultimate outcomes, and even recognize the
truth that both individually and collectively humanity transcends
the end of life.

Niebuhr identified and critiqued two views of history that he
found inadequate to the human experience of time. The first was
the idea of history as positive, a model that saw it as the realm of
meaning in which humans move toward ever fuller and more perfect knowledge of life's essential meaning (Niebuhr 1943: 2). The

second model of history conceived of history negatively, representing a model that saw history as expressive of human finitude and "creatureliness." In this second model, history and materiality are to be escaped or overcome (Niebuhr 1943: 3). Niebuhr discerned these models of history both in religions and in philosophical views of existence.

But Niebuhr pointed out that the paradoxical nature of humanity, both subject to time and able to transcend it, tempted humans. Humans may joke that nothing is certain but death and taxes, but humans also place enormous effort into escaping both. No single medical category takes up a larger slice of the medical spending pie in America than efforts at end-of-life care. But escaping death is not the only way that humanity seeks to escape finitude. Empires have sought to claim an immortality as well, and humans constantly pursue the technological idol that promises one day to release humanity from death and oblivion. Niebuhr saw this effort as profoundly sinful, as well as being impossible (Niebuhr 1952: 132). Finally, Niebuhr was keenly aware of the paradoxical character of human efforts to control history—that the exact behaviors and efforts that sought to chain history's capriciousness to human control were the most likely to drive history in ways that escaped all control.

Obama's Anthropology

Obama's anthropology differs starkly from that of Niebuhr. Although at times his rhetoric can sound uncannily Niebuhrian, such as in his Nobel Peace Prize acceptance speech, his basic view of the human condition is far more optimistic than Niebuhr's. Obama frequently hides the anthropological observations that he does make under the guise of reflections on American values, but his rhetoric makes clear that he's talking about fundamentals that are substantial.[9] Obama can write that "at the core of the American experience are a set of ideals that continue to stir our collective conscience; a common set of values that bind us together despite our differences; a running thread of hope that makes our improbable experiment in democracy work" (Obama 2006: 11). Obama believes that the American values are:

---

9. Obviously, Obama is a politician, not a philosopher writing a treatise. But his core beliefs are discernible, although in a rhetorical form different than that generally used by Niebuhr.

. . . rooted in a basic optimism about life and a faith
in free will—a confidence that through pluck and sweat
and smarts, each of us can rise above the circumstances
of our birth. But these values also express a broader
confidence that so long as individual men and women
are free to pursue their own interests, society as a whole
will prosper. (66)

That basic optimism about life and free will is a clear statement about what humans are by nature. Writing about the American values that endure, Obama (2006) wrote that they are what
makes us ". . . who we are as a people" (83).[10] These include a
basic decency and generosity (Obama 2008). Furthermore, Obama
believes politicians can turn to this set of human constants in order
to gain acceptance for specific programs that are valuable (Obama
2006: 71). Beyond that, he believes that although humans occasionally will fail to follow their best instincts because of their particular contexts, when given freedom to change, groups of people will
follow their best impulses.

However, this is exactly where Niebuhr finds that the idea of
collective action experiences its greatest difficulties. First, Niebuhr
sees the creative tension within humanity, but always holds onto
its root at the heart of sin, rebellion, and injustice. Furthermore,
while Niebuhr finds that the possibility of individual commitment
and ethical action from the basis of Christian morality a possibility, his analysis of group action finds the idea of a society working on the basis of its highest values either impossible or even
laughable. Groups larger than those held together by the most
intimate bonds will allow economic interest to interpenetrate their
ideals, and will work from that starting point (Niebuhr 1932a: 5).
Where Obama finds the greatest source of hope, Niebuhr denies
the possibility of it, and searches for other methods of achieving
a proximate and tolerable justice.

Analysts have been much slower to take on this comparison
between Niebuhr and Obama. Although Jean Bethke Elshtain has
noted the enormity of the importance of a serious anthropology

---

10. Obama also set forth his list of virtues that seem to be linked to the substance
of Americans in his inaugural address, listing faith, determination, selflessness,
courage, and willingness to nurture as the enduring values that mark the
character of Americans.

for governing, and how this gift of Niebuhr's deserves more attention, she spends no effort at linking this critical recognition to the
thought or policies of Obama (Elshtain 2010: 42ff). Liam Julian
has considered these kinds of issues in his investigation of Obama
and Niebuhr, but does not set out Niebuhr's perspective on the
human condition clearly enough to explicate plainly the kinds of
difference that matter (Julian 2010).

Obama's Doctrine of History

Obama's conception of history differs from that of Niebuhr as well.
The difference does not appear to be as stark as that in their
anthropologies. Obama can state that:

> We can acknowledge that oppression will always be with
> us, and still strive for justice. We can admit the intracta-
> bility of depravation, and still strive for dignity. We can
> understand that there will be war, and still strive for
> peace. We can do That—for that is the story of human
> progress; that is the hope of all the world; and at this
> moment of challenge, that must be our work here on
> Earth. (Obama 2009)

However, that balanced, striving-in-the-face-of-reality voice is not
the only accent that the president has. At times, his rhetoric can be
positively giddy at the abilities of humans (especially Americans)
to form the future they want.

One example is obvious—Obama's campaign slogan was
"Yes We Can." One might argue that it is inappropriate to read
too much into any politician's campaign rhetoric—but at least it
is worthwhile to consider what message he chose. Furthermore,
Obama can be optimistic about human control of the shape of history in more measured contexts. In 2007, he said, "Never forget
that we have it within our power to shape history in this country.
It is not in our character to sit idly by as victims of fate or circumstance, for we are a people of action and innovation, forever
pushing the boundaries of what's possible" (Obama 2007). The
president's notion of history suggests that things are at times difficult, and that progress may be slow. There is none of Niebuhr's
notion of the paradox of history, that the best efforts of humanity to control history are just as likely to turn into tyranny and
destruction as they are to bring world peace.

Conclusion

Given this admittedly brief sketch of Obama's anthropology and his idea of history and their points of departure with Niebuhr, we are left with a picture of a president who seems to accept some of the conclusions of the philosopher-theologian, but for very different reasons than Niebuhr set them forth. We see Obama closely echoing Niebuhr's concern about large economic interests taking advantage of the weaker and less-privileged members of the society. We also see Obama seemingly echoing Niebuhr's Christian-tinged pragmatism about the use of force in the international sphere. But when we examine the roots of Niebuhr's thought, the analysis demonstrates a sizeable chasm between the positions that Niebuhr took and those of the president.

This difference indicates a significant difference between Barack Obama and Reinhold Niebuhr. Obama cannot be seen as a Niebuhrian disciple when his most basic and foundational commitments veer away from those of Niebuhr. Their relationship, thus, becomes more complex than some commentators have sought—knowing Niebuhr's position on a topic does not give full insight and predictive capacity for anticipating Obama's position on that topic. What this analysis suggests, then, is that Obama's use of Niebuhr is considered and pragmatic.

Before we go further, it is important to consider the nature of political speech. Might Obama be a true disciple of Niebuhr, but one who is constrained by political necessity from making that whole-hearted statement of allegiance? Of course. Politics is the art of the possible, and it may not be possible to take the American electorate to a place where the acceptance of the ironic character of our history replaces the triumphal cast that reassures voters and wins elections. But even if that is true, it only strengthens my thesis. Obama's use of Niebuhr's thought is a pragmatic choice, rather than a full-fledged philosophical acceptance.

Obama uses Niebuhr in various ways as a particularly helpful tool, but one that may be set aside when circumstances dictate. Just as one does not use a hammer when a chisel is called for, so too Obama seems to use Niebuhr's models of thinking at some points, while dropping his influence at other moments. At times, Obama may present a Niebuhrian face for his policies. But his political efforts will probably largely avoid the irony and paradox in which Niebuhr reveled, and his confidence in the ability of his nation and his government to effect positive change will depart from Niebuhr.

What does this mean about the Obama–Niebuhr synthesis? First, it will allow analysts to dispense with some of the more ambitious efforts to divine what the Obama administration will do in both general and particular terms by investigating Niebuhr on the topic. Although this is a pleasurable intramural sport for intellectual historians, it fails to achieve much explanatory or predictive power in the real world. Second, this insight may drive scholars and pundits to consider Obama as something more or less than the idealist (for his supporters) or ideologue (for his detractors). As this analysis demonstrates, Obama proves to be a pragmatic president, seeking a way forward through a complicated terrain. Although the Christian philosophy of a Reinhold Niebuhr or Martin Luther King will gain a seat at the table, that seat will compete for ideological and practical significance in the rough and tumble of governing and campaigning, and thus sometimes will be strategically silenced.

Works Cited

Editorial, "Marching into the past." *America* (4 Jan. 2010), 5.

Baker, Peter. "How Obama came to plan for 'surge' in Afghanistan." *The New York Times* (5 Dec. 2009).

Brooks, David. "Obama: Gospel and verse." *New York Times* (26 April 2007).

———. "Obama's Christian realism. *New York Times* (15 Dec. 2009).

Bullert, Gary B. "Reinhold Niebuhr and the Christian Century: World War II and the Eclipse of the Social Gospel." *Journal of Church and State* Vol. 44 (2002): 271–290.

CNN. "How Obama's Favorite Theologian Shaped His First Year" (2 Feb. 2010).

Cordesman, Anthony. Afghanistan and Obama: Transparency, Credibility, and a Long War. *Center for Strategic & International Studies* (12 April 2010).

Cooper, John W. and Brackley, Dean. "On the Economics of Maritain and Niebuhr." *Journal of the American Academy of Religion* Vol. 56 (1988): 321–323.

Elshtain, Jean Bethke. "Niebuhr's 'nature of man' and Christian realism." Eds. Richard Harries and Stephen Platten. *Reinhold Niebuhr and Contemporary Politics: God and Power.* London: Oxford University Press, 2010.

Finstuen, Andrew. "This American mess: Where is Reinhold Niebuhr when we need him?" *Christian Century* (1 Dec. 2009), 11–12.

Gibson, David. "Of Niebuhr and nobels: Divining Obama's theology." *Politics Daily* (12 Dec. 2009).

Judis, John B. "Obama, Niebuhr, and U.S. politics." *The New Republic* (13 Dec. 2009).

Julian, Liam. "Niebuhr and Obama." *Policy Review* (23 Feb. 2010).

Kaplan, Fred. "Obama's war and peace: How the president accepted the Nobel while sending more troops to fight in Afghanistan." *Slate.com* (10 Dec. 2009).

Loconte, Joseph. "Obama contra Niebuhr." *The American: A Magazine of Ideas* (14 Jan. 2010).

Lovin, Robin. "Christian Realism for the Twenty-First Century." *Journal of Religious Ethics*. Vol 37 (2009), 669–682.

Nelson, Lynn D. "Religion and Foreign Aid Provision: A Comparative Analysis of Advanced Market Nations." *Sociological Analysis*. Vol. 49 (1988), 49S–63S.

Niebuhr, Reinhold. "The Church and the Middle Class." *The Christian Century* Vol. 39 (1922), 1513–1515.

———. "Henry Ford and Industrial Autocracy." *The Christian Century* Vol. 43 (1926a), 1355.

———. "How Philanthropic is Henry Ford?" *The Christian Century* Vol. 43 (1926b), 1516–1517.

———. "Why We Need a New Economic Order." *The World Tomorrow* Vol. 11 (1928), 397–398.

———. *Leaves from the Notebook of a Tamed Cynic*. San Francisco: Harper & Row, 1929; Reprint, Louisville: Westminster John Knox Press, 1980.

———. "Property and the Ethical Life." *The World Tomorrow* Vol. 14 (1931), 19–21.

———. *Moral Man and Immoral Society: A Study in Ethics and Politics*. New York: Charles Scribner's Sons, 1932a; Reprint, Louisville: Westminster John Knox Press, 2001.

———. "Must We Do Nothing?" *The Christian Century* Vol. 47 (1932b), 416–417.

———. "If America is Drawn into the War, Can You, as a Christian, participate in it or Support it?" Reinhold Niebuhr, 3rd in a series of Ten Answers. *The Christian Century* Vol. 57 (1940), 1578–1580.

———. "Repeal the Neutrality Act!" *Christianity and Crisis* Vol. 1 (1941), 1–2.

———. *The Nature and Destiny of Man: A Christian Interpretation*, Vol. 1. New York: Charles Scribner's Sons, 1941; Reprint, Louisville: Westminster John Knox Press, 1996.

———. *The Nature and Destiny of Man: A Christian Interpretation*, Vol. 2. New York: Charles Scribner's Sons, 1943; Reprint, Louisville: Westminster John Knox Press, 1996.

————. *The Irony of American History*. New York: Charles Scribner's Sons, 1952; Reprint, Chicago: University of Chicago Press, 2008.

Obama, Barack. *The Audacity of Hope: Thoughts on Reclaiming the American Dream*. New York: Vintage Books, 2006.

————. "The Time Has Come for Universal Health Care," speech made to Families USA Conference (25 Jan. 2007). http://obamaspeeches.com/097–The–Time–Has–Come–for–Universal–Health–Care–Obama–Speech.htm (accessed 6 July 1010).

————. "A More Perfect Union" (The Race Speech). (18 March 2008) http://obamaspeeches.com/E05–Barack–Obama–A–More–Perfect–Union–the–Race–Speech–Philadelphia–PA–March–18–2008.htm (accessed 6 July 2010).

————. "A Just and Lasting Peace." (2009). http://www.huffingtonpost.com/2009/12/10/obama–nobel–peace–prize–a_n_386837.html (accessed 2 July 2010).

————."Obama's remarks on House Health Bill passage." *New York Times* (22 March 2010a).

————. "Obama's remarks at the signing ceremony." *New York Times* (21 July 2010b).

Osborn, Ronald. "Obama's Niebuhrian moment." *First Things* (Jan. 2010).

Plaskow, Judith. *Sex, Sin and Grace: Women's Experience and the Theologies of Reinhold Niebuhr and Paul Tillich*. Washington, DC: University Press of America, 1980.

Saiving, Valerie (Goldstein). "The Human Situation: A Feminine View." *Journal of Religion*. Vol. 40 (1960), 100–112.

Smith, Gary Scott. "A Pilgrim's Progress: Review of The Faith of Barack Obama." *Christianity Today*. Vol. 52 (2008), 103–104.

Yamin, Alicia Ely. 'Suffering and Powerlessness: The Significance of Promoting Participation in Rights–Based Approaches to Health.' *Health and Human Rights*. Vol. 11 (2009), 5–22.

Chapter 5

Obamania in Europe

Marie des Neiges Léonard

The Ambiguities of an American Dream

Obama's election in 2008 was undoubtedly an historic event both in the United States and around the world, and the election itself was closely watched by media worldwide. Numerous articles, editorials, and political commentaries in the European press reacted to Obama's election with strong emotions. For instance, on November 5, 2008, *The Times of London*'s front page showed a picture of President Barack Obama with the words "THE NEW WORLD" emblazoned in block letters, while the French newspaper *Libération* showed a close-up of Obama with the headline "An American Dream."

Most political observers and polls point to the Europeans having generally positive reactions and attitudes to Obama's election. Opinion polls in Europe show that, had Europeans been the ones voting, the former Illinois senator would have won the election with an enormous margin. Indeed, as political observers have noted, Obama's election to the presidency encouraged Europeans to dream of a new era in transatlantic relations and of a new America, not the least because he embodies the image of a pluralist America that Europeans admire. In this sense, the attitudes of Europeans have been compared to something of an infatuation or elation, which translates into the idea of "Obamania." It has even been suggested that Obama is somewhat of a political pop star in Europe.

This chapter examines Europe's love affair with Obama from the time of his campaign, through his 2008 election, and during the first two years of his presidency. Through a media analysis of the European press, it appears that the euphoria toward Obama in Europe can be linked to two main factors: 1) a counter-reaction to the negative attitudes and perceptions Europeans had of George W. Bush's character and administration, as Obama seems to represent the "Other" America; and 2) the positive hopes and expectations of European minority populations for whom Obama embodies American democracy as well as the America of pioneers and possibilities, and the New American Dream.

However, although the love affair between Obama and Europe seems steady, political observers have argued the following:

1. There seems to be a disconnect between the longing for an "other" America based on an opposition to Bush and the attitudes of Europeans toward the U.S. foreign policy.

2. There seems to be a disconnect between what Europeans admire, and perhaps idealize, in Obama (what he represents to them) and what is happening at their own borders (regarding the access of minorities to power).

This chapter explores those ambiguities and what they might mean for future transatlantic relations.

Obama as the Antithesis of Bush

Under the Bush presidency, the United States experienced a deficit of positive political image around the world. Several scholars (Forsberg 2010; Gordon 2004) argued that the negative attitudes and criticisms against the United States really come from a reaction to and rejection of the Bush administration's policies and Bush's personal image, rather than resentment toward America in general. As Philip Gordon writes: "the European public is not as 'anti-American', as is often assumed, but it is quite anti-Bush" (Gordon 2004: 188). Indeed, the Bush era can be characterized by negative attitudes and distrust toward the United States, and an anti-American bias. In fact, claims Forsberg (2010: 218), "'Anti-Americanism' became the catchword in transatlantic relations during the George W. Bush presidency." And these strong negative views deteriorated between 2002 and 2009.

So it seems that the disapproval of U.S. leadership is not based on fundamental differences in values, but rather—or at least in part—on views the Europeans have of the president of the United States, which they distinguish from their views of the United States as a country. As Robert Singh (2006: 43) notes, "there exists a pronounced tendency among non-Americans to associate—and judge—the nation according to the incumbent in the Oval Office." This is true even to the point that supporting the "wrong" American presidency might prove costly politically, as argued by Dorman (2010). Indeed, Dorman claims that Blair's connection to Bush did tremendous "damage to him domestically" (Dorman 2010: 81). It is even argued that Blair's allegiance to Bush drove him out of office because of the public dissatisfaction with his government's support of George W. Bush (House of Commons, Foreign Affairs Committee 2010). In 2002, 64 percent of Europeans viewed the United States as desirable, whereas only 38 percent approved Bush's international policies (Transatlantic Trends 2008). In 2003, after the Iraq war had started, Europeans who were unfavorable to the United States identified the problem more as being "Bush" than the country in general (Gordon and Shapiro 2004). In 2008, before the presidential elections, the number dropped to only 19 percent of Europeans who approved of Bush's international policies (Transatlantic Trends 2008). So there is something salient about the actual personality of the president and who is in power, versus the country itself.

Europeans' negative and critical views of the U.S. leadership in world affairs had remained unchanged since 2004. But given that the image of the United States has declined in the past several years (Transatlantic Trends 2008), at the time of the 2008 presidential elections, it looked like the next American president, regardless of who was going to be elected, would have an opportunity to improve transatlantic relations. That said, in pre-election polls, Europeans already preferred Obama to McCain and expected that transatlantic relations would improve if Obama were elected. It seemed as if Obama's election was enough to remove this negative bias and bring positive attitudes toward America. Another event that illustrates this point is Sen. Obama's speech in Germany in July 2008 at the Tiergarten in Berlin in front of more than 250,000 people.

Prior to this speech, Obama had been criticized for not showing enough interest in Europe. Going to Germany, and more specifically Berlin, was in itself a rebuttal to those criticisms. Indeed, the choice of Berlin was a strategic one: Berlin is the bridge between the East and the West; it is also the place where previous American presidents have gone to deliver memorable speeches—Ronald

Reagan in 1987 with the famed "Mr. Gorbachev, tear down this wall!" and, earlier, John F. Kennedy in 1963 and the legendary "Ich bin ein Berliner!" speech. In fact, according to Daum (2008), when JFK visited Berlin, it was a really big deal for the Republic of West Germany and West Berliners. Kennedy's visit was a way to demonstrate "transatlantic solidarity and American commitment to Western Europe," when the image of the United States had deteriorated in Germany due to policies giving the impression of abandonning the idea of a unified Germany (Daum 2008: 215). For younger West Germans in particular, Kennedy represented the hope of getting out of the old ways produced by the bipolarity of the Cold War (Daum 2008). Similarly, for Europeans, Obama represents a break with the "old" ways of Bush in a transatlantic relationship locked in opposing policies on Iraq, but more importantly for racial minorities in Europe, Barack Obama represents a positive, hopeful image of a different America with which they can identify.

So Berlin is indeed the place to establish foreign policy credentials. Here came Sen. Obama (before he had even received the Democratic Party nomination) and his words: "People of Berlin, people of the world, this is our moment. This is our time!" Later, the German (and European) press proclaimed that Obama was in fact "The New Kennedy" (in *Berliner Morgenpost*), or compared him to Lincoln, Kennedy, and Roosevelt (in *Frankfurter Rundschau*). For Germans, as for Europeans, the image that Obama conveyed was that of the "good America" and the "other America" (not Bush's America), perhaps a "European" America, with the "correct" candidate they would like to see lead America and Europe together.

At this point, Obama was made an "honorary European" by the European media (Meunier 2009: 29). As argued by Thomas Risse (2008: 10), "there is no other country in the world whose leaders can still serve as a projection space for these emotional desires among Europeans." What Europeans wished for or desired was a clean break from the Bush presidency and an America that stood for human rights and liberal values they have identified before in political figures like Kennedy. In that regard, says Risse (2008: 10), "George W. Bush and Barack Obama represent two ends of the emotional spectrum that Europeans invoke to relate to America." By electing Obama as its president, it seems that America, in the eyes of Europeans, has made a step toward redemption.

For Europeans, the very fact that he was elected president was reason enough to celebrate America's ability to basically reinvent itself. It was, in fact, one of Obama's vows during his campaign in 2008 to restore America's image and decrease the anti-U.S. sentiment abroad. Indeed, 47 percent of Europeans believed that relations between the United States and Europe would improve if Barack Obama was elected. And 69 percent of Europeans viewed Sen. Obama favorably, compared with 26 percent who viewed Sen. McCain favorably (Transatlantic Trends 2008).

Among the Europeans who felt that U.S. leadership in world affairs was undesirable, 50 percent believed relations would actually improve if Obama were elected. Public opinion in Europe actually was transformed dramatically with Obama's election. In 2009, the Transatlantic Trends study (2008) showed an increase in approval of U.S. leadership in the area of handling foreign policy (from 19% in 2008 to 77% in 2009 when the respondents were asked about assessing Bush and Obama). For example, only 12 percent of Germans and 11 percent of French approved of Bush's policy in 2008, whereas a whopping 92 percent of Germans and 88 percent of French approved Obama's policy in 2009. So, generally, the perception of the role of the United States in world politics changed from negative to positive as Obama became president. Scholars like Sophie Meunier (2009: 21) claim that Obama's election appeared to be the "strongest factor influencing" the improvement of anti-Americanism. Most Europeans have indeed expressed their confidence in Obama both in general and in terms of his leadership in world affairs.

In 2010, Western European nations continued to demonstrate a favorable view of Obama's international policies (88% in Germany, 84% in France, 76% in Spain, 64% in Britain). The median approval rate of U.S. leadership in Europe during 2010 rose to 50 percent, which reflects a continuation of a high level of approval throughout the years of Obama's presidency.

In Europe, Obama's victory was therefore constructed in opposition terms to Bush. The perception, then, is that of Obama the global president versus Bush the provincial president. The Europeans' reaction to the Nobel Peace Prize awarded to Obama shows that they see him as sort of powerful ambassador of the United States/Peace Corps leader rather than an imperial(ist) president. As Gary Younge writes in *The Nation* (2009: 13), Obama was perceived as "wordly where Bush was parochial, consensual where Bush was confrontational, nuanced where Bush was brash." Bush, was the "toxic Texan," but Obama was the anti-cowboy (Forsberg 2010: 218).

After a steep decline during the Bush years, views of the United States improved dramatically under Obama. And, the confidence ratings (in world affairs) remained virtually unchanged from 2009 through 2010 in countries like France, Germany, and Britain. This continued approval of U.S. leadership does stand in contrast to George W. Bush's last year in office: That year, disapproval rates were high among members of the European Union (Gallup 2010).

Therefore, it should come as no surprise that the announcement of the Nobel Peace Prize awarded to President Obama in 2009 immediately received public approval and considerable media interest all over Europe. This also revealed that Europeans continued to be captivated by the public image of the U.S. president, regardless of his actual achievements in the world after only nine months in office. It was in Germany that the Nobel news was given the most space in the media. Headlines such as "Still a Dream" (in *Die Zeit*) or "Good Hope Award" (in *Säddeutsche Zeitung*) reflected the expression of hope and encouragement that Obama would reverse the Bush-era policies and deliver change.

On the one hand, the fact that Obama was not Bush was enough in itself; on the other hand, it has been argued that Europeans were reacting positively to his willingness to simply reach out. Relatedly, underscoring such impressions was a fundamental shift in U.S. relations with Europe, and one that resonated well with Europe. Indeed, one of Obama's understated achievements is that he has changed the attitude of many Europeans about the United States. At the same time, Obama helped to reconcile the United States with much of the rest of the world and he gained an important capital of trust.

An African American in the White House

When Barack Obama was elected, German newspapers such as *Berliner Morgenpost* and *Bild* saw him as the "New Kennedy," or a black Kennedy. The French newspaper *Le Monde* proclaimed (November 5, 2008): "First we must write these words. Read them slowly out loud to take measure of the scale of the event, its emotional and historical charge: The American people have just elected, in the White House, a man with a black skin." Most of the European press at the time portrayed Obama as a symbol of change, but did so from a racial perspective by describing him as the multicultural president.

Overwhelmingly in Europe, Obama's victory was seen as a sign that race relations were changing in America. During the campaign, most Europeans expressed doubt about Obama's chances because they perceived America as too racist to elect a black president. Therefore, the election of Obama showed Europeans that "racial identity politics" in America were not as "fixed" as they thought (Forsberg 2010: 7). As the Swiss newspaper *24 Heures* observed, Europeans applauded the fact that America had seemingly overcome racial prejudices. It was therefore within this context that Obama was seen as the embodiment of the American pioneer and optimistic spirit, the very spirit that many Europeans could only dream about.

The enthusiasm was particularly striking in France, where festivities on election night were grandiose (notably by the French Support Committee for Barack Obama). In contrast, it was in France where the disillusionment over Bush's foreign policy was the strongest among Western European allies. France also possesses the Continent's largest community of African immigrants and ethnic minorities. After the 2005 ethnic riots in the French suburbs, new political organizations were created by minorities to prompt a national conversation on race. For the first time in French history the issues of racism and discrimination had entered the national debate, and Obama's election reignited questions on the politics of race in Europe.

A few days before the U.S. election, polls were showing that 80 percent of the French would vote for a black presidential candidate, but only 47 percent thought one actually could be elected. As Rama Yade (then secretary of state for human rights in the French government) declared: "This is the fall of the Berlin Wall times 10" (Poggioli 2009b). After the U.S. election, Patrick Lozès (founder and president of the Conseil Représentatif des Associations Noires de France, a grassroots umbrella organization for black associations in France) noted that "what's so extraordinary about Barack Obama's election is that this was the first time we didn't hear only negative things about us." He also added that "young people now believe they can conquer the world. . . . A black can be an ambassador, a doctor, anything" (Poggioli 2009c). In other words, Obama's election demonstrated that being a minority does not lock one into a preset status or a low status in society. It gave minorities a new self-consciousness about what is achievable.

In fact, this "miracle" as it was sometimes called, motivated Yazid Sabeg (an Arab French businessman serving as commissioner for diversity and equality of chances, a service attached to the Cabinet of the prime minister in France) to launch "A Manifesto for Real Equality. Yes, We Can!" which was published in a weekly newspaper in France (*Le Journal du Dimanche* 2008). This passionate manifesto basically seeks to learn the lessons of Obama's election. As Sabeg writes, "America has confirmed the validity of a democratic model founded on equity and diversity; and therefore it's no surprise that Obama is so popular in France, his popularity demonstrates the aspirations of all the children of the Republic." Sabeg also urged France (and the government) to adopt policies equivalent to that of affirmative action without saying it (affirmative action is called "positive discrimination" in France, which has raised linguistic controversies). "Positive actions," as Sabeg calls them, in the United States have enabled "the black middle class to emerge."

In Germany, the context is different. The blood line has long been the criteria for entering political life in Germany. For example, ten years ago Germans with foreign backgrounds were absent from the political landscape. Today, eleven sit in the 612-seat Bundestag. Cem Ozdemir, of Turkish origin, has become co-head of the Green Party, "Bündnis 90/Die Grünen," which won more than 10 percent of the votes at the last election for the Bundestag. Furthermore, Chancellor Angela Merkel's government began slowly changing. In 2005, after years of denying participation to non-Germans, the government officially acknowledged Germany as a country of immigrants. And so, Germany's citizenship law, traditionally based on the principle of *jus sanguinis* (blood line), was recently modified to reflect the demographic composition of the country, making it somewhat more open for children of immigrants born in Germany to acquire German citizenship. In that regard, Obama has been an important symbol in Germany, especially when he gave a speech in Berlin in front of some 250,000 people. The "yes we can" attitude had a crucial effect. His election gave German minorities a boost in self-confidence and prompted them to work to open German society to minorities. Minorities in Germany generally see Obama's victory as their victory. To German migrants and minorities, Obama's election was less about race than personal ability.

So the biggest impact of Obama's victory in Europe, as far as attitudes and perceptions go, can be seen among minorities of Europe. For them, Obama is an example of the possibilities of social mobility and breaking the racial barrier. What has happened in parts of Europe is that Obama's success has created a new rhetoric based on ability rather than on race or skin as the rationale for change. Europe has taken note that whites in America voted for a black man for the highest office and the election has been credited for pushing a wave of optimism throughout Europe. As France's former Socialist minister of culture, Jack Lang, has put it, Barack Obama represents "the America we love . . . the youth and racial mix of an America under transformation and in movement" (*The Times* 2008).

However, there seems to be a paradox in the praise given by Europeans to America and its black president: Obama is the minority president they (the Europeans) will never elect. Basically, Europe applauds Obama but believes that he succeeded because he was in America, and it could only have happened in America. Certainly, Obama has restored the belief in the American dream. Unfortunately for Europeans, it seems to be a dream out of their reach, at least for now.

Obama as the New American Dream

Obama has enjoyed a significant degree of sympathy in Europe and this political capital has helped him in his foreign policy. Indeed, most Europeans reacted extremely favorably to his election. Polls have shown that his honeymoon in Europe lasted through the first two years in office. However, right after the elections, the European press also encouraged its readership to be a bit more realistic about the expectations and challenges ahead for the Obama administration. Editorials espoused cautious optimism and listed a number of obstacles for Obama.

Part of the expectation for Obama was that he should break with the Bush era and usher in a new foreign policy. But, that was no simple task. This was evident to the Russian business newspaper *Vedomosti*, which commented that "he is not to be envied." Therefore, it appears that simply not being Bush might not be enough to fully satisfy Europe. The European press also became a bit skeptical about Obama's chances to achieve his agenda. Indeed, after the elation over Obama's election, many Europeans quickly sobered up. One of the issues responsible for tempering the enthusiasm was Obama's silence during Israel's conflict with Palestinians in the Gaza Strip. Another example is Obama's support for the death penalty in some circumstances and the right to own guns.

There is little support for such policies in parts of Europe such as Germany and France. Also, there is a clear disconnect between the image of a "global" president, which Obama enjoys in Europe, and the administration's policy in Afghanistan. While Obama delivered on his campaign promise to withdraw 90,000 American combat troops from Iraq by late summer 2010, some Europeans were disappointed in his surge of troops in Afghanistan. The awarding of the Nobel Peace Prize to Barack Obama in 2009 provides an illustration of this paradox. Although most Western European nations were enthusiastic about the award, not all reactions were positive in Europe. In Poland and Slovakia, comments were skeptical. News outlets suggested of the award: "Too soon," "What for?" For some Europeans indeed, the prize comes with a "price tag" (German Marshall Fund 2009) for the transatlantic relationship.

Not all Europeans approve of Obama and there seems to be a divide between the "old Europe" and the "new Europe." This may actually reflect a more cautious attitude among Eastern Europeans toward Obama because they have the impression that America is withdrawing its engagement in this part of Europe. If Obama's policies conflict with European interests and values, there might be some thawing of the Obamania that has gripped Europe. Yet, Forsberg, for instance, predicts that Europeans might become more critical of Obama but would still not resort to anti-American sentiment such as during the Bush years "in any deeper sense" (Forsberg 2010: 225).

An Ambiguous Icon

Probably the most significant part of the "Obama effect," however, is that his victory suddenly forced Europeans to look into the mirror, and they realized that it could take a while before a "European Obama" emerges out of the growing minority populations. It could be years before an ethnic minority is elected to the highest office in Europe. This prompted, in the words of Sylvia Poggioli (2009a), a "soul-searching" for the European nations. America had a black leader and Europeans wonder if the same will happen for them.

Obama's improbable victory revived the essence of American exceptionalism. But it is an ambiguous icon for Europe. Obama was (able to be) elected president precisely because he is an American in America. Some European analysts and news outlets wondered if this could only happen in America; hence, the paradox and disconnect between what Obama represents and the social/political realities in European nations. In Europe, the press started to reflect on their own failure to even think about the possibility of electing non-white leaders. An editorial in Russian daily newspaper *Vedomosti* focused on Russia's inability to elect a minority in power. In Russia, minorities constitute 20 percent of the population (versus 31 percent in the United States). But the majority of ethnic Russian citizens are against someone of a different ethnioc background heading the government. Europeans admire Obama's success only so far as they need not question their own racial politics. This was seen, for example, in France's failed and controversial national debate on French identity that took place in 2009. European societies have yet to reconcile their egalitarian ideals with the failures of their systems when confronted with realities of racism and discrimination.

One of the issues is that concepts of national identity in most European nations are actually founded on exclusion (excluding those who are not German, French, or Italian, for example), whereas America's national identity is founded on diversity and inclusion.

Obama's election thus directly questioned the political systems of Europe, particularly in France. These structures are often traditionally closed to minorities and, after Obama's election, they came under scrutiny. Fadela Amara (former secretary of state for urban policies, 2007–2010), for example, suggested that the public in France might be ready for a black president of France, but that the French political parties are not. It is a paradox because France is supposed to be the "egalitarian" nation and France's constitution is supposed to assure as much. France is the country, after all, that was once considered to be the haven for black Americans such as writers and jazz musicians. It was the country where "negritude," a black pride movement, was very much part of French culture.

One of the problems in France is that grassroots politics for minorities are not very strong. Indeed, France does not have a strong community of minority politicians in small towns. Part of this comes from the fact that local officials simply do not encourage such organization. So the data for political participation is disappointing for minority groups. This is one of the reasons there is no "French Obama." Additionally, there is only one black parliamentarian in France's National Assembly and only a few black deputies from overseas territories. Very few minorities are represented among the 36,000 mayors in France. Certainly no minorities are present in the highest military ranks, the Foreign Service, or the Judiciary.

As Yazid Sabeg concluded, "French society is frozen." Racial barriers have yet to be broken. In the manifesto that Sabeg published shortly after Obama's election, he claims that Obama's victory has actually shed some light on "the failures of the French Republic and the gap separating (France) from a country whose citizens were able to transcend the racial question and to elect a man who happens to be black." His text points to the frustration with the French system that many minorities feel, and it offers a warning that if France does not change and engage in actual public policies promoting diversity and equality, France might end up at the periphery of "democracy . . ." even "retrograde, out of place, obsolete." Other indicators of the failures of the French integration system include the ethnic riots of 2005 that followed the death of two young minorities. This spilled over into the suburbs of Paris and other cities in France. Sabeg and other political observers in France acknowledge that several impoverished, marginalized projects on the outskirts of the big cities are seething with pent-up sentiment. They are described as a "social bomb."

Bertrand Cabedoche (2009) argues that, in some ways, the French praise of Obama, the "black president," reflects a deeper attempt to free themselves from the guilt they have about their own striking lack of diversity in the political arena. Despite the call made by Rachida Dati (former minister of justice, 2007–2009) for a "positive discrimination" (the equivalent of affirmative action) in an editorial of French newspaper *Le Monde* (December 30, 2010), most scholars agree that France does not seem to be ready to turn away from its illusion of a color-blind society. This is true even if such an objective is implied in its constitution. Obama's election highlighted the fact that France is not America.

In Germany, despite the progress made by Angela Merkel's coalition government, many Turkish minorities do not feel German and cannot really imagine a Turkish Obama. Although German immigration and citizenship laws have changed a bit, the perception that minorities have is that non-white politicians in Germany are seen as foreigners, and that religion is still a factor in blocking access to political opportunities. In Germany, many of the minorities of African descent (500,000) and Turkish descent (3 million) feel that they are still treated as foreigners despite having lived in Germany for many generations. They do not see any national debate on racism taking place and they perceive Germany as a mono-racial nation where whites do not even see themselves as racists and do not even "see" other races.

As in other European nations, in Germany it seems that the concept of national identity is based on exclusion. The blood rule for citizenship (granting citizenship only to those with German blood) was abolished less than a decade ago. And it still appears in language with the term *people of migrant origin,* which shows the difficulty Germany has in accepting that 20 percent of its population is not of German "blood." Minorities are mostly absent from the mainstream media, police, judiciary, and political office. And only 10 percent of minorities in Germany are able to pursue higher education.

Italy has some of the most restrictive immigration and citizenship laws in Western Europe. Immigrants have to live in the country for ten years before applying, and children born in Italy are not guaranteed citizenship when they turn eighteen even if they have lived in the country for their entire lives. Yet, Italy has an estimated 4 to 5 million immigrants. Surveys show that Italians are indeed the most suspicious (of all Europeans) of immigrants, and the common rhetoric in Italy connects immigration to "invasion" and the issue prompts debates on security. There is only one black member in the Italian parliament. The European Commission on Racism and Intolerance and organizations such as Amnesty International have denounced Italian politicians for legitimizing the use of racist and xenophobic language in politics. After Barack Obama was elected, Italian Prime Minister Silvio Berlusconi described the newly elected American president as "young and 'tanned.'"

So the argument promoted by the Europeans themselves about the fact that Obama's election is not about racial politics but about personal capability ignores the very social realities of racism and discrimination that European minorities face on a daily basis. Much like the argument of a post-racial society that emerged in the United States in the wake of Obama's election, it ignores the very racial politics that were present throughout the 2008 campaign. So once again, Europeans have not married perception to reality when it comes to the image of a post-racial America or an open racial society in Europe. The sharp contrast between the ideals and the reality of what young minorities can hope for politically, shows that perhaps the magical thought of "yes we can" is after all an illusion. And perhaps, in the end, Obama's victory is a bittersweet one for Europeans who may have realized that such an outcome may not be possible in Europe.

Conclusion

Despite the fact that Obama's job approval ratings declined in the United States during his first two years in office, he has remained popular in most parts of the world (Pew Global Attitudes Project 2010). Additionally, the opinion of the United States around the world improved significantly after Obama's election and remained positive during his first two years. Particularly, ratings of America are very favorable in Western Europe, with 73 percent favorability in France and 63 percent favorability in Germany, for example. Overall, two years into the Obama presidency most polls showed that President Obama remained popular and the image of the United States remained positive in Europe (Pew Global Attitudes Project 2010, Transatlantic Trends 2010).

When Obama was elected, Europeans saw it as a sign of hope and renewal for transatlantic relations. Since his election, Obama has retained the political capital he received from Europeans, and views of America have improved. From numerous polls and surveys, Obama can be credited with rebuilding the capital of trust the previous U.S. president had lost, and he has repaired America's credibility in Europe and the world. Indeed, political observers were surprised by such a dramatic change in the image of the United States in Europe after Obama's election, as most believed it would take years to repair the poor relations resulting from the Bush years. The image Europe has of the United States is important for transatlantic relations, but overly high expectations regarding America's "new role" must be tempered. Yet, two years into Obama's presidency, even when Europeans disagree with U.S. foreign policy they do not necessarily disapprove of the United States (Pew Global Attitudes Project 2010).

Obama's election was seen by Europeans as a new American revolution, the renewal of the American Dream, the ultimate proof that racial barriers could be overcome. Obama became the symbol of success and optimism for an entire generation of disenfranchised minorities in Europe. However, as reflected in the European press, there is ambivalence in this European Obamania. The image that Europeans had of America was that of a country with a segregationist past and persisting issues of racism; at the same time, Europeans thought they were more enlightened in matters of race relations. France particularly prided itself as the birthplace of human rights and the country that abolished slavery twenty years before the United States. But when Europeans asked themselves if a minority could be elected as head of state, the overwhelming answer was that it could not happen any time soon.

Therefore, European attitudes toward the Obama victory are more ambiguous than a simple blind love affair—Europeans may reject U.S. foreign policies, but they admire and praise the American values and way of life that they cannot replicate at home. In that regard, Obama's election has taught a lesson to Europe in that a radical transformation is needed in European societies. Europe can no longer see itself as monocultural and monoethnic. So perhaps the promise that Obama represents in Europe goes beyond historic reconciliation between races and beyond his particular incarnation of a new America. In this sense, American presidential elections are not just a domestic affair, but a global one. Perhaps Europe benefits most from an American black president because this has produced self-reflection on Europe's own paradoxes and ambiguities.

Works Cited

Cabedoche, B. "L'obamania à la française, consécration d'une stratégie open source ou nouvel olympisme?" *Les Cahiers du Journalisme* Vol. 20 (2009), 166–193.

Daum, A. *Kennedy in Berlin*. Cambridge: Cambridge University Press, 2007.

Dorman, A. "Transatlantic relations: The United Kingdom." Ed. A. Dorman and J. Kaufman. *The Future of Transatlantic Relations. Perceptions, Policy and Practice*. Stanford University Press, 2010, 78–95.

Forbrig, J. "The Peace Prize has a price tag—for Europe." *German Marshall Fund Blog* (13 Oct. 2009). http://blog.gmfus.org/2009/10/13/the-peace-prize-has-a-price-tag-%E2%80%93-for-europe/.

Forsberg, T. "The rise and fall of criticism towards the United States in transatlantic relations: From anti-Americanism to Obamania." Ed. B. Germond, J. Hanhimäki, and G.-H. Soutou. *Handbook of Transatlantic Relations*. Abingdon: Routledge, 2010, 218–230.

Gordon, P. and J. Shapiro. *Allies at War. America, Europe and the Crisis over Iraq*. New York: McGraw-Hill, 2004.

House of Commons, Foreign Affairs Committee. Global Security: UK-US Relations. Sixth Report of Session 2009–10. Stationery Office, 2010.

Manchin, A. "U.S. approval stable at 50% in European Union." *Gallup* (7 Dec. 2010). http://www.gallup.com/poll/145100/approval-stable-european-union.aspx.

Meunier, S. *Anti-Americanism and the Financial Crisis*. Paper presented at the meeting of the American Political Science Association, Toronto, 2009.

"Obama: The color of change for both Russia and Europe." *Vedomosti*, Russia, via translation by WorldMeets.US (6 Nov. 2008). http://worldmeets.us/vedomosti000001.shtml.

Poggioli, S. "Obama's election prompts soul-searching in Europe." *NPR* (9 Jan. 2000a). http://www.npr.org/templates/story/story.php?storyId=99189120.

———. "'Obama effect' instills hope in Europe's minorities." *NPR* (12 Jan. 2009b). http://www.npr.org/templates/story/story.php?storyId=99247328&ps=rs.

———. "French minorities push for equality post-Obama." *NPR* (14 Jan. 2009c). http://www.npr.org/templates/story/story.php?storyId=99298290.

Singh, R. "Are we all Americans now? Explaining anti-Americanisms." Eds. B. O'Connor and M. Griffiths. *The Rise of Anti-Americanism*. New York: Routledge, 2006, 25–47.

Transatlantic Trends: Key Findings 2008. *German Marshall Funds* (2008). http://www.gmfus.org/trends/doc/2008_english_key.pdf.

Transatlantic Trends: Key Findings 2010. *German Marshall Funds* (2010). http://www.gmfus.org/trends/doc/2010_English_Key.pdf.

The Pew Global Project Attitudes. "Obama More Popular Abroad than at Home, Global Image of U.S. Continues to Benefit". (17 June 2010). http://pewglobal.org/2010/06/17/obama-more-popular-abroad-than-at-home/.

Younge, G. "What Obama means to the world." *The Nation* (2 Feb. 2009).

III

Politics and Leadership

Chapter 6

The First Hundred Days

FDR and Obama

Sean J. Savage

FDR and Obama

In his 1933 inaugural address, Franklin D. Roosevelt (FDR) did not state that the first hundred days of his presidency would have any policymaking or historical significance (Woolley and Peters 2010: 14473). Shortly after becoming president, FDR decided not to let Congress adjourn as scheduled. Instead, he called it into special session, which lasted one hundred days until June 16, 1933 (Burns 1956: 166). Much of the so-called "early" or "first" New Deal legislation and programs, including the National Industrial Recovery Act (NIRA), Agricultural Adjustment Act, Civilian Conservation Corps, Works Progress Administration, Tennessee Valley Authority, and Federal Deposit Insurance Corporation, were enacted during FDR's first hundred days as president (Alter 2006: 304–307). This frenzied period of policymaking productivity also made Americans familiar with FDR's leadership and rhetorical styles, namely his "fireside chats" through radio broadcasts and such dramatic executive actions as his proclamation of a national "bank holiday" (Cohen 2009: 2–14).

Barack Obama was aware of the comparisons that would be made between FDR combating the Great Depression during his first hundred days and Obama combating the Great Recession during his first hundred days as president. In an interview given

85

shortly after he won the 2008 election, Obama stated that he was reading history books about FDR's first hundred days and would especially emulate FDR's willingness to experiment with different policies in trying to stimulate and reform the troubled economy (Chernus 2008). *The New York Times* columnist, Paul Krugman (2008), however, warned Obama "to learn from FDR's failures as well as from his achievements: the truth is that the New Deal wasn't as successful in the short run as it was in the long run." Krugman then urged Obama to be bolder and spend more than FDR in his economic policies, especially those proposed or executed during his first hundred days.

A comparison between the first hundred days of Obama's presidency and those of FDR's presidency must especially consider the following differences: 1) The more extreme and pervasive economic suffering and chaos in 1933; 2) the broader range and diversity of noneconomic issues, such as abortion and the wars in Iraq and Afghanistan, that Obama addressed during his first hundred days; and 3) the longer and more difficult transition period between Herbert Hoover and FDR than that between George W. Bush and Obama. Nonetheless, the most important ideological and policy similarity between FDR and Obama during each president's first hundred days is that one particular bill that was enacted during this period encapsulated and signified how this president wanted to revive and reform the American economy. For FDR, it was the NIRA creating the National Recovery Administration (NRA). For Obama, it was the American Recovery and Reinvestment Act (ARRA) detailing and implementing the American Recovery and Reinvestment Plan (ARRP).

The Only Thing We Have to Fear . . .

FDR's inaugural address of March 4, 1933, is distinguished more by its solemn yet confident tone and its religious and martial allusions than by a coherent economic philosophy prescribing unique, specific policies. FDR understood that one of his duties as president during the Great Depression was to restore his fellow Americans' faith in their government's ability to improve the economy and in their own self-confidence and optimism about the future. Thus, the most famous and frequently quoted phrases from FDR's first inaugural address are "the only thing we have to fear is fear itself" and "This great nation will endure as it has endured." In blaming big business, bankers, and stock brokers for causing or at least contributing to the widespread misery of the Great Depression, FDR combined biblical references with condemnations of big business similar to those of Theodore Roosevelt. He used such phrases and statements as "plague of locusts" and "the money changers have fled from their high seats in the temple of our civilization" (Woolley and Peters 2010: 14473).

Despite FDR's stern denunciation of big business in his inaugural address, he did not initially intend the New Deal to have an antagonistic relationship with big business. The overall tone and several policy changes expressed in his 1932 Commonwealth Club address suggested that FDR wanted the gradual recovery and permanent reform of the American economy to be based on rational economic planning achieved and implemented through the cooperation of government, business, labor, and agriculture (Savage 1991: 111). Although government would usually play the role of arbiter and coordinator among these economic actors from the private sector, it would ultimately have the power to define the public interest in the economy and effectively punish those who violated it.

FDR's refusal to make explicit, binding agreements with Hoover and issue joint statements about the future World Economic Conference was primarily based on his disagreement with Hoover and some of his fellow Democrats about the causes of and remedies for the Great Depression (Hawley 1966). FDR's so-called Brains Trust, especially Raymond Moley, Rexford Tugwell, and Adolf Berle, persuaded the president-elect that the Great Depression needed to be addressed through domestic policy, not foreign policy (Rosen 1977: 209). Berle's book, *The Modern Corporation and Private Property*, influenced FDR's Commonwealth Club address and the later creation of the NRA and the Securities and Exchange Commission. Although Berle advocated stricter government regulation of big business, especially the stock market, Moley emphasized a substantial reduction of unemployment through direct relief instead of federal loans to states and accepted the temporary use of deficit spending (Moley 1939). As FDR's top economic advisor on agricultural issues, Tugwell wanted the federal government to plan and coordinate agricultural production controls in order to stabilize farm prices and save as many small farms as possible. Despite their occasional disagreements and different priorities in economic policy, these three members of FDR's original Brains Trust agreed that the early New Deal and especially

the legislation passed and executive orders issued during the first
hundred days should reflect economic nationalism.

More so than the Brains Trust, FDR realized that he needed to immediately and dramatically demonstrate this economic
nationalism shortly after his inauguration. On the day of FDR's
inauguration, the governors of Illinois and New York had closed
the banks of their states. At various times, the governors of other
states had declared so-called "bank holidays." It was not clear,
however, if the president had the authority to declare and implement a national bank holiday. Attorney General Homer S. Cum-
mings interpreted a section of the Trading with the Enemy Act
of 1917 to mean that a president could close the banks and stop
the further exportation of gold out of the United States. This wartime executive power coincided with and substantiated Roosevelt's
assertion in his Inaugural Address that he would need the same
broad, discretionary powers that a president needs and has during
a war. Thus, the four-day national "bank holiday" was the basis of
FDR's first major executive action of the first hundred days and of
his first "fireside chat" broadcast to the public on March 12, 1933
(Badger 2008: 24–26).

FDR decided that he needed to continue a momentum of vigorous action, at least in order to improve the public's shattered
confidence in the ability of the federal government to respond to
this unprecedented economic crisis (Davis 1986: 42–45). Therefore,
FDR decided not to let Congress adjourn and called it into special session on March 9. On that same day, Congress passed the
Emergency Banking Act of 1933, which was the first New Deal
bill to be passed by Congress during the first hundred days. This
law's provisions, strongly influenced by Hoover's economic advisors, included granting authority to the secretary of the treasury
to determine which closed banks could be reopened, the issuance
of emergency currency, and the distribution of Reconstruction
Finance Corporation (RFC) funds to solvent banks so that they
could quickly reopen. The Banking Act of 1933, also known as
the second Glass-Steagall Act, was not enacted until the last two
weeks of the first hundred days on June 16, 1933.

By the third week of his presidency, FDR responded to the
unemployment problem. On March 21, 1933, he sent a message to
Congress asking it to pass legislation that would include provisions
to create an office of Federal Relief Administration, "a broad public works labor-creating program," grants to the states for "relief
work," and a focus on temporary jobs that would help to conserve

natural resources, such as through reforestation, flood control, and soil erosion projects (Woolley and Peters 2010: 14596). The recommendations of this message influenced legislation that became the Federal Emergency Relief Act, the Reforestation Relief Act which created the Civilian Conservation Corps, and the Tennessee Valley Authority Act. All of these laws were enacted during FDR's first hundred days (Freidel 2006: 100).

The following legislation was also enacted during FDR's first hundred days: The Agricultural Adjustment Act; Federal Securities Act; National Employment System Act; Home Owners Refinancing Act; Farm Credit Act; Emergency Railroad Transportation Act; and NIRA. To a great extent, the NIRA of 1933 was the primary intellectual and legislative product of FDR's Commonwealth Club address and the economic philosophy of the early New Deal. The NIRA emphasized planning, cooperation, and reform of the economy through codes established by business, labor, and agriculture and enforced by the NRA. It also included the Works Progress Administration (PWA) supervised by the Department of the Interior. Congress passed the NIRA legislation on June 16, 1933, the last day of its special session. The complex details and controversial implementation of NIRA foreshadowed the Supreme Court decision that ruled it to be unconstitutional.

Critics of the New Deal in general and FDR's first hundred days in particular claim that Roosevelt's policies worsened and prolonged the Great Depression (Powell 2003; Shlaes 2007). Scholars, political commentators, and the general public will undoubtedly continue to question and debate the economic effectiveness of the early New Deal. What is far less doubtful, however, was the impressive, inspiring leadership that FDR demonstrated during his first hundred days as president. FDR's leadership became the standard by which future presidents in general and Barack Obama in particular would be compared.

Obama and the Great Recession

In his inaugural address of January 20, 2009, Barack Obama, like FDR, attributed the causes of the Great Recession to "greed and irresponsibility on the part of some" (Woolley and Peters 2010: 44). However, unlike FDR, Obama partially attributed the causes of the Great Recession to "our collective failure to make hard choices and prepare the Nation for a new age" (44). A more consistent similarity between the 1933 and 2009 inaugural addresses was the new president's public recognition that the faith of many Americans in their government's ability to solve the current economic crisis had been shaken. Whereas FDR expressed his confidence that Americans would survive and successfully end the Great Depression, Obama assured his fellow Americans that, although their economic challenges were serious and complex, "They will be met" (44).

FDR's inaugural address barely mentioned international relations and seemed to perceive the causes of and cures for the Great Depression to be entirely domestic. Obama's address covered a broader range and greater diversity of issues. In U.S. foreign policy toward Muslim countries, Obama vowed that "we seek a way forward based on mutual interest and mutual respect" (44). He assured the world "that America is a friend of each nation and every man, woman, and child who seeks a future of peace and dignity, and we are ready to lead once more" (44). He explained how the use of military force to protect American security interests in Afghanistan and Iraq must be influenced by and conducted according to American principles of justice and idealism. Obama stated, "Our security emanates from the justness of our cause, the force of our example, the tempering qualities of humility and restraint" (44). By contrast, FDR briefly and blandly stated that he wanted the United States to be a good neighbor to other nations.

Consequently, when Obama began his first hundred days as president, his use of executive orders, presidential proclamations, and memoranda, as well as his advocacy or signing of major legislation, reflected his inaugural address's greater breadth and diversity of issues compared to FDR's first hundred days. Although FDR proclaimed a "bank holiday" shortly after becoming president, Obama proclaimed a National Day of Renewal and Reconciliation on January 20, 2009. According to Obama, the purpose of this proclamation was "to call upon all of our citizens to serve one another and the common purpose of remaking the Nation for our new century" (Woolley and Peters, 2010: 85668). Having criticized Bush's conduct of the Iraq war and the use of Guantanomo Bay naval base for the detention of enemy combatants and controversial interrogation methods, Obama issued three executive orders on January 22, 2009. They ordered reviews of Guantanomo Bay and detention policy options and the requirement that interrogation techniques comply with U.S. and international law.

Obama's use of executive orders and presidential memoranda on social issues such as abortion and, to a lesser extent, on some foreign policy issues such as Cuba, expressed differences with and departures from the presidency of George W. Bush. Unlike FDR, however, Obama experienced a cordial and generally cooperative transition with his Republican predecessor (Gibbs 2008). In his study of presidential transitions, Carl M. Brauer stated, "Transitions are filled with peril and with opportunity. The ability of newly elected Presidents to avoid the former and make the most of the latter goes a long way toward determining their success in office and affects a great deal besides that" (Brauer1986: xiv). Of course, in addition to Obama's relationship with Bush, the transition in the presidency from Bush to Obama was facilitated by $8.5 million in federal funds and an additional $3.5 million in private donations raised by Obama (Pika and Maltese 2010: 463). Furthermore, a relatively smooth transition with the Bush administration regarding foreign and defense policies in Iraq and Afghanistan was bolstered by Obama's decision to ask Robert Gates, a Bush appointee, to continue as secretary of defense. According to journalist Michael Shear (2008), "Shortly after the election, Obama signaled that he would spend the 11-week transition largely in the background, deferring to his predecessor. But when it comes to the economy, he has been anything but a political wallflower."

Indeed, long before his inauguration, Obama was issuing press releases and making speeches throughout the United States about his administration's plans for stimulating and reforming the recession-plagued economy. Like his fellow Democrats in Congress, Obama had supported the Troubled Assets Relief Program (TARP) and, in general, the Bush-approved bailouts of the automobile, banking, and insurance industries. Likewise, FDR had supported the Hoover-created RFC and continued and expanded its use during his presidency. During the first year of his presidency, Obama decided to retain Ben Bernanke, a Bush appointee, as chairman of the Federal Reserve Board.

Obama's rhetoric and actions during the transition and first hundred days may have suggested continuity with Bush's most recent anti-recession economic policies. Obama, however, emphasized a major economic policy difference with Bush and Republicans in Congress by promoting a major stimulus package in public statements before his inauguration. On January 8, 2009, Obama spoke at George Mason University in Virginia. In this speech, he proposed an American Recovery and Reinvestment Act (ARRA). The president-elect claimed that this plan would save or create 3 million jobs while improving such priority areas as health care, energy, and education (Woolley and Peters 2010: 85361). The more specific details of this plan included computerizing all medical records in the United States within five years, expanding broadband and Internet access in rural areas, creating more "green jobs" by improving the energy efficiency of federal buildings, and doubling the production of alternative energy within five years. On January 16, 2009, Obama, while visiting Bedford Heights, Ohio, spoke again about the ARRA. The president-elect spoke about how companies that make wind turbines would benefit from this plan. In this speech, Obama stated, "We started this year in the midst of a crisis unlike any we've seen in our lifetime" (Woolley and Peters, 2010: 85450). He promised that, after the ARRA is implemented, "We'll put nearly 400,000 people to work by repairing our infrastructure—our crumbling roads, bridges and schools. And we'll build the new infrastructure we need to succeed in this new century" (85450).

Although the Lilly Ledbetter Fair Pay Act was the first bill that Obama signed into law on January 29, 2009, Obama did not sign the ARRA into law until February 17, 2009. The House of Representatives passed the ARRA on January 28, 2009, but the Senate did not pass it until February 10, 2009. Although Obama had emphasized bipartisan continuity with Bush's TARP policies, most Republicans in Congress opposed the ARRA. Furthermore, two days after the Senate vote on this legislation, Republican Sen. Judd Gregg of New Hampshire, Obama's nominee for secretary of commerce, announced the withdrawal of his nomination partially because of his disagreements with details of the ARRA legislation.

Because of Republican opposition to and some media criticism of the pending ARRA legislation, Obama traveled to Elkhart, Indiana, on February 9 and Fort Myers, Florida, on February 10 in order to advocate the ARRA and generate greater public support for it. In Elkhart, which had been suffering the highest local unemployment rate in the nation because of its dependence on the depressed recreational vehicle industry, Obama promised that the ARRA would save or create 3 to 4 million jobs over the next two years. But not just any jobs,

> jobs that meet the needs we've neglected for too long,
> jobs that lay the groundwork for long-term economic

growth, jobs fixing our schools and computerizing our medical records to save costs and save lives; jobs repairing our roads and our bridges and levees; jobs investing in renewable energy to help us move towards energy independence. (Woolley and Peters 2010: 85742)

At a news conference later held on February 9, Obama told the nation that there were even foreign policy implications for the enactment and successful implementation of the ARRA. He stated, "We find ourselves in a rare moment where the citizens of our country and all countries are watching and waiting for us to lead" (Woolley and Peters 2010: 85728). In his February 10 speech in Fort Myers, Obama concluded his speech on the ARRA and other economic policies by emphasizing the moral responsibility of contemporary Americans for the economic, educational, technological, and environmental quality of life for future generations. He stated, "This is a responsibility that we did not ask for, but it is a responsibility we will accept for the sake of our future and our children's" (Woolley and Peters 2010: 85755). Likewise, in his February 14, 2009, address to the nation, Obama expressed confidence that the ARRA would help to revive and reform the economy because Americans "will prove equal to this task" and "will turn this crisis into opportunity and emerge from our painful present into a brighter future" (Woolley and Peters 2010: 85780).

After this extensive, vigorous rhetorical effort to generate public support and favorable media coverage of the ARRA legislation, Obama signed the American Recovery and Reinvestment Act of 2009 into law on February 17, 2009, in Denver, Colorado. Obama made it clear that he had traveled to Denver to sign the bill because it was the same city that hosted the 2008 Democratic national convention where he had been nominated for president. He connected the ARRA to his acceptance speech in which he promised to stimulate and reform the American economy in order to reduce economic suffering and improve the lives and futures of Americans. Obama summarized the ARRA as "a balanced plan with a mix of tax cuts and investments. It's a plan that's been put together without earmarks or the usual pork barrel spending. It's a plan that will be implemented with an unprecedented level of transparency and accountability" (Woolley and Peters 2010: 85781).

Because only three Republican senators and no Republicans in the House of Representatives voted for the ARRA bill, Obama may have believed that the content and tone of his speech at the bill signing ceremony needed to be more defensive in responding to criticism of this legislation than his previous speeches had been. In particular, Republicans and conservative media commentators criticized ARRA for contributing to higher deficits, mostly subsidizing unionized public-sector jobs in state and local governments, and expanding social welfare benefits. On February 23, 2009, less than one week after signing the ARRA into law, Obama addressed the Fiscal Responsibility Summit. Responding to Republican arguments that the ARRA would sharply increase deficits and hamper economic growth, Obama stated, "This administration has inherited a $1.3 trillion deficit—the largest in our nation's history—and our investments to rescue our economy will add to that deficit in the short term" (Woolley and Peters 2010: 85794).

This speech served as a prologue to Obama's address to a joint session of Congress on February 24, 2009. As he had done in his inaugural address and as FDR had in his 1933 inaugural address, Obama partially blamed the economic crisis on the selfish, socially irresponsible behavior of some Americans. "In other words, we have lived through an era where too often short-term gains were prized over long-term prosperity, where we failed to look beyond the next payment, the next quarter, or the next election" (Woolley and Peters 2010: 85753). He warned Wall Street, banks, and mortgage companies that tougher future regulations would require more ethical and responsible behavior from them. Later in this speech, Obama stated that the budget bill that he would soon submit to Congress would fulfill his campaign promise for greater accuracy and transparency in the federal government's policy behavior, especially on spending. Consequently, he revealed that "this budget looks ahead 10 years and accounts for spending that was left out under the old rules" (85753). In an implied criticism of how federal spending had sharply increased under Bush, Obama promised that his budget bills would clearly disclose the short-term and long-term costs of the wars in Iraq and Afghanistan.

In his February 26, 2009, remarks about his $3.55 trillion budget proposal, Obama contended that his budget was fiscally responsible and necessary both for the current economic crisis and for long-term reforms in such policy areas as health care, education, and energy. He also emphasized that his administration was actually reducing some areas of federal spending through cost cutting and greater efficiency. In particular, he specified savings of $20 million by the Department of Agriculture, $200 million by the Department of the Interior, and tens of millions of dollars by the Department of Education (Woolley and Peters 2010: 85803).

For the next two weeks, Obama mostly concentrated on foreign policy matters. On February 27, he announced his plan for troop withdrawals from Iraq. Obama met with Gordon Brown, Britian's prime minister, on March 3 and Ban Ki-Moon, the UN secretary general, on March 10. On March 12, Obama renewed economic sanctions on Iran and met with the president of Brazil on March 14 and the prime minister of Ireland and first minister of Northern Ireland on March 17, 2009. Later that month, Obama also met with the secretary general of NATO and Mikhail Gorbachev, former Soviet premier, and announced a new strategy for American foreign policy in Afghanistan and Pakistan.

On March 11, 2009, Obama signed the Omnibus Appropriations Act of 2009. This appropriation of $410 billion included spending on approximately 8,500 individual projects (commonly and pejoratively known as earmarks or pork barrel projects) worth $7.7 billion (Weisman 2009). According to the Taxpayers for Common Sense, these earmarks included $22 million for the John F. Kennedy Library and $200,000 to fund the removal of tattoos from members of criminal gangs. In remarks to the media made shortly before he signed this bill, Obama assured the public that he would continue to develop and apply budgetary reform to reduce the use of earmarks and make government spending more transparent. He warned Congress, "Along with that reform, I expect future spending bills to be debated and voted on in an orderly way and sent to my desk without delay or obstruction, so that we don't face another massive, last-minute omnibus bill like this one" (Woolley and Peters 2010: 85847). After stating this implied criticism of Congress and ambivalence about some of the content of this bill, Obama proceeded to assert his determination that this omnibus spending bill "must mark an end to the old way of doing business and the beginning of a new era of responsibility and accountability that the American people have every right to expect and demand" (85847).

The last major domestic policy legislation Obama signed during his first hundred days as president was the Edward M. Kennedy Serve America Act on April 21, 2009. This bill's provisions included the creation of four new service corps, an increase in the number of volunteers from 75,000 to 250,000, and the establishment of Youth Engagement Zones. In his remarks on signing this legislation, Obama stated, "What this legislation does, then, is to help harness this patriotism and connect deeds to needs" (Woolley and Peters 2010: 86032). According to Paul Light (2010), "Even though the Serve America act clearly encourages older Americans to pursue encore careers, most colleges and universities have yet to build programs to attract them to service" (81).

Legacies

On April 29, 2009, Obama held a prime time news conference to discuss the first hundred days of his presidency. He noted that on that day Congress had passed a budget resolution that "builds on the steps we've taken over the last 100 days to move this economy from recession to recovery and, ultimately, to prosperity" (Woolley and Peters 2010: 86069). He claimed that the ARRA "has already saved or created over 150,000 jobs" and provided tax relief to most Americans. Obama acknowledged that more progress in public policy needed to be made to end the Great Recession and reform the economy. He concluded his opening statement by thanking "the American people for their support and their patience during these trying times, and I look forward to working with you in the next 100 days and the 100 days after that, all the hundreds of days to follow, to make sure that this country is what it can be" (86069).

Future presidents will continue to disagree about what significance, if any, should be attributed to the first hundred days of their administrations. Since the Great Recession of 2008–2009 was widely perceived and experienced as the worst recession since the Great Depression, comparisons between the first hundred days of FDR and Obama were inevitable. Obama understood this inevitable comparison and did not publicly reject it. However, through his policy behavior and rhetoric, he also made it clear that he had a broader, more diverse range and quantity of non-economic issues, especially those in foreign and defense policy, to address in his first hundred days than FDR had (Dye 2010: 91–102). Although a larger number and variety of major economic policy bills were enacted during FDR's first hundred days, each president's first hundred days produced one major new economic policy, the NIRA for FDR and the ARRA for Obama, that summarized and signified each president's perception and policy agenda for reviving and reforming the American economy.

Works Cited

Alter, J. *The Defining Moment: FDR's Hundred Days and the Triumph of Hope*. New York: Simon and Schuster, 2006.

Badger, A.J. *FDR: The First Hundred Days*. New York: Hill and Wang, 2008.

Brauer, C.M. *Presidential Transitions: Eisenhower Through Reagan*. New York: Oxford University Press, 1986.

Burns, J.M. *Roosevelt: The Lion and the Fox*. New York: Harcourt, Brace, 1956.

Chernus, I. "The first hundred days or the last hundred days?" *The L.A. Progressive* (18 Dec. 2008). http://www.laprogressive.com/political-issues/the-first-hundred-days-or-the-last-hundred-days/.html (accessed 6 Nov. 2010).

Cohen, A. *Nothing to Fear: FDR's Inner Circle and the Hundred Days That Created Modern America*. New York: Penguin Press, 2009.

Davis, K.S. *FDR: The New Deal Years, 1933–1937*. New York: Random House, 1986.

Dye, T.R. *A Full Pate: The Obama Policy Agenda, in Obama: Year One* (T.R. Dye, ed.). New York: Longman, 2010, 91–102.

Freidel, F. *Franklin D. Roosevelt: A Rendezvous with Destiny*. Newtown, DE: American Political Biography Press, 2006.

Gibbs, N. "When new president meets old, it's not always pretty." *Time* (10 Nov. 2008). http://www.time.com/time/politics/article/0,8599,1857862,00.html (accessed 6 Nov. 2010).

Hawley, E. W. *The New Deal and the Problem of Monopoly*. Princeton, NJ: Princeton University Press, 1966.

Krugman, P. "Franklin Delano Obama?" *The New York Times* (10 Nov. 2008). http://www.thenewyorktimes.com/2008/11/10/opinion/10krugman.html (accessed 5 Nov. 2010).

Leuchtenburg, W.E. *Franklin D. Roosevelt and the New Deal, 1932–1940*. New York: Harper and Row, 1963.

Light, P.C. Obama and the Federal Bureaucracy. Ed. T. R. Dye. *Obama: Year One*. New York: Longman, 2010, 73–84.

Moley, R. *After Seven Years*. New York: Harper, 1939.

Pika, J.A. and J.A. Maltese. *The Politics of the Presidency*. Washington, DC: CQ Press, 2010.

Powell, J. *FDR's Folly*. New York: Three Rivers Press, 2003.

Rosen, E.A. *Hoover, Roosevelt, and the Brains Trust*. New York: Columbia University Press, 1977.

Savage, S.J. *Roosevelt: The Party Leader, 1932–1945*. Lexington, KY: University Press of Kentucky, 1991.

Shlaes, A. *The Forgotten Man*. New York: Harper, 2007.

Shear, M.D. "Obama's one president gambit." *The Washington Post* (31 Dec. 2008). http://www.washingtonpost.com/wp-dyn/content/article/2008/12/30/AR2008123003104.html (accessed 28 Oct. 2010).

Weisman, J. "Obama outlines plan to curb earmarks." *The Wall Street Journal.* (12 March 2009). http://online.wsj.com/article/ SB123680763049200481.html (accessed 7 Nov. 2010).

Woolley, J.T. and G. Peters. *The American Presidency Project* (online). 2010. Santa Barbara, CA. http://presidency.ucsb.edu/ws/?pid=.html (accessed 24 Oct. 2010).

Chapter 7

Legislative Leadership

Max J. Skidmore

Evaluating Presidents

Barack Obama came to the presidency vowing to work with Congress. Headlines in blogs and newspapers all over the country reported variations of the theme, even before his inauguration, that as president-elect he had gone out of his way to consult (see, e.g., "Obama Builds" 2009). A few months later, reports indicated that he was working diligently to encourage Congress, itself, to develop the details of the health care plan, rather than to submit a White House version, which in the Clinton administration had been unsuccessful (Bai 2009).

Later, however, David Broder reported on a January meeting between Obama and House Republicans, in which a Chicago Republican, Peter Roskam, complained that Speaker Pelosi had "stiff-armed" Republicans. Conceding that the president cannot govern the House, Roskam, according to Broder, nevertheless was issuing "an invitation to govern differently in his second year" (Broder 2010). Many sources, less credulous than Broder, spoke of Republican refusal to work with Democrats except on Republican terms. "Top House Republicans Throw Cold Water on Health-Care Summit," read one headline in *The Washington Post*. The article included a letter (February 8) from House Republican leaders refusing to engage in talks unless the whole process would start anew, with all existing proposals abandoned (Shear 2010). Thus, Obama's efforts to work with Congress were complicated by united

Republican opposition (echoing their famous 1994 "Bill Kristol strategy" of refusal to cooperate with President Clinton under any circumstance) and by opposition from conservatives within his own party. Although Republicans complained that Obama was "ramming his program through," leftist critics condemned him for conceding too much. Certainly, his relations with Congress were complex.

However defined, "leadership" normally overwhelms other considerations in evaluations of presidential administrations, and success with Congress is paramount. This is not to say that legislative leadership, by itself, is the only measure of presidential success, or indeed that it even is a necessary factor.

Two of our most successful and significant presidents, Abraham Lincoln and Theodore Roosevelt—although each signed a number of important laws—are better known for executive actions than legislative leadership. Conversely, George W. Bush, because of unusual circumstances, was quite successful with Congress. Owing to the consequences of his administration, however, Bush is unlikely ever to be high on many lists of presidential greatness. Presidents most noted as legislative leaders include Woodrow Wilson, Franklin D. Roosevelt, and Lyndon B. Johnson.

For a charismatic politician, Obama's legislative accomplishments passed without generating much enthusiasm—or even broad awareness. Consider taxes, for example. Roughly one-third of the stimulus package was tax reduction. In September 2010, *Time Magazine's* Joe Klein, in Kansas City, quipped that Obama and his staff should be found guilty of political malpractice because he had reduced the taxes of 95 percent of Americans, yet few recognized it. Indeed, many detractors complained that Obama *raised* their taxes. Such misunderstanding undoubtedly influenced the massive Republican victories in 2010, along with other factors, including a prominent one that the voters understood very clearly: high unemployment.

Obama and the Midterm Elections

Regardless of whether the defeats reflected flaws in Obama's leadership or the slowness of the economic recovery, the drubbing Democrats took was not inevitably fatal, nor was it unique. Three of the last dozen presidents besides Obama found both houses shifting from their party's control, while Obama's party lost only the House.

The voters hammered Harry Truman in 1946, changing control of both House and Senate to Republican. In 1954, they did the same to Dwight Eisenhower, changing control of both House and Senate to Democratic, and repeated the reversal for Bill Clinton in 1994, changing control of both House and Senate to Republican. Each was re-elected.

Republicans who then said that Obama must heed "the will of the American people" and change course, were hardly consistent; they had ignored that "will of the people" following the two previous Democratic landslide elections, and opted to oppose all significant actions of the then victorious Democrats. Nor does analysis demonstrate that the Democrats were "too liberal," and thus needed to appeal to "the center," yet retiring Sen. Evan Bayh said in Kansas City that their votes for health care had brought defeat to sixty House Democrats. Those Democrats, he said, would no longer be in Congress, and therefore would be unable to support progressive legislation. Lest this sound plausible, note that although the Democrats did lose just more than sixty House seats, a huge defeat, those losses included a number of vacancies. There were not sixty House Democratic incumbents who lost, and those who did lose included twenty-nine "blue dog," conservatives out of fifty-four in the 111th Congress. Moreover, Bayh's argument that Democrats should have cast their votes against progressive measures in order to be able to vote progressively in the future is obvious nonsense as strategy. It also assumes that a legislator's duty is to gain re-election, not to effect policy.

"Pundits" and conservative Democrats advanced the equally strained argument that Nancy Pelosi should have stepped aside, and not run for minority leader, because she had been "polarizing." They forgot the harsh polarization of former speaker Dennis Hastert who supported only bills receiving "a majority of the majority."

Even the generally more sober *New York Times* in a brief editorial on November 8, 2010, said that Pelosi had been an extraordinarily gifted speaker, without whose skills Obama's legislative program would have foundered, but that she should step out of the leadership for the sake of harmony. Undoubtedly, the Republicans were largely successful in demonizing her, but to charge Pelosi with being "polarizing" because of Republican attacks is to ignore the reason for those attacks.

It is precisely because Pelosi used power so effectively that her opponents professed outrage. The Democrats would have been foolish (as well as churlish) to punish her has a result—especially inasmuch as she previously was a brilliant minority leader before the Democrats took control of the House following the 2006 elections, a fact that the "pundits" either forgot or ignored.

Obama as Legislative Leader

The purpose here is to look at Obama's legislative record, not the midterm elections. Whether he is likely to achieve re-election is beyond the purview of this chapter.

In his first month in office, Obama signed into law three significant measures: On January 29, he signed the Lilly Ledbetter Fair Pay Act (in response to a 2007 decision by the Supreme Court, *Lilly Ledbetter* v. *Goodyear Tire and Rubber Co,.* which held that women could not sue for pay discrimination unless they did so soon after the discrimination took place, even if they had been unaware of the discrimination); on February 4, the Children's Health Insurance Reauthorization Act (expanding health insurance coverage for children, an act that George W. Bush had twice vetoed); and on February 17, the American Recovery and Reinvestment Act (the stimulus program).

By November, the *Wall Street Journal* could title an article, "Democrats' Quiet Changes Pile Up" (Weisman 2009). New legislation included:

- The Matthew Shepard and James Byrd Jr. Hate Crimes Prevention Act: An act expanding hate crime laws to include gender identification and sex crimes, which, said the *Journal*, had first been introduced twelve years previously (October 28, 2009).

- The Weapon Systems Acquisition Reform Act of 2009: This act eliminated a number of weapon systems that the military had agreed were unnecessary, but for which contractors had lobbied strongly, and which members of Congress long had protected (May 22, 2009,).

- The Omnibus Public Lands Management Act of 2009: This act reversed Bush administration land policy. It set aside millions of acres of public land in the west from development, shifting policy toward conservation, and encouraging solar power (March 30, 2009).

- The Family Smoking Prevention and Tobacco Control Act: An act subjecting tobacco for the first time to FDA regulation (June 22, 2009).

- The Worker, Home Ownership, and Business Assistance Act of 2009: This act extended unemployment benefits for those who had exhausted them, extended the tax credits for home buyers, and provided for additional tax write-offs for business losses (November 6, 2009).

These legislative accomplishments constituted what the Republicans termed, "Obama's liberal agenda." It continued into the next year as Congress, at Obama's urging, passed the following acts:

- The Health Care and Education Reconciliation Act: An act increasing efficiency and significantly lowering costs by removing private banks from the student loan process, and doubling funding for Pell Grants (March 20, 2010).

- The Dodd-Frank Wall Street Reform and Consumer Protection Act: This act reversed years of deregulation of the financial industry, and provided consumer protections (including curbs on credit-card abuses) through a new Consumer Financial Protection Bureau (July 21, 2010).

- The Restoration of Emergency Compensation Act of 2010: An act further extending unemployment benefits (July 22, 2010). The signing took place after the Democrats succeeded in breaking a months-long Republican filibuster, and after Obama had "lambasted Senate Republicans . . . for blocking a $33.9 billion extension of jobless benefits and leaving more than 2.5 million Americans without jobs or unemployment checks" (Wiseman 2010).

- The Tax Relief, Unemployment Insurance Reauthorization, and Job Creation Act of 2010: This law extended the Bush tax cuts; Obama reluctantly accepted Republican demands that the most wealthy must benefit, but secured additional payments for the unemployed, and further stimulus for the economy (December 17, 2010).

With a flurry of last-minute activity in the lame-duck Congress, Obama secured four pieces of landmark legislation:

1. Eliminating the military's exclusion of gays (the Don't Ask Don't Tell Repeal Act of 2010);

2. Enacting the 9/11 First Responders' Health Bill that Republicans had been blocking;

3. Overcoming opposition by many Republicans including their leader, Sen. Mitch McConnell, to achieve ratification of the New Strategic Arms Reduction Treaty ("New START") (reducing Russian and U.S. nuclear stockpiles and providing mutual inspections) by the required vote in the Senate of two-thirds; and

4. Passing the Food Safety and Mobilization Act.

Then, there is his crowning legislative achievement: the Patient Protection and Affordable Care Act (ACA), for health care reform (March 23, 2010).

These accomplishments must place Obama among the most successful legislative leaders in American presidential history. Considering the century of failed efforts to reform America's health care delivery system, passage of the ACA alone secures him this status.

The Patient Protection and Affordable Care Act

Although the right is furious at having lost at last its struggle to stifle health care reform, many on the left are irate that the reforms are disappointing. Misinterpretation predominates. Conservatives, decrying Obama's alleged "socialism," complain that "Obamacare" gives "the government control over one-sixth of the economy," and bemoan "government seizure of America's healthcare system, the best in the world."

This is nonsense, as is the argument that anyone can get needed care from an emergency room. Emergency rooms constitute not only one of the most expensive ways possible to deliver care, but they do not deliver "health care" at all—they care for emergency situations, and are not prepared to provide for overall health care needs.

Complaints from the left are understandable. There is no single-payer system, and the reforms subsidize the current health care industry. Undoubtedly, a single-payer system would be more economical and more efficient. Certainly, the reforms catered to the major segments of the industry, and the new system will be highly complex and most probably cumbersome.

Leftist criticism, however, overlooks or ignores the millions of additional Americans who will ultimately get coverage because of ACA. According to numbers usually cited, some 45 to 47 million people currently have no health insurance—although recently there were numerous articles quoting comments on November 9, 2010, from Dr. Thomas Frieden, director of the Centers for Disease Control and Prevention, that nearly 59 million people were uncovered for at least part of 2010. Many of these, contrary to frequent allegations, were neither poor nor healthy (Fox 2010). Moreover, many of those who had insurance—or thought they did—had been underinsured, or had policies cancelled if they became too expensive for their companies.

Much of the general public was disgusted by the protracted process that resulted in the final act. There were deals, disputes, special arrangements, charges and countercharges, and the bill was long and complex. However unseemly the process, though, it was not unusual except that the opposition was so united and so determined to prevent passage of a program that the elected majority favored. In general, all large, complex, and controversial programs that pass are based on similar deals, disputes, and special arrangements; all go through long and complicated processes. What was unusual in this instance is that it was all out in the open, and that the continuous news cycle today revealed, and sometimes magnified, each step forward, backward, sideways, and eventually across the finish line. For details, see the brilliant study by Jacobs and Skocpol (2010).

Charges that "no one read the bill," or that things were "rushed through in secret," added to the public's discomfort—but the charges were completely false. The process was extraordinarily open. All versions of the bill were available to policymakers throughout the process; everything was posted online to provide for complete public information. The cry that legislation was "shoved down the throats of the American people" simply meant that the minority was unable, after extensive delay, to prevent the majority from acting. True, polls showed increasing public skepticism—but it also is true that the public tended to favor the specific provisions of the bill. It is not true that the Constitution or the political process demands that policymakers follow polls—as Republicans were quick to point out over a decade ago when they controlled Congress, and when—in a lame-duck session, it should be noted—they impeached a president in the face of public disapproval.

Although critics on the right greatly exaggerate their charges against ACA, they are correct that it is very substantial legislation. The act is far more substantial than many critics on the left acknowledge. Undoubtedly, it represents the most conservative way possible in which to move toward universal health coverage, but despite its faults, the ACA provides the first serious, national, regulation of health insurance companies. It empowers the government to eliminate the most notorious abuses by the insurers, to ensure adequate and permanent levels of coverage, and to require that insurers return a satisfactory level of benefits to their customers. This will come from regulating what the industry calls "medical loss ratios" (a phrase that, itself, speaks volumes). Companies writing group policies will now have to return 85 percent of their premium income to their policyholders in the form of benefits. For those writing individual policies, which are less efficient and more expensive, the companies must provide benefits in the amount of 80 percent of income. These requirements will mean that no more than 15 to 21 percent of health care premiums can be used for administrative costs, including executive salaries, or profits. The rest must go actually for health care. Most companies today pay far less, and retain far more, diverting money away from health care and into profits and huge salaries, bonuses, and other benefits to their top officials. Thus, this should be a definite control on health costs.

What follows are highlights, and an implementation timeline, for the ACA. These are taken from the Kaiser study (Kaiser 2010), and the complete text of the ACA is available online.

2010

- Implemented federal–state processes requiring insurers to justify unusual rate increases, with grants to states for review programs.

- Required that productivity be considered when calculating Medicare reimbursement rates.

- Provided additional funding to include assessments of adult services in Medicaid.

- Established a nonprofit institute to conduct research comparing and evaluating the effectiveness of various medical treatments.

- Appropriated funds for public health and prevention programs.

- Provided a $250 rebate to help Medicare recipients who reach the "doughnut hole" prescription drug coverage gap in Part D. Subsidies will increase annually until they eliminate the gap.

- Began tax credits to employers with fewer than fifty employees and average annual wages of no more than $50,000 who provide health insurance to subsidize the insurance.

- Began an option (later a requirement) to extend Medicaid to adults without children, up to 133 percent of the federal poverty level.

- Created a temporary program for employers to provide for retirees aged fifty-five or older before they are eligible for Medicare.

- Established a plan for those who have preexisting conditions and are not currently eligible for health insurance.

- Created a consumer Website to inform the public regarding health care options.

- Levied a 10 percent tax on indoor tanning services.

- Beginning September 23, mandated that adult children may remain on parents' health insurance policies until the age of 26.

- Required that new health plans must include preventive services, including immunizations, and preventive care for children through adolescence and screenings for women, all without extra patient charge.

- Banned lifetime caps on coverage; banned rescinding policies except in cases of true fraud; banned denial or exclusion of coverage for children because of preexisting conditions; placed restrictions on annual coverage limits; beginning in 2014, will completely eliminate annual limits.

2011

- Implements minimum medical loss ratios for insurers.

- Requires drug manufacturers to provide 50 percent discount on brand-name prescription drugs in the Part D "doughnut hole"; and begins subsidies for generic prescriptions used in the coverage gap.

- Implements Medicare bonus payments of 10 percent for primary care services; also provides them to general surgeons in areas with physician shortages.

- Eliminates cost-sharing for preventive services in Medicare; eliminates deductibles for colorectal cancer screening; pays for "personalized prevention plan," including "comprehensive health risk assessment."

- Creates a Center for Medicare & Medicaid services to test new payment, delivery, and cost-reduction models that maintain or improve quality.

- Begins reduction of extra payments to Medicare Advantage Plans.

- Reduces Medicare Part D subsidy for higher income beneficiaries, and increases Part B payments from higher income beneficiaries.

- Increases incentives for home health care and lifestyle programs in Medicaid.

- Provides grants to small employers to establish wellness programs.

- Encourages primary care residency programs and patient care centers.

- Authorizes grants to states to "develop, implement, and evaluate alternatives to current tort litigations."

- Provides grants to states to plan for American Health Benefit Exchanges and Small Business Health Options Program Exchanges, to assist in purchasing of health insurance.

- Increases medical training opportunities, and encourage straining in outpatient settings.

- Establishes an "Independent Advisory Board" to recommend reduction in per capita cost of Medicare, if spending exceeds targets.

2012

- Allows Accountable Care Organizations that meet quality standards to share in the Medicare cost savings they achieve.

- Reduces subsidies to Medicare Advantage Plans, and provides bonuses to high-quality plans.

- Establishes procedures to counter fraud and abuse.

- Imposes fees on pharmaceutical manufacturers.

- Reduces Medicare payments for preventable re-admissions.

2013

- Begins phasing-in of subsidies for brand-name prescription drugs to move toward closing of the Part D coverage gap.

- Encourages coverage of preventive services under Medicaid with increases in matching payments to states and no patient cost sharing.

- Brings payments for Medicaid primary care up to the level provided in Medicare.

- Decreases deductions of medical expenses from income taxes.

- Increases Medicare taxes on earnings over $200,000 for individuals, or over $250,000 for joint filers.

- Imposes tax on sale of medical devices.

- Requires disclosure of possible conflicts of interest among providers and manufacturers.

- Creates Consumer Operated and Oriented Plan to encourage creation of "non-profit, member-run health insurance companies."

2014

- Expands Medicaid coverage to all with incomes under 133 percent of poverty level, who are under the age of sixty-five and not eligible for Medicare.

- Requires all U.S. citizens and legal residents to have "qualifying health coverage," with a phased-in tax penalty for noncompliance.

- Requires certain employers who offer coverage to employees to give certain employees the option of vouchers to purchase insurance.

- Creates state-based exchanges and Small Business Health Options Program Exchanges through which some individuals and businesses can purchase insurance.

- Guarantees insurance availability, issuance, and renewals with fees that do not vary, except for age, geographic area, tobacco use, and family circumstances, with limits to the variations permitted.

- Creates a package of required basic services.

- Requires exchanges to include at least two multistate plans, at least one of which must be nonprofit.

- Assesses fees on employers who do not offer insurance unless exempted.

- Requires Medicare Advantage Plans to have medical loss ratios no lower than 85 percent.

2015

- Increases federal matching for Children's Health Insurance Program

2016

- Permits states to form compacts, and allows insurers to sell policies in any participating state.

2018

- Imposes tax on "Cadillac" plans.

In their study of the ACA's tortuous path to passage, Jacobs and Skocpol (2010) provide a more succinct and accessible summary of the timeline.

What are the prospects for the future of health reforms, given Republican takeover of the House, gains in the Senate, and lawsuits against health reforms? Jacobs and Skocpol remark that the Republicans would like simply to repeal ACA, making its fate the same as the short-lived Medicare Catastrophic Coverage Act of 1988, but conditions now have changed. "Democrats, as of 2009 and 2010, learned lessons from the Catastrophic episode. Drafters of Affordable Care front-loaded widely popular features. Between the March enactment of the new system and the November 2010 elections, many small businesses are claiming tax credits to help pay for employee health coverage; millions of senior citizens are cashing $250 checks (the first of an expanding new benefit) to help pay for prescription drugs that fall into the previous 'doughnut hole' gap in Medicare coverage; millions of young adults are signing up to stay on parents' insurance coverage until age 26; and millions of families are discovering ways to access insurance, despite serious health problems." Already, they note, Republicans changed their cries from "repeal," to "repeal and replace." The Republicans could be highly effective over time in their opposition, but despite their success in "immediately and loudly demonizing 'Obamacare,' . . . the American public seems to be moving in the direction of 'keep it and fix it'" (Jacobs and Skocpol 2010).

Conclusion

Although Obama has given the impression of being "hands off," it is his agenda that Congress has passed. Admittedly, it has been weakened, and certainly skillful leadership by Majority Leader Harry Reid in the Senate and Speaker Nancy Pelosi's unparalleled guidance of the House were crucial. President Obama's accomplishments nevertheless have been substantial. Even before he has served half of a term his legislative record is highly impressive when judged by any reasonable criterion. As he remarked, "I am persistent."

Works Cited

Bai, Matt. "Taking the hill." *New York Times Magazine*. (2 June 2009).

Broder, David. "Obama need not wait to change relations with Congress." *The Washington Post.* (7 February 2010).

Fox, Maggie. "Nearly 59 Million Lack Health Insurance: CDC" (9 Nov. 2010); http://www.reuters.com/assets/ (retrieved 10 Nov. 2010).

Jacobs, Lawrence R. and Theda Skocpol. *Health Care Reform and American Politics: What Every American Needs to Know*, New York: Oxford University Press, 2010.

Henry J. Kaiser Family Foundation. "Implementation timeline," *Health Reform Source* (2010) <http://healthreform.kff.org/timeline.aspx>; [retrieved 8 Nov. 2010].

"Obama Builds Relationship with Congress," http://www.msnbc.msn.com/id/28732342/ns/politics-white_house/t/obama-builds-relationship-congress/; retrieved 25 May 2011.

Shear, Michael D. "Top House Republicans throw cold water on health-care summit." *The Washington Post.* (8 February 2010).

Weisman, Jonathan. "Democrats' quite changes pile up." *Wall Street Journal.* (2 Nov. 2009).

Wiseman, Paul. "Obama blasts Republicans for employment benefits block." *USA Today.* (19 July 2010).

Chapter 8

The Firing of General Stanley McChrystal

Douglas M. Brattebo

Obama versus McChrystal

On Monday evening, June 21, 2010, the nation's capital began to buzz over the impending release of an article in *Rolling Stone* magazine, "The Runaway General," by freelance writer Michael Hastings. In the piece, Gen. Stanley A. McChrystal, a four-star officer and the commander of U.S. and NATO forces in Afghanistan, and his aides spoke disparagingly of almost every senior member of President Barack Obama's national security team. Indeed, Hastings, who had been granted close access to McChrystal's staff, stated in the article, "In private, Team McChrystal likes to talk shit about many of Obama's top people on the diplomatic side" (Hastings 2010: 94). Unsurprisingly, the most egregious comments in the piece were not attached to particular speakers, but variously to "one aide," a "top adviser," an "adviser," and the like (Editorial Desk 2010). From the moment the story broke, two things were clear: 1) McChrystal, who had been in his post for one year, and who had made previous blunders, had almost certainly committed a career-ending mistake; and 2) the episode, however it turned out, was likely to reveal a great deal about the state of civil–military relations in the still-young twenty-first century. Obama rightly concluded that the best course of action was to remove McChrystal from command, and he did so. The president's quick handling of the thirty-six-hour affair shored up the bedrock American principle of civilian control over the military. It also highlighted how thorny that tenet has become in recent decades due to the rise of a class of senior officers in the U.S. Armed Forces whose jobs require them to be just as involved in and skilled at politics and diplomacy as in military strategy and tactics.

As Obama consulted his advisers that first evening, the prospect of firing McChrystal emerged quickly as the most likely—if not quite inevitable—outcome. According to one administration official, "A lot of us were arguing that the message of letting McChrystal's comments roll off our backs would be enormously harmful" (Cooper and Sanger 2010). Five senior officials figured most prominently in the president's deliberations: Robert M. Gates, defense secretary; Joseph R. Biden Jr., vice president; Rahm Emanuel, chief of staff; Gen. James L. Jones, national security adviser; and Adm. Mike Mullen, chairman of the Joint Chiefs of Staff (Landler 2010). The next morning Obama ordered McChrystal to fly back to Washington for a meeting in the Oval Office on Wednesday, June 23. "I think it's clear that the article in which he and his team appeared showed poor judgment," said the president. "But I also want to make sure I talk to him directly before I make a final judgment" (Cooper and Shanker 2010). Gates was McChrystal's biggest defender in the administration, encouraging the president to retain the general in Afghanistan in order to ensure "continuity, momentum, and relations with the allies" (Landler 2010). From abroad, the Afghan president, Hamid Karzai, spoke via telephone with the president to voice his strong support for McChrystal, whom he considered to be a reliable partner whose departure would disrupt the war effort (Rubin 2010). Obama fixed swiftly on the idea of replacing McChrystal with Gen. David H. Petraeus, also a four-star officer, and McChrystal's boss as head of the U.S. Central Command, and arranged for Petraeus to meet with him Wednesday morning following his meeting with McChrystal (Landler 2010). Gates later said that his mind was eased by the president's idea that Petraeus, former commander of the Iraq war during its most trying phase, should take the helm in Afghanistan (Shanker 2010b).

Obama met with McChrystal for twenty minutes in the Oval Office that Wednesday morning. The general "apologized, offered his resignation and did not lobby for his job" (Landler 2010). After accepting McChrystal's resignation, Obama held a forty-minute meeting with Petraeus to offer him the job, which Petraeus accepted without even an opportunity to consult his wife (Baker 2010). The president then met with his national security team, lighting into the members and ordering them to cease their backbiting in the interests of the larger cause in Afghanistan (Cooper and Sanger 2010). Finally, Obama made a statement in the Rose Garden, announcing his firing of McChrystal and his appointment of Petraeus. Three themes came through in the president's remarks: 1) he had acted not out of "any sense of personal insult" resulting from Team McChrystal's trash talk in *Rolling Stone*, but because he deemed greater unity a prerequisite to progress in Afghanistan. "I welcome debate," Obama said, "but I won't tolerate division"; 2) members of the U.S. military had to observe "strict adherence to the military chain of command and respect for civilian control over the military chain of command"; and 3) the essential approach in Afghanistan would not be adjusted, despite gathering disquiet within the president's domestic political coalition and from the leaders of some allied countries (Cooper and Sanger 2010). The president had switched generals, but he was determined to lash his national security team together and search out a way to reverse the trends on the battlefront in order to stick to his timetable to begin drawing down troops by July 2011.

Sources in the military offered a dual critique of the president's performance, noting that McChrystal's behavior had been intolerable and warranted dismissal, but also that the administration's national security team was dysfunctional, producing an incoherent approach to Afghanistan (Cooper and Sanger 2010). The White House was careful not to demonize McChrystal. Emanuel said the president "likes Stan and thinks Stan is a good man, a good general and a good soldier. But . . . this is bigger than any one person" (Landler 2010). McChrystal announced before the end of June that he planned to retire. The president decided to allow McChrystal to retire with four stars, despite the fact that the general had not served the required span of three years at that rank. This was an important signal to the Pentagon that the administration did not hold a grudge, and it also told defense contractors that might wish to employ McChrystal that he was not considered toxic (Bumiller 2010). The Obama versus McChrystal chapter revealed civil–military antagonism, but the White House's deft handling of it may actually have reduced this problem (Baker 2010). According to Stephen Biddle of the Council on Foreign Relations, "Ironically enough, the McChrystal firing helped a lot because Obama handled it exactly the way most senior military officers would have handled it if they had been in his shoes" (Baker 2010). It was a silver lining of sorts, but a far cry from the high hopes for McChrystal's command in Afghanistan when Gates had announced on his appointment on May 11, 2009.

McChrystal's Infelicities During the Afghanistan Policy Review

Bruce O. Riedel, a senior fellow at the Brookings Institution, was surprised that Gates, in announcing McChrystal as Gen. David D. McKiernan's replacement, also seemed to be suggesting that the new commander should undertake a full-fledged reexamination of the basic strategy in Afghanistan (Woodward 2010: 119). Riedel, who had spent twenty-nine years with the CIA, Pentagon, and National Security Council staff, had become the leader of the South Asia advisory team for Obama's presidential campaign in 2007. At the president's request, Riedel had undertaken a review of Afghanistan policy in early February 2009, and he ended up laying out three basic options in mid-March: 1) add no more troops beyond the 17,000 that Obama had approved in February, thus limiting the scope of the U.S. commitment in Afghanistan and focusing it on a counterterrorism strategy; 2) add 4,000 troops as trainers for the Afghan army, a move that McKiernan, Petraeus, and Gates had recommended; and 3) commit the United States to a fully resourced, nationwide counterinsurgency in Afghanistan by adding 100,000 troops (Woodward 2010: 102–103). In late March the president decided in favor of Riedel's second, middle course and dispatched another 4,000 troops to train the Afghan security forces. Obama, just over two months into his term, had already authorized 21,000 more troops for the U.S. war effort in Afghanistan. On top of troop requests approved by George W. Bush before he left office, the total increase in U.S. forces in Afghanistan would be 33,000.

But some among both the civilian and military wings of the president's national security team thought the Riedel review had not gotten at the fundamental complexities at play in Afghanistan. This was the tension that Riedel had picked up on in Gates's comments as McChrystal was put in charge of the war effort. On the military side, Petraeus was alarmed that the president appeared to have become skeptical about applying the general's strategy of counterinsurgency, which had succeeded in Iraq, to the war in Afghanistan (Woodward 2010: 111–112). The possible inference was that Afghanistan was a war only to be managed until the United States could find a way to extricate itself, rather than won. On the civilian side, Richard Holbrooke, the career diplomat whom Obama had selected as the State Department's special representative for Afghanistan and Pakistan, had both procedural and substantive problems with the Riedel report. First, Riedel had presented his recommendations privately to the president, in a one-hour meeting, without an opportunity for other administration officials to cross-examine Riedel or even keep a record of the meeting (far from an ideal process). Second, the report did not adequately acknowledge that political reconciliation—finding a way to make peace with elements of the Taliban—would be one of the keys to concluding the conflict (Woodward 2010: 169–170).

By July, a gulf had opened up between the Pentagon and the White House. McChrystal, finding firsthand that things on the ground in Afghanistan were not going well, was preparing to request more resources (Woodward 2010: 143). McChrystal's assessment of in-theater resource needs reached the Pentagon at the end of August, and both Pentagon and administration officials immediately began to characterize and frame its content for articles in major newspapers (Woodward 2010: 153–154). The president ordered a second, more comprehensive review of U.S. policy in Afghanistan. It unfolded across ten sessions, from September to early December 2009. But one week after the opening session, the full, final report by McChrystal was leaked to Bob Woodward, who analyzed it in a *Washington Post* article (Wolffe 2010: 240–241). The leak raised the hackles of Obama's inner circle, who considered it a purposeful attempt to box the president in and narrow his range of options on Afghanistan. Gates later acknowledged the damaging effects the leak had on the broader policy review process, saying, "If I had been in the White House, I would have been suspicious" (Baker 2010). The report itself was noteworthy because McChrystal clearly had taken primary authorship—Woodward later characterized its tone as "a cry from the heart" (Woodward 2010: 176)—and also because it painted a grim portrait across nearly all dimensions of the U.S. war effort. McChrystal laid out three options for the president, ranging from adding 10,000 to 11,000 additional troops at the low end to 85,000 at the high end, and the general endorsed the middle path of adding 40,000 (Woodward 2010: 192).

In late September, just prior to the second meeting of the policy review, McChrystal appeared in a prerecorded interview on the CBS television show *60 Minutes*. The general noted that he had only spoken once with Obama, by secure video, in the seventy days since he had assumed command in Afghanistan (Woodward 2010: 193). Understandably, a media tempest ensued. The White House arranged a meeting between the president, who would be heading to Denmark to promote Chicago as a venue for the 2016 Olympics, and McChrystal, who was to make a speech in London to the International Institute for Strategic Studies. Mullen had encouraged McChrystal to accept the speaking engagement but had warned him to be careful (Woodward 2010: 193).

McChrystal's October remarks in London went badly wrong. The general's opening joke fell flat, and in the body of his remarks he emphasized that only a counterinsurgency strategy, coupled with decisiveness and firmness, could succeed in Afghanistan (Woodward 2010: 193). McChrystal may also have leaked, without authorization, classified information about Afghanistan from a CIA report (Rich 2010). But it was in the question-and-answer period that McChrystal went completely off the rails, stating flatly that a limited, counterterrorism effort could not succeed in Afghanistan, and predicting it would create "Chaosistan" (Sanger 2010). And he jokingly suggested that his candid input, welcomed so far in the policy review process, might be curtailed if those in the White House "change their minds, and crush me someday" (Woodward 2010: 193–194). The president's advisers were livid, and Obama, en route to Denmark, concluded, "We got to stop this. This is not helping" (Woodward 2010: 194). McChrystal told Petraeus he knew he had made a mistake and resolved to keep a lower profile; Petraeus then spoke with Gates, who assured Obama that the general knew the error of his ways (Woodward 2010: 194).

The president and the general met for twenty-five minutes the next day aboard Air Force One in Denmark for what proved to be a calm exchange. They agreed on the impropriety of the general's London speech, and that such behavior could not recur, but the incident did not dominate their discussion. McChrystal made it clear that, whatever the president ultimately decided on in terms of Afghanistan strategy, the military would carry it out. Obama came away feeling as though McChrystal was fit to command the war in Afghanistan, but it was up to the president and Gates to provide the general with orders that took into account the broader picture, particularly the spillover effects from instability in Pakistan. The president concluded, "I like him. I think he's a good man" (Woodward 2010: 194).

As more than one commentator has observed, the president would have been wholly justified in firing McChrystal immediately after the general's remarks in London (Dowd 2010). By conveying disrespect for the commander-in-chief, and disagreeing with him over strategy, McChrystal had enflamed civil–military tensions and left Obama feeling as though his policy options were being purposefully narrowed. The president brought up McChrystal's London performance with Mullen and Gates in their next weekly meeting. Mullen went to pains to reassure Obama that "It will never happen again" and "We would never do that intentionally" (Woodward 2010: 197). The fact that McChrystal's attitudes and words had become the basis for a tense exchange among the president, the secretary of defense, and the chairman of the Joint Chiefs of Staff should have been ample warning to curb McChrystal's behavior.

In late November, Obama reached closure on the strategy review for Afghanistan. The president would sign on to sending an additional 30,000 troops, to which a maximum of 3,000 could be added, to cope with exceptional circumstances, at the discretion of the secretary of defense (Woodward 2010: 308–309). This meant that, in addition to the 33,000 troops already flowing into Afghanistan from earlier decisions by Obama and Bush, another 33,000 would be added (Woodward 2010: 332). Thus, 66,000 U.S. troops would swell the U.S. war effort in Afghanistan by the end of the first half of 2010, bringing the total U.S. military presence there to more than 100,000. Obama took the exceptional step of providing six pages of detailed orders to accompany his decision. This constituted, in the estimation of one of his advisers, "an assertion of presidential and civilian control of the military" (Woodward 2010: 316). The president, moreover, secured from the high-ranking civilian and military members of his national security team direct, spoken commitments of support for the plan (Woodward 2010: 326–329). Obama's plan for Afghanistan was crafted to provide an extended surge of forces, and thus break the Taliban's momentum (Woodward 2010: 317). A strategy review, to be conducted in December 2010, would assess the effort's success. The military campaign, whose ultimate purpose was to set the stage to begin to draw down U.S. forces in July 2011, was decidedly "not a nationwide counterinsurgency strategy" in Obama's words to McChrystal and others, because, "We're not making Afghanistan a long-term protectorate" (Woodward 2010: 329). On December 1, 2009, Obama spelled out his administration's new strategy for Afghanistan in a speech at West Point, from which Stanley McChrystal had graduated in 1976.

McChrystal's Career Prior to Command in Afghanistan

After four years at the U.S. Military Academy, McChrystal's career traversed many assignments and stations, and he spent a large, crucial portion of it in Special Operations. From 2003 to 2008, he led the Joint Special Operations Command, the armed services' opaque group of commandos whose job it is to "kill terrorists, and stay quiet about it" (Filkins 2010a). During his time in this post, McChrystal was involved in a sordid sequence of events following the death of Army Ranger and former professional football player Pat Tillman, which could have ended his career. Tillman, a safety for the Arizona Cardinals, enlisted in the Army after the events of September 11, 2001, foregoing a contract worth millions of dollars in the process. Tillman was killed in combat in April 2004 in Afghanistan, in a friendly fire incident in which he was shot by fellow soldiers.

McChrystal and other officers took part in an extensive cover-up concerning Tillman's death that involved lying to Tillman's family and the public and fraudulently awarding him a Silver Star (Filkins 2009; Krakauer 2010). The investigation into the conspiracy found that McChrystal had put forward "inaccurate and misleading assertions" in its furtherance (Rich 2010). Having received his second star while being promoted to major general nine days after Tillman's death, McChrystal's career nevertheless moved forward. This may have been, as Tillman's mother believes, because McChrystal was a favorite of both President Bush and Defense Secretary Don Rumsfeld, who appreciated his ability to get things done, even if not strictly by the book (Hastings 2010). When he was elevated to command U.S. and NATO forces in Afghanistan in May 2009, McChrystal had been serving as director of the Joint Staff for three months. Obama, who had not met McChrystal at that point, accepted the opinion of Mullen and Gates that McChrystal was right person for the job (Woodward 2010: 120). Obama held a ten-minute meeting with McChrystal in the Oval Office one week later (Woodward 2010: 120).

Comparisons with Truman's Firing of MacArthur

From the moment the *Rolling Stone* story broke, the media fluttered with comparisons of Obama's dilemma over McChrystal and President Harry S. Truman's firing of Gen. Douglas MacArthur in April 1951 during the Korean War. Truman's dismissal of MacArthur was the most recent, comparable analog, and the two cases actually had much more in common than many people appreciated. Some military sources contended that the two cases were unalike, on the rationale that McChrystal had never refused to implement the orders given by the commander-in-chief, but had (merely) spoken negatively about the president and his approach to the war in Afghanistan (Cooper, Shanker, and Filkins 2010). But that line of argument—portraying the Truman–MacArthur episode as being mainly about refusal to follow orders, and the Obama–McChrystal episode as being mainly about indecorous banter—was flat-out mistaken. Similarly, a senior administration official's statement that McChrystal's dismissal was "not about policy" but "about judgment and conduct, and working well with others" painted only part of the picture (Sanger 2010). The truth is that both cases were about insubordination that became evident due to three behaviors by a senior commander: making public a disagreement over strategy, conveying disdain for the president and his office, and displaying bad judgment in the process.

Despite disagreeing with Truman's policy in Korea and loudly advocating a widening of the war into China, MacArthur did in fact do what he was ordered to do. "The problem," noted Eliot A. Cohen, professor at the School of Advanced International Studies at Johns Hopkins University, "was that [MacArthur] let his disagreements become clearer than they should have been." McChrystal's essential and unforgiveable mistake thus was very much like MacArthur's: making his variance with the president over strategy visible to the world. Like MacArthur, McChrystal also did this disrespectfully, if not quite so colorfully as MacArthur, "with his corncob pipe, open shirt and insouciant conviction that he was working for idiots." McChrystal, who had skated up to and probably over the edge in his London speech, "crossed that fine line between Mr. Obama's encouragement of dissent and his no-drama management style." Successful presidents value the respectful articulation of different opinions in the Situation Room. Disrespectful expressions of divergences, provided to journalists, are less likely to inspire confidence (Sanger 2010).

A New Brand of Military Leaders
in a New Environment

After McChrystal's disastrous remarks in London in fall 2009, Obama's advisors had wondered whether the general's time in relative isolation at the Special Operations Command had rendered him clueless about public relations (Woodward 2010: 194). Mullen, who had told McChrystal to accept the invitation to speak, later observed that every new four-star officer has to grow into the role, but McChrystal had the disadvantage of having to do so before a global public (Woodward 2010: 193). And Colin Powell, former chairman of the Joint Chiefs of Staff, who early in his career had worked with McChrystal's father, emailed McChrystal to tell him to avoid the limelight (Woodward 2010: 195). Powell's outreach was telling, for he was the personification of a general who had risen to the pinnacle of command during the latter stages of the Cold War and its immediate aftermath—and had gone on to become secretary of state under the administration of George W. Bush. Powell had achieved these things by mastering the complexities of politics, navigating with utmost skill the shoals that could undermine a high-profile officer at any moment. In this sense, Powell was also emblematic of a new breed of savvy, sophisticated military officers who must be every bit as politically adept as their civilian masters. One author has referred to these new military leaders as "America's viceroys," and explored the implications of their rise (Reveron 2007).

Gen. Petraeus, who is the most vivid embodiment of this new type of leader, has called them "pentathlete" leaders (Shanker 2010c). Natural leadership abilities and tactical expertise on the battlefield are now necessary, but not sufficient, characteristics to rise to the highest levels of command. As Thom Shanker has written: "Generals and other top officers are now expected to be city managers, cultural ambassadors, public relations whizzes and politicians as they deal with multiple missions and constituencies in the war zone, in allied capitals—and at home" (Shanker 2010c). The tempo of war is faster now than in previous eras, the stream of information that must be assimilated is relentless, and survival and success require a commander to build a web of relationships spanning sectors. The most demanding task for senior officers is learning how to build and manage relationships with their civilian officials atop the chain of command and also with the media, with its nonstop news cycles. Importantly, this new environment places a premium on mastering political skills, because today's commanders must move seamlessly between military and nonmilitary worlds (Filkins 2010a).

Hastings, author of the *Rolling Stone* piece, was amazed that the general's staff invited him to spend a total of nearly a month with McChrystal and his intimates in Afghanistan, with almost everything on the record. Hastings reflected: "The amazing thing to me was that no ground rules were set" (Peters 2010). Some analysts have concluded that McChrystal left the ground rules open because he hoped doing so would help produce an incendiary article that would challenge the White House. Historian Robert Dallek has taken this position: "It is impossible to believe that General McChrystal didn't know exactly what he was doing. Surely he understood that an interview with a left-of-center magazine would produce headlines across the country. He was reading the president the riot act" (Dallek 2010). Perhaps this is true. It is more likely, however, that the general was seeking a milder result, not expecting the final article to have so strong an edge—or such political impact. This opposing conclusion takes into account the lack of familiarity that some senior officials have with the relatively new "culture of exposure" in which it is rare for any journalist to protect a subject from his or her own spontaneous and potentially damaging remarks—a courtesy that journalists more willingly extended decades ago (Brooks 2010).

Nine days after McChrystal's firing, Gates moved forward on issuing orders requiring senior Pentagon and military leaders to get clearance from the Defense Department's assistant secretary of public affairs "prior to interviews or any other means of media and public engagement with possible national or international implications" (Shanker 2010a). This step was a reaction to McChrystal's missteps and the resulting firestorm. Even more so, it was direct acknowledgement of the complex environment in which senior commanders would continue to find themselves operating. It showed the damage that could be done, by leaders and subcontractors alike, to the time-honored ideas of civilian control of the military and respect for the chain of command.

Petraeus Succeeds McChrystal, and Fates Intertwine

Petraeus, who had served under Gen. David D. McKiernan during the 2003 invasion of Iraq, had taken an unmistakable, unsettling point from his former boss's dismissal in May 2009, even though he agreed with it: "Generals were expendable. Center stage one day, gone the next" (Woodward 2010: 119). Petraeus undoubtedly suffered genuine anguish at McChrystal's fate, too, no matter how self-inflicted it was. Now Petraeus was effectively taking a demotion, stepping down as commander of U.S. Central Command to assume a post whose holder had reported to him, to bring all of his ambition and media savvy to bear on the War in Afghanistan. Almost no one thought a repeat immolation was possible. As the only four-star officer whose profile was higher than McChrystal's, there was almost universal regard for his record of military leadership—and for his political adroitness. The Senate confirmed him by a vote of 99–0.

Petraeus was confident that he could do in Afghanistan what he had done in Iraq (Woodward 2010: 263). He was, after all, the originator of the counterinsurgency strategy that had succeeded there, and which was to continue as the approach taken by U.S. and NATO forces under his command in Afghanistan. By late 2008, in wake of the effective surge of forces in Iraq, he had salvaged the war, even while noting presciently, "I've always said that Afghanistan will be the tougher fight" (Rubin and Filkins 2010). The Washington establishment was hopeful that his leadership style would refocus and reenergize the war effort by "reaching out to allies and the civilian leadership," as Sen. Jack Reed of Rhode Island put it (Cooper and Sanger 2010). Afghanistan was a very different country, though, more problematic in terms of its geography, economy, history, demographics—and the way its insurgency was dispersed in rural areas (Rubin and Filkins 2010). This situation would require Petraeus to draw on his vast store of goodwill and political capital in Washington in order to turn the war around, assuming that it could be turned around by June 2011 (Rubin and Filkins 2010). And it was clear from the start that Vice President Biden would be the central figure in the administration with whom the general was likely to butt heads over Afghanistan strategy in the coming months (Landler and Cooper 2010).

Petraeus acted quickly to retain and even tighten rules put in place by McChrystal to restrict the use of artillery and airstrikes, a crucial aspect of minimizing Afghan civilian deaths that had endeared McChrystal to Afghan leaders but had been skeptically received by U.S. and NATO forces (Oppel and Nordland 2010). By mid-August, Petraeus was already saying in interviews that he was opposed to a premature withdrawal from Afghanistan. The general also was predicting that, despite skepticism within the administration, he would ultimately get more time and materiel needed to win (Filkins 2010b). Perhaps most strikingly, the general went on record as saying that it was not his intent to simply manage a "graceful exit" of U.S. forces from Afghanistan (Herbert 2010a). By mid-October, the allied forces were stepping up the pace and intensity of the war, utilizing more frequent airstrikes and raids by Special Forces in the hopes of opening up a diplomatic approach to make terms with the Taliban, or elements of it (Dao 2010). The urgency was in no small measure a sign of Petraeus's judgment that he was in danger of running out of time to convince the Pentagon and the president that the United States should not begin to withdraw from Afghanistan in July 2011, the president's six-page binding orders notwithstanding. In the November midterm elections, Afghanistan was anything but a major issue, "virtually an afterthought in American politics" (Dao 2010). Yet it would have to reemerge at some point, perhaps in spring 2011, as the fighting season resumed and everyone, at home and abroad, looked nervously ahead to the July deadline.

An interesting dynamic emerged during fall 2010 between Obama and Petraeus: The president was much more deferential toward his new general, occasionally asking during meetings what the general thought about specific matters. Having allowed Gen. McKiernan to be forced out in 2009, and having removed Gen. McChrystal from the same job in 2010, the president may well have decided that he could not bank on support in Washington or among the public if he were to cycle through a third Afghanistan commander, particularly one as prominent as Petraeus (Cooper, Sanger, and Shanker 2010). Petraeus, who had had a direct line to the White House during George W. Bush's administration, and whose Iraq surge then-Sen. Obama had opposed in 2007, now enjoyed closeness with President Obama, who valued the general's judgment (Baker 2010). The irony of the situation was not lost on Riedel, who had led Obama's first review of Afghanistan strategy. "He, like Bush before him, has put all his bets down on the table on one guy," said Riedel, "and it's the same guy" (Baker 2010). Leslie H. Gelb, president emeritus of the Council on Foreign Relations, observed, "They are joined at the hip, but the leverage lies with Petraeus" (Cooper et al. 2010).

Truman, reflecting later on his run-in with MacArthur, wrote: "If I allowed him to defy the civil authorities in this manner, I myself would be violating my oath to uphold and defend the

Constitution" (Dallek 2010). More than half a century later, Obama came to the Constitution's defense under similar circumstances. The president recognized that McChrystal was, in one writer's colorful phrase, "chronically insubordinate" (Herbert 2010b). Obama looked past shrill warnings such as that offered by former Clinton adviser George Stephanopoulos that he might come off looking "thin-skinned and petulant" if he dismissed the general (Rich 2010). That Obama did not waver was especially important, for he was confronting one member of a class of contemporary military leaders who have become, for better and worse, quite comfortable with politicking.

Almost every president finds it challenging to get comfortable dealing with the military brass. Obama showed that he learned quickly when he gave the military an eighteen-month time limit in Afghanistan and put on record his determination to stick to it (Baker 2010). That fact, coupled with the president's appreciation of what was at stake in the showdown with McChrystal, bodes well for his ability to handle the vexing decisions that lie in store in Afghanistan. There is, however, no guarantee that a quagmire will be avoided or even that closure will be attained in any form. A quick scan of the Korean peninsula serves as a bracing reminder that the war during which Truman fired MacArthur "remains the running sore of Asia, a conflict as unresolved today as it was the day the armistice was signed" (Sanger 2010). Yet it would be rash to bet against limited progress in light of the determination, deliberateness, and tenacity that have been Obama's hallmarks in contending with the Afghan war. Obama's unerring sense that the national interest requires the substantial disentanglement of U.S. forces from Afghanistan is likely to bring about in late 2011 the first phase of an inevitably protracted drawdown.

Works Cited

Baker, Peter. "A wartime chief's steep learning curve." *The New York Times* (29 August 2010).

Brooks, David. "The culture of exposure." *The New York Times* (25 June 2010).

Bumiller, Elisabeth. "Mentor says McChrystal is 'crushed' by the change in his circumstances." *The New York Times* (3 July 2010).

Cooper, Helene and David E. Sanger. "Obama fires commander, citing need for unity in the war." *The New York Times* (24 June 2010).

Cooper, Helene, David E. Sanger, and Thom Shanker. "Once weary, Obama relies on Petraeus." *The New York Times* (17 Sept. 2010).

Cooper, Helene, and Thom Shanker. "General's job is in doubt in exposing Afghan rifts." *The New York Times* (23 June 2010).

Dallek, Robert. "General uproar; the other Truman doctrine." *The New York Times* (23 June 2010).

Dao, James. "In midterm elections, Afghan war barely surfaces." *The New York Times* (30 July 2010).

Dowd, Maureen. "Seven days in June." *The New York Times* (23 June 2010).

Editorial Desk. "The president and his general." *The New York Times* (23 June 2010).

Filkins, Dexter. "The good soldier." *The New York Times* (8 Sept. 2009).

———."In Afghanistan, a new breed of commander stepped in." *The New York Times* (23 June 2010a).

———."General opposes a rapid pullout in Afghanistan." *The New York Times* (16 Aug. 2010b).

———. "U.S. uses attacks to nudge Taliban toward a deal." *The New York Times* (25 Oct. 2010c).

Hastings, Michael. "The runaway general." *Rolling Stone* (8–22 July 2010), 94.

Herbert, Bob. "No graceful exit." *The New York Times* (17 Aug. 2010a).

———."Worse than a nightmare." *The New York Times* (26 June 2010b).

Krakauer, John. *Where Men Win Glory: The Odyssey of Pat Tillman.* New York: Anchor Books, 2010.

Landler, Mark. "Short, tense deliberation, then a general is gone." *The New York Times* (24 June 2010).

Landler, Mark and Helene Cooper. "As generals change, Afghan debate narrows to 2 powerful voices." *The New York Times* (25 June 2010).

Oppel, Richard A. Jr. and Rod Nordland. "Petraeus to expand efforts to protect Afghan civilians." *The New York Times* (4 Aug. 2010).

Peters, Jeremy W. "The fury of a general, released by nature." *The New York Times* (23 June 2010).

Reveron, Derek S. *America's Viceroys: The Military and U.S. Foreign Policy.* New York: Palgrave Macmillan, 2007.

Rich, Frank. "The 36 hours that shook Washington." *The New York Times* (27 June 2010).

Rubin, Alissa J. "Afghan leaders defend McChrystal." *The New York Times* (24 June 2010).

Rubin, Alissa J. and Dexter Filkins. "New mission for Petraeus: Make his own plan work." *The New York Times* (24 June 2010).

Sanger, David E. "McChrystal tests Obama's priorities." *The New York Times* (24 June 2010).

Shanker, Thom. "Defense secretary tightens rules for military's contacts with news media." *The New York Times* (3 July 2010a).

————."From Pentagon, messages of dismay and support." *The New York Times* (25 June 2010b).

————. "Win wars? Today's general must also meet, manage, placate, politick and do PR." *The New York Times* (13 Aug. 2010c).

Wolffe, Richard. *Revival: The Struggle for Survival Inside the Obama White House*. New York: Crown Books, 2010.

Woodward, Bob. *Obama's War*. New York: Simon & Schuster, 2010.

Chapter 9

2010 Midterm Election

Matthew N. Green

An Electoral "Shellacking"

The 2010 midterm election served as a decisive coda to Barack
Obama's first two years as president. His party not only lost its
majority in the U.S. House of Representatives but did so in a spec-
tacular fashion, surrendering more House seats to the opposition
than any party in a congressional election in over sixty years. And
although Democrats still controlled the U.S. Senate, the party's
majority of fifty-three seats was a far cry from the sixty seats that
it had held in 2009.

Inevitably, questions arise over the impact of the election on
Obama's legislative program and whether the results represent a
repudiation of the president and his agenda. Although many pundits claimed that it constituted such a rejection, other factors were
at least as important—and probably more so—than the president's
leadership. It is also worth considering whether the new balance of
power brought by the election, which imposed obvious constraints
on Obama, could offer the president opportunities as well.

2008 versus 2010

In the 2008 elections, Democrats were the big winners. Obama
defeated John McCain, winning the presidency with 53 percent
of the vote—a greater percentage than any Democratic candidate since 1964. House Democrats had taken the chamber from

Republicans in 2006, and in 2008 they won an additional twenty-one seats (just above the average nineteen seats captured by the party that wins the White House). And after Democrats won a hotly contested recount of a Senate race in Minnesota, the party had expanded its Senate majority from fifty-one to sixty—the magic number needed to beat a minority party filibuster. Democrats were triumphant; Republicans, demoralized.

But it was a different story two years later. Obama probably best summed up the 2010 election from his party's perspective when he described it as a "shellacking" (White House 2010). Republicans won 242 seats in the House of Representatives, the most held by the GOP in that chamber since 1946. Its sixty-three-seat gain was more than double the average House seat loss by a president's party in a midterm[1] and greater than what either party had won in a midterm election since 1938. In the Senate, the Democrats lost six seats, twice the historical average for a midterm, and Obama's reduced Senate majority not only included conservatives and independents, whose party loyalty was less than ironclad, but was also significantly smaller than the sixty-seat supermajority necessary to overcome a filibuster.

Things were no better for Democrats at the state level. Previously in control of a majority of governorships and state legislatures, the party was reduced to majority status in the bicameral legislatures of just sixteen states (and controlled one of the two chambers of the legislature in another eight states), while only twenty governors remained Democrats. These losses were in themselves not a complete surprise because state elections tend to track national ones fairly closely (Sides 2010b). But the state-level results presented several tough challenges to Obama and the Democratic Party, including potential for greater state resistance to the implementation of health care reform and, more ominously, a diminished influence over the impending state and congressional redistricting process.

In short, the 2010 midterm was, even more so than the 2008 election, a "wave"—or, perhaps more accurately, a "tidal wave"—election. Historic in its scope, it had halted, if not wiped out, the careers of countless incumbent Democratic politicians, both in state and national government, and had sapped the Democratic Party of much of its governing power throughout the country.

---

1. Between 1902 and 2006, presidential parties lost an average of twenty-nine House seats and three Senate seats in midterm elections.

Explaining the Wave

Once the election was over, Washington pundits quickly turned to one of the city's favorite parlor games: debating why the election turned out as it did. For many, Obama was to blame, and for several reasons: 1) The president is the highest-profile politician in the country and considered the leader of his party; 2) Obama's approval ratings had fallen into negative territory prior to the election; and 3) the president had faced strident critics from both ends of the political spectrum for perceived leadership failings. Even Obama placed himself square in the middle of things, telling the press the next day that "I'm not recommending for every future President that *they* take a shellacking, like . . . I did last night" (White House 2010).

But this is not the only possible explanation for the 2010 midterm results. Looking more closely at several widely cited reasons for the outcome, one finds that the presidency-centered account of the election is only partially accurate and cannot in itself explain the sheer scale of the Republican victory.

Macro Factors

The two most important factors that contributed to the wave election were national in scope. The first was the Democratic Party's inherent electoral disadvantages. Being in the majority, of course, the party had more offices to defend at both the state and national levels, and midterm elections almost always result in losses for the president's party in Congress. Many Democrats in Congress also represented conservative constituencies, including forty-eight House members and three Senators who were up for reelection in states or districts that had voted for John McCain in 2008. Additionally, more than sixty House Democrats were either freshmen, typically the most vulnerable incumbents in Congress, or sophomores who had been the beneficiaries of a Democratic "wave" in 2006 and Obama's electoral coattails in 2008. (A good number of Democrats faced the "double-whammy" problem of both being junior members and representing conservative districts.)

The Democratic Party in Congress was thus badly exposed to electoral tides (Oppenheimer, Stimson, and Waterman 1986) and faced a difficult environment from day 1. And Republicans proved quite successful at winning seats away from these vulnerable lawmakers, capturing 75 percent of the House seats and two of the three Senate seats representing "McCain country" and more than thirty House seats represented by freshman or sophomore Democrats.

The second important "macro" condition that led to the mammoth Republican election victory was the poor state of the national economy. Although the recession had officially ended in the latter half of 2009, the nation's unemployment rate remained stubbornly high—more than 9.5 percent—through most of 2010, and elevated home foreclosure rates continued to plague many parts of the country. Results from repeated studies over the past decades have shown that poor economic conditions hurt incumbent congressional parties at the polls, and 2010 was no exception (e.g., Grier and McGarrity 1998; Kramer 1971; Rees, Kaufman, Eldersveld, and Freidel 1962; Tufte 1978). In fact, several statistical models that predicted big wins for the GOP that year included one or more economic indicators that pointed in the negative direction (e.g., Cuzán 2010; Klarner 2010; Lewis-Beck and Tien 2010; Masket 2010).

Evidence that voter worry about the economy was both widespread and translated into votes against Democrats can be found in exit surveys of voters taken after they cast their ballots in the midterm. According to one such poll, a survey of more than 17,500 people casting ballots in House races, the national economy was the top concern of 63 percent of respondents, and 54 percent of those voted for Republican candidates. Even more telling, in both that CNN exit poll and one from 2008, virtually the same percentage of respondents indicated that they were "very worried" about the economy (50 percent in 2008, 49 percent in 2010), yet such voters shifted their ballot preferences starkly from Democrats in 2008 (60 percent) to Republicans in 2010 (68 percent) (CNN 2008, 2010).

One could make the case that Obama should have taken some blame for the nation's sluggish economic recovery in his first two years in office. Economist Paul Krugman, for instance, asserted forcefully that the stimulus bill enacted in early 2009 was far too limited in scope to fully restore the nation's economic health (see e.g., Krugman and Wells 2011). But this claim is debatable. According to a trio of different economists, the bill was already "the largest stimulus package in modern U.S. economic history" (Auerbach, Gale, and Harris 2010), and it is difficult to imagine whether an even bigger bill—assuming Obama could have marshaled the votes for one in Congress—might have created more jobs or improved personal incomes early enough to appease anxious voters.

Campaign-Related Factors

Two additional explanations have been suggested related to campaign tactics undertaken by the Republican Party or its campaign allies: strong Republican candidates and massive non-party campaign spending. It is unlikely, however, that either of these was anywhere near as important as both the economy and the Democrats' overexposure in bringing about the GOP's electoral blowout.

A candidate's "quality," at least as measured by her prior electoral experience, has been shown to have a nontrivial relationship with her share of the two-party vote (Jacobson 2004), and the GOP did attract an unusually high number of experienced candidates to run in competitive House races (Nyhan 2010). Yet, candidate quality does not explain why many incumbent House Democrats were defeated by politically inexperienced candidates, such as a pizzeria owner (Bobby Schilling), a former NFL linebacker (Jon Runyan), a nurse (Renee Ellmers), and a funeral home owner (Steve Southerland). More generally, it is difficult to separate the decision of a strong candidate to run for office from larger variables, like the economy, that might have encouraged such candidates to run in the first place.

The other campaign-related explanation for the Republican sweep was increased spending by outside groups. The midterm election was quite expensive: An estimated $3.7 billion was spent on the election at the national level, nearly $1 billion more than in the 2006 midterm. Congressional election spending by non-party groups in particular grew: They more than doubled from 2008, totaling $280 million, and most importantly the majority of that money was spent to help Republican candidates (The Campaign Finance Institute 2010; Center for Responsive Politics 2010).

But although most people believe that money buys elections, causal relationships between campaign spending and election outcomes are notoriously tough to establish with certainty. For instance, the preexisting vulnerability of some Democratic incumbents might have attracted high levels of spending by pro-Republican organizations, instead of the increased spending making safe incumbents vulnerable. In "wave" elections like 2010, furthermore, campaign expenditures may have only a limited influence on the overall outcome. Paul Herrnson, an elections scholar who argues that money does matter in elections, nonetheless notes that congressional incumbents can fall prey to "national partisan tides, which are beyond any one candidate's control," and shows that such tides can affect candidates' vote share independently of how much money is spent on their campaigns (Herrnson 2008, 251). Also, even if large amounts of money are spent on behalf of candidates, how those campaign dollars are spent matters a great deal. Expenditures by outside conservative groups in 2010 were on advertising, which tends to have less of a per-dollar impact on voter turnout than grassroots, get-out-the-vote activities (Green and Gerber 2004).

Presidential Leadership Style and Agenda

Then there is the possibility that Obama himself contributed to the massive GOP wave. Voter perceptions of the president do correlate with midterm congressional election results, and presidential job approval ratings, another common feature of forecasting models for the 2010 election, had dropped over the course of the year to below 50 percent (Jones 2010a, 2010b; Lewis-Beck and Tien 2010; Masket 2010).[2] Interestingly, the 2010 CNN exit poll found that 60 percent of respondents intended their vote to signal their views of the president (CNN 2010).

Survey data suggest that whatever impact Obama's leadership did have on the election almost certainly affected liberal voters far less than conservative, and maybe independent,[3] voters. To be sure, some Democrats complained vehemently that the president had compromised too much with conservatives or had been insufficiently aggressive in responding to crises or Republican attacks (see e.g., Krugman and Wells 2010). Although those complaints may be valid, Obama's overall approval rating actually remained high among Democrats, upwards of 75 percent through

---

2. Obama's job approval ratings are problematic as a means of measuring the independent effect of presidential performance on the election because they actually may be a proxy for other, more fundamental factors that influenced the election, like voters' view of the state of the economy (Blumenthal 2010). As noted here, Obama's average Gallup approval rating was actually higher than President Bill Clinton's had been in 1994, yet Obama suffered much larger seat losses in Congress.

3. Professor John Sides is among those who are highly skeptical of the attention given to independents in the election. Many independents are self-identified and merely eschew party labels while maintaining strong ideological predispositions. Furthermore, data suggest that "true" independents are more sensitive to the state of the economy than are other voters, suggesting that their vote choice in 2010 reflected economic worries rather than views about presidential leadership per se (Sides 2010a).

Election Day. By contrast, it sank among Republicans early in the president's tenure (to a mere 20 percent by July 2009) and a majority of self-declared independents had turned against Obama by the end of 2009 (Huffpost Pollster 2010).

President Obama was held responsible in two specific ways for the rout of his party at the polls. First, he was accused of having a poor style of public leadership by ignoring issues of greatest concern to voters, such as the economy and the mid-2010 oil spill in the Gulf of Mexico, and failing to effectively "sell" his administration's achievements. But Obama's average public approval ratings in mid-October 2010, as measured by Gallup, were higher than those of Bill Clinton and Ronald Reagan—two other rhetorically agile presidents—at the same time in each of their first terms (Jones 2010b). Also, among conservatives and independents, the shift in public opinion away from Obama came well before many of Obama's alleged communication missteps on such matters as the final passage of health care or the Gulf oil spill. Nor did Obama ignore the public's concerns about the economy or fail to tout his administration's successes. Figure 9.1 shows the number of public appearances by Obama in September and October 2010 (and, as a comparative benchmark, in the same months of 2009) in which either health care or the economy was mentioned. Obama dedicated far more attention to the subject of the economy as the election approached, but he also more frequently praised health care reform as well. Although this metric cannot capture how well the president framed either issue, Obama cannot be faulted for giving them insufficient attention, at least in the last two months before the election.

A stronger case can be made, however, for a second possibility: that Obama's legislative agenda hurt his party's standing among right-leaning voters. Political scientist Eric McGhee found that incumbents who cast votes in favor of several high-profile and controversial measures supported by the Obama White House, such as environmental regulation and health care reform, saw their share of the two-party vote decline from 2008 to 2010. In fact, enough congressional Democrats voted with Obama often enough, and then lost by sufficiently narrow margins, for the agenda to have possibly cost the party control of the House (McGhee 2010).[4]

---

4. McGhee is not alone in finding a similar relationship between key votes in Congress and subsequent electoral outcomes. Others have found such a pattern for votes on the economic bailout in late 2008 (Green and Hudak 2009), on high-profile issues in the mid-1990s (Ferejohn 1998), and more broadly over time (Canes-Wrone, Brady, and Cogan 2002).

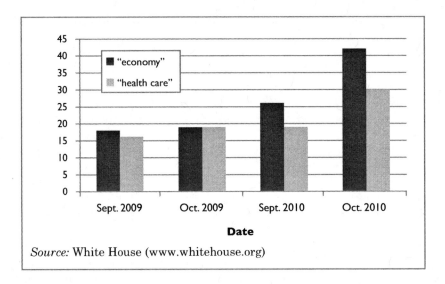

Figure 9.1. Number of Presidential Speeches Mentioning the Economy or Health Care.

This finding does not preclude the important role of the economy or Democrats' structural disadvantages; for instance, McGhee found that the effect was greater for incumbents who were representing conservative districts and thus already electorally vulnerable. But it is nonetheless compelling evidence that incumbent congressional Democrats who supported Obama were punished at the polls.

Another Explanation?

It also provides a plausible explanation for one of the most striking features of the midterm, a feature that helped make the election more of a tsunami than a wave: the tremendous turnout by conservative voters. Even before Election Day, pollsters had discovered that the GOP electorate was unusually galvanized. A Gallup survey taken shortly before the midterm found that 68 percent of Republican voters were highly enthusiastic about the election—the largest ever seen by Gallup—whereas only 44 percent of Democrats felt the same way (Jones 2010c). Conservatives acted on their enthusiasm: On the day of the election itself, older Americans, who tend to vote Republican at a higher rate than younger voters, cast ballots in record numbers. Figure 9.2, which charts exit poll data on election turnout by age between 1994 and 2010, shows that voters between ages forty-five and sixty-four, and those sixty-five and older, each made up an unusually high proportion of the electorate in the midterm election. Their decision to come to the polls in such numbers resulted in the highest turnout for any midterm since the last Republican wave election in 1994,[5] and their support for Republican candidates was essential to the GOP's success.[6]

Deep dissatisfaction with Obama and the policies of a unified Democratic government is the most likely reason so many older and conservative Americans felt motivated to participate in the election. Other explanations for their high turnout are less compelling. Given the older tilt of the electorate, for instance, one may speculate that certain generational issues were at play, although what those might have been is unclear. Perhaps older voters were more upset about health care reform than about other items on Obama's agenda—although, of the meager 18 percent of respondents in the exit poll who put health care at the top of their list of concerns, 51 percent actually voted Democratic, not Republi-

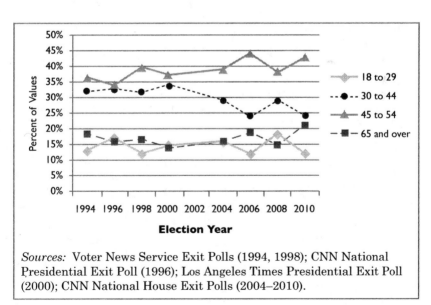

Sources: Voter News Service Exit Polls (1994, 1998); CNN National Presidential Exit Poll (1996); Los Angeles Times Presidential Exit Poll (2000); CNN National House Exit Polls (2004–2010).

Figure 9.2 Percent of the U.S. Electorate By Age

can (CNN 2010). Nor did older voters have more reason to be anxious about the economy than younger ones; in fact, economic hardship was actually felt more keenly by younger citizens. From January to October 2010, for instance, the average unemployment rate among those ages twenty to twenty-four was 15.5 percent, and among twenty-five to forty-four-year-olds it was 10 percent; whereas it was 6.9 percent for those aged forty-five to fifty-four and 7.1 percent among those aged fifty-five and older (Bureau of Labor Statistics 2010). It is possible, however, that fears about the economy by older voters were amplified by their conservatism and dislike of Obama's agenda because studies have found that people tend to view objective economic data differently depending on their ideological leanings (e.g., Bartels 2008). Interestingly, according to the CNN 2010 exit poll, voters who were "very worried" about the economy voted GOP 68 to 30 percent, yet those from a household with one or more job losses in the past two years voted Democratic 50 to 46 percent (CNN 2010).

Making Sense of the Results

The science of explaining election results remains primitive. Voters make their choices for all sorts of reasons, and "when there are only two ways of expressing a hundred varieties of feeling," as Walter Lippman noted, "there is no certain way of knowing what the decisive combination was" (Lippman 1922: 149). Exit polls, presumably the solution to this problem, have their limits, dependent as they are on not only proper methodology but voter honesty. Even Warren Mitofsky, the pioneering developer of exit polls, once declared that they "are not that good. They're approximate" (Morin 2006).

Nonetheless, the evidence that is available strongly suggests that three factors were the most important in explaining Democrats' crushing losses in November 2010: the party's electoral overexposure, the weak domestic economy, and Republican voters' intense distaste for Obama's legislative agenda. Obama could do nothing about the first factor, and his responsibility for the second is disputable. One could argue that the president might have been able to limit, if not stave off, the massive GOP wins had he better tempered the outrage of conservative voters by pursuing a different set of legislative initiatives. Yet doing so would almost certainly have come at the steep price of disillusionment and repudiation by his own partisans, both in and outside of government, and with no guarantee, given the highly partisan nature of contemporary Washington politics, of garnering enough cooperation from Republicans to enact nearly as much significant legislation as he did.

What Comes Next?

When the new Congress was sworn in on January 5, 2011, Obama entered a difficult situation that resembled what the last Democratic president, Bill Clinton, faced following his own "shellacking" after two years in office: being caught between liberal Democrats, who lack institutional power but remain ardent guardians against perceived party disloyalty by the president, and ascendant Republicans, who have both the eagerness and a perceived mandate to turn back Obama's previous legislative achievements, hinder his efforts to enact policy, and cripple his chances of reelection. It is a situation that can easily lead to legislative stalemate and a diminished reputation for the president.

Then again, just as the 1994 election proved politically helpful to Clinton, so too did the 2010 midterm offer Obama some important, if uncertain and limited, political and policy-related opportunities. For one thing, the president—who at times appears more comfortable pursuing less-confrontational and more bipartisan leadership than many Democrats would care for—was given an excuse to pursue cooperative legislative strategies with Republicans, much as he did on a major budget bill in the lame duck session of the 111th Congress. The GOP may even feel some pressure to meet Obama part way on legislation, not only because it is in partial control of Congress and want to avoid a "do-nothing" label going into the 2012 election, but also because many of its freshmen members represent states and districts won by Obama in 2008. Obama can also profit politically from the fact that Republicans find themselves in a challenging spot: Conservative party activists are bound to rebel at any perceived cooperation with the White House by the GOP, and the ardent conservatism of many of the new congressional Republicans creates an opportunity to brand the Republican Party as "extremist."

Whether Obama can successfully navigate the dangerous shoals of this changed political environment, steering to the center on some issues to enact desired legislation while tarnishing the Republican Party's reputation by partaking in more of the symbolic politics he seems to find distasteful, is an open question.

Regardless, the president's second two years in office will almost certainly be filled with even more partisan rhetoric, confrontation, and heated drama than pervaded his first two. For Obama, and also for leaders of the Republican Party, the new dynamic threatens to fulfill the apocryphal Chinese curse: "May you live in interesting times."

Works Cited

Auerbach, Alan J., William G. Gale, and Benjamin H. Harris. "Activist Fiscal Policy." *Journal of Economic Perspectives*, Vol. 24, No. 4 (2010), 141–164. http://pubs.aeaweb.org/doi/pdfplus/10.1257/jep.24.4.141 (accessed 2 Jan. 2011).

Bartels, Larry M. *Unequal Democracy: The Political Economy of the New Gilded Age.* New York: Russell Sage Foundation, 2008.

Blumenthal, Mark. Obama's Problem Is Not About 'Connecting.' It's The Economy. *Huffpost Pollster* (30 Dec. 2010). http://www.huffington-post.com/2010/12/30/obama-overblown-connectin_n_802775.html (accessed 1 Jan. 2011).

Bureau of Labor StatisticsTable A-10: Household Data Seasonally Adjusted, 2010. ftp://ftp.bls.gov/pub/suppl/empsit.cpseea10.txt (accessed 1 Jan 2011).

Cable News Network. U.S. House National Exit Poll, 2008. http://www.cnn.com/ELECTION/2008/results/polls/ (accessed 1 Jan. 2011).

———. U.S. National House Exit Poll, 2010. http://www.cnn.com/ELEC-TION/2010/results/polls.main/# (accessed 30 Dec. 2010).

The Campaign Finance Institute. Non-Party Spending Doubled in 2010 but Did Not Dictate the Results. Press Release, 5 Nov. 2010.

Canes-Wrone, Brandice, David W. Brady, and John F. Cogan. "Out of Step, out of Office: Electoral Accountability and House Members' Voting." *The American Political Science Review.* Vol. 96, No. 1 (2001), 127–140.

Center for Responsive Politics. Election 2010 to Shatter Spending Records as Republicans Benefit from Late Cash Surge. *OpenSecretsblog* (27 Oct. 2010). http://www.opensecrets.org/news/2010/10/election-2010-to-shatter-spending-r.html (accessed 3 Jan. 2011).

Cuzán, Alfred G. "Will the Republicans Retake the House in 2010?" *PS: Political Science and Politics.* Vol. 43, No. 4 (2010), 639–641.

Ferejohn, John. A tale of two congresses: Social policy in the Clinton years. Ed. Margaret Weir. *The Social Divide: Political Parties and the Future of Activist Government.* Washington, DC: Brookings Institution Press, 1998, 49–82.

Green, Donald P. and Alan S. Gerber. *Get Out the Vote! How to Increase Voter Turnout.* Washington, DC: Brookings Institution Press, 2004.

Green, Matthew N. and Kristen Hudak. "Congress and the Bailout: Explaining the Bailout Votes and Their Electoral Effect." *Extension of Remarks, Legislative Studies Section Newsletter*. Vol. 32, No. 1 (2009).

Grier, Kevin B. and Joseph P. McGarrity. "The Effect of Macroeconomic Fluctuations on the Electoral Fortunes of House Incumbents. *Journal of Law and Economics*." Vol. 41, No. 1 (1998), 143–162.

Herrnson, Paul S. *Congressional Elections: Campaigning at Home and in Washington*. Washington, DC: Congressional Quarterly Press, 2008.

HuffPost Pollster. National Job Approval: Barack Obama. 2010. http://www.huffingtonpost.com/2009/01/06/jobapproval-obama_n_726319.html (accessed 2 Jan. 2010).

Jacobson, Gary C. *The Politics of Congressional Elections,* 6th ed. New York: Pearson Longman, 2004.

Jones, Jeffrey M. Avg. Midterm Seat Loss 36 for Presidents Below 50% Approval. *Gallup* (9 Aug. 2010a). http://www.gallup.com/poll/141812/Avg-Midterm-Seat-Loss-Presidents-Below-Approval.aspx (accessed 2 Jan. 2011).

———. "Obama's approval rating at new low in most recent quarter." *Gallup* (21 Oct. 2010b). http://www.gallup.com/poll/143921/Obama-Approval-Rating-New-Low-Recent-Quarter.aspx (accessed 2 Jan. 2011).

———. "Record midterm enthusiasm as voters head to polls." *Gallup* (2 Nov. 2010c). http://www.gallup.com/poll/144152/Record-Midterm-Enthusiasm-Voters-Head-Polls.aspx (accessed 2 Jan. 2011).

Klarner, Carl. "Forecasting the 2010 State Legislative Elections." *PS: Political Science and Politics*. Vol. 43, No. 4 (2010), 643–648.

Kramer, Gerald H. "Short-Term Fluctuations in U.S. Voting Behavior, 1896–1964." *The American Political Science Review*. Vol. 65, No. 1 (1971), 131–143.

Krugman, Paul and Robin Wells. "Where do we go from here?" *The New York Review of Books* (13 Jan 2011).

Lewis-Beck, Michael S. and Charles Tien. "The Referendum Model: A 2010 Congressional Forecast." *PS: Political Science and Politics*. Vol. 43, No. 4 (2010), 637–638.

Lippman, Walter. *Public Opinion*. New York: Penguin Books, 1922.

Masket, Seth. "Weak growth means the House is in play." *Enik Rising* (30 July 2010). http://enikrising.blogspot.com/2010/07/weak-growth-means-house-is-in-play.html (accessed 3 Jan. 2011).

McDonald, Michael. Election data. *United States Elections Project*. 2010 http://elections.gmu.edu/index.html (accessed 2 Jan. 2011).

McGhee, Eric. "Did controversial roll call votes doom the Democrats?" *The Monkey Cage* (4 Nov. 2010). http://www.themonkeycage.org/2010/11/did_controversial_roll_call_vo.html (accessed 29 Dec. 2010).

Morin, Richard. "The pioneer pollster whose credibility you could count on." *The Washington Post* (6 Sept. 2006).

Nyhan, Brendan. "How much are Tea Party candidates hurting the GOP?" *Brendan Nyhan blog* (21 Oct. 2010). http://www.brendan-nyhan.com/blog/2010/10/did-the-tea-party-weaken-gop-candidate-quality.html (accessed 29 Dec. 2010).

Oppenheimer, Bruce I., James A. Stimson, and Richard W. Waterman. "Interpreting U. S. Congressional Elections: The Exposure Thesis." *Legislative Studies Quarterly.* Vol. 11, No. 2 (1986), 227–247.

Rees, Albert, Herbert Kaufman, Samuel J. Eldersveld, and Frank Freidel. "The Effect of Economic Conditions on Congressional Elections 1946–1958." *The Review of Economics and Statistics* Vol. 44, No. 4 (1962), 458–465.

Sides, John. "Do Democrats understand political independents?" *The Monkey Cage* (Online, 16 Nov. 2010a). http://www.themonkeycage.org/2010/11/do_democrats_understand_politi.html (accessed 30 Dec. 2010).

Sides, John. 2010b. "Seat losses everywhere." *The Monkey Cage* (Online, 1 Nov. 2010b). http://www.themonkeycage.org/2010/11/seat_losses_everywhere.html (accessed 31 Dec. 2010).

Tufte, Edward R. *Political Control of the Economy.* Princeton, NJ: Princeton University Press, 1978.

White House. Press Conference by the President, 3 Nov. 2010. http://www.whitehouse.gov/the-press-office/2010/11/03/press-conference-president (accessed 30 Dec. 2010).

IV

Domestic Policy

Chapter 10

U.S. Auto Industry Rescue

Steve A. Stuglin

The presidency of Barack Obama began with high expectations
built up over a heated and historic campaign. The president was
presented with a number of challenges when he took office and
any one of them could be used as a metric to determine his success. The rescue of the domestic automobile industry is particularly
well suited to this endeavor because the contemporary case has
historic parallels that can be used for comparison. Jimmy Carter,
Ronald Reagan, and George W. Bush all rescued the auto industry
in some form while in office, providing three cases against which
the Obama intervention can be measured.

In each case, direct presidential influence on these rescues
was limited but there are important rhetorical elements that
are well within presidential control. In this chapter, four cases
of government intervention in the auto industry are examined.
Highlights of how each president justified the public expense are
provided, as are the ways in which they established a desired
outcome for the intervention. These rhetorical influences on the
rescue policies have important consequences in the likely event
of a future need for government aid to the automakers. President
Obama, in a skillful use of praise and blame, was able to shift
away from the historical tendency to justify aid only on economic
terms. Obama established a mandate for government to aid automakers that will act as a precedent in the future, whether aid
is requested or not.

The chapter proceeds in five parts:

1. The first part briefly reviews the historical arc of the domestic auto industry, including the four instances of public government aid at issue.

2. Part 2 discusses presidential influence on policy broadly and on economic policies specifically.

3. Obama's decision to act and his justification for aid are compared with the parallel cases during the Carter, Reagan, and Bush administrations in part 3.

4. The fourth section considers the consequences of Obama's shift in rhetorically negotiating the rescue of 2008 and 2009.

5. The analysis concludes by offering a view of Obama's handling of the auto rescue.

Rescuing the Domestic Auto Industry

Since the Model T brought the motorcar within reach of the American public, automobiles have been an integral part of everyday lives. Manufacturing of these vehicles was once the largest domestic industry in the United States, directly and indirectly employing tens of millions of workers. Following World War II, many industries in the United States entered a new boom era that corresponded with the economic rise of the country as a whole. At the time, General Motors posted staggering 25 percent returns on investments (Taylor 2010: 15). With little foreign competition and an exploding domestic market automakers expanded, borrowing in the process.

The era of unchecked growth began to erode in the 1960s when presidential and congressional actions imposed a series of new regulations on auto manufacturing. By the early 1970s, new models were required to conform to standards of safety, fuel emissions, and fuel efficiency. These regulations involved engineering challenges that inflated the cost of production even though they enhanced consumer safety and environmental quality (Crandall et al. 1986). Foreign competition, chiefly from Europe and Asia, began to increase and erode the domestic market share (Teaford 1994: 217–222). With the oil shocks of 1973 and 1979, the cost of production and ownership of vehicles skyrocketed, pushing consumers toward smaller makes and models (Reich and Donahue 1985: 55). Stagflation and high interest rates complicated industry responses to these challenges.

By the end of the 1970s, Chrysler's position had become so precarious it asked for government aid to stay in business. The Carter administration matched $2 billion in stakeholder concessions with $1.5 billion in guaranteed federal loans. Later, Reagan instituted less visible aid in the form of tax subsidies, foreign trade subzone status, and voluntary import quotas against Japan. Chrysler rebounded, paying back the government loans early and buying back warrants from the Treasury for a $311 million profit to taxpayers (Reich and Donahue 1985: 254–257). By 1984, the domestic auto industry had ridden the regulatory relief and import protection enacted by Carter and Reagan into a new golden age. The economic prosperity and comparatively cheap gasoline of the Clinton era meant much of the 1990s were good years for Chrysler, Ford, and General Motors. Throughout, domestic automakers were buoyed by the rise of minivans, sport-utility vehicles, and the continued popularity of light trucks.

In 2006, the industry showed signs of trouble again. Rapidly rising gasoline costs during the Bush administration again pushed consumers toward smaller cars. Toyota, Honda, and other manufacturers were still making higher-quality small cars for lower prices than Detroit automakers could match. By 2008, with gasoline at $4 a gallon, Ford posted an $8.7 billion quarterly loss, General Motors lost $15.5 billion in the second quarter, and Chrysler explored merger options (Rattner 2010: 17). Gasoline costs continued to rise and the industry as a whole went to the government for help. In December, George W. Bush signed a $17.4 billion bridge loan for General Motors and Chrysler. The Obama administration, under pressure for further aid, led General Motors and Chrysler through special bankruptcy procedures. Between the Bush and Obama administrations, $82 billion had been spent to save the auto industry.

Over the past half century, the auto industry has endured times of boom and bust, largely as a result of changing macroeconomic forces and the response of company leadership to them. The Carter, Reagan, Bush, and Obama administrations each provided significant material aid to the industry during these periods of flux. In each case, presidential action influenced the broader rescues of the industry even though direct presidential engagement with the rescues was minimal at best. To fully understand this point we must briefly discuss presidential influence generally before moving to an analysis of presidential influence on the auto rescues.

Presidential Influence

To make a case that Carter, Reagan, Bush, or Obama influenced the rescues of the automobile industry we must first establish that a president can have influence over this level of policy. Modern presidents are the head of a vast bureaucracy. The president directs more attention to some policies and less attention to others. Yet, most of the work done, with most policies, is carried out below presidential attention, by people ranging from staffers to cabinet level officials. Even in the case of heightened presidential attention to an individual policy the president requires cooperation from a host of other agencies to implement and monitor it (Wood 2004: 573). Presidential influence on the intricacies of policy is generally, by necessity, limited.

The limits of presidential influence are evident in the domestic auto industry rescues. A detailed account of the 1980 rescue shows that most of the decisions about how to help Chrysler were made by lawyers, staffers at the Treasury, Federal Reserve (Fed), and members of the Council of Economic Advisors (CEA) (Reich and Donahue 1985). After the agreement on the process had been made between Chrysler and government, a Loan Advisory Board was established to validate that loan conditions were met and to oversee the funds. In 2008, the bridge loan provided by the Bush administration was a product of Henry Paulson, secretary of the Treasury, Joel Kaplan, White House deputy chief of staff for policy, and Keith Hennessey, director of the National Economic Council (NEC) (Rattner 2010: 35–42). The Obama administration rescue, built on top of the Bush bridge loan, was designed and implemented by "Team Auto" under the joint supervision of Timothy Geithner, secretary of the Treasury, and Lawrence Summers, director of the NEC (Rattner 2010). For the most part, these members of the Treasury, the Fed, CEA, and NEC decided how to rescue the automakers.

Presidential influence was limited in these rescues, as it usually is in matters of policy. However, an important aspect of presidential influence on policy is one not often evident from a structural perspective. As Richard Neustadt (1960) argued, presidential power is the power of persuasion. Samuel Kernell (1997) added that presidents go public for support of decisions or plans, and Kimberly Maslin-Wicks (1998) argued that presidents have a heresthetical influence wherein the president structures the world to win. Presidential influence is thus the rhetorical act of arguing for or against policy, appealing to the public and Congress for support, and framing the entire issue along agreeable lines. To consider the potential for presidential influence on a multibillion dollar government intervention in private enterprise we must focus on the rhetorical choices made by the president as the action was being advocated or defended.

This potential for rhetorical influence is particularly important when discussing an issue of economic policy. Government intervention in the auto industry is complex and implicates related issues of labor, foreign trade, credit, and the money supply. Discussions of economic policy at this level are, by definition, rhetorical enterprises that require usage of metaphors and narrative structures (Montanye 2005). The president, as chief metaphor and narrative maker in these moments, can either further complicate the situation or make sense of it in a way that benefits the stance of the administration.

Presidents have little actual control over the economy. Still, the public tends to think that the president can control or guide the economy through policy. There are a number of studies that document the link between presidential approval ratings and the perceived strength of the economy (Clark and Stewart 1994; Edwards et al. 1995; MacKuen et al. 1992; Monroe 1978). This leads to a paradox: "One of the president's greatest responsibilities is the one over which he exerts relatively little independent authority" (Lewis 1997: 391). Presidents resort to speaking out on the economy, using rhetorical strategies in place of the executive control over the economy we imagine presidents have.

These rhetorical efforts might actually work. According to David Rankin (2006), the public tends to give more weight to the presidential voice on complex issues like the economy and foreign policy, in turn reinforced by a media that highlights the presidential perspective instead of those of other political actors. Presidents *can* provide economic leadership by speaking in positive tones to sell a particular economic policy or the broader economic climate. It appears to work because, simply put, the positive or negative tone a president adopts affects how we make decisions (Wood 2004: 574).

Although direct presidential influence on the particulars of a given policy may be limited, economic policies are an ideal venue for the kind of indirect rhetorical influence that the chief executive is suited to. This also makes economic policies an ideal site to observe the influence in action. We can observe two forms of presidential influence over the domestic auto rescues and judge the broader presidential influence on the rescues by comparing how Carter, Reagan, Bush, and Obama handled each of the two forms differently.

Presidents Influencing the Rescues

Before each president could exercise rhetorical influence each first had to decide to act. It was ultimately an executive decision, even if only to preempt congressional action. The decision to act was based in part on a desire to avoid the perceived economic fallout of a company or industry collapse.[1]

In 1979, based on the economic justification of saving jobs, Carter chose between the options presented to him for dealing with Chrysler: Chapter 11 bankruptcy or loan guarantees. According to Reich and Donahue (1985), "The way the issue came to be posed—a bailout or collapse—effectively dictated the administration's choice. . . . There were too many hostages for the administration to consider letting the automaker go" (131). For Reich and Donahue, the decision to act was not really a decision at all. This would also be the case in early 1981 when the Reagan administration took over the now-approved and halfway-disbursed loan guarantee program. Reagan could not realistically choose to end the public bailout program he had so adamantly opposed during the campaign. In fact, he may not have wanted to. Although it played well politically for Reagan to be opposed to government intervention, he actually advocated a different *kind* of intervention. Publicly, Reagan put low-level staffers in charge of the Loan Advisory Board until its mandate expired. Privately, or perhaps quietly, Reagan helped to expand the foreign trade subzone status for industrial companies (including automakers) and maintained Carter-era programs to help General Motors, such as a $90 million Department of Housing and Urban Development grant used to relocate residents from an area earmarked for a new plant (Rubenstein 1992: 205–206). Reagan also helped the auto industry get tax subsidies and $68 million in profits from safe-harbor lease transactions while protecting the industry from Japanese imports (Reich and Donahue 1985: 243–245).

In 2008, when the Bush administration had to decide whether or not to help the auto industry, the decision was similarly framed by the economic situation. The president was presented with four options, of which three were some form of government intervention, whereas the last was to do nothing and let the automakers fail. Like Reagan, Bush found the idea of a rescue distasteful, "yet he'd already decided that letting the companies fail was off the table, and he had said so in public on December 12" (Rattner 2010: 40). On December 19, 2008, President Bush explained these were "not ordinary circumstances" and that government should act (Bush 2008: ¶4). The conditions of the bridge loan Bush provided automakers demanded that each company submit revised business plans to the new Obama administration in three months, effectively guaranteeing that the next administration would have to publicly consider the matter. Obama decided to act as well, extending conditional aid to the industry with a mandate for restructuring plans and an ultimatum for bankruptcy (Rattner 2010: 132).

In each instance, the president at the time was given the final say in whether or not to use public funds to intervene. Once the decision to intervene had been made, and in each case the economic problems of a collapsing auto industry made the decision all but a foregone conclusion, the rescue could proceed. As noted, much of the work before and after this decision would fall to staffers and officials at the Treasury, the Fed, or elsewhere. However, once the decision was made, the president was able to exercise rhetorical influence in at least two important ways. First, the president would have to justify the large expense of public funds to the American people. Second, the president would have to establish a desired goal to be achieved by this public expense, which often entailed a certain process of intervention. These rhetorical choices did not always reflect the fiscal or legal reality of the intervention. Yet, because of the importance of the presidential voice in discussions of economic policy, these rhetorical choices have important consequences.

Justifying the Public Expense

The public justification of spending taxpayer money is an important element of presidential influence on policy. How the president chooses to defend a large public expense may affect how the public perceives that expense and what level of support the policy will gain (Cohen 1995; Corrigan 2000; Hogan et al. 2008; Koch 1998; Zarefsky 2004). In each of the following cases the president chose to publicly justify the expense of aiding the auto industry by making clear the fiscal reality of the situation. The economic importance of a healthy auto industry was, in each case, used as a reason to spend money to create or maintain one.

For Carter, Chrysler deserved government attention and taxpayer money because "It has the most diversified workforce of any corporation in America. Its suppliers and dealers and its manufacturing plants touch almost every major community in our country" (Carter 1980: ¶4). Chrysler was so large and diverse that any continued economic decline would surely influence the entire country. To stop this depicted catastrophe, the government rescue would use taxpayer money so that "200,000 American jobs can be preserved" (1980: ¶8).

During the Reagan administration, the aid provided to the auto industry was less public and merited less public justification. Still, Reagan defended his much smaller expenditure of public funds to help the industry by referencing the dire need: "The American automobile industry is vital to our nation's economy," and is "in serious trouble. Our national economic condition and strangling regulations have helped cause the layoff of an estimated 500,000 workers in automobile and related industries" (Reagan 1981: ¶11, 1). Like Carter, Reagan needed only to show just how bad the situation was for the auto industry and how it might link to a broader national economy to justify executive attention and public expense.

This trend continued in the Bush administration's initial aid during the 2008 auto industry collapse. The president justified interfering in the free market: "If we were to allow the free market to take its course now, it would almost certainly lead to disorderly bankruptcy and liquidation for the automakers" (Bush 2008: ¶3). If this were to happen the reverberations for the broader economy would be severe. According to Bush, "Such a collapse would deal an unacceptably painful blow to hard-working Americans far beyond the auto industry . . . worsen a weak job market and exacerbate the financial crisis. It could send our suffering economy into a deeper and longer recession". (2008: ¶7). In light of the consequences of inaction, Bush decided government intervention was justified.

Obama's justification of aid demonstrates a significant shift from his predecessors. Of course, Obama made it clear that the intervention in private enterprise was economically justified, as had his predecessors: "Over the past year, our auto industry has shed over 400,000 jobs, not only at plants that produce cars, but at the businesses that produce the parts that go into them and the dealers that sell and repair them. More than 1 in 10 Michigan residents is out of work" (Obama 2009b: ¶2).

Yet, this economic justification was only the foundation upon which Obama layered further defense of aid for the industry:

> It is an emblem of the American spirit, a once and future symbol of America's success. It's what helped build the middle class and sustained it throughout the 20th century. It's a source of deep pride for the generations of American workers whose hard work and imagination led to some of the finest cars the world has ever known. (2009b: ¶5)

Embedded in this glowing praise of the industry are themes of indebtedness, American exceptionalism, and symbolic imagery more common during ceremonial occasions. Rather than only defending the economic importance of an industry or company too big to fail, as had past presidents, Obama chose to also praise that industry, even while preparing to spend tens of billions of dollars to save it. In the second form of presidential influence on the rescues, wherein the president establishes a goal for the aid, Obama's response entails a similar rhetorical shift.

Establishing the Intended Goal

Once each president decided to aid the auto industry and justified that aid, for the most part on economic grounds, he had to establish a clear goal for the public. This would often prefigure a particular process for attaining that goal. By establishing what outcomes were to come out of the intervention program the president would be able to later argue that the act had been a success. In this sense, it would be wise for the president in any given case to set significant but attainable goals rather than strive for an unlikely but more ideal outcome.

The preservation of Chrysler was the primary stated goal for the Carter administration's aid package. Carter said "it's important to have Chrysler preserved as a viable, competitive entity not only to protect jobs involved but to protect the competitive nature of the American automobile manufacturing industry" (Carter 1980: ¶5). Given that the mission was to preserve Chrysler the process

of guaranteeing loans to match stakeholder sacrifice made sense.
If everyone did their part, the government included, Chrysler could
continue as it had. Based on the goal established for the public this
act would protect the jobs and competition that already existed,
rather than trying to improve either.

Reagan was less interested in preserving the industry than
in getting out of its way. The goal of government intervention
for Reagan was deregulation, which would "remove the Federal
shackles and improve the economic environment within which the
automobile industry operates" (Reagan 1981: ¶10). In keeping with
most of his other economic policy, Reagan argued that the best
way to help the auto industry in 1981 was to let it help itself.
In accordance with this policy of removing the "federal shackles,"
Reagan itemized the regulatory relief that would clear the way for
the auto industry to succeed. He also mentioned briefly the coming
voluntary import quota agreement with Japan that would shield
domestic automakers from foreign competition.

Seventeen years later, when the Bush administration decided
to aid the auto industry, President Bush said that the goal of the
rescue package was to buy the industry time. In a nationally televised address he said "U.S. auto executives say that their companies are nearing collapse and that the only way they can buy time
to restructure is with help from the Federal government" (Bush
2008: ¶1). Since the auto executives needed to buy time to restructure and, as he had argued earlier, an auto industry collapse would
reverberate painfully throughout the rest of the economy, the government should act. The government should help the auto industry
buy time because "government has a responsibility to safeguard
the broader health and stability of our economy. . . . Allowing the
U.S. auto industry to collapse is not a responsible course of action"
(2008: ¶2, 4). The action taken by the Bush administration aligns
with the publicly stated goal of buying time. The bridge loan provided time to come up with plans that were to be presented to the
new Obama administration.

Bush's rescue of the auto industry did buy time for automakers, funding the companies until the Obama administration could
set up "Team Auto." According to Obama, the comparatively intri-
cate operation and exponentially larger amount of money spent
were designed to meet a new kind of goal that was based on a
problem that had always been there:

> The pain being felt in places that rely on our auto indus-
> try is not the fault of our workers; they labor tirelessly

and desperately want to see their companies succeed. It's not the fault of all the families and communities that supported manufacturing plants throughout the generations. Rather, it's a failure of leadership—from Washington to Detroit—that led our auto companies to this point. (2009b: ¶3)

Leaders in Washington and Detroit, former administrations, and auto industry executives, had failed to live up to the expectations of auto workers and the communities in which they operated. These leaders were aware of the problems but chose not to deal with them: "Year after year, decade after decade, we've seen problems papered over and tough choices kicked down the road, even as foreign competitors outpaced us" (2009b: ¶4). Since leaders in Washington and Detroit knew of the problems but chose not to deal with them, resulting in ruin, government would have to step in and deal with those problems itself: "We've reached the end of that road. We as a nation cannot afford to shirk responsibility any longer. Now is the time to confront our problems head on and do what's necessary to solve them. . . . We cannot, and must not, and we will not let our auto industry simply vanish" (2009b: ¶5). Government's goal was to fix the industry, to deal with the problems past officials and executives had "papered over," and government "must not" fail. This rhetorical shift in public goal will have consequences for the rest of Obama's term in office and for future administrations.

The Consequences of Presidential Influence

Insider accounts of auto industry rescues examine the financial implications of government intervention in private enterprise (Rattner 2010; Reich and Donahue 1985; Taylor 2010). Each also considers the consequences of the rescues in moral terms, as the rescue sets a potentially dangerous precedent for other companies in the future: If you fail government will rescue you. The presidents discussed did have the final say in whether or not to intervene but as has been pointed out, this may have been a foregone conclusion. If we are interested in the influence that presidents had on the rescues we must look to the rhetorical strategies used by each when justifying the expense of public funds and establishing a goal for them.

As shown, the justification employed by each president tended to be grounded in the repercussions of a collapse for employees and the broader economy. Obama, in justifying a more involved and extensive expenditure of public funds, also praised the industry on a number of different levels. Carter, Reagan, and Bush have all done so at other times, but chose to avoid painting too positive an image of the automakers they were spending taxpayer money to save from disaster. Perhaps the decision to avoid praising the industry on the occasion of a rescue was an intentional rhetorical choice. If so, Obama has made the opposite choice.

This praise of the industry has the potential to create a mixed message for the public, a flaw of which Carter, Reagan, and Bush were likely aware. A company worthy of such praise should not need government aid to survive. Obama created the rhetorical trap and then sprung it himself. The *industry* and its *workers* are praiseworthy but the *leaders* in Detroit and Washington have let them down. By praising the whole and blaming a part Obama has created a new, stronger justification for government intervention. A praiseworthy industry and worker base deserving of success has been thwarted by blameworthy leaders. Due to the economic importance of the industry and the symbolic importance of the worker government must step in and make it right. Government is obligated to act.

That action creates a new goal, dependent on the shift in justification and usage of praise and blame. If the goal is only to preserve a company, the need for government to step in only arises when that company is not preserving itself. If the goal is to get out of its way, government can theoretically do so and never deal with the company again. If the goal is to buy time for the company to accomplish some process like restructuring, once the process is complete government is no longer needed. With the Obama administration, the goal of government intervention changed. Government became obligated to step in and fix the problem. Even though in the past auto rescues have involved high levels of government involvement in the day-to-day decisions of the company this was never made a public part of the process by the president at the time. Obama publicly announced that government would step in and fix the companies. He even provided a guarantee of success: "If you buy a car from Chrysler or General Motors, you will be able to get your car serviced and repaired, just like always. Your warranty will be safe. In fact, it will be safer than it's ever been, because starting today, the United States Government will stand behind your warranty" (2009b: ¶19). The difference between the goals of preservation during the Carter era, nonintervention during the Reagan era, buying time during the Bush era, and Obama's notion of fixing the company is an important one. We fix what is broken, but we also must maintain things with small fixes to avoid larger, more expensive fixes. Regulation of the auto industry is not a static thing, nor is the national or global economy. Government will be obligated to step in to ensure the industry is handling new regulations properly or prospering during inevitable periodic recessions. With the rhetorical shift from a government agreement to help preserve the industry or get out of its way to a responsibility to provide some time and funds to restructure, Bush came close to creating a mandate for future occasions of need. Obama solidified this mandate by rhetorically establishing a government imperative for fixing the industry, through the praise of one aspect and the blame of another. Later, Obama said "I don't want to run auto companies . . . I've got more than enough to do" (Obama 2009a: ¶47). The implications of this rhetorical shift have provided a precedent for government to do just that for a long time to come if it so chooses.

Conclusion

In this chapter it has been argued that presidential influence over the domestic auto industry rescue policies was limited, but presidents could and did shape the way those policies were justified and the goals established for the public. President Obama's justification and establishment of his goal represent a rhetorical shift from past presidents in parallel situations. This rhetorical shift involved the public praise and blame of the auto industry simultaneously. With the economic importance of so large an entity, government would be obligated to step in on behalf of those praised and do what those blamed could not or would not do—fix the companies. In the future administrations can rely on this shift to intervene in auto industry operations even if automakers do not ask for aid. It is not difficult to imagine this justification setting the stage for more in-depth regulation of the industry to benefit consumers, the economy or the environment.

This case also points out the importance of presidential epideictic in analysis of policy. Praise and blame are best suited to ceremonial situations rather than the more legislative examples examined here. Yet, praise and blame do occasionally arise in policy discussions and this usage may be strategic, as with Obama's handling of the 2008 auto rescue. As is evident, this praise and blame can work in interesting ways to shift a policy discussion or recast justifications and goals. Since it is employed and may have consequences the next step is to determine to what extent praise or blame extends over time, across administration and party. To answer this question, we should look to longstanding enterprises that hold historical or symbolic significance in our culture, such as the auto industry or agriculture.

This chapter began by posing that one way to consider the success of the Obama administration is to examine the rescue of the auto industry against historic parallels. In material terms, the rescue has been a success. The industry rebounded after "Team Auto" guided General Motors and Chrysler through section 363 bankruptcies. Taxpayers stand to profit from the deal and, at the time of this writing, have already done so (Calmes 2010; Shepardson 2010). Obama was able to attempt what Carter could not do, Reagan did not want to do, and Bush would not do—change the industry from the outside in. This was made possible by the rhetorical influence the president wielded over the policy. The true implications of this rhetorical shift may only be evident in the future, if and when government calls on its new intervention obligation when it deems the industry to be failing. Whether we call this a success depends on our personal views of the expansion of government power.

Works Cited

Bush, G. W. "Remarks on the American automobile industry." Ed. J. T. Woolley & G. Peters. *The American Presidency Project,*2008. http://www.presidency.ucsb.edu/ws/index.php?pid=85276 [Accessed: 1 Oct. 2010].

Calmes, J. "Tarp bailout to cost less than anticipated." *New York Times* (September 30, 2010 and October 1, 2010), p. B1.

Carter, J. "Remarks on signing into law H.R. 5860, the Chrysler Corporation Loan Guarantee Act of 1979." Ed. J. T. Woolley & G. Peters. *The American Presidency Project*, 1980. http://www.presidency.ucsb.edu/ws/index.php?pid=32978 [Accessed: 1 Oct. 2010].

Clark, H. D. and Stewart, M. C. "Prospections, Retrospections, and Rationality: The 'Bankers' Model of Presidential Approval Considered." *American Journal of Political Science.* Vol. 38 (1994), 1104–1123.

Cohen, J. E. "Presidential Rhetoric and the Public Agenda." *American Journal of Political Science.* Vol. 39 (1995), 87–107.

Corrigan, M. "The Transformation of Going Public: President Clinton, the First Lady, and Health Care Reform." *Political Communication*. Vol. 17 (2000), 149–168.

Crandall, R. W., H. K. Gruenspecht, T. E. Keeler, and L. B. Lave. *Regulating the Automobile*. Washington DC: The Brookings Institution, 1986.

Edwards, G. C. I., W. Mitchell, and R. Welch. "Explaining Presidential Approval: The Significance of Issue Salience." *American Journal of Political Science*. Vol. 39 (1995), 108–134.

Hogan, J. M., G. C. I. Edwards, W. C. Hall, et al. "Report of the national task force on the presidency and public opinion. Ed., J. A. Aune and M. J. Medhurst. *The Prospect of Presidential Rhetoric*. College Station: Texas A&M University Press, 2008.

Kernell, S. *Going public: New strategies of presidential leadership*. Washington DC: CQ Press, 1997.

Koch, J. W. "Political Rhetoric and Political Persuasion: The Changing Structure of Citizens' Preferences on Health Insurance During Policy Debate." *Public Opinion Quarterly*. Vol. 62 (1998), 209–229.

Lewis, D. "The Two Rhetorical Presidencies: An Analysis of Televised Presidential Speeches, 1947–1991." *American Politics Quarterly*. Vol. 25 (1997), 380–395.

MacKuen, M. B., R. S. Erikson, and J. A. Stimson "Peasants or Bankers? The American Electorate and the U.S. Economy." *American Political Science Review* Vol. 86 (1992), 597–611.

Maslin-Wicks, K. "Two Types of Presidential Influence in Congress." *Presidential Studies Quarterly*. Vol. 28 (1998), 108–126.

Monroe, K. R. "Economic Influences on Presidential Popularity." *Public Opinion Quarterly*. Vol. 42 (1978), 360–369.

Montanye, J. A. "Rhetoric and Economic Policy." *The Independent Review*. Vol. 9 (2005), 328–338.

Neustadt, R. *Presidential Power*. New York: Wiley, 1960.

Obama, B. The President's News Conference: April 29, 2009. Ed. J. T. Woolley & G. Peters.*The American Presidency Project,* 2009a. http://www.presidency.ucsb.edu/ws/index.php?pid=86069 [Accessed: 1 Oct. 2010].

———. Remarks on the United States automobile industry. Ed. J. T. Woolley & G. Peters.*The American Presidency Project,* 2009b. http://www.presidency.ucsb.edu/ws/index.php?pid=85927 [Accessed: 1 Oct. 2010].

Rankin, D. M. "Featuring the President as Free Trader: Television News Coverage of U.S. Trade Policies." *Presidential Studies Quarterly*. Vol. 36 (2006), 633–659.

Rattner, S. *Overhaul: An Insider's Account of the Obama Administration's Emergency Rescue of the Auto Industry*. Boston: Houghton Mifflin Harcourt, 2010.

Reagan, R. Statement on assistance for the domestic automobile industry. Ed. J. T. Woolley & G. Peters. *The American Presidency Project,* 1981.

http://www.presidency.ucsb.edu/ws/index.php?pid=43793 [Accessed: 1 Oct. 2010].

Reich, R. B. & J. D. Donahue. *New Deals: The Chrysler Revival and the American System.* New York: Penguin, 1985.

Rubenstein, J. M. *The Changing U.S. Auto Industry: A Geographical Analysis.* New York: Routledge, 1992.

Shepardson, D. "GM Buying Back $2.1 Billion in U.S. Preferred Stock." *Detroit News* (October 28, 2010).

Taylor A. III. *Sixty to Zero: An Inside Look at the Collapse of General Motors and the Detroit Auto Industry.* New Haven, CT: Yale University Press, 2010.

Teaford, J. C. *Cities of the Heartland: The Rise and Fall of the Industrial midwest.* Bloomington: Indiana University Press, 1994.

Wood, B. D. "Presidential Rhetoric and Economic Leadership." *Presidential Studies Quarterly* Vol. 34 (2004), 573–606.

Zarefsky, D. "Presidential Rhetoric and the Power of Definition." *Presidential Studies Quarterly.* Vol. 34 (2004), 607–619.

Chapter 11

Environmental Policy and Global Climate Change

Byron W. Daynes
Glen Sussman

Although there have been at least six modern presidents since Franklin D. Roosevelt (FDR) who have had a positive impact in shaping environmental policy, no one president has been so successful that we could call him *the* environmental president. Conservation was a high priority for FDR, and, as a result, he was given credit for ushering in the "Golden Age of Conservation." Harry Truman became a conservationist because he believed that conserving resources was a key to a strong and viable economy. John F. Kennedy's time in office was cut short, but he, nevertheless, became interested in the resource potential for both the ocean and outer space. Lyndon B. Johnson and his wife, Lady Bird Johnson, focused their attention on "beautifying America," making its highways, bridges, parks, and dams more attractive and environmentally cleaner. Richard Nixon, the only Republican among these presidents, declared the 1970s to be the "decade of the environment" (Owen 1968). Jimmy Carter focused his attention on cleaning the air and water and preserving public land, while Bill Clinton enjoyed his greatest successes in his second term in responding to environmental concerns.

But no president to date has been able to achieve all that he set forth on his environmental agenda. This chapter examines the extent to which President Barack Obama comes near the goal of being *an environmental president* and addressing the challenge of global climate change.

Assessment

At the core of the analysis we examine the following factors:

1. political communication, including all references made by the president to conservation and the environment in speeches and informal references;

2. legislative leadership, focusing on the president's relationship with Congress and its environmental output;

3. administrative actions, looking at administrative appointments, executive orders, and proclamations related to the environment; and

4. environmental diplomacy, examining the president's international activity.

Political Communication

In the 2008 presidential campaign, Obama made it clear that a substantive response to global warming and the environment was going to be his No. 1 priority on entering office. In November 2008, for example, he stated that "Few challenges facing America and the world are more urgent than combating climate change. My presidency will mark a new chapter in America's leadership on climate change" (Selin and Vandeveer 2008: 336).

At that time, Obama felt that the key for resolving the climate-change dilemma was to act *now* and act *boldly* (Obama 2007), but then later that same month he qualified his statement suggesting in an interview with Joe Klein of *Time Magazine* that his priority focus would depend on whether "we have done enough to just stabilize the immediate economic situation" (Klein 2008).

A careful examination of Obama's radio and television speeches as president, comparing them with those delivered by his predecessor, George W. Bush—no friend of the environment or advocate for addressing climate change—for the same period, reveals that Obama's six radio speeches on the environment (Figure 11.1) ranked third among the 105 speeches he delivered in terms

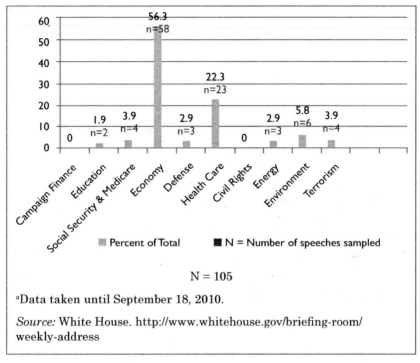

Figure 11.1. Obama's national radio addresses, first term[a]

of the frequency of the topic addressed; Bush's environmental radio addresses (Figure 11.3, page 165) placed sixth overall in terms of frequency among his 87 speeches. As far as his 107 television speeches were concerned, Obama's environmental addresses again placed third (Figure 11.2, page 164), whereas Bush's environmental television addresses were ninth in importance, among the 136 addresses given (Figure 11.4, page 166). Moreover, another important difference was that Bush's public comments on the issue typically were intended to make a case against acting to protect the environment. Overall, however, one might conclude that both Obama and Bush viewed environmentalism as somewhat peripheral to the other more pressing issues they addressed. In Obama's case, apparently, he was more interested in trying to stabilize the economy which has prevented him from fulfilling his climate control promise.

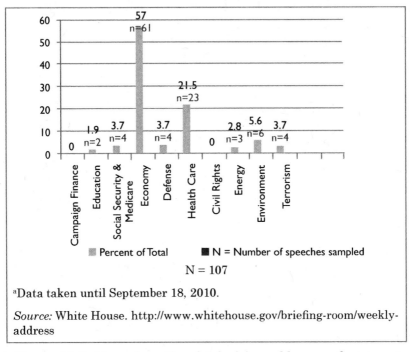

[a]Data taken until September 18, 2010.

Source: White House. http://www.whitehouse.gov/briefing-room/weekly-address

Figure 11.2. Obama's national television addresses, first term[a]

Obama also has shown a reluctance to speak out from the Oval Office on the environment. For this he has been criticized by environmentalist Jeremy Hance, who faulted Obama for his "... general reticence to talk about climate change ..." and for playing it politically "safe," given the potential consequences of moving too slowly (Hance 2009). But Obama's focus on the environment may still come about while he is in office if one believes what he said in an October 2010 interview with Peter Baker in *The New York Times Magazine*, where he pointed out that on his "checklist" he thought he had "accomplished 70 percent of the things that we talked about the during the campaign. And I hope as long as I'm president, I've got a chance to work on the other 30 percent." Although Obama implemented a few environmental measures, it remains to be seen if environmental concerns will be among the remaining 30 percent yet to be accomplished.

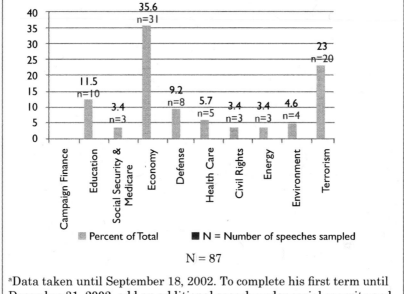

Figure 11.3. Bush's national radio addresses, first term[a]

Legislative Leader

During Obama's presidency, members of Congress from his own party have been somewhat supportive of his positions in support of the environment, but Republicans have been adamantly opposed to any environmental initiatives on global climate change, energy, natural resources, or even clean air. Partisan debate has stalled many of the president's initiatives and Republicans have largely rejected scientific arguments on behalf of the existence of climate change and human activity contributing to such problems.

Republican opposition became even stronger as a result of the 2010 midterm elections. As John Broder indicated, "(m)any of the newly elected members (of Congress) have expressed skepticism about the existence of global warming and say they strongly oppose government action to combat it." He also added that John Boehner,

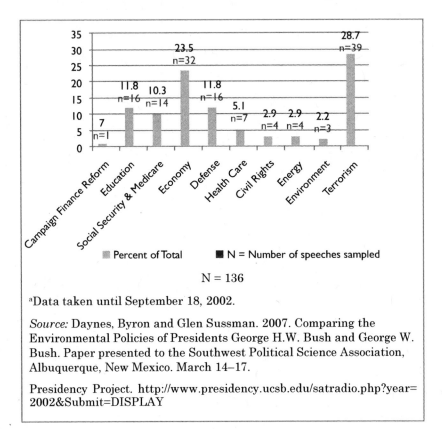

N = 136

[a]Data taken until September 18, 2002.

Source: Daynes, Byron and Glen Sussman. 2007. Comparing the Environmental Policies of Presidents George H.W. Bush and George W. Bush. Paper presented to the Southwest Political Science Association, Albuquerque, New Mexico. March 14–17.

Presidency Project. http://www.presidency.ucsb.edu/satradio.php?year=2002&Submit=DISPLAY

Figure 11.4. Bush's national television addresses, first term[a]

Republican Speaker of the House, "dismissed the idea that carbon dioxide is affecting the climate and has characterized cap and trade and other proposed solutions to global warming as job-killing energy taxes" (Broder 2010).

As a result, Congress moved very slowly on Obama's initiatives on the environment and climate change. As Table 11.1 suggests, there has been but one major environmental bill affecting climate change voted on in Congress in the past two years (and only one chamber voted). The bill was The American Clean Energy and Security Act of 2009 (H.R. 2454)—that passed the House by the slim margin of 219 to 212, but was not voted on by the Senate on account of Republican opposition. It is a bill that put tight limits

Table 11.1. Environmental Legislation Proposed, passed in U.S. House and Senate, 2009–2010

Legis ID	Description	When Proposed	Committee Jurisdiction	Floor Vote	Presidential Action
H.R. 1262	Water Quality Investment Act of 2009	March 3, 2009	Senate—Environment and Public Works House—Transportation and Infrastructure	Passed House March 12, 2009	
H.R. 1580	Electronic Waste Research and Development Act	March 18, 2009	Senate—Environment and Public Works House-Science and Technology	Passed House, April 22, 2009	
S. R. 121	A Resolution designating May 15, 2009, as "Endangered Species Day"	April 30, 2009	Senate—Judiciary	Senate Passed, May 12, 2009	None needed
H.R. 2454	American Clean Energy and Security Act of 2009	May 15, 2009	House-Science and Technology House-Transportation and Infrastructure . . .	Passed House, June 26, 2009	
H.R. 2093	Clean Coastal Environment and Public Health Act of 2009	April 23, 2009	Senate-Environment and Public Works House-Transportation and Infrastructure House-Transportation . . .	Passed House, July 29, 2009	

continued on next page

Table 11.1. (Continued)

Legis ID	Description	When Proposed	Committee Jurisdiction	Floor Vote	Presidential Action
H. R. 710	Supporting the goals and ideals of "National Estuaries Day"	July 31, 2009	House-National Resources—Insular Affairs, Oceans and Wildlife	Passed House, October 6, 2009	
H.R. 3650	Harmful Algal Blooms and Hypoxia Research and Control Amendments Act of 2010	September 25, 2009	House-Science and Tech. House-National Resources—Insular Affairs, Oceans and Wildlife House-Science and Technology-Energy and Environment House—Natural Resources	House Passed, March 12, 2010	
H.R. 4715	Clean Estuaries Act of 2010	March 2, 2010	Senate-Environment and Public Works House-Transportation and Infrastructure House-Transportation and Infrastructure-Water Resources and Environment	House Passed, April 15, 2010	
S.R. 3473	A bill to amend the Oil Pollution Act of 1990 to authorize advances from Oil Spill Liability Trust Fund for the Deepwater Horizon oil spill	June 9, 2010	n/a	Senate Passed, June 9, 2010 House Passed, June 10, 2010	President Signed, June 15, 2010

Bill	Title	Date Introduced	Committee(s)	Progress	Final Action
H.R. 2693	Oil Pollution Research and Development Program Reauthorization Act of 2010	June 3, 2009	House—Science and Technology; House—Homeland Security; Senate—Commerce, Science and Transportation; House—Science and Technology	House Passed, July 21, 2010	
S.R. 3372	A bill to modify the date on which the administrator of the Environmental Protection Agency and applicable States may require permits for discharges from certain vessels	May 13, 2010	Senate-Environment and Public Works	Senate Passed, July 14, 2010; House Passed, July 29, 2010	President Signed, July 30, 2010
H.R. 5320	Assistance, Quality, and Affordability Act of 2010	May 18, 2010	Senate—Environment and Public Works; House—Energy and Commerce-Environment and Hazardous Materials; House—Energy and Commerce	House Passed, July 30, 2010	

Source: http://www.govtrack.us/congress/subjects.xpd?type=crs&term=Environmental%20Protection
http://www.opencongress.org/

on greenhouse gas emissions with a "17% cut from 2005 levels by 2020, and 80% by 2050" (Goldenberg 2010).

Both critics and supporters agree that the House legislation would transform the energy sector of the economy in major ways. The Environmental Defense Action Fund, for example, described it as "the most important environmental measure of the past 20 years" (Yarnold 2010).

So what happens if Congress fails to pass a bill to control greenhouse gas emissions during Obama's presidency? If this should happen, the Environmental Protection Agency (EPA) is ready to act. It has indicated that, as a result of the Supreme Court decision in *Massachusetts v. EPA* (2007), it has the authority to respond to climate change and protect the public health. Lisa Jackson, Obama's EPA administrator, has made it quite clear that she, along with the president, and the Democratic leadership in Congress, would prefer a wide-ranging legislative approach, but the EPA is ready to act if necessary. Republican leaders in both Houses during both the 111th and 112th congresses, along with a few Democrats and state attorney generals have made it clear they will try to "block the EPA from regulating carbon dioxide and other greenhouse gasses" (Broder 2010). This Republican opposition had some affect in delaying its response to carbon emission until January 2011, despite what Jackson has called a "tactical decision" (Broder and Stolberg 2010).

Obama also showed his reluctance to gravitate from his desire to procure legislation when he refused to give any support to a Supreme Court global warming lawsuit, *Connecticut v. American Electric Power Co., et al* (2009) that demanded new limits on carbon pollution from coal-burning power plants. Although this is what the administration has sought from the Congress and the EPA, the president made it quite clear that "courts should step aside." Environmentalists were not only surprised but also angered and disappointed at this reaction (Savage 2010).

Administrative Actions

Appointments are key to advancing a president's environmental goals. George W. Bush selected his environmental and interior appointees from the fossil fuel industry, mining, ranching, and timber. This posed a major problem for environmental interests. In contrast, appointments made by Obama were more likely to include individuals with a pro-environmental orientation support-ive of a green agenda (cf. Tables 11.2 and 11.3).

Table 11.2. Key Appointments to Bureaucratic Positions (Bush 43 Administration)

Name	Position	Background	Philosophy
Dick Cheney	Vice president & head of the administration's National Energy Policy	CEO of Halliburton oil company; U.S. Senator pushing for oil development	Pro-fossil fuel industry/support for drilling in Alaska's Arctic National Wildlife Refuge (ANWR)
James Connaughton	Chair, Council on Environmental Quality (CEQ)	Energy industry lawyer and environmental advisor	Worked to reduce regulations on energy industry clients
Christie Todd Whitman	EPA administrator	Former governor of New Jersey	Business-friendly approach but supported expanding open spaces by millions of acres
Gale Norton	Secretary of the Interior Department; Colorado Attorney General	Associate solicitor at the Interior	"Protégé" of former Secretary of the Interior, James Watt; senior attorney for the pro-mining/ranching/timber interests Mountain States Legal Foundation
J. Steven Griles	Deputy secretary of the Minerals Management in the Interior Department under James Watt; mining industry lobbyist	Assistant Secretary of Lands and Interior	Pro-fossil fuel industry; lobbyist coal, oil, gas, mining

continued on next page

Table 11.2. (Continued)

Name	Position	Background	Philosophy
Fran Mainella	Director of the National Park Service	Head of Florida's Parks and Recreation Service	Supported expansion of public lands conservation
Spencer Abraham	Secretary of Energy U.S. senator, Michigan; lost re-election bid in 2000	Aide to Vice President Dan Quayle;	Supported oil drilling in ANWR; opposed higher fuel efficiency for SUVs
John Ashcroft	Attorney general	Former U.S. senator, Missouri	Anti-environmental voting record; as senator opposed increased funding for air and water quality and cleanup of hazardous waste sites

Table 11.3. Key Appointments to Bureaucratic Positions (Obama Administration)

Name	Position	Background	Philosophy
Nancy Sutley	Chair, CEQ Environment for Los Angeles; energy advisor to California Gov. Gray Davis; senior policy advisor in President Clinton's EPA	Deputy mayor for Energy & where she championed environment, energy, and water policy; experience in inter-governmental relations; known for dogged work ethic	Strong background in California politics
Lisa Jackson	EPA administrator Gov. Jon Corzine; commissioner of New Jersey's Department of Environmental Protection; Worked in EPA's hazardous waste cleanup operations	Chief of state to New Jersey priorities include reducing greenhouse gases, improving air and water quality, cleanup of hazardous waste sites, environmental justice	Open dialogue between stakeholders;
Carol Browner	Assistant to the president for Energy and Climate change; former Administrator under Clinton	Consultant on energy, environment, climate	Known for coalition building with government and business to solve environmental problems and helped put climate change on Clinton's agenda
Heather Zichal	Deputy assistant to the president for Energy and Climate Change	Energy and environment advisor for Obama's campaign and transition team; worked on Capitol Hill for two members of Congress	Highly involved in creating green jobs, addressing climate change, reducing oil dependence, Arctic National Wildlife Refuge

continued on next page

Table 11.3. (Continued)

Name	Position	Background	Philosophy
Ken Salazar	Secretary of the Interior Colorado	U.S. senator and attorney	As U.S. senator pushed renewable energy policy; as attorney general established environmental crimes unit
Jonathan Jarvis	Director of the National Park Service (NPS)	Worked at NPS since 1976	Considerable experience in park resource management and service as a biology ranger
Steven Chu	Secretary of Energy	Nobel prize-winning scientist in physics; director of Lawrence Berkeley National Lab; professor of physics and molecular biology	Advocate for renewable energy technologies and reducing greenhouse gases while addressing global climate change policy

Such key appointments as Lisa Jackson, selected to direct the EPA, Nancy Sutley, who was appointed as chair of the Council on Environmental Quality, and Carol Browner, who was selected to be an assistant to the president for energy and climate change, are examples. Two other noteworthy examples are former U.S. Sen. Ken Salazar of Colorado, selected as secretary of the interior, and Steven Chu, Nobel Prize winner and advocate for alternative and renewable energy sources, who was appointed secretary of energy. The League of Conservation Voters called these appointments a "green dream team" (Fahrenthold 2008).

Environmental Diplomacy

The 2000 presidential election proved to have a profound impact on U.S. policy regarding global climate change. President Bush refused to offer leadership on this issue reneging on his campaign promise to reduce carbon emissions despite the fact that the United States, at that time, was the major producer of greenhouse gases. The Kyoto Protocol, a multination agreement requiring mandatory limits on greenhouse gasses, was signed by President George H. W. Bush in 1992, and was supported by the Clinton administration, but was never ratified by the Senate owing to Republican opposition. Two months into his presidency, George W. Bush renounced the Kyoto Protocol, arguing that the agreement was a threat to the U.S. economy and that the United States would not support it until developing countries such as China, India, and Brazil limited their emissions. Thus, the Bush presidency continued to promote reliance on fossil fuels and energy consumption rather than focusing on conservation and the reduction of greenhouse gas emissions.

In contrast, President Obama engaged in several initiatives during his first two years in office. In January 2009, the newly elected president made it clear that it was the policy of the United States to offer leadership to confront global climate change. When meeting with Canadian Prime Minister Stephen Harper in May 2009, the two leaders informed the global community that they would work together in order to "advance carbon reduction technologies" and to "develop an electric grid that can deliver clean and renewable energy in the U.S. and Canada" (Horsley and Siegel). In July 2010, Michael Levi, director of the Program on Energy Security and Climate Change at the Council on Foreign Relations, contrasted the Bush and Obama administrations on global climate change in this way: "The United States spent the better part of the last decade being pilloried for its lack of action on climate. The last year and a half has seen a new attitude from much of the rest of the world" (Levi 2010).

The UN climate talks that took place in Copenhagen in December 2009 included delegates from 194 countries, and offered both the potential for progress as well as the prospects for disagreement. Although no formal agreement resulted, Obama was able to talk with a number of world leaders stating his position in support of collectively doing something to confront climate change.

The results at the UN climate gathering on November 28, 2010 in Cancún, Mexico seem much more promising. In all, 193 countries agreed to continue to use the UN as a negotiating forum where every nation has a say in the agreements. Developed nations agreed to set up a "Green Climate Fund" to be administered by the World Bank to assist poorer nations to develop clean energy and preserve their rain forests (Eilperin and Booth 2010). Bolivia was the only nation that refused to support the agreement because it did not feel the agreement went far enough. Additionally, 191 nations agreed that the Kyoto Protocol limitations on gases would continue until a new agreement is written at the 2011 conference in Durban, South Africa . The major developed and developing nations of China, India, Brazil, South Africa, and the United States agreed to subject their efforts to cut greenhouse gases to "international scrutiny" for the first time (Eilperin and Booth 2010). Continuing on the work of the Copenhagen Conference in 2009 and Cancun Conference in 2010, the UN Convention on Climate Change in Durbin in late 2011 continued the push for developing countries to reduce carbon emissions through a $30 billion fund provided by the UN and developed nations. Although Obama continued to feel pressure from his political Right against a legally binding agreement to reduce emissions, he did join other conferees in the widespread agreement about international cooperation to address climate change and the need to continue meeting because the Kyoto Treaty on reducing greenhouse gases expires at the end of 2012.

It has been the domestic debate that continues to restrict the president in what he can contribute to the international arena on climate change. The partisan split between the Obama and Sen. James Inhofe (R-OK) has nowhere been more strained that between these two men. Obama, however, repeatedly stated that he hopes that he is able to prove Inhofe incorrect when he claims "Mr. Obama is handcuffed by Senate fractiousness on the issue and new doubts among some about the basic science underpinning the talks" (Broder 2009). But until the president is able to support the U.S. regulation of gas emissions and exert a more forceful leadership in that direction, he can expect few world leaders to take confidence in his climate leadership.

Conclusion

So how might we evaluate the president's environmental efforts at midterm? It is clear that there is an important distinction between Presidents Obama and Bush in their political rhetoric about the environment. When Bush communicated information regarding the environment and global climate change in particular, there was an attempt to mislead and obfuscate. In contrast, President Obama was much more likely to argue that change was needed due to the threat posed by increasing greenhouse gases especially from the burning of fossil fuels (Table 11.4, page 178).

President Obama's relationship with the Congress has been the most difficult environmental impedance to the president. Obama first faced a Democratic majority in the Congress that had mixed views on global climate change legislation. As a result of the increased number of House Republicans elected in the 2010 midterm elections, Obama has been forced to change his strategy. He also has indicated a willingness to move from narrowly focused projects such as federal incentives for the building of electric cars to a more comprehensive legislative approach.

As far as appointments to key environmental positions, Obama appointed persons who were serious environmentalists compared to the Bush appointments from business and industry. Likewise, internationally, Bush showed his lack of sensitivity to the rest of the world in renouncing the Kyoto Protocol that represented world agreement on the importance of limiting global climate change, while Obama has been supportive of other nations at Copenhagen and in the more promising Cancún gathering.

Opposition exhibited from an unenthusiastic public was another problem for Obama. Although during the Bush years most Americans indicated they wanted to do something about global warming (Nordhaus and Shellenberger 2009), there has not been that same support for Obama's climate-change proposals. For instance, 57 percent of U.S. citizens in a 2009 *Washington Post-ABC News* poll opposed Obama's plan to contribute $10 billion a year to assist developing countries to help in reducing the amount

Table 11.4. A Midterm Evaluation of President Barack Obama and Global Climate Change

	Evaluation
Electoral Campaign	Climate change as a major issue of the twenty-first' century and therefore an important part of his environmental agenda
Global Warming as a Threat	Fundamental agreement that there is a threat and it is time to take substantive action
View of Scientific Evidence	Accepts the proposition that there is consensus among members of the scientific community that global climate change is, in part, a human-induced problem that needs to be addressed
Basic Principles of the Kyoto Protocol	Supported the international agreement and has pushed for a post-Kyoto agreement; despite flaws it is considered a basis to promote action
Target Preference	Supports a cap and trade system: Given the results of the 2010 midterm elections, the president has focused on a "chunk's" approach to promoting climate change efforts through legislation
Presidential Leadership at Home	The president faces a stiff challenge by members of Congress, organized interests, and a confused public
U.S. International Role on Global Climate Change	United States intends to be in a leadership position: Supports multi-lateralism and cooperation with other countries/Challenged by several domestic constraints on foreign policy and criticism by global leaders about a lack of leadership by the United States.

of greenhouse gases (Agiesta and Cohen 2009). Additionally, there are those in the media who have criticized Obama's global climate-change policy including Fox News, Glenn Beck, George Will, *National Review*, and the *Washington Times* (Best 2005); so too have these individuals and outlets argued against the notion of human-induced climate change. And it was Rush Limbaugh who called the global warming movement a "fraud" and a "hoax," suggesting that "militant environmentalism" has become the "home of displaced communists after the Berlin Wall came down" (2009).

A number of observers have argued that the climate change deniers have done a better job than Obama and the scientific community in making their case and educating the people. To be the sort of environmental leader Obama suggested he wanted to be when he first came into office, he must do a more effective job in convincing the Congress, an antagonistic conservative press and media, and a confused public concerned more about the economy at home and two wars abroad than about climate change.

Works Cited

Agiesta, Jennifer and John Cohen. "Political polarization on environmental science." *Washington Post* (18 Dec. 2009) http://www.washingtonpost.com/wp-dyn/content/graphic/2009/12/18.GR2009121800213 (accessed 18 Dec. 2009).

Associated Press. "EPA issues greenhouse gas warning despite concerns over leaked e-mails." *Fox News* (7 Dec. 2009). http://www.foxnews.com/politics/2009/12/07/republicans-slam-epa-decision-declare-public-health-danger (accessed 6 Jan. 2010).

Baker, Peter. "What does he do now?" *The New York Times Magazine* (17 Oct. 2010), 42.

Best, Joseph L. "Michael Crichton is right!" *The Heartland Institute* (11 Jan. 2005) http://www.hearland.org/policybot/results/16260/Michael_Crichton (accessed 30 Jan. 2010).

Broder, David. "Senate poses obstacles to Obama pledge on climate." *The New York Times* (13 Dec. 2009). http://livingstories.googlelabs.com/lsps/climatechange (accessed 16 Dec. 2009).

Broder, John M. "Obama to face new foes in global warming fight." *The New York Times* (4 Nov. 2010), B4.

Broder, John and Sheryl Gay Stolberg. "EPA Delays Tougher Rules on Emissions." (9 Dec. 2010) http://www.nytimes.com/2010/12/10/ . . . /10epa.html. (accessed 14 Dec. 2010).

Brune, Michael. "Standards on smog." Letter to the Editor, *New York Times* (16 Dec. 2010) http://www.nytimes.com/2010/12/17/.../17epa. htm . . . (accessed 16 Dec. 2010).

Connecticut v. American Electric Power Co., et al, U.S. Court of Appeals for the Second Circuit (2009), Docket Nos. 05-5104-cv, 05-5119-cv

Eilperin, Juliet and William Booth. "Cancun agreements put 193 nations on tract to deal with climate change." *The Washington Post* (11 Dec. 2010). http://www.washingtonpost.com/ . . . /AR201021202 (accessed 13 Dec. 2010).

Fahrenthold, David. "Ready for challenges: Obama's environmental team: No radicals." *The Washington Post National Weekly* (22 Dec. 2008– 4 Jan. 2009).

Hance, Jeremy. "Environmental Disappointments under Obama." (24 Aug. 2009) http://www.mongabay.com/0823-hance_obam . . . (accessed 7 May 2010).

Horsley, Scott and Robert Siegel. "In Canada, Obama Pledges Stronger Ties." *National Public Radio.* http://www.npr.org/templates/story. php? story Id =100885544&ft=1003 (accessed 20 Nov. 2009).

Hudson, Paul. "What Happened to Global Warming?" *BBC News* (9 Oct.2009) http://newsvote.bbc.co.uk/mpapps/pagetools/print/news. bbc.co.uk/1/hi/science/nature/829 . . . (accessed 10 Dec. 2009).

Klein, Joe. "Obama's First Priority." *TAPPED—blog of The American Prospect* (23 Oct. 2008) http://www.prospect.org/csnc/blogs/tapped_ archive . . . (accessed 7 May 2010).

Levi, Michael A. "Gloom Awaits U.S. Climate Diplomacy." (23 July 2010) http://www.cfr.org/publication/22689/gloom_awaits_us_climate_ diplomacy.html (accessed 4 Nov. 2010).

Limbaugh, Rush. "From the Climate Hoax to Health Care to "Hope"— Liberalism is Lies." (23 Nov. 2009) http://www.rushlimbaugh.com/ home/daily/site_112309/content/01 . . . (accessed 9 Feb. 2010).

Nordhaus, Ted and Michael Shellenberger. "Apocalypse Fatigue: Losing the Public on Climate Change." *Environment360* (16 Nov. 2009) http://e360.yale.edu/content/feature.msp?id=2210. (accessed 18 Dec. 2009).

Obama, Barack. "Promoting a Healthy Environment." Portsmouth, N.H. (Online, 8 Oct. 2007) http://www.barackobama.com (accessed 26 May 2010).

Owen, Anna Lou Riesch. "Conservation under Franklin D. Roosevelt." Ed., Roderick Nash. *The American Environment: Readings in the History of Conservation.*Reading, MA: Addison-Wesley, 1968, 150–151.

Savage, David G. "Obama Administration Leaves Climate Change to Congress, not theCourts." *Los Angeles Times,* (18 Sept. 2010) http://www. latimes.com/ . . . ./la-na-climate-obama-2

The White House. "Energy and the Environment." (25 Oct. 2010) http:// www.whitehouse.gov/issues/energy-and-environment (accessed 25 Oct. 2010).

Selin, Henrik Selin and Stacy D. Vandeveer. "Multilevel Governance and Transatlantic Climate Change Politics." Ed., Barry G. Rage. *Greehnouse Governance: Addressing Climate Change in America*. Washington, DC: Brookings Institution Press, 2010, 336.

Chapter 12

Food and Agricultural Policy

Julie A. Lester

Although there are an awful lot of farms in Illinois, in the neighborhood where I live, the main livestock is squirrels. . . . So I don't pretend to know everything there is to know about agricultural issues.

—Presidential candidate Barack Obama

Planting the Seeds of Change

The United States is no longer a nation of farmers, but the food and agricultural policymaking process is important as all Americans are stakeholders in those policy outcomes. Most presidents have an opportunity to shape food and agricultural policy, primarily through general farm legislation (the Farm Bill), but the Obama administration's efforts to influence food and agricultural policy have gone beyond the Farm Bill. As a candidate, Obama campaigned with the rhetoric of change and proposed policy initiatives that could bring about various changes in food and agricultural policy. As president, how has Obama delivered on his rhetoric of policy change? Through a consideration of candidate Obama's campaign proposals for food and agricultural policy and some of the policy initiatives he pursued during the first two years of his presidency, a few observations can be made regarding the Obama administration's efforts to implement food and agricultural policy changes.

Obama on the Campaign Trail

As the road to the White House goes through Iowa and because every American is affected by food and agricultural policy decisions, those policy issues play a role in presidential campaigns. Candidate Obama recognized the importance of reaching out to agricultural interests early in his campaign, especially family farmers, whom he called "the cornerstone of American democracy" ("Real Leadership" 2007). Obama stated, "we need to set priorities that reflect our values. . . . Well it's time to stand up to these lobbyists and tell them we're putting family farmers first, we're putting conservation of land and water first" (CBS News 2007). Keenly aware of the importance of winning the Iowa caucus and crafting a message that would resonate with rural voters, Obama often invoked preservation of the family farm at rural campaign events. In an effort to reach out to farmers and rural voters, Obama's campaign team participated in a summer 2007 "listening tour" of more than thirty different events in rural Iowa (CBS News 2007). The tour allowed his campaign team to gather ideas that undoubtedly influenced the development of his platform for agricultural and rural policy, a thirteen-page document entitled "Real Leadership for Rural America." The document outlined Obama's priorities, which included strengthening family farms and rural businesses, through four broad policy goals: 1) "ensure economic opportunity for family farmers"; 2) "support rural economic development"; 3) "promote rural America's leadership in developing renewable energy"; and 4) "improve rural quality of life." In addition to identifying his campaign's policy goals, the document also introduced programs to strengthen agriculture and rural America.

Although the Obama campaign's food and agricultural policy platform provided many policy ideas, there was concern about his lack of experience in those policy areas. Political scientist James Gimpel observed, "the concern would be that he doesn't understand or would have much sympathy for their interests at all. . . . And that rural Americans would not be a very high priority in an Obama administration" (Berkes 2008). Candidate Obama's comment at a July 2007 Iowa campaign stop did not alleviate the concerns of those who questioned his experience. His attempt to address a primary concern of agricultural producers—receiving a fair price for their product—turned into an embarrassing campaign gaffe. Obama asked his audience, "anybody gone into Whole Foods lately and see what they charge for arugula?" (Zeleny 2007). His statement led to criticism for being out of touch with farmers and rural voters because of the linkage of their concerns to a high-end grocery chain that did not have a store in Iowa.

Obama's critics were quick to point out his potential short-comings in understanding food and agricultural policy, but his supporters were enthusiastic about the potential policy changes an Obama administration would work to implement. In an interview for the *Missoula News,* Obama brought attention to the American obesity crisis and stated that, through the use of the "bully pulpit of the office," he would "encourage parents to devote more time to ensuring that their children are eating healthy meals" (LeVaux 2008). Those advocating for change may have also found hope when Obama acknowledged reading Michael Pollan's "Farmer in Chief."

> I was just reading an article in *The New York Times* by Michael Pollan about food and the fact that our entire agricultural system is built on cheap oil. As a conse-quence, our agriculture sector actually is contributing more greenhouse gases than our transportation sector. And in the meantime, it's creating monocultures that are vulnerable to national security threats, are now vulner-able to sky-high food prices or crashes in food prices, huge swings in commodity prices, and are partly responsible for the explosion in our healthcare costs because they're contributing to type 2 diabetes, stroke and heart disease, obesity, all the things that are driving our huge explo-sion in healthcare costs. (Klein 2008)

Food blogger Eddie Gehman Kohan remarked, "people are so inter-ested in a massive change in food and agriculture that they are dining out on hope now" and to have a president "who might actually have eaten organic food" may open up opportunities for policy reform (Severson 2008). Chef Rick Bayless was optimistic that Obama would "recognize that we need to do what we can in our country to encourage real food for everyone" (Jalonick 2009). Obama's campaign rhetoric may have brought hope to those that have sought change in food and agricultural policy, but considering the complex nature of American food and agricultural policy, would Obama be capable of implementing policy change?

Obama's election to the presidency may have been viewed as a victory for those seeking reform of American food and agricultural policy, but there continued to be skepticism about his knowledge of the realities of American agriculture and the policymaking process. Former Department of Agriculture (USDA) secretary and Nebraska senator, Mike Johanns, expressed concern that "there seems to be, from the current administration, an idyllic vision of the countryside, without much of a realistic understanding of how modern-day agriculture feeds an ever-growing population" (Burros 2010). From the early days of his presidency, Obama worked to implement policy changes, but he has had to work within the existing policy structures that have been dominated by special interests that reformers believe have, for years, negatively influenced food and agricultural policy. Aware of the challenges facing him in the policymaking arena and the challenges facing rural America, in June 2009 Obama announced that his administration would embark on a listening tour in rural towns across America. Administration officials, including cabinet secretaries, engaged in discussions with citizens on issues related to rural health, education, infrastructure, natural resources, and energy (White House 2009a). Obama also demonstrated his commitment to rural America through the creation of the White House Rural Council, which would work to promote and strengthen efforts to ensure policies beneficial to rural Americans (White House 2011).

Ensuring Economic Opportunity for Family Farmers

Obama's campaign platform set forth many ideas to promote economic opportunity for America's family farmers, but some of the policy ideas are specifically tied to the Farm Bill that is not scheduled to be reauthorized until 2012. Although much work in food and agricultural policy will come with the drafting of the next Farm Bill, the Obama administration did not wait to implement new policy initiatives. With the enactment of the American Recovery and Reinvestment Act of 2009 (ARRA), farmers and rural Americans benefited from stimulus monies. According to the USDA's Recovery Website, the ARRA provided the agency with almost $28 billion for recovery programs. In addition to the programs funded by the ARRA, the administration has worked to promote economic opportunity for America's family farmers through the pursuit of policies promoting food safety and organic, sustainable, and local agriculture.

Obama stated that one of the government's responsibilities is to ensure a safe food supply and, as a response to the need to update food safety laws that have not been significantly overhauled since the early twentieth century, in March 2009 he announced the creation of the Food Safety Working Group (FSWG) (Eggen 2009). A collaborative effort of multiple government entities, including the USDA, Commerce, Health and Human Services (HHS), Homeland Security and State as well as the Centers for Disease Control and Prevention (CDC), the Food and Drug Administration (FDA), the Food Safety and Inspection Service (FSIS) and the Environmental Protection Agency (EPA), the FSWG hosted a public listening day in May 2009 to identify food safety concerns and principles that would guide the group's activities. The three guiding principles of the FSWG are: 1) "prioritizing prevention" so that consumers are not harmed by an unsafe food supply; 2) "strengthening surveillance and enforcement" of current and future legislation; and 3) "improving response and recovery" to illness outbreaks or food supply contamination (Food Safety Working Group 2009).

Through the creation of the FSWG, the Obama administration empowered government agencies to ensure a safe food supply. Efforts to "prioritize prevention" included the establishment of a collaboration among the FSIS, CDC, and state agencies to strengthen response to food safety incidents as well as strengthening public communication. Through the use of Facebook, Twitter, and the Website Foodsafety.gov, the government now provides consumers with instant information about food safety issues. To "strengthen surveillance and enforcement" of current and future legislation, the Obama administration challenged the FDA to develop systems that would allow for tracking outbreaks of food-borne illness so that all agencies involved in mitigating a response to an emergency could more effectively collaborate in their outbreak response. In August 2009, the FDA established an Office of Foods to achieve the goal of "improving response and recovery." This office was charged with building a "unified FDA foods program that can best achieve the agency's public health mission" (U.S. Food and Drug Administration 2009). With the creation of the Office of Foods, the FDA assumed a more active role in promoting food safety.

Although the Obama administration has made strides in addressing issues related to food safety, there is still concern that the government is not doing enough to prevent outbreaks of food-borne illness. According to a 2010 Union of Concerned Scientists survey of more than 1,700 FDA and USDA employees, approximately 38 percent of respondents believed that "public health has been harmed by their agencies deferring to business interests." Twenty-seven percent of respondents "personally experienced instances where public health has been harmed by businesses withholding food safety information from agency investigators in the past year." Twenty-five percent reported "they personally experienced corporate interests forcing their agency to withdraw or significantly modify a policy or action designed to protect consumers in the past year." The results of the survey reflect many of the criticisms of the government's efforts in food safety, primarily the belief that the agencies responsible for protecting America's food supply are captured by special interests and real policy change may be difficult to achieve.

The role of the FDA in regulating the American food supply also expanded significantly with passage of the Food Safety Modernization Act, which was the first comprehensive food-safety legislation passed since the 1930s. The legislation empowered the FDA in its regulation of food production, such as granting the agency the power to implement food recalls, but would not apply to food activities that fall under the jurisdiction of the USDA, such as meat, poultry, and certain egg products (Doering 2010, Layton 2010). The legislation was supported by "an eclectic array of groups across the political spectrum" (Layton 2010) and supporters called it "a big victory for consumers that finally brings food-safety laws into the 21st century" (Doering 2010). The legislation was met with concern because of the level of control the FDA would have over food production facilities and the estimated $1.4 billion it would cost to implement to law (Layton 2010).

While passage of food-safety legislation has garnered much attention, other actions proposed to ensure economic opportunity for farmers and rural Americans included programs to promote organic, sustainable, and local agriculture. The USDA has encouraged employees to establish "People's Gardens" in communities nationwide. When Abraham Lincoln created the USDA in 1862, he referred to it as "the people's department," so it was fitting that on February 12, 2009, the 200th anniversary of Lincoln's birth, the groundbreaking for the very first "People's Garden" occurred at the USDA's Washington, DC headquarters. At the ceremony, Secretary Vilsack stressed the Obama administration's commitment to environmental preservation and assured the public that through this project the federal government would "lead the way in enhancing and conserving our land and water resources" (USDA 2009a). Since the program's inception, more than 1,200 gardens have sprouted up across the nation and, in addition to providing green space in communities as well as wildlife habitat, many of the People's Gardens are providing locally grown foods to communities in need (USDA 2010b).

The "Know Your Farmer, Know Your Food" initiative was established in September 2009 to support programs authorized in the 2008 Farm Bill to promote local and regional food systems and to strengthen rural economies. Secretary Vilsack stated:

> An American people that is more engaged with their food supply will create new income opportunities for American agriculture. . . . Reconnecting consumers and institutions with local producers will stimulate economies in rural communities, improve access to healthy, nutritious food for our families, and decrease the amount of resources to transport our food. (USDA 2009b)

At the launch of the initiative, the USDA announced awards total- ing $65 million for programs that would assist "socially disad- vantaged and underserved farmers" with marketing development, providing rural cooperatives with opportunities to improve and expand their markets, and funding to schools, to assist with the purchase of local produce (USDA 2009b). The program has expand- ed significantly since its inception and has provided funding to numerous projects across the nation, but the initiative has been criticized. In an April 2010 letter to Secretary Vilsack, Senators Saxby Chambliss (R-GA), John McCain (R-AZ), and Pat Roberts (R-KS), expressed concern that, "in the name of promoting local food systems, the Department appears to be prioritizing Rural Development grant and loan programs for local projects in urban areas, apparently at the expense of rural communities with docu- mented rural development needs." This letter served as a reminder of the opposition the Obama administration would face in pursuing policies that may challenge the status quo in food and agricultural policy.

The People's Garden and Know Your Farmer, Know Your Food initiatives brought attention to issues of importance to both president and First Lady Michelle Obama, namely the promotion of access to locally grown foods to encourage nutritious eating habits while strengthening the rural economy. Mrs. Obama planted the first White House garden since the 1940s and believed that "the garden was an important first step—just sort of exploring the ideas around nutrition and children" (Hall and Hellmich 2010). She expressed hope that "through children, they will begin to educate their families and that will, in turn, begin to educate our communities" (Burros 2009). The first lady also has been involved with the White House Task Force on Childhood Obesity and the Let's Move initiative, a collaborative effort between the White House, HHS, the Department of Education, and the USDA. Along with the president, she has met with leaders across the country to discuss issues related to school nutrition and has worked to promote access to healthy meals at schools for all children (Obama 2010). The Obamas celebrated a policy victory with the passage of the Healthy, Hunger-Free Kids Act of 2010, which reauthorized and reformed child nutrition programs and the national school lunch program. The legislation, which included $4.5 billion in new funding over ten years will, in part, give the USDA more authority to improve nutritional standards and expand access to drinking water for school children as well as strengthen the relationship between schools and local farmers to provide access to healthy foods (White House 2010b).

Supporting Rural Economic Development

Candidate Obama's plans for supporting rural economic development included incentives for small businesses and policies to improve access to communications technology, such as broadband. According to the USDA's Recovery Website, more than half of the agency's recovery fund allocation would be invested in rural development and USDA loan and grant programs focusing on rural business development, community facilities, water and waste disposal, broadband infrastructure, and housing would benefit from those funds. According to the USDA's report, "Rural Development and the Recovery Act: Working for Rural Communities," rural development projects were funded by approximately 95,000 loans and 2,500 grants in 2,962 counties and it is estimated that those projects created or saved more than 300,000 jobs. Examples of the ARRA's impact in rural American include the following:

- Homeownership became a reality for 93,000 families ($11.4 billion investment).

- 854 water and waste projects served 1.7 million people ($3.3 billion investment).

- 2.8 million people benefited from 563 public safety facilities ($176 million investment).

- 180 health facilities cared for 3.5 million people ($590 million investment).

- 312 cultural and educational facilities provided for 4.2 million people ($271 million investment).

- Access to broadband Internet for 7 million people was improved ($3.5 billion investment).

- 2,000 small businesses received approximately $1.6 billion in funds.

Although it will take years to identify the full economic impact of programs funded by the ARRA, the USDA has acknowledged that recovery funds have had an immediate, beneficial impact on rural communities.

Promoting Rural America's Leadership in Developing Renewable Energy

The Obama campaign's platform focused on a variety of methods through which to improve America's investment in renewable energy as well as increasing standards for energy efficiency. President Obama affirmed his commitment to increase renewable energy production and recognized that "providing incentives for energy-efficiency and clean energy are the right thing to do for our future because the nation that leads the clean energy economy will be the nation that leads the global economy" (White House 2010a). With the passage of the ARRA, the Obama administration allocated $786.5 million for investment in biofuels research and development (White House 2009b). In May 2009, the president signed a directive to create the Biofuels Interagency Working Group (IWG), co-chaired by the secretaries of agriculture and energy and the administrator of the EPA. The group's responsibilities include the coordination and development of policies to improve biofuel infrastructure, marketing, and conservation. The Biofuels IWG February 2010 report, "Growing America's Fuels," outlined the administration's plans for advancing the American biofuels industry. In 2010, the USDA announced the establishment of USDA Regional Biomass Research Centers. This was part of a plan "to include as many U.S. rural areas as possible to maximize the economic benefits of biofuel production across the country." Funding would also be provided to establish biofuels refineries in each of the five regions where the research centers are located (USDA 2010a). In addition to developing new energy sources, the renewable energy policies of the Obama administration also have the potential to benefit rural economies.

Improving Rural Quality of Life

To improve the quality of life for rural Americans, Obama focused on a variety of issues, including improving rural health care and education. Kathleen Sebelius, secretary of HHS, stressed that "the President is committed to improving health care in rural communities" (US HHS 2009). Under the ARRA, funding was provided to improve access to health care in rural communities through funding upgrades to existing health care facilities as well as monies for new construction (USDA Rural Development 2010). According to the healthcare.gov Website, provisions in the Affordable Care Act would provide funding for community health centers in underserved rural areas, as well provide incentives, such as scholarships and loan repayment, to encourage doctors and nurses to practice in rural communities. In August 2010, Sebelius announced that $32 million would be allocated to programs to improve access to and the quality of rural health care services (US HHS 2010)

Candidate Obama pledged to improve rural education in a variety of ways, such as providing incentives to attract teachers to rural schools and bringing farms to schools and the administration's "A Blueprint for Reform" outlined efforts that would improve education in rural America. The Rural School and Community Trust (2010) acknowledged that although the Blueprint did mention rural schools more frequently than other federal documents, few policy ideas were targeted directly to rural educational needs. Using ARRA funds, improvements in rural education have been made to improve access to broadband Internet, upgrade existing facilities, and build new educational facilities. Additionally, the

People's Garden program has worked to provide healthy, local foods to school across the nation.

A Preliminary Assessment

Presidents have high aspirations for policy initiatives they would like to implement and Obama has been no exception. His campaign set forth a detailed plan to change food and agricultural policy and to revitalize rural America. Although Obama faced many challenges during his first two years in office, he did not abandon his campaign platform for change in food and agricultural policy. Comprehensive in nature, the campaign platform set forth many policy ideas that the Obama administration has worked to implement. The ARRA provided funding for numerous programs that benefited farmers and rural Americans. Additionally, the Obama administration success-fully implemented a variety of programs that promote sustainable agriculture and local foods, improved nutrition, and rural develop-ment. Working with a Congress controlled by his political party, Obama also signed legislation to overhaul the food-safety system and the national school lunch program. With budget shortfalls and a Congress characterized by divided party control after the 2010 elections, Obama will continue to face many challenges during the remaining years of his presidency and many of those challenges in food and agricultural policy will come while drafting the next Farm Bill. In drafting future legislation, the administration will have to balance the demands of Americans who desire changes in food and agricultural policy while addressing the needs of the constituencies served by agricultural special interests. Although it is difficult to predict Obama's future successes, contentious battles will continue to be fought in food and agricultural policy.

Works Cited

The Affordable Care Act—what it means for rural Americans. n.d. http:// www.healthcare.gov/center/brochures/rural_america.pdf (accessed 10 Dec. 2010).

Berkes, H. "How will an urban president handle farm policy." *National Public Radio* (23 Nov. 2008) http://www.npr.org/templates/story/ story.php?storyId=97309054 (accessed 15 Dec. 2010).

Bioenergy Interagency Working Group. "Growing America's fuel." (2010) http://www.whitehouse.gov/sites/default/files/rss_viewer/growing_ americas_fuels.PDF (accessed 17 Dec. 2010).

Burros, M. "Obamas to plant vegetable garden at White House." *The New York Times* (20 March 2009) http://www.nytimes.com/2009/03/20/dining/20garden.html?_r=1&pagewanted=print (accessed 19 Oct. 2010).

———. "Obama ag policies sow confusion." *Politico* (11 Feb. 2010) http://www.politico.com/news/stories/0210/32812.html (accessed 9 Sept. 2010).

CBS News. "Obama talks agriculture in rural Iowa." *CBS News* (17 Dec. 2007) http://www.cbsnews.com/stories/2007/12/17/politics/main3627120.shtml (accessed 12 Oct. 2010).

Doering, C. "House passes reform of food safety system." *Reuters* (21 Dec. 2010) http://www.reuters.com/article/idUSN3014097720101221 (accessed 23 Dec. 2010).

Eggen, D. "Obama targets food safety." *The Washington Post* (15 March 2009) http://www.washingtonpost.com/wp-dyn/content/article/2009/03/14/AR2009031401600.html (accessed 15 Oct. 2010).

Food Safety Working Group. "President's food safety working group: Delivering results." (2009) http://www.foodsafetyworkinggroup.gov/FSWG_Fact_Sheet.pdf (accessed 15 Oct. 2010).

Hall, M. and Hellmich, N. "Michelle Obama aims to end child obesity in a generation." *USA Today* (9 Feb. 2010) http://www.usatoday.com/news/health/weightloss/2010-02-09-1Afirstlady09_CV_N.htm (accessed 9 Sept. 2010).

Jalonick, M.C. "For top chefs, food policy is on menu." *The Boston Globe* (25 Jan. 2009) http://www.boston.com/news/nation/washington/articles/2009/01/25/for_top_chefs_food_policy_is_on_menu/ (accessed 12 Oct. 2010).

Klein, J. "The full Obama interview." *Time* (23 Oct. 2008) http://swampland.blogs.time.com/2008/10/23/the_full_obama_interview/ (accessed 5 Oct. 2010).

Layton, L. "Food-safety measure passes Senate in Sunday surprise." *The Washington Post* (19 Dec. 2010) http://www.washingtonpost.com/wp-dyn/content/article/2010/12/19/AR2010121904032.html (accessed 28 Dec. 2010).

LeVaux, A. "Flash in the pan: Obama talks food, farming and chili." *Missoula Independent* (29 May 2008) http://missoulanews.bigskypress.com/missoula/flash-in-the-pan/Content?oid=1138250 (accessed 5 Oct. 2010).

McCain, J., Chambliss, S. and Roberts, P. "Letter to secretary of agriculture Vilsack." (27 April 2010). http://www.agri-pulse.com/uploaded/KnowYourFarmers.pdf (accessed 5 Oct. 2010).

Obama, M. "A food bill we need." *The Washington Post* (2 Aug. 3009) http://www.washingtonpost.com/wp-dyn/content/article/2010/08/01/AR2010080103291.html?wprss=rss_opinions (accessed 9 Sept. 2010).

Real leadership for rural America. (2007). http://www.barackobama.com/pdf/issuesRuralPlanFactSheet.pdf (accessed 5 Oct. 2010).

The Rural School and Community Trust. Quick and dirty: The RPM take on a blueprint for reform. (2010) http://www.ruraledu.org/articles. php?id=2437 (accessed 22 Dec. 2010).

Severson, K. "Is a new food policy on Obama's list." *The New York Times* (23 Dec. 2008) http://www.nytimes.com/2008/12/24/dining/24food. html (accessed 9 Sept. 2010).

Union of Concerned Scientists. "FDA and USDA scientists say U.S. food system needs strengthening; hundreds say corporations wield undue influence." (13 Sept. 2010) http://www.ucsusa.org/news/press_ release/fda-and-usda-scientists-survey-0402.html (accessed 15 Oct. 2010).

United States Department of Agriculture (USDA). n.d. Overview of USDA recovery act funds. http://usda.gov/wps/portal/usda/arrapie? navid=USDA_ARRA_OVEW (accessed 17 Dec. 2010).

USDA. Vilsack establishes the people's garden project on bicentennial of Lincoln's birth. (12 Feb. 2009a) http://www.usda.gov/wps/portal/ usda/usdahome?contentidonly=true&contentid=2009/02/0042.xml (accessed 17 Dec. 2010).

USDA. USDA launches 'Know Your Farmer, Know Your Food' initiative to connect consumers with local producers to create new economic opportunities for communities. (15 Sept. 2009b) http://www.usda. gov/ (accessed 21 Oct. 2010).

USDA. USDA farm to school tactical team monthly report—October-November (2009c). http://www.fns.usda.gov/cnd/F2S/pdf/F2Sreport_ 11-09.pdf (accessed 22 Dec. 2010).

USDA. Agriculture secretary Vilsack announces renewable energy initiatives to spur rural revitalization throughout the country. (21 Oct. 2010a) http://www.usda.gov/wps/portal/usda/usdahome?contentidonl y=true&contentid=2010/10/0545.xml (accessed 5 Nov. 2010).

USDA. Keep America Beautiful and the Department of Agriculture team up to grow nearly 700 people's gardens. (7 Dec. 2010b) http://www. usda.gov/ (accessed 17 Dec. 2010).

USDA Rural Development. Rural development and the Recovery Act: Working for rural communities. (2010) http://www.rurdev.usda.gov/ publications/USDA_ARRA-Report_single-pg_413pm_LOW-res.pdf (accessed 22 Dec. 2010).

United States Department of Education. A blueprint for reform. (2010) http://www2.ed.gov/policy/elsec/leg/blueprint/blueprint.pdf (accessed 22 Dec. 2010).

United States Department of Health and Human Services. Top Obama administration officials hold rural health community forum. (20 July 2009) http://www.hhs.gov/news/press/2009pres/07/20090720a. html (accessed 15 Dec. 2010).

US HHS. Secretary Sebelius announces $32 million to support rural health priorities. (23 Aug. 2010) http://www.hhs.gov/news/press/2010 pres/08/20100823a.html (accessed 15 Dec. 2010).

United States Food and Drug Administration Office of Foods. FDA foods program overview and mission. (2009) http://www.fda.gov/AboutFDA/CentersOffices/OC/OfficeofFoods/default.htm (accessed 7 Oct. 2010).

White House. President Obama announces rural tour with cabinet secretaries and administration officials. (30 June 2009a) http://www.whitehouse.gov/the-press-office/president-obama-announces-rural-tour-with-cabinet-secretaries-and-administration-of (accessed 17 Dec. 2010).

White House. President Obama announces steps to support sustainable energy options, departments of agriculture and energy, environmental protection agency to lead efforts. (5 May 2009b) http://www.whitehouse.gov/the_press_office/President-Obama-Announces-Steps-to-Support-Sustainable-Energy-Options/ (accessed 17 Dec. 2010).

White House. Remarks by the president in state of the union address. (27 Jan. 2010a) http://www.whitehouse.gov/the-press-office/remarks-president-state-union-address (accessed 15 Oct. 2010).

White House. President Obama signs Healthy, Hunger-Free Kids Act of 2010 into law. (13 Dec. 2010b) http://www.whitehouse.gov/the-press-office/2010/12/13/president-obama-signs-healthy-hunger-free-kids-act-2010-law (accessed 17 Dec. 2010).

White House. Executive Order—Establishment of the White House Rural Council. (9 June 2011) http://www.whitehouse.gov/the-press-office/2011/06/09/executive-order-establishment-white-house-rural-council(accessed 13 June 2011).

Zeleny, Mark. "Obama's down on the farm." *The New York Times* (27 July 2007) http://thecaucus.blogs.nytimes.com/2007/07/27/obamas-down-on-the-farm/ (accessed 15 Oct. 2010).

Chapter 13

Health Care Reform

Michael K. Gusmano

Constraints of the Past

After a century of failed efforts, President Barack Obama signed the Patient Protection and Affordable Care Act (ACA) into Law on March 23, 2010. The health reform law regulates private health insurance and extends public and private insurance to millions of Americans. Nevertheless, the full implementation of the new law is uncertain. Its complexity and long implementation timeline limited the political gains that the Democrats hoped to enjoy as a result of this legislative success. Passing health reform in 2010 was a remarkable accomplishment and required effective leadership on the part of the president. The limits of this reform reflect the lack of consensus on health policy, the influence of our fragmented political institutions, and, ironically, the strategy adopted by the president to achieve a legislative victory.

This chapter provides a brief overview of the problems associated with the U.S. health care system and the history of health care reform in the United States. Next, I recount the journey of health care reform from the presidential election campaign of 2008 through its adoption in 2010. Finally, the chapter closes with reflections on what this case tells us about the importance, and limits, of presidential leadership.

The U.S. Health Care System: "Excess and Deprivation"

Opponents of health care reform insist that the United States has the "best health care system in the world," but few experts agree with this assessment. The "system" is a complex patchwork of public and private insurance with large gaps in coverage. It is the most expensive health care system in the world. Health care expenditures in the United States were $2.3 trillion in 2008, which amounted to about 16.2 percent of gross domestic product (GDP). By 2019, U.S. health care spending is projected to reach $4.5 trillion—or about 19 percent of GDP (CMMS 2010). Even with all of this spending, more than 47 million people are uninsured and health care expenses cause half of the personal bankruptcies in the United States (Himmelstein 2005).

A host of studies document access problems faced by people without health insurance. People without insurance are less likely to have a regular source of care (Schoenet al. 2007), are more likely to delay necessary care due to cost, are less likely to receive timely diagnoses for life-threatening conditions (Ayanianet al. 2000), are less likely to receive surgical interventions and other specialty services once they are diagnosed with a serious illness (Gusmano, Rodwin, and Weisz 2010), and are more likely to be admitted to the hospital for ambulatory care sensitive conditions—like pneumonia, congestive heart failure, asthma, and diabetes—that can be managed with access to timely, effective primary care (Brown, Goldacre, and Hicks 2001).

Racial and ethnic minorities and women also face significant barriers to care, regardless of insurance status (Gusmano et al. 2010; Gusmano and Allen 2011). Although some areas enjoy a significant concentration of medical resources, many rural areas have few medical professionals. There are also huge variations in the practice of health care that cannot be explained easily by differences in patient need. Regions that spend more on health care services also do not enjoy better results than lower spending regions (Fisher, Bynum, and Skinner 2009).

Health Care Reform: The "Hardy Perennial"

The issue of health care reform is no stranger to the American political agenda. The United States has flirted with the idea of comprehensive national health insurance for nearly a century. John Kingdon refers to national health insurance (NHI) proposals as "hardy perennials" (Kingdon 1995: 7). From the time of the Progressive Era, opponents categorized NHI as a dangerous "foreign" idea. Conservative critics during the late 1940s and early

1950s, succeeded in associating NHI with the Soviet Union. It was characterized as "socialized medicine."

Presidents John F. Kennedy and Lyndon B. Johnson (LBJ) shifted the Democratic strategy to focus on Medicare, a proposal to provide limited hospital insurance for older people. Following the 1964 election, which resulted in a landslide victory for LBJ and large Democratic majorities in Congress, a more expansive version of Medicare, which included hospital (Part A) and physician (Part B) insurance, as well as Medicaid—a federal-state health insurance plan for the very poor—were adopted in 1965.

By 1974, national health insurance was back on the agenda. Before the Watergate scandal led to President Richard Nixon's resignation, he nearly reached agreement with Sen. Ted Kennedy (D-MA) on a health reform bill based on an employer mandate (Skocpol 1996: 21). President Carter proposed NHI, but he clashed with Kennedy and other congressional leaders on how to proceed. NHI died without a vote in Congress. After fading away during the presidency of Ronald Reagan, health care reform burst back onto the national policy agenda in 1991 with the election of Harris Wofford (D-PA) to the U.S. Senate (Peterson 1992).

Between 1989 and 1992, more than 3 million workers and more than 1 million nonworkers lost their health insurance. Middle-class workers earning between $25,000 and $50,000 had the largest increase in the number of uninsured between 1990 and 1991 (Business and Health 1993).

Wofford and his campaign advisor, James Carville, capitalized on growing middle-class anxiety. In a November 1991 special election to fill the seat of the late senator John Heinz, Wofford defeated the heavily favored Richard Thornburgh, former Pennsylvania governor and U.S. attorney general. Wofford made the need for NHI a central part of his campaign and his election put the issue back on the political agenda.

After the Wofford election, Democrats came to believe health care reform would be an effective theme to use against their Republican counterparts. Before Carville reached the conclusion that "it's the economy stupid," he and Gov. Bill Clinton planned to make health care the central theme of the 1992 presidential campaign.

Although health care reform was back on the agenda, Clinton rejected the idea of pursuing a so-called "single-payer option," which had been favored by Democrats for decades. He claimed that even though a single-payer system would produce greater savings, it would be difficult to get the bill passed by Congress (Clinton

1994). When discussing health reform, Clinton often referenced the failure of President Truman.

Another argument against single-payer involved Clinton's assessment of the political feasibility of enacting a program that called for a large new bureaucracy and new taxes. Clinton ran for office as a "new" Democrat. Advocating a single-payer solution to the health care crisis did not fit this image. Yet, despite his desire to craft a bill that relied on market competition, the final product was remarkably complex.

The White House also recognized that the Congressional Budget Office (CBO) would not accept a plan that relied on so-called "managed competition" alone to control costs. These concerns were well founded because the CBO later estimated that the implementation of the managed care aspects of the Clinton plan would result in minimal savings (CBO 1994). The CBO argued that the market forces used by the Clinton plan would have limited effectiveness because employer-paid premiums would continue to be excluded until 2004, and more importantly, "the proposal would substantially expand the income tax subsidy for premiums paid by the self-employed" (CBO 1994). Instead, the plan's main cost control features involved the regulation of provider fees (Starr 1995). Not only did this make the Clinton plan appear to be bureaucratic and regulatory, it contributed to the fear that it would limit access to care through government "rationing." These cost-control features helped undermine support for the plan among medical providers, the insurance industry, the public, and congressional Democrats.

The political strategy of the Clinton administration also received a great deal criticism. The administration cut members of Congress out of the process of crafting their health reform proposal. The Health Care Task Force, led by First Lady Hillary Clinton, took nine months to craft a plan so it was not unveiled until September 1993 (Epstein 2009). The delay allowed opponents to generate public fear and one year later "Senate Majority Leader George Mitchell (D-Me.) pronounced the reform effort dead" (Shah and Rosenberg 1996). Health care reform, however, was off the policy agenda until the presidential election campaign of 2008.

Toward the Affordable Care Act

Health care reform reemerged as an important issue in the 2008 presidential election campaign. Before the fall of Lehman Brothers on September 14, 2008 (Sorkin 2008) shifted attention to the state of the economy, health care was the top domestic issue for much of the public and all of the major presidential candidates produced health reform plans (Oberlander 2007).

Following Obama's victory, some Democrats argued that the president should focus on the economic crisis and put health care reform on the back burner (Benen 2009). Although he rejected the incremental approach in public statements, behind closed doors Chief of Staff Rahm Emmanuel also argued for it (Milbank 2010).

Health reform efforts also took a hit on January 30, 2009 when the president's choice for secretary of Health and Human Services (HHS), former senator Tom Daschle, was forced to withdraw his name from nomination due to a tax scandal. Setbacks notwithstanding, the president did not waiver from his commitment to pursuing a more comprehensive health reform bill. Obama and many Democratic leaders in Congress argued that health care reform was necessary to strengthen the economy.

The view that economic recovery required further investment in health care coverage was reflected in the American Reinvestment and Recovery Act (ARRA), signed into law by President Obama on February 17, 2009. ARRA included health investments designed to lay the groundwork for broader health care reform. The act included money for the development of health information technology, money to expand the primary care workforce, and more than $1 billion to fund comparative effectiveness research that would provide a better evidence base for treatment decisions. It provided $87 billion for a temporary increase in the federal share of Medicaid costs to counter declines in state revenue and increases in the number of people eligible for the program as a result of the recession. The president also signed a reauthorization of the State Children's Health Insurance Program (SCHIP), which was vetoed by Bush and would have expired on March 1, 2009. This included funding to cover an additional 4 million children and was consistent with the administration's broader health care reform strategy to extend coverage by building on existing programs.

The president established an Office of Health Reform to coordinate administrative efforts on national health reform and hosted a Health Reform Summit with key stakeholders. Because he hoped to avoid the delays associated with the Clinton health reform effort, the president called on the Congress to produce a bill by October 2009.

Rather than develop a detailed health reform proposal, Obama outlined eight broad principles for health reform in his fiscal year 2010 budget:

1. Protect families' financial health;

2. Assure affordable, quality health coverage for all Americans;

3. Provide portability of coverage;

4. Guarantee choice of doctors;

5. Invest in prevention and wellness;

6. Improve patient safety and quality of care;

7. End barriers to coverage for people with preexisting medical conditions; and

8. Reduce the long-term growth of health care costs for businesses and government (Orzag 2009).

The administration and Democratic congressional leaders also met with officials from several stakeholder groups in an effort to bring about consensus in support of an individual mandate and other dimensions of the Democratic health reform ideas (Pear 2009). The Chamber of Commerce was one of the least cooperative groups and became a vocal opponent of the health plan, but the level of cooperation among stakeholders was unprecedented.

The administration was able to reach compromises with the Pharmaceutical Research and Manufacturers of America and the American Hospital Association on reductions in Medicare and Medicaid payments. This did not stop the rhetoric around health care reform from becoming particularly nasty, nor did it prevent an active misinformation campaign on the part of opponents. But the well-financed opposition of powerful stakeholders that marked previous health reform campaigns was clearly minimized by the administration's efforts.

Within Congress, the Democratic leadership worked to avoid internal divisions. The chairmen of the three House committees with jurisdiction over health care—Energy and Commerce, Ways and Means, and Education and Labor—sent a letter to Obama on March 11 in which "they promised to move to pass 'similar' health care reform bills" in 2009 (Kaiser 2009). Speaker Nancy Pelosi worked with the rest of the House leadership and negotiated the relatively minor differences among the bills reported out by each committee. In the Senate, Ted Kennedy, chair of the Health, Education, Labor and Pensions Committee, played an important role early in the process, but Sen. Christopher Dodd (D-CT) took over as Kennedy's health deteriorated. Some, including Kennedy's long-time colleague, Orin Hatch (R-UT), argue that Kennedy's absence from the process made it more difficult to achieve bipartisan consensus. Others argue that bipartisan consensus was impossible because the majority of Republicans refused to support any version of health reform. Nevertheless, Sen. Max Baucus (D-MT), who chaired the Senate Finance Committee, attempted to forge a compromise with conservative, "blue dog" Democrats and Republicans on the committee. The efforts to forge a bipartisan compromise took time and "breached Obama's timelines" (Morone 2010: 1097).

During the summer recess, public debate was marked by a great deal of misinformation, including former Republican vice presidential candidate Sara Palin's infamous suggestion in August that the president's health reform proposal would create "death panels" that would deny life-sustaining care to patients (Bank 2009). Later, the *Investor's Business Daily* published an editorial on July 31, 2009 in which it claimed that the Obama health care plan would lead to the sort of rationing found in the United Kingdom: "People such as scientist Stephen Hawking wouldn't have a chance in the UK, where the National Health Service (NHS) would say the life of this brilliant man, because of his physical handicaps, is essentially worthless" (*Investor's Business Daily* 2010). In response, Professor Hawking pointed out that he has received all of his health care from the English NHS!

Although this rhetoric was baseless, it fed into long-standing fears about government "rationing" that have been used to undermine public support for previous health reform efforts. Republican opponents of reform hoped "to capitalize on the unrest displayed at the meetings to highlight their discontent with other aspects of the health legislation" (Adamy 2009).

Although the summer town hall debates did undermine public support for health care reform, they did not deter the president or congressional Democrats from pushing forward on the issue in the fall. The House finally adopted a health care reform bill on November 7 by a vote of 220 to 215—with only one Republican vote. The Senate adopted a health reform bill on December 24 by a vote of 60 to 39 without a single Republican vote. The main difference between the bills was the public option. The House bill called for a new public health insurance plan to compete with private health insurance plans, but the Senate bill did not. Before congressional leaders were able to complete informal negotiations about how they would bridge the differences in conference, the special election in Massachusetts nearly derailed the entire effort.

On January 19, 2010, Republican state senator Scott Brown defeated Democratic Party candidate Martha Coakley in a special election to fill the seat of Sen. Kennedy, who died in August (Morone 2010: 1114). The results of this election shifted the balance of power within the U.S. Senate (Nagourney 2010). Until that time, the Democrats—along with independents Bernie Sanders of Vermont and Joe Lieberman of Connecticut—enjoyed a sixty-vote majority that, in theory, was capable of ending a filibuster.

The election of Sen. Brown led some Democrats to believe that comprehensive health reform would have to be abandoned, but the administration decided not to give up on reform. There are conflicting accounts about what led to this decision. Some argue that the president made the decision to do so on his own. Others stress the role of Speaker Pelosi in encouraging the president to move forward with health care reform. Regardless, Obama did choose to push for a congressional vote without the comfort of a sixty-vote majority in the Senate.

One development that bolstered the president's decision was the announcement in early February 2010 by Anthem Blue Cross and Blue Shield of California that they planned to increase premiums in the individual health insurance market by 39 percent. This gave credibility to the claim that the consequences of failure would be dire for the economy (Manos 2010).

At this point, the president played a more aggressive public role. The president and his advisors met regularly with Speaker Pelosi, Sen. Majority Leader Harry Reid, and other congressional leaders on a regular basis throughout the process, but they did not get bogged down in the details of the legislation and they stayed further in the background than had the Clinton team (Morone 2010: 1099). By the end of February, Obama released his own proposal for health care reform that pulled together the features of the House and Senate bills. On February 25, 2010, Obama hosted a second nationally televised Health Care Summit at Blair House. It did not produce a compromise, but allowed Obama to make his case for reform.

Equally important, the president and Congressional leadership decided that they were willing to use the reconciliation process. Reconciliation bills cannot be filibustered, so they only require a simple majority, rather than a sixty-vote super-majority, to pass. Because the Democrats no longer had sixty votes in the Senate, they would not be able to pass a bill that emerged from the conference committee. To get around this, the House Demo-crats agreed to pass the Senate version of health reform with the promise that some of the features in the Senate bill would be "fixed" in a reconciliation bill.

Republicans cried foul over the proposed use of reconcilia-tion. Senator Minority Leader Mitch McConnell (R-KY) wrote a letter signed by all forty-one Senate Republicans in which they argued that the budget reconciliation mechanism was intended to facilitate deficit reduction, not to "to pass a partisan bill that is opposed by the majority of Americans." The use of reconciliation to overcome partisan opposition was not, however, without precedent. Republicans had used this mechanism to adopt many aspects of the *Contract with America* in the mid-1990s and they used it again to adopt tax cuts in 2001, 2003, and 2005.

The agreement to use the reconciliation process required additional lobbying and negotiation by the president with reluc-tant members of the House. During a flight on Air Force One, the president convinced Rep. Dennis Kucinich (D-OH) to support the bill. Rep. Bart Stupak (D-MI) was also a holdout, but finally agreed to vote for the bill after the president agreed to issue an Executive Order stating that federal money could not be used to pay for abortions. On March 21, 2010, the House adopted the Senate health care reform bill by a vote of 219 to 212 and the reconciliation bill (Health Care and Education Reconciliation Act of 2010) by a vote of 220 to 211.

The Senate parliamentarian ruled that the president must sign the original law before the Senate could vote on the reconcili-ation bill designed to change the original law, so two days later President Obama signed the Patient Protection and Affordable Care Act (P.L. 111-148). Two days after that, the Senate passed the final version of the Health Care and Education Reconciliation Act of 2010 with two small amendments related to education by a vote of 56 to 43 and the House adopted the bill as amended by the Senate by a vote of 220 to 207. Finally, on March 30, 2010, Obama signed the Health Care and Education Reconciliation Act of 2010 (P.L. 111-152), amending P.L. 111-148.

Overcoming the Barriers:
Institutions, Interests, and Leadership

Opposition by powerful interest groups in the context of fragment-ed institutions and a public that is skeptical of big government solutions have combined to thwart health reform in the United States for a century (Brown 2008; Steinmo and Watts 1995). The American Medical Association and other representatives of organized medicine have often opposed government intervention in medical care. Similarly, the United States has a large and powerful commercial health insurance industry that is opposed to government regulation of private insurance or an expansion of public insurance that would limit (or eliminate) their market share. Business associations are also skeptical of government intervention in health care because they worry that interventions designed to improve access will raise the cost of doing business.

The existence of powerful interests that oppose health reform is not unique to the United States. Organized medicine opposed health care reform in the Canada before it was enacted in 1965 and in the England before the NHS was created in 1948 (BBC 1998). In the United States, however, reformers must combat these interests in a political system designed to limit major policy change. Our "government of separated institutions sharing powers" (Neustadt 1960), bicameral legislature, equal representation of states within the Senate, committee system in Congress, and the need for a supermajority to overcome the threat of filibuster in the U.S. Senate, are all potential veto points that make it difficult to enact major policy change (Peterson 1992; Steinmo and Watts 1995). The ACA, like previous health reform proposals, had to negotiate a legislative "gauntlet" that included three House committees, the House Rules committee, and two Senate committees (Morone 2010).

Although President Obama enjoyed significant Democratic majorities in both houses of Congress, a complete lack of support by Republicans and divisions within the Democratic Party meant that health reform was far from inevitable. The interests that took advantage of the fragmented institutions to block change in the past may well have done so this time around. The adoption of the ACA was due in large part to the administration's efforts to "work around" these veto points.

Leadership and Strategy

In almost every respect, the strategy President Obama used to bring about change was the opposite of the Clinton administration. Along with working closely with the congressional leadership, a crucial lesson that Obama learned from Clinton's experience was the importance of reassuring the public that they could keep their existing health insurance coverage (and doctors) if they were happy with them. The "Harry and Louise" ads financed by the Health Insurance Association of America during the Clinton reform debate invoked fears that patients would no longer be able to access their doctors. Obama tried to preempt this by emphasizing that he intended to build on the existing system rather than replace it with something less familiar.

Obama also worked hard to co-opt stakeholders, particularly those who had worked against reform in the past. Although Clinton did so as well, Obama was more successful because he placed much less emphasis on cost control. The Clinton administration addressed concerns about a CBO score by incorporating physician payment regulation. In contrast, the ACA included few cost controls that threatened the interest of industry.

The more explicit cost control components of the bill are proposed reductions in payments to Medicare Advantage plans and a reduced update factor for Medicare hospital reimbursement rates. Rates paid to Medicare Advantage, for example, represent a significant source of savings and have been cut before, when the government found that the rates were not sufficiently "risk-adjusted" and plans were making a profit by enrolling beneficiaries that were, on average, healthier than those in the traditional Medicare program. Proponents of rate cuts say that they would not reduce service to Medicare beneficiaries, but merely eliminate profit taking by insurance companies. Regardless of the merits of these cuts, they were highly controversial and have undermined support for the law among Medicare beneficiaries.

Obama was able to avoid some of the negative reaction faced by the Clinton plan because he relied on a long implementation period, rather than provider fee regulation or some other mechanism that would have threatened entrenched interests, to receive a good score from the CBO. The most costly provisions of the new law will not be implemented until 2014.

Would it have been possible to enact a law that did more to constrain costs? Perhaps, but the administration clearly did not believe so. Unfortunately, the strategy that helped overcome a century of legislative failure and frustration raises questions about the long-term success of health reform. Without creditable efforts to control the health care inflation rate, premiums for decent health insurance will not be affordable for many Americans. Moreover, the long implementation time frame poses at least two threats to the long term success of the law.

First, before the ACA will expand insurance coverage in a significant way, there will be a presidential election in 2012 and a mid-term election in 2014. If President Obama is not re-elected and/or if the Republican Party gains more seats in the Congress, there is a chance that the law could be underfunded, changed significantly, or perhaps even repealed. The law's expanded role of the federal government in health care has made it an obvious target of the "Tea Party." In the 2010 midterm congressional elections, Republicans, particularly those affiliated with the Tea Party, made the repeal of "Obamacare" a central component of their campaign. Rep. Michele Bachmann (R-MN) claimed, without producing evidence, "that the new law is already harming the economy and killing jobs" (Steinhauer and Pear 2011). Claims that the law is harming the economy and requires irresponsible government spending are likely to be repeated by the next Republican presidential candidate.

Second, because many of the benefits of the new law will not be felt for several years, opponents have an opportunity to generate fears about the potential impact of the law before most people have any experience with its provisions. The president has acknowledged that opinion polls indicate low support for the new health reform law. Nevertheless, he argued that, once people experience the changes in the new law, they "will have a 'fair shake' in dealing with insurance companies and will realize that their 'worst fears' are 'groundless'" (Alarkon 2010). The president's optimism notwithstanding, polls indicate that Americans remain confused about the new law and their lack of enthusiasm about this historic policy achievement continues to threaten its future" (Marmor 2010).

Works Cited

Adamy, J. "Obama heads to town-hall meetings." *The Wall Street Journal* (11 Aug. 2009): A2.

Alarkon, W. "Obama tells Dems that economy, healthcare will help in midterms." *The Hill* (2010). (accessed 2 Jan 2011).

An Analysis of the Administration's Health Proposal. Washington, DC: Congressional Budget Office, 1994.

Andrews, M. "Voters see very different healthcare plans from Obama, Clinton and McCain." *US News & World Report* (18 April 2008). (accessed 10 Dec. 2010).

Ayanian, J.Z., J.S. Weissman, E.C. Schneider, J.A. Ginsburg, and A.M. Zaslavsky. "Unmet Needs of Uninsured Adults in the United States." *Journal of the American Medical Association*. Vol. 284, No. 16 (2000), 2061–2069.

Bank, J. "Palin vs. Obama: Death Panels." FactCheck.org, A Project of the Annenberg Public Policy Center (2009). (accessed 2 Dec. 2010). http://www.factcheck.org/2009/08/palin-vs-obama-death-panels.

Benen, S. "Clyburn hitting the brakes on healthcare." *Washington Monthly* (26 Jan. 2009). http://www.washingtonmonthly.com/archives/individual/2009_01/016615.php (accessed 5 Dec. 2010).

Brown, A.D., M.J. Goldacre, N. Hicks. "Hospitalization for Ambulatory-Care Sensitive Conditions: A Method for Comparing Access and Quality Studies Using Routinely Collected Statistics." *Canadian Journal of Public Health*. Vol. 92 (2001), 155–159.

Brown, L.D. "The Amazing Noncollapsing U.S. Health Care System—Is Reform Finally at Hand?" *New England Journal of Medicine*. Vol. 358, No 4 (2008), 325.

Business and Health. "Number of uninsured rises to 35.4 million, report says." *Business and Health News Brief* (10 Feb. 1993).

Centers for Medicare and Medicaid Services. "National Expenditure Projections 2009–2019. (accessed 30 Dec. 2010).

Clinton, W.J. "Remarks in a Town Meeting in Minneapolis, April 8." *Compilation of Presidential Documents*, 30 WCPD 754. Washington, DC: GPO, 1994.

Daschle, Tom. *Critical: What We Can Do About the Health-Care Crisis*. New York: Thomas Dunne Books, 2008.

Epstein, A. "Introduction: Health care reform in perspective." *New England Journal of Medicine* (4 Dec. 2009): 1.

Fisher, Elliott S., Julie P. Bynum, Jonathan S. Skinner. "Slowing the Growth of Health Care Costs—Lessons from Regional Variation." *New England Journal of Medicine*. Vol. 360, No. 9 (2009), 849–852.

Gusmano, M.K., S. Allen. "Health Care for Older Persons in England and the U.S.: A Contrast of Systems and Values." *Journal of Health Politics, Policy and Law*. Vol. 36, No. 1 (2010).

Gusmano, M.K., V.G. Rodwin, D. Weisz. *Health Care in World Cities: New York, London, and Paris*. Baltimore, MD: Johns Hopkins University Press, 2010.

Himmelstein, D.U., E. Warren, D. Thorne, S. Woodhandler. "Illness and Injury as Contributors to Bankruptcy." *Health Affairs Web Exclusive* (Feb. 2005): W5–W63.

"How the House Bill Runs Over Grandma." *Investor's Business Daily* (31 July 2009). <http://www.investors.com/newsandanalysis/article.aspx?id=503058 (accessed 2 Jan. 2011).

Kingdon, John W. *Agendas, Alternatives and Public Policies*, 2nd ed. New York: Longman, 1995: 7.

"Making Britain Better." BBC News (1998). <http://news.bbc.co.uk/2/hi/events/nhs_at_50/special_report/119803.stm (accessed 1 Jan. 2011).

Manos, D. "Anthem Blue Cross Takes Additional Heat Over 39 Percent Premium Increase." *Healthcare Finance News* (11 Feb. 2010). (accessed 1 Jan. 2011).

Marmor, T.R. "The Undisciplined Economist: Health Reform and the Obama Administration: Reflections in Mid-2010." *Healthcare Policy.* Vol. 6, No. 1 (2010), 15–21.

Milbank, Dana. "Why Obama needs Rahm at the top." *The Washington Post* (21 Feb. 2010): A13.

Morone, J.A. "Presidents and health reform: From Franklin D. Roosevelt to Barack Obama." *Health Affairs.* Vol. 29, No. 6 (2010), 1097.

Nagourney, A. "A year later, voters send a different message." *The New York Times* (20 Jan. 2010).

Neustadt, Richard. *Presidential Power: The Politics of Leadership.* New York: John Wiley & Sons, 1960.

Numbers, Ronald. *Almost Persuaded: American Physicians and Compulsory Health Insurance.* Baltimore, MD: Johns Hopkins University Press, 1978.

Oberlander, J. "Presidential Politics and the Resurgence of Health Care Reform." *New England Journal of Medicine.* Vol. 357 (2007), 2101–2104.

Orzag, P. R. "FY 2010 Budget and Health Care Reform." Testimony before the Committee on Finance, U.S. Senate (10 March 2009).

Pear, R. "Health care industry in talks to shape policy." *The New York Times* (20 Feb. 2009): A16.

Peterson, M.A. National Health Care Reform in the 1990s: Politics, Structure, and Change from Iron Triangles to Policy Networks. Center for American Political Studies, Harvard University. Occasional Papers 92 (1992): 2.

Schoen, C, R. Osborn, M.M. Doty, M. Bishop, J. Peugh, N. Murukutla. "Toward Higher-Performance Health Systems: Adults' Health Care Experiences in Seven Countries, 2007." *Health Affairs Web Exclusives.* Vol. 26, No. 6 (2007), W717–W734.

Shah, M.C. J.M. Rosenberg. "Essay: Health Care Reform in the 103rd Congress—A Congressional Analysis." *Harvard Journal on Legislation.* Vol. 33 (1996), 581–585.

Skocpol, T. "The Political Challenge that May Undermine Health Reform." *Health Affairs.* Vol. 29, No. 7 (2010), 1288–1292.

———. *Boomerang: Health Care Reform and the Turn Against Government.* New York: W.W. Norton and Co., 1996: 21.

Sorkin, A.R. "Lehman files for bankruptcy: Merrill is sold." *The New York Times* (14 Sept. 2008): A1.

Starr, Paul. "What Happened to Health Care Reform?" *The American Prospect.* Vol. 20 (1995), 20-31.

Steinhauer, J and R. Pear. "G.O.P. newcomers set out to undo Obama victories." *New York Times* (3 January, 2011): A1.

Steinmo, S. and J. Watts. "It's the Institutions, Stupid." *Journal of Health Politics, Policy and Law.* Vol. 20, No. 2 (2008), 395–438.

Chapter 14

Response to the Gulf Oil Spill

Matthew A. Williams
Brian Richard

The Spill

Directly following an explosion on the Deepwater Horizon oil rig on April 20, 2010 substantial quantities of oil began to flow from a partially drilled well on the Gulf of Mexico's seafloor. Following the initial days of the Gulf oil spill (or the Deepwater Horizon oil spill), political debate centered on questions over who should take the lead in the short- and long-term response and clean-up efforts. It was obvious British Petroleum (BP), the owner of the rig, and the private sector in general, were better equipped than the federal government to deal with the immediate technological necessities for repairing the ruptured underwater pipeline. Public opinion, however, was divided over whether the government or BP should take the lead. President Barack Obama allowed BP to take the lead but eventually established roles for the federal government, including the transfer of federal oversight to the U.S. Coast Guard (USCG), placing Adm. Thad Allen in charge. Allen has since resigned the post.

The Gulf oil spill could hardly have occurred at a worse time for the president or the country, which was dealing with a bewildering array of domestic and foreign policy challenges and embroiled in two overseas conflicts—Iraq and Afghanistan. Moreover, the manmade disaster was made worse because there was no easy or obvious solution either politically or in terms of plugging the leak. There were—and remain—important implications of the leak on the nation's oil supply, the future of drilling and alternative energy, the ecosystems of the entire Gulf, and the economic viability of the region. But there also were ramifications on national politics and Obama's public approval.

The press, public, and scholars are still trying to make sense of the spill and the president's handling of it. There are parallels to and lessons from presidential responses to other oil spills and disasters. However, initially, it appears that the federal government relinquished disproportionate levels of control to the private sector relative to the limited accountability mechanisms for the immediate response and clean-up efforts following the Deepwater Horizon oil spill. Moreover, increased federal involvement and oversight, converse to what had been implemented in previous comparable situations, was necessary in the direct aftermath of the spill. This spill was unlike any other in the country's history in that oil continued to flow for several months. As such, unfamiliar scenarios require stricter mechanisms of federal accountability and involvement, as the American public will invariably look to the government for resolutions when none seem to be present. Also, because this spill was ongoing, it required heightened and continuous executive-level attention. Ultimately, the Obama administration's failure to recognize the complexity of the Deepwater spill early on slowed and complicated response and recovery efforts.

Responses to disasters vary based on the type of disaster. Generally, disasters are man-made or natural, but oil spills are considered anthropogenic or natural environmental disasters (Enzler 2006). A man-made or technological disaster generally contains an intentional or accidental failure of a man-made system or technology. A natural disaster is the effect of a natural hazard, such as a hurricane or tornado, which affects the natural environment and leads to losses on the economic or human level. Oil spills are difficult to define by type because causes differ from situation to situation, hence the overarching complexity in establishing accountability—be it public or private—in the aftermath. It is clear, however, the Deepwater event was a result of a failed man-made containment system by BP and a failure of federal regulators and regulations.

With the Deepwater event, the Obama administration was faced with a gradual disaster caused by a failed man-made system and made worse by poor decision making. Although the failures of BP—in deepwater drilling technology and engineering as well as in safety systems and leadership—have been widely discussed, there is also a role for the federal government. The American public rightly needs and demands accountability for the handling of situations that have a potential effect on a wide population of citizens. Whether or not the private sector is to blame or is better equipped to handle the situation can be debated, but the limits of federal regulations and decisions on safety systems is evident. The next section discusses regulations emanating from formal mandates that set guidelines for response efforts

Official Executive Role

Legislation governing the federal response to an oil spill is defined primarily by the Oil Pollution Act (OPA), under which the executive role during and after such disasters is outlined in the National Oil and Hazardous Substances Pollution Contingency Plan (NCP), a subsequent three-tiered expansion of the NCP, the National Response Framework, and the National Response Plan (NRP).

OPA

President George H. W. Bush signed OPA into law in August 1990 as a response to the Exxon *Valdez* oil spill. The act sought to expand the authority and resources of the federal government to respond to oil spills (EPA 2009). OPA's vast framework provided new requirements for oil spill contingency planning that government and industry leaders had to observe.

The essential purpose of OPA was to condense the scattered and disjointed federal oil spill laws under one roof. Thus, federal "spill response authority" was a primary aspect of OPA. Section 4201 of OPA provides three options to the president when faced with an oil spill: 1) "Perform cleanup immediately ('federalize' the spill); 2) monitor the response efforts of the spiller; or 3) direct the spiller's cleanup activities" (Ramseur 2010). After the Gulf oil spill, the Obama administration appeared to focus its response efforts on monitoring the actions of BP and other liable private sector parties, but by the end of May 2010 the role was expanded to direct BP's activities.

OPA provides mechanisms for the federal government to determine the liable parties and, on December 15, 2010, the Obama administration filed a lawsuit against BP claiming violations of environmental laws. The lawsuit was the first brought forward by the government and was filed in New Orleans. The named defendants in the case were BP, Transocean, Ltd., MOEX Offshore 2007 LLC, and QBE Insurance Group Ltd (Blum and Fisk 2010). The first three of these defendants were sued under the Clean Water Act (CWA)—an action granted under OPA framework—while the last is being sued under OPA alone (Blum and Fisk 2010). Some of the violations that contributed directly or indirectly to the spill included:

> . . . failing to take necessary precautions to keep the well under control leading up to the explosion; failing to use the best and safest drilling technology to monitor well conditions; failing to maintain continuous surveillance; and failing to use and maintain equipment to ensure the safety and protection of personnel and the environment. (Blum and Fisk 2010)

The Department of Justice reportedly suggested the potential to add more defendants in the coming months. Numerous civil penalties continue to accumulate as of 2011 and will continue to unfold over time.

NCP

The NCP is the federal government's blueprint for responding to both oil spills and hazardous substance releases. The NCP developed from an acknowledged need for the federal government to improve its national response capability and to promote "overall coordination among the hierarchy of responders and contingency plans" (EPA 2009).

Since its inception, the NCP has expanded and now reflects a three-tiered approach: 1) "The Federal government is required to direct all public and private response efforts for spill events"; 2) "Area Committees—composed of federal, state, and local government officials—must develop detailed, location-specific Area Contingency Plans (ACP)"; and 3) ". . . owners or operators of vessels and certain facilities that pose a serious threat to the environment must prepare their own Facility Response Plans" (EPA 2009). Although considerable responsibility is delegated to local and state authorities during a spill event, the NCP holds the federal government as the primary response coordinator. Primary accountability for "implementation plans." however, is unclear. Mechanisms intended to bridge gaps in accountability were implemented under OPA, such as the designation of a regional response team, which assesses ACPs through a "review process" aimed at maintaining consistency on all levels of response (federal, regional, and local).

This raises a fundamental question of the relevance of an accountability mechanism that is intended to provide consistency of "implementation plans" for ACPs when the point of OPA's division of contingency planning was to respond to and account for various regional and local inconsistencies in terms of relative and available oil spill countermeasures. Candidly, these accountability mechanisms are contradictory and bare no relevance on the actual regional and local response efforts, which constitute the main points of public and private scrutiny during and after an oil spill. The development of ACPs was motivated by a recognition that improved strategy and coordination at the local level during a spill was critically lacking prior to OPA 1990. The ACPs tailor the implementation strategy and tactics to the anticipated spill scenarios, environmental resources at risk, available response assets, and the expectations and policies of agency officials within the designated response area (Douligeris et al. 1997: 4).

NRP

The National Response Framework (NRF) defines the federal government as a "key player" responsible for providing "capabilities and resources" to aid the response of state governments, including the support of numerous federal departments and agencies (NRF 2008). Under the auspices of the NRF, the NRP outlines the general governmental approach to disaster events, whether resulting from natural or unnatural circumstances. According to NRP, the emphasis for initial response to emergency or disaster situations is placed on local governments, while state agencies and the Department of Homeland Security coordinate logistics operations (NRF 2008). However, the NRP also "provides mechanisms for expedited and proactive federal support to ensure critical life-saving assistance and incident containment capabilities" for "high-impact" but "low-probability" incidents, such as the Deepwater Horizon spill.

The questions remain whether such expedited and proactive federal support, beyond the scope of federal contingency planning, to contain the incident was present following the spill, and if so, was it adequate? The nature of the federal response to a major oil spill should be central as outlined by OPA, NCP, NRP, and subsequent modifications of these guidelines. The fact that federal, state, and local governments have an official response and contingency plan for oil spills implies a certain level of accountability, but such accountability is rife with unclear, divisive, or overlapping responsibilities. Moreover, the level of federal accountability is especially difficult to measure given that contingency planning differs based on the region's circumstance. Likewise, the necessary level of executive involvement is difficult to determine and is linked to social, political, economic, and technical circumstances surrounding the spill. Such circumstances shaped a much different scenario for President Bush in 1989.

Comparing *Exxon Valdez* and Deepwater Horizon

In March 1989, the *Exxon Valdez* ran aground spilling 250,000 to 750,000 barrels of crude oil into Prince William Sound, Alaska. At the time, multiple federal and state statutes defined oil spill governance, whereas certain federal agencies were tasked with developing and implementing oil spill regulations (Ramseur 2010: 7). In considering the actions of President Bush during *Exxon Valdez,* it is essential to note federal authority for oil spills at that time. According to a 2010 Congressional Research Service report, there were five primary federal authorities when *Exxon Valdez* occurred: 1) the CWA (1972); 2) the Deepwater Port Act (DWPA; 1974); 3) the Trans-Alaska Pipeline Authorization Act (1973); 4) the Outer Continental Shelf Lands Act Amendments (1978); and 5) the NCP (1968) (Ramseur 2010: 7–8).

The CWA provided the "broadest authority" for oil spill response and facilitated the creation of the "311 Fund" which appropriated federal funds for restoration and remediation (Ramseur 2010: 7). The DWPA and the Trans-Alaska Pipeline Authorization Act outlined response procedures for oil spills in deepwater ports and around the Trans-Alaska Pipeline System, respectively. The Outer Continental Shelf Lands Act Amendments, of all pre-*Exxon Valdez* oil spill governance, pertains most directly to the Deepwater Horizon incident. This act responded to concern over spills by "oil extraction facilities in federal offshore waters" and established federal parameters for determining liability in such situations (Ramseur 2010: 8). Finally, the NCP, discussed earlier, was first established in 1968 after U.S. officials observed the *Torrey Canyon* spill off the coast of England. The NCP highlighted the federal government's response procedures during oil spills or other releases of hazardous material (Ramseur 2010: 8). With these five primary authorities for oil spill response, Bush turned to his newly appointed administration for a response.

Much like the Gulf oil spill's unexpectedly burdensome impact on Obama's agenda, the *Exxon Valdez* spill was one of the first major challenges for the Bush presidency. The American public, however, seemed to have a different set of expectations for Bush than they did for Obama two decades later. Such a difference in public expectation creates two very different scenarios when comparing *Exxon Valdez* and Deepwater Horizon. According to Fareed Zakaria, the Bush administration denied the federal government had any responsibility for the clean-up effort (Zakaria 2010). Zakaria points to the rise in arguments for increased government control surrounding Deepwater in the current political arena, although, as he also suggests, officials in the Bush administration asserted government involvement would be counterproductive during the *Exxon Valdez* spill (Zakaria, 2010). Zakaria argues that more pressure was on Obama than was on his counterpart in the only comparable oil spill in U.S. history. The pressure centered on a public call to express emotion, or to "emote" as Zakaria puts it. The public was frustrated and looked for a "kick-butt" attitude rather than measured leadership. Indeed, there was no effort to implicate Bush in the 1989 accident (Zakaria 2010).

Scholars such as Daniel Drezner argue that, although parallels are drawn between Obama and Bush, and the *Exxon Valdez* and Deepwater incidents, the situations are too distant for accurate comparison. As Drezner points out, although it seems necessary to compare actions of presidents in similar situations, this is not necessarily a sound methodology for rating Obama's handling of the Gulf oil spill. The Deepwater spill was predicated by unique circumstances so it is difficult to compare them.

Yet, according to a 1989 NBC report, the *Exxon Valdez* spill was viewed as a test for the incoming president's claim that he was the "environmental president" (Palmer and Miklaszewski 1989: 1–2). Similar to the public dissatisfaction with BP's efforts to diminish or mitigate the impact of the Deepwater oil leak, the public was "increasingly disillusioned" by Exxon's efforts (Palmer and Miklaszewski 1989). Like Obama, Bush faced critics who questioned his position to increase domestic offshore drilling (this was Obama's pre-oil spill position). But unlike Obama, Bush was only three months into office and had the benefit of still being on his presidential "honeymoon." Bush claimed the spill had not changed his position in support of drilling. Obama, however, approved a formal moratorium on offshore drilling on May 28, 2010 (Clayton 2010: 1). The moratorium was set for six months and applied to pending and current operations in waters deeper than 500 feet (Clayton 2010). During the moratorium, offshore drilling operations were forced to comply with new regulations aimed at preventing another Deepwater incident until the ban on deepwater drilling was lifted by the Obama administration on October 12, 2010, citing industry's compliance with modified standards and the inevitable negative impact on Gulf Coast economies (Cohen 2010: 1–3).

Confusion over authority characterized many aspects of the public and private sector's response to the Deepwater disaster. On July 14, 2010, Joe Stephens, a journalist for *The Washington Post*, succinctly captured the confusion over who was in charge in the immediate aftermath of both the *Valdez* and Deepwater spills:

> In the immediate aftermath of the Alaska spill, as in the gulf, there was confusion over who was in charge—oil companies or government officials. Federal authorities eventually asserted themselves but lacked the equipment and personnel to stem the damage. Storms slowed the response and spread contamination. Cleanup technology was old and ineffective. Environmentalists questioned the toxicity of dispersants and asked whether oil companies were using chemicals to hide damage. (Stephens 2010)

Reports and Public Opinion on the Oil Spill

A litany of reports following the 1989 disaster recommended "strengthening government preparedness, clarifying lines of authority and improving cleanup technology" (Stephens 2010). Afterward, Bush's supportive rhetoric was manifested within legislation such as the OPA and its expansion of NCP. Interestingly, Bush's Environmental Protection Agency (EPA) head, William Reilly, later co-chaired a presidential commission investigating the liability of BP and others for the Gulf oil spill. The report was released on January 11, 2011 and produced several conclusions:

1. Deepwater energy exploration and production, particularly at the frontiers of experience, involve risks for which neither industry nor government has been

adequately prepared, but for which they can and must be prepared in the future.

2. To assure human safety and environmental protection, regulatory oversight of leasing, energy exploration, and production require reforms beyond those already initiated and in the areas of regulatory oversight and decision-making process.

3. Because regulatory oversight alone will not be sufficient to ensure adequate safety, the oil and gas industry will need to take its own, unilateral steps to increase safety (Graham et al. 2011: vii).

The first of these conclusions highlights the lack of government preparedness for situations involving ruptures in deepwater oil operations, particularly ones with unique characteristics such as Deepwater. The next two indicate the need for increased oversight and accountability in both government and private industry. These suggestions help validate the notion that the federal government allowed the private sector too much control relative to the industry's limited public accountability mechanisms. It must also be noted that the relaxation of such regulations occurred under President George W. Bush. Furthermore, the government's options for legitimizing their accountability were and remain subject to the limitations of OPA and NCP.

Undoubtedly, numerous factors contributed and will continue to contribute to the successes and failures of a government's response to an instantaneous or ongoing disaster. Ali Farazmand discusses three variables complicating emergency management and response that apply to the responses by Bush in 1989 and Obama in 2010. First, "task complexity" is based on the notion that response and recovery tasks can be "too complex" for any random agency to handle and specialized skill sets may be necessary for unique circumstances (Farazmand 2001). Farazmand argues that "differences in skills, resource availability, organization orientations or legal jurisdictions can impede initial response efforts." (During the *Valdez,* the primary clean-up concern rested with salvaging the spilled oil. Both the USCG and Exxon were better equipped and possessed more experience with salvage than state, local, or environmental organizations, and were consequently tasked with the clean-up responsibility (Farazmand 2001). Similarly, during the Deepwater leak, specialized deepwater technology needed to repair the ruptured well was available through BP and other private-sector actors. In disaster situations, the president's responsibility should be to coordinate and manage tasks as well as resources.

Second, "organizational incompatibility" refers to the lack of "open channels of communication, information sharing and coordination" among public and private response organizations leading to flawed response on the organizational level (Farazmand 2001). Such concerns plagued both the Bush and Obama administrations. After gaps in the national government's preparedness for natural and man-made disasters were exposed during the terror attacks of 9/11 and four years later in 2005 after Hurricane Katrina, the federal government became quite conscious of the importance of interagency and interorganizational communication. Thus, many of the organizational incompatibility issues have been improved in the past five years.

Third, "political incompatibility" means that "responding organizations may not operate according to the same processes or decision-making criteria" (Farazmand 2001). For instance, BP, a private company, and the USCG, the on-sight federal authority in charge, have completely different processes for accomplishing tasks and making decisions. Such disconnects lead to miscommunication and a public perception that the response is being poorly handled. Political incompatibility helps make the case that a scenario like Deepwater Horizon requires the president to act as a leader, coordinating the complex response hierarchy that emerges from a litany of laws (OPA 1990) and practical abilities (deepwater technology). Bush was criticized for not taking a more central or expedient role during Katrina (Sylves 2006). The same critique can be leveled at Obama's actions during the Gulf oil spill.

Public Opinion

Also useful in analyzing Obama's handling of the spill is public opinion. Indeed, the American public is demanding accountability for the oil spill from both BP and the federal government.

Gallup has tracked public approval of both Obama's and BP's handling of the oil spill. In early June 2010, 40 percent of Americans approved of the Obama administration's handling of the spill, 46 percent disapproved, and 13 percent had no opinion (Gallup 2010). A little more than two months later, in mid-August, a Gallup poll revealed that 44 percent of Americans approved of the president's actions (Gallup, 2010). As expected, the early two-month mark of the oil spill reflected the lowest presidential approval rating, due mostly to the failure to cap the leaking well.

In mid-June, Gallup also polled Americans on their opinions of BP's handling of the spill. The polls indicated that 16 percent of Americans approved of BP's handling, 76 percent disapproved, and 8 percent had no opinion (Gallup 2010). The approval ratings doubled two months later with 31 percent of Americans approving of BP's action, but 64 percent still disapproved (Gallup 2010). As with the public's perception of Obama's handling of the spill, BP's approval rating was lower at the earlier two-month mark than at the four-month mark, meaning federal and private-sector actions were largely seen as ineffective during the initial two months following the spill. Beyond the question of the public's view of the handling of the spill, Americans seem to be closely divided over who should lead the spill response and remediation efforts. On June 15, 2010, 45 percent of Americans expressed their preference for the federal government to lead the spill response and 49 percent favored BP (Gallup 2010). Taken together, public opinion indicated that BP and the federal government were perceived as almost equally responsible for the clean-up effort.

Oil Spill Lessons

Obama appears to have relinquished too much authority to the private sector and demanded too little accountability in the immediate aftermath of the spill, leading to a troubled response effort.

As discussed earlier, an atmosphere of confusion over who should be in charge was present during both the *Exxon Valdez* and Deepwater spills. However, the circumstances surrounding the *Valdez* spill were completely different than those surrounding Deepwater, as outlined previously. It was made clear, however, by Obama on May 27, 2010, that his administration was in charge and had been directing BP's activities from the beginning. However, because some aspects of the scenario were comparable to *Exxon*, especially the initial confusion over who should lead the clean-up efforts, the Obama administration clearly neglected to incorporate all lessons from the *Valdez* incident.

Initially, the USCG was indecisive about various issues, including whether or not to burn the surfacing oil, which in the long-term has less environmental impact on the air than it would on water. It is believed that early opportunities to burn the oil were passed up due to reluctance to act over pollution concerns (Lieberman 2010). Additionally, coordination was lacking, as Obama's administration failed to enlist the Department of Defense in deploying deepwater equipment and technology until ninety days had passed since the beginning of the spill (Lieberman 2010). OPA provides that the president appoint either the USCG or EPA as the federal response authority, but holds the executive accountable for the actions of either actor. President Obama gave too much leeway to the USCG in the initial Deepwater response and ultimately failed to recognize its limitations early on.

A 2010 opinion piece argued that "the exceedingly adversarial tone and relationship that Obama has established with BP and its partners will, at best, slow the response and recovery effort" (McNeill and Walsh 2010). These authors argued that Obama was posing a serious risk to the future of cooperation between government and the private sector, citing the negative tone administration officials have expressed with BP and other liable private-sector actors in the wake of Deepwater. At the same time, the public was clamoring for Obama to "get tough" on BP. Either way, the argument highlights the vital importance and inevitability of a workable relationship between the federal government and the private sector.

Many critics level the argument that a lack of a clear command structure prevented the movement of critical resources, such as booms and skimmers, into the Gulf at the most critical times. A *Christian Science Monitor* journalist even described the response command structure as a "'Gordian Knot' for local officials requesting help and resources" (Jonsson, 2010). The Obama administration failed to clarify the command structure of the Deepwater response, which increased tension in the effected region by stalling the deployment of workers to initiate the clean-up efforts.

By allowing BP to have full reign in decision making, the federal ultimately undermined local efforts (Tilove, 2010). Some even claimed that the Coast Guard's role was more "protective" of BP than anything else (Tilove, 2010). One local authority reported:

> Instead of embracing the local authorities' involvement and resource capacity, local authority was met with resistance, exclusion and power struggles. . . . This decision, contemplated or not, resulted in adversarial relationships between the local agencies, the state and

governor's office, and BP and the United States Coast Guard. (Tilove 2010)

Zakaria and other respected analysts argue that Obama should "lead, not emote." Obama's actions, according to Zakaria, amounted to "government as theater," which resulted in only the "impression of resolution" (Zakaria, 2010). Yet, at the same time, the president was criticized for not showing enough passion or anger over the spill. The public and media attitude toward Bush during the *Exxon Valdez* incident was unemotional compared with the same attitudes expressed toward Obama. The media and public demanded an unrealistic and impractical reaction of Obama, urging an "emotionally charged, angry response from Obama, demanding that he kick butt rather than meet with experts and advisors" (Zakaria 2010).

On May 27, 2010, Obama claimed the federal government had been in charge of the response effort from the disaster's beginning and that BP was operating at Obama's direction. This announcement marked a change in tone, as the administration had previously claimed to be overseeing BPs operations, but taking a limited role as BP was better equipped to handle the situation (Staff writer, 2010). The question remains whether this assertion was helpful or not. It is undoubtedly good and necessary, and consistent with federal guidelines, that the president asserts himself as the primary leader of the response effort, but to do so after criticisms started to surface,—a little over a month into the spill—was perceived by some to be forced and artificial. From some perspectives, Obama's late May announcement only made the administration appear weaker.

Conclusion

Most oil spill disasters are a discrete event. But in the case of the Deepwater Horizon, oil flowed from the ruptured well for three and a half months. Thus, it seemed inaccurate to draw on previous experience in responding to some aspects of it, although not all. The complexities and contradictions of this event include the fact that the private sector had much more appropriate technology to try to stop the leak than did the government, so the president had to rely on BP. At the same time, the administration failed to recognize that these unique circumstances demanded enhanced executive attention early on and thus slowed the response. Additionally, the OPA seems to have the assumption that a spill will be more of an instantaneous event, rather than something that goes on for months. Thus, components of OPA are more focused on clean-up and remediation rather than stopping a leak.

Ultimately, the private sector was granted too much managerial power (or control of the details) in the immediate response following the Deepwater incident, especially considering the limits and contradictions of accountability mechanisms related to spill response and spill contingency plans. This was especially true of the public relations response to the spill. Given that the private sector had more appropriate technology for dealing with the problem, President Obama should have been visible in at least informing the public regarding the response efforts. The public was angry over the lack of resolution and looked to the president to at least acknowledge this anger. Whether this delay was an attempt to avoid emerging rhetorical stereotypes (i.e., the "angry black man") or an attempt at working more effectively with the private-sector response, the public viewed it as a lack of concern. A more forceful public response earlier in the disaster would have given Americans more confidence in the government's efforts.

Works Cited

Blum, J. and M. Fisk. "BP sued by Obama administration over worst oil spill." *Bloomberg* (15 Dec. 2010). http://www.businessweek.com/news/2010-12-15/bp-sued-by-obama-administration-over-worst-oil-spill.html.

Clayton, M. "Offshore drilling moratorium: good for the Gulf, bad for the economy?" *The Christian Science Monitor* (27 July 2010). http://www.csmonitor.com/USA/Politics/2010/0727/Offshore-drilling-moratorium-good-for-the-Gulf-bad-for-the-economy.

Cohen, T. "Obama administration lifts deep-water drilling moratorium." *CNN* (12 Oct. 2010). http://articles.cnn.com/2010-10-12/us/drilling.moratorium_1_deep-water-drilling-drilling-rig-oil-drilling/3?_s=PM:US.

Department of Homeland Security. National Response Framework. (2008). http://www.dhs.gov/xlibrary/assets/NRP_Brochure.pdf.

Douligeris, C., P. Tebeau, S. Snedoker, et al. "Study of Gulf Coast oil spill contingency plans with respect to remediation and restoration." *Sea Grant Alabama-Mississippi* (Oct. 1997). http://www.masgc.org/pdf/masgp/97-024.pdf.

Environmental Protection Agency "National Contingency Plan overview." *U.S. Environmental Protection Agency, Emergency Management* (Dec. 2009). http://www.epa.gov/oem/content/lawsregs/ncpover.htm.

Enzler, S.M. "Top 10 anthropogenic and natural environmental disasters." *Lenntech* (Sept. 2006). http://www.lenntech.com/environmentaldisasters.htm#5._Major_oil_spills_of_the_20th_and_21st_century.

Farazmand, A., ed. *Handbook of Crisis and Emergency Management.* New York, NY: Mareel Dekker, Inc., 2001.

Gallup. Oil Spill in the Gulf of Mexico. *Gallup* (2010). http://www.gallup.com/poll/140978/Oil-Spill-Gulf-Mexico.aspx.

Graham, B., W. Reilly, F. Beinecke, D. Boesch, T. Garcia, C. Murray, F. Ulmer. (Jan. 2011). "Deep Water: The Gulf oil disaster and the future of offshore drilling: Report to the President." *National Commission on the BP Deepwater Horizon Oil Spill and Offshore Drilling* (Jan. 2011). https://s3.amazonaws.com/pdf_final/DEEPWATER_ReporttothePresident_FINAL.pdf

Jonsson, P. "Top five bottlenecks in the Gulf oil spill response." *The Christian Science Monitor* (1 July 2010). http://www.csmonitor.com/USA/2010/0701/Top-five-bottlenecks-in-the-Gulf-oil-spill-response.

Lieberman, B. "The federal response to the oil spill: lessons to be learned." *Heritage Foundation* (18 May 2010). Retrieved from http://www.heritage.org/research/reports/2010/05/the-federal-response-to-the-oil-spill-lessons-to-be-learned.

McNeill, J.B. and B. Walsh. "Oil spill response sets poor precedent for public–private cooperation." *Heritage Foundation* (22 June 2010). http://www.heritage.org/research/reports/2010/06/oil-spill-response-sets-poor-precedent-for-public-private-cooperation.

National Oil and Hazardous Substances Pollution Contingency Plan (NCP). *Department of the Interior* http://www.doi.gov/oepc/response/ncp.htm.

Palmer, J. and J. Miklaszewski. "George H.W. Bush on Exxon Valdez and ANWR." *NBC Today Show* (29 March 1989).

Ramseur, J.L. "Oil spills in U.S. coastal waters: background, governance, and issues for Congress." *Congressional Research Service* (30 April 2010). http://fpc.state.gov/documents/organization/142741.pdf.

Staff writer. "Obama: U.S. in charge of oil spill response." *CBS New* (27 May 2010). http://www.cbsnews.com/stories/2010/05/27/politics/main6524264.shtml.

Stephens, J. "Lessons from Exxon *Valdez* spill have gone unheeded." *The Washington Post* (14 July 2010). http://www.washingtonpost.com/wp-dyn/content/article/2010/07/13/AR2010071306291.html

Sylves, R.T. "President Bush and Hurricane Katrina: A Presidential Leadership Study." *The ANNALS of the American Academy of Political and Social Science.* Vol. 604, No. 26 (2006).

Tilove, J. "Gulf of Mexico oil spill response guided too much by BP, St. Bernard president says." *NOLA.com* (22 Sept. 2010). http://www.

nola.com/news/gulf-oil-spill/index.ssf/2010/09/gulf_of_mexico_oil_
spill_respo_3.html.
Zakaria, F. "Presidential pony show." *Newsweek* (13 June 2010). http://
www.newsweek.com/2010/06/13/presidential-pony-show.html.

Foreign Policy and National Security

Chapter 15

Inherited Wars

Afghanistan and Iraq

Tom Lansford
Jack Covarrubias

Throughout U.S. history, newly elected presidents have inherited conflicts from their predecessors. The regularity of presidential elections every four years has meant that wars or conflicts have overlapped the terms of U.S. chief executives. This trend accelerated in the twentieth century as the United States assumed a broader role in regional and global affairs and then emerged as a superpower in the post-World War II era. In general, presidents who come into office in the midst of a conflict have tended to fall into one of two broad categories: successors, those who continued the strategies of their predecessors, or innovators, those who implemented broad shifts in strategy different from their predecessors. The majority of chief executives have fallen into the first category because of the inherent risks and dynamics associated with changing paths in the middle of a campaign. However, one tendency that has been fairly constant is the trend for these twentieth century inherited conflicts to end in either a stalemate or defeat for the United States.

President Barack Obama assumed office in the middle of two specific conflicts, Afghanistan and Iraq, and the broader, less defined war on terror. In many ways, Obama faced foreign and security challenges that were very reminiscent of the Cold War. However, the new president also faced major domestic problems, including the worst economic recession since the 1930s. The economic downturn constrained policy options and exacerbated the general tendency for presidents to concentrate on domestic policy in their first years in office (Light 2009). Thus, the new president had a great deal of incentive to be an innovator by finding a way out of Iraq and then Afghanistan, a position that many assumed he would take. However, President Obama inherited a solid plan put together by the Bush administration in January 2007 that was beginning to show unexpected success on the ground in Iraq by the time he assumed office. With the risk for complete failure seemingly lessened, the Obama administration in its first years in office generally adopted the successor approach by keeping many of the strategic choices of President Bush.

Inherited Conflicts

As aforementioned, U.S. history in the twentieth century is rife with inherited conflicts. Harry S. Truman inherited the management of World War II following the death of Franklin D. Roosevelt on April 12, 1945. Truman left office in 1953 in the midst of the Korean War, leaving the conclusion of the conflict to his successor, Dwight D. Eisenhower. The Vietnam War spanned the presidencies of John F. Kennedy, Lyndon B. Johnson, Richard M. Nixon, and Gerald R. Ford. A number of smaller conflicts also transcended presidential administrations, including the Somali conflict from George H. W. Bush to William J. Clinton.

Of the significant conflicts (more than one hundred U.S. casualties, wounded or dead) since World War II, the Korean War (1950–1953), Vietnam War (1955–1975), Somali Intervention (1992–1993), Afghan conflict (2001–present), and the Iraq War (2003–present) were inherited conflicts. The interventions in the Dominican Republic (1965–1966), Beirut (1982–1984), and Grenada (1983), as well as the invasion of Panama (1989) and the Persian Gulf War (1990–1991) were resolved within a single presidency. Inherited conflicts pose particular domestic and international risks for incoming presidents. First, in most cases, the management of the ongoing conflict was a major campaign issue. In the elections of 1952, 1968, and 2008, the winning candidates' campaigns were highly critical of the incumbent administration's military strategy. Consequently, incoming chief executives such as Obama faced significant pressure to change the fortunes of war and implement new strategies and tactics. Likewise, all of the inherited conflicts in the post-World War II era involved a change in the party in power in the White House (with the exception of Kennedy to Johnson). Second, incentives to end a conflict or withdraw military forces can be constrained by international factors, ranging from geo-strategic calculations to the need to maintain alliances. For example, the Korean War took on connotations related to the broader Cold War. Both Iraq and Afghanistan have repercussions associated with the War on Terror.

Approaches to Inherited Conflicts

Presidents who enter office in the midst of an ongoing conflict are typically either successors or innovators in their approach to the war. Successor presidents continue the main tenets of military and political strategies utilized by their predecessors. Innovators attempt to implement dramatic changes to the nation's wartime military strategies and tactics. Presidents can be innovators and successors simultaneously when dealing with different conflicts. For instance, Clinton significantly changed the mission and scope of the U.S. forces during the intervention in Somali, but generally maintained the Bush-era efforts to contain the Iraqi regime of Saddam Hussein through enforcement of UN sanctions and no-fly zones in northern and southern Iraq.

Successors

Most presidents tend to be successors even if they campaigned on pledges to dramatically alter the nation's approach. There are a number of factors that underlie this trend, including institutional inertia among either the executive and legislative branches, or both. The effort to formulate, enact, and implement new approaches to a conflict can be stymied by the bureaucracies of the executive branch, including the military. Additionally, and especially if the United States is losing or stalemated in a conflict, Congress is often risk-adverse in terms of backing bold or innovative new approaches (for additional conversation on the role of Congress see Lindsay 1994; Powell 2006; Stevenson 2007) There also are military factors that constrain the implementation of new policies. For instance, there may be domestic political limitations on the number of troops that can be deployed. Alternatively, the military may not be able to develop and implement effective tactics to defeat an enemy because of domestic factors (as was the case during the Vietnam War).

Presidents who inherit a conflict also face the fear of failure and the concurrent political risks associated with a military defeat in the early period of a new presidency. There also are very significant international repercussions from a military defeat, or even the perception of a loss. Defeat undermines the credibility of the U.S. military abroad and may raise the threshold for future military action to unacceptable levels. The most ardent example of this phenomenon would be the "Vietnam Syndrome" which emerged in the aftermath of the U.S. withdrawal from Vietnam in 1974.

The final major factor in prevalence of successor-type presidencies is the preservation and promotion of U.S. interests. There are interests that prompt a president to use military force (even if the decision to enter a conflict involves a miscalculation of interests or of the repercussions of the conflict). The same interests that compel the use of force by one president remain when a new president enters office. Additionally, once engaged in combat, victory itself, or at least the avoidance of defeat, becomes a powerful interest that limits the policy options available to chief executives.

Innovators

Although incoming presidents often claim they will develop and implement sweeping changes in the management of a conflict, true innovators are rare. Instead, presidents tend to adopt only marginal changes. Innovators have to change the nation's goals or interests in the conflict. They also must develop new military strategies and tactics in order to pursue new goals. Often, this includes a change in military leadership through the appointment of a new theater commander or secretary of defense. Innovators typically will change the level of commitment by the United States. That could mean the deployment of new troops or the withdrawal of forces. Finally, there is a notable change in rhetoric and perception within the administration.

Eisenhower is the best example of an innovator in his management of the end of the Korean War. Eisenhower had been very critical of the Truman administration's management of the conflict and he was elected partially because of the American public's confidence that the former general's military experience would ensure a U.S. victory. In a major speech on October 25, 1952, Eisenhower declared:

The biggest fact about the Korean War is this: It was never inevitable, it was never inescapable, no fantastic fiat of history decreed that little South Korea—in the summer of 1950—would fatally tempt Communist aggressors as their easiest victim. . . . There is a Korean war—and we are fighting it—for the simplest of reasons: Because free leadership failed to check and to turn back Communist ambition before it savagely attacked us. The Korean war—more perhaps than any other war in history—simply and swiftly followed the collapse of our political defenses. There is no other reason than this: We failed to read and to outwit the totalitarian mind. (Eisenhower 1952)

Before he was inaugurated, Eisenhower traveled to the Korean Peninsula on an information-gathering effort. He met with senior military officers and South Korean political leaders and came home convinced that the Chinese and Koreans could not be defeated without unacceptable U.S. casualties (Smith 2009). Once in office, Eisenhower replaced Gen. James Van Fleet, who supported an expansion of the conflict, with Gen. Maxwell Taylor. Eisenhower exerted additional pressure on the Chinese and North Koreans by deploying more troops and launching limited military offensives. Meanwhile the U.S. explosion of a hydrogen bomb changed the strategic balance of power between the United States and the Soviet Union and Eisenhower signaled a willingness to use nuclear weapons, a dramatic reversal of Truman's stance on the issue. While increasing pressure, Eisenhower also signaled a willingness to restart negotiations. The resumption of talks was aided by the death of Soviet premier Joseph Stalin in March 1953 and the desire of the new Soviet regime to end the conflict in light of what appeared to be Eisenhower's willingness to escalate the war. An armistice was signed on July 26, 1953.

The peace deal involved significant political risks for the president. The former general was opposed by many of his closest advisors, including Secretary of State John Foster Dulles and Secretary of Defense Charles Wilson (Smith 2009) who both asserted that the United States had to achieve a military victory in the conflict in order to maintain credibility. He faced significant criticism from Congress and the press for agreeing to allow Korea to remain divided. The peace deal that Eisenhower approved would not have been political feasible for his predecessor, but the former general's military stature allowed him to generally deflect the domestic political costs and maintain the public's confidence in his administration's ability to lead the nation in the Cold War.

Obama's Inherited Conflicts

Obama entered office confronted by two ongoing and highly complicated specific conflicts and a broader and less defined global campaign against terrorism. Obama had been highly critical of the Bush administration's conduct of the ongoing wars. In a July 2008 op-ed for *The New York Times,* Obama wrote about Iraq:

> Ending the war is essential to meeting our broader strategic goals, starting in Afghanistan and Pakistan, where the Taliban is resurgent and Al Qaeda has a safe haven. Iraq is not the central front in the war on terrorism, and it never has been. As Adm. Mike Mullen, the chairman of the Joint Chiefs of Staff, recently pointed out, we won't have sufficient resources to finish the job in Afghanistan until we reduce our commitment to Iraq. (Obama 2008)

During the campaign, Obama repeatedly promised to withdraw forces from Iraq and to bolster the anti-Taliban and anti-al-Qaeda efforts in Afghanistan and Pakistan. Obama was specifically critical of the Bush administration's military "surge" in Iraq whereby the United States deployed an additional 30,000 troops in order to end the ongoing insurgency.

Once in office, in April 2009, Obama, in an action reminiscent of Eisenhower, traveled to Iraq to meet with military and political leaders in an effort to gain a better understanding of the situation as he and his administration developed a promised new approach. Obama faced considerable constraints, along with some unexpected advantages. First, by the time he entered office, the insurgency in Iraq had significantly diminished by a combination of the U.S. troop surge and a change in tactics whereby the U.S.-led coalition and the Iraqi government empowered Sunni groups to take on a larger role in providing security (the effort was dubbed the Sunni Awakening, as Sunni tribal and religious leaders increasingly rejected terrorism and the anti-regime insurgency in exchange for a range of incentives including greater autonomy and direct payments). Second, Obama's military strategies and tactics faced relatively little opposition in Congress. From 2006 to 2010, the Democrats had commanding majorities in both houses of Congress. Additionally, Republicans supported Obama's efforts to increase the number of U.S. troops in Afghanistan and to expand U.S. military and intelligence operations against the Taliban and al-Qaeda in Pakistan. Third, Obama kept the Bush administration's senior defense leadership in place. Secretary of Defense Robert Gates remained secretary under Obama and the senior field commanders were initially left in place. These actions represented a pragmatism that Obama endeavored to apply to both Afghanistan and Iraq. Yet, they also underscored the new president's decision to not undertake dramatic changes in the basic strategy and tactics employed in both conflicts.

Obama and Iraq

Obama entered office as violence in Iraq had significantly declined. Meanwhile, the Bush administration had begun negotiations with the Iraqi government of Prime Minister Nouri al-Maliki over the withdrawal of U.S. forces from Iraq. The Iraqis had applied increasing pressure on the United States to withdraw forces, although the Bush administration had been reluctant to set a precise timetable for the redeployments, asserting that such a schedule would allow the insurgents to bid their time. However, in the waning days of the administration, talks over a timetable were finalized. The result was a status of forces agreement that was approved by the Iraqi parliament in November 2008. Bush and Maliki signed the accord on December 15 of that year. The agreement called for the withdrawal of U.S. combat forces in 2010 and the complete withdrawal of U.S. troops by the end of 2011.

Obama ultimately adopted a successor approach to Iraq. The main goals of Obama's Iraq policy were the measured withdrawal of U.S. forces, concurrent with the solidification of a strong, democratic government in the country. These goals were in line with those of the Bush administration in 2008. Of course, the initial objectives of the Bush administration in 2003 had been the removal of the regime of Saddam Hussein, the destruction of Iraq's weapons of mass destruction (WMD) programs, and the creation of stable, democratic Iraqi government. The Saddam regime was toppled, but the lack of WMDs undermined U.S. creditability and eroded both domestic and international support for the Bush administration. Significantly, Obama did not immediately withdraw troops from Iraq or greatly accelerate the planned withdrawals negotiated under the Bush administration.

On the contrary, the Bush administration instituted a number of significant changes in Iraq strategy in the waning months of his administration that were originally opposed by then senator and candidate Obama and opposition within the congress, but subsequently embraced as the way forward by the Obama administration. Granted, the policy changes represented in what was dubbed "The New Way Forward" and presented by President Bush in January 2007 reflected the lessons learned from the hard realities of several years of war in Iraq at that stage and had yet to show significant improvement of circumstances on the ground. Likewise, candidate Obama was in the midst of a presidential primary election and found it necessary to distinguish his policy differences from the front runner Democratic candidate, Hillary Clinton. In a campaign speech in Iowa in September 2007, candidate Obama presented his primary objectives:

My plan for ending the war would turn the page in Iraq by removing our combat troops from Iraq's civil war, by taking a new approach to press for a new accord on reconciliation within Iraq; by talking to all of Iraq's neighbors to press for a compact in the region; and by confronting the human costs of this war.

Obama would go on to demand the immediate beginning of a phased "combat" troop withdrawal among other significant changes—a position that at least tacitly allowed room for a continued presence of U.S. forces within the country. He had maintained since at least 2004 that the United States had an obligation to see Iraq through although he did move away from it as the 2008 election cycle heated up and sectarian violence in the region was flaring. This is in line with Obama's opinion on war with Iraq as early as 2002. In a speech at an anti-war rally in October 2002, then-senate candidate Obama espoused:

I know that even a successful war against Iraq will require a U.S. occupation of undetermined length, at undetermined cost, with undetermined consequences. I know that an invasion of Iraq without a clear rationale and without strong international support will only fan the flames of the Middle East, and encourage the worst, rather than best, impulses of the Arab world, and strengthen the recruitment arm of al-Qaeda. I am not opposed to all wars. I'm opposed to dumb wars.

By the end of 2007 and throughout 2008, it became increasingly clear that circumstances in Iraq had significantly changed for the better with much of the change attributed to the revised strategy put in place in January 2007 by the Bush administration; namely, the troop surge that Obama opposed and a change in senior military leadership and revised strategy on the ground. By Obama's inauguration in January 2009, the Obama strategy proposed in the rhetoric running up to the presidential election was clearly outdated and counterproductive. The immediate institution of a phased withdrawal from Iraq and U.S. military leadership change would more likely setback the rapid gains on the ground up to the point. Namely, sectarian violence was at an all-time low, combat-related deaths of U.S. forces was on the decline, and life was returning to some semblance of normalcy after six years of warfare.

To President Obama's credit, in February 2009 in a speech at Camp Lejeune, a preference is apparent to maintain the Bush strategy that had proven itself successful in Iraq. Although he does not directly acknowledge Bush's strategy, he does acknowledge the great amount of progress that has been made and embraces the major steps forward that were initially made by Bush. Most importantly, Obama kept the Bush strategy team that had been waging the campaign in Iraq; he acknowledged the need for a large military presence in Iraq in a post-"combat" environment; and he maintained the timeline for withdrawal that was negotiated by the Bush administration.

As part of President Bush's shift in strategy in 2007, a number of personnel changes were made that directly impacted the strategy on the ground in Iraq and where held over by the Obama administration in important politically charged positions. Most notably, Gen. David Petraeus, who first saw combat in the Iraq War in 2003 and later commander of Multi-National Force-Iraq and United States Central Command, and Gen. Raymond T. Odierno, who succeeded Petraeus as commander of Multi-National Forces-Iraq and its transition to United States Forces-Iraq continued to receive the support of the president. Obama also kept Gates who succeeded Donald Rumsfeld as secretary of defense in December 2006. These three key positions promoted and executed the bulk of the 2007 Iraq War troop surge and subsequent Bush era Iraq strategy. It is clear that by keeping these key leaders, no drastic change in strategy was expected to occur moving into the Obama administration.

Likewise, the timeline for withdrawal was essentially the same as that agreed by in late 2008 by President Bush and Iraqi Prime Minister Nuri al-Maliki. President Obama ordered U.S. combat troops to cease combat operations by August 2010. What seems more pressing, however, are the stark similarities between both presidents' commitment to Iraq. In both cases, Bush and Obama supported the continued presence of U.S. forces in the region to prosecute terrorism, to continue training Iraqi security forces, and to protect the sovereignty of Iraq in case of new sectarian violence. Indirectly said is the benefit of having a large robust U.S. presence in the Middle East. Current policy expects up to 50,000 American troops to maintain a presence in Iraq until the end of 2011. The big question that Obama will face going into the 2012 presidential election is whether that time line has been kept. The Obama administration has already indicated that it may be interested in maintaining a larger U.S. presence than expected after the December 2011 deadline. Speaking before the House Armed Service Committee on February 16, 2011, Gates stated: "There is certainly on our part an interest in having an additional presence" in reference to keeping more than the 150 military trainers who are slated to stay post-December 31, 2011.

Obama and Afghanistan

The situation in Afghanistan that President Obama inherited from President Bush was different than in Iraq in 2008. Although the January 2007 strategy in Iraq was bearing fruit in Iraq, by January 2009, Afghanistan was in the midst of an upswing in insurgent violence from the Taliban. The failure of the Afghan government to develop adequate governance outside of the main strongholds coupled with the failure to eliminate the Taliban as a rival force in the rural area of the state left an abundance of space for insurgent growth (Jones 2008). Jones looks at the growth of the Afghan insurgency from 2002 to 2008 reporting a rise of more than 400 percent during this time frame and a rise in related deaths over 800 percent.

In a paper written in 2009, Najibullah Lafraie succinctly defines the problem as it existed that is summarized here. First, the Bush strategy did not want to repeat the failures of the Soviet occupation of a decade before. Therefore, in an effort to minimize exposure of American forces, Bush chose to minimize the number of forces used. This process essentially reinforced itself as commitments to Iraq beginning in 2003 increasingly absorbed materials and resources. Concurrently, Bush supported traditional regional warlords to make up for the shortfall in in-theater forces further eroding the credibility of the central government. Third, the Taliban were capable of maintaining a significant operational depth by using the logistical support of cross-border bases and training camps "hidden" within Pakistan. Finally, the Karzai government itself had some significant structural problems that are exacerbated by an under commitment of financial and logistical support by the international community.

The end result is that by the presidential elections in 2008, much of the initial ground won against the Taliban in the early years of the conflict had been lost to a lack of resources and a lack of focus by the United States (Rohde and Sanger 2007). Despite rising force levels since 2002, efforts to contain the Taliban were meeting with little success. Once Obama took office, there was no real immediate change to this particular status quo and if anything, as portrayed in Bob Woodward's 2010 book *Obama's Wars*, was the cause of a great deal of internal divide within the administration.

As early as January 2008, the Bush administration began to focus more in Afghanistan most noticeably in the number of ground forces stationed in the region. In the first half of 2008, U.S. troop levels close to doubled moving from 26,602 in January to 48,250 in June, indicating an interest in solving the declining security situation within the region. By the end of September, Bush had ordered several additional units into Afghanistan that would later be upheld and increased by the incoming Obama administration in February 2009. However, it was noted that despite the increasing clamor of U.S. senior military officers for at least 30,000 additional troops, the Obama administration was reluctant to go any further than this 17,000 additional troops until an appropriate policy for Afghanistan could be developed (Woodward, 2010).

The first succinct policy on Afghanistan was delivered in March 2009 and highlighted key changes in existing policy at the time but was also noted for some similarities to his predecessor. Most notably, President Obama announced an additional 4,000 U.S. troops for Afghanistan on top of the 17,000 that had been approved in February, which several media outlets noted looked remarkably like the 2007 surge in Iraq and the direction that Bush policy was heading for Afghanistan in 2008. Obama also discussed only vague commitments to a time line for withdrawal or an exit strategy in Afghanistan, which served to remind many of the debates over the lack of an Iraq exit strategy that Obama championed in the 2008 election campaign. Likewise, President Obama emphasized the need to seduce the loyalties of insurgents that were not die hard ideologues that proved to be reminiscent of the efforts to quell sectarian violence in Iraq in what was termed the Sunni Awakening. Other notable tweaks in strategy in Afghanistan was a re-emphasis on training Afghani security forces, the linking of Afghanistan with the worsening situation along the border regions in Pakistan, and the commitment to expand the civilian mission in the region.

By August, however, the debate continued to rage within policy circles over the effectiveness of the commitment of the Obama administration to Afghanistan and the failure to significantly increase troop levels. In a sixty-six-page strategy document submitted to the administration at the end of that month by Gen. Stanley McChrystal, then commanding U.S. and international forces in the region, recommendations were made that seemed to indicate the need for a massive troop expansion, a position that politically President Obama was hesitant to embrace at the time. However, in December 2009, the new strategy for Afghanistan was announced along with the commitment to drastically expand the ground mission for U.S. and coalition forces on the ground. The new strategy's most important shifts in policy were the rapid deployment of 30,000 additional troops into Afghanistan and the announcing of July 2011 as the beginning of withdrawal for U.S. forces in the region, and as later emphasized by the administration, provided that circumstances on the ground warranted.

Conclusions

This early attempt to look at the Obama administration's efforts in Afghanistan and Iraq seems to indicate that the president largely followed the Bush administration with the notable exception of declaring timelines. Thus, at least for this model, he seems to be more of a "successor" rather than an "innovator." In the four-pronged metric of rhetoric, goals, strategy, and commitment there is little that separates President Bush in 2007–2008 from the current President Obama in either case. This is not such a bad thing. Clearly, the Bush team took the lessons of several years of warfare to develop a winning campaign that reflected the best thinking at the time. It makes little sense that Obama would make drastic strategic changes to what was working on the ground.

For the Obama administration, in the case of both Iraq and Afghanistan, rather than a drastic change in goals, the new normal meant embracing a lowered expectation of what a viable future for these two states might hold. In both cases, the Bush administration took on an early hubris that assumed that nothing short of an open and free democracy could be acceptable. However, by 2009 the challenges in both states proved too much for an American and international audience tired from too many years of warfare and a worldwide recession that made bleeding away the lives and treasure seem little worth it. Speaking at a Pentagon news conference on January 23, 2009, Gates highlighted this point: "One of the points where I suspect both administrations come to the same conclusion, is that the goals we did have for Afghanistan are too broad and too far into the future."

Likewise, perhaps the biggest difference between Bush and Obama is a shift in commitment strategies. Bush embraced an open commitment that did not set any time lines for the withdrawal of U.S troops from either Iraq or Afghanistan which sparked a fairly wide political debate as early as the 2004 presidential election but was a highlight of the 2007 campaign season. Significantly, candidate Obama campaigned on setting a sixteen-month time line for withdrawal from Iraq and a recommitment to efforts in Afghanistan. In this case however, both Bush and Obama succeed in these goals. The Bush-era Status of Forces Agreement with Iraq signed in December 2008 called for a withdrawal time line that fell mostly in line with the campaign promises of then candidate Obama.

In both the case of Afghanistan and of Iraq, Obama either kept the strategies of the previous administration as a whole or adopted them to changing circumstances on the ground. For example both eventually supported a troop surge as part of an exit strategy. Bush recommended a surge of 20,000 troops in January 2007 in Iraq, a move that then-Sen. Obama initially opposed. By the middle of 2008, then-candidate Obama was recommending a surge in Afghanistan as well. However, although President Obama approved initial troop-level increases in Afghanistan after his election, he was largely hesitant for a rapid expansion. He eventually gave way to stiff resistance within the bureaucracy of the military supporting a troop-level increase of 30,000 in December 2009. Thus, Obama presided over an increase of boots on the ground in Afghanistan from levels in the thirty-thousands in January 2009 to more than 100,000 by January 2010. Likewise, President Obama largely kept President Bush's senior military team that had so effectively waged the renewed 2007 efforts in Iraq and eventually Afghanistan assuring that many of the same tactics would cross over into his administration.

Is it necessarily a bad thing to be a successor? Does it mean that we should look at the Obama presidency in a negative light for his failure to formulate a unique strategy more in line with the rhetoric of his pre-presidency years? Certainly not. Obama, as all presidents eventually come to, did not fully understand the broad picture of events on the ground in either Iraq or Afghanistan until he was placed in that position. No president truly becomes the president he thought he would be. In each case, the underlying issues that brought the United States into these conflicts and has kept the country there through several years has not changed. All presidents must come to grips with both the need to preserve the basic interests of the state and also the consequences involved in failure to do so. President Bush put together a solid team and a solid plan that President Obama should be commended for embracing despite the potential political backlash associated with doing so.

Works Cited

Eisenhower, Dwight D. "I Shall Go to Korea." Speech. (25 Oct. 1952).

Jones, Seth G. "The Rise of Afghanistan's Insurgency: State Failure and Jihad." *International Security.* Vol. 32, No. 4 (2008), 7–40.

Lafraie, Najibullah. "Resurgence of the Taliban Insurgency in Afghanistan: How and Why?" *International Politics.* Vol. 46, No. 1 (2009), 102–113.

Light, Paul. *The President's Agenda: Domestic Policy Choice From Kennedy to Clinton.* 3rd ed. Baltimore: Johns Hopkins, 2009

Lindsay, James M. *Congress and the Politics of U.S. Foreign Policy.* Baltimore: John Hopkins University Press, 1994

Obama, Barack. "Remarks of Illinois State Senator Barack Obama Against Going to War with Iraq." (2 Oct. 2002).

———. "Turning the age in Iraq." Speech. (11 Sept. 2007).

————. "My plan for Iraq." *The New York Times.* (14 July 2008).

Powell, Robert. "War as a Commitment Problem." *International Organizations.* Vol. 60 (2006), 169–203.

Rohde, David and David Sanger. "How a 'good war' in Afghanistan went bad." *New York Times.* (12 Aug. 2007).

Smith, Jean Edward. "How to end a war, Eisenhower's way." *The New York Times.* (11 April 2009).

Stevenson, Charles. *Congress at War: The Politics of Conflict since 1789.* Herndon, VA: Potomac Books, 2007.

Woodward, Bob. *Obama's Wars* New York: Simon & Schuster, 2010.

Chapter 16

Iran Policy

Robert J. Pauly Jr.

Threats to U.S. National Security

As a presidential candidate in 2008, Barack H. Obama pledged to employ constructive engagement as a means to help reduce the threats adversaries posed to the interests of the United States and its allies, placing an emphasis on one such state in particular—Iran. Yet, since his election as America's forty-fourth president, Obama has refined that approach in dealing with Iran. He has done so because Iran has maintained its pursuit of the development of nuclear weapons, support for terrorist organizations, and repression of domestic opposition groups, actions that represent significant threats to both U.S. interests and those of Washington's allies within—and beyond—the Persian Gulf and Greater Middle East.

Obama began his presidency with promises of change in U.S. policy toward Iran. However, the approach his administration has employed in practice is one that reflects continuity in attempting to contain the threats Tehran presents to Washington, its allies, and the broader international community. Following initial expressions of interests in open, high-level dialogue with Iran, Obama changed course and charted a path comparable to that of predecessors such as presidents George H. W. Bush (1989–1993), William J. Clinton (1993–2001), and George W. Bush (2001–2009), one that seeks to contain Iran through the use of economic and political sanctions of the unilateral, bilateral, and multilateral sorts. With this synopsis of the Obama administration's basic approach to the variable policy challenges that grow out of Tehran's actions providing a necessary contextual foundation, this chapter examines and assesses three research questions:

1. What are the most significant strains of continuity and change in the approaches of the administrations of both Bushes, Clinton, and Obama to containing the threats Iran poses to the interests of the United States and its allies?

2. To date, how effective have the Obama administration's policies been in mitigating the threats Iran poses to those interests?

3. What policy options are available to the Obama administration to attempt to mitigate, if not eliminate, Iranian threats in the future?

In response to the aforementioned questions, three central arguments are articulated and assessed:

1. Since the end of the Cold War, variable strains of containment have been the policy options of choice for the United States to mitigate the threats Iran poses to the interests of the United States and its allies.

2. To date, the United States has used containment effectively to slow the pace of Iran's development of nuclear weapons, but has not been effective in either eliminating Tehran's nuclear weapons program or in convincing the regime to moderate its support for terrorist organizations or curb its repression of opposition groups within the Iranian population.

3. Moving forward, the United States must work to exert ever greater economic, political, and as a last resort, military pressure on Iran in an attempt to mitigate the threats Tehran poses. The Obama administration should craft policies that target the regime in Tehran, while limiting the potential for the Iranian leadership to engender more pronounced anti-Western sentiments within the Iranian population.

Continuity and Change: Containing Iran, 1989–2010

Notwithstanding some subtle differences in their policies toward Iran, the past four American presidential administrations have used the same basic approach—containment. Essentially, and not surprisingly, when dealing with Iran, U.S. policymakers have relied on the predominant U.S. Cold War strategy, but applied it regionally, within the Persian Gulf, and, to an extent, the broader Middle East, rather than at the global level (Pauly 2005). What has changed over the past decade in particular is the nature and extent of the threats entailed by Iran's pursuit of the development of nuclear weapons and the missile systems to deliver them, the increasingly aggressive tone of its anti-Israeli and anti-American rhetoric, and its capacity to influence the politics of the Persian Gulf and Greater Middle East.

The George H. W. Bush administration's foreign policy began with an emphasis on managing a peaceful conclusion to the end of the Cold War in Europe, one followed rapidly by a shift to coalition building and subsequent prosecution of the 1991 Persian Gulf War against Iraq (Baker and DeFrank 1995; Bush and Scowcroft 1998). After expelling Iraqi forces from Kuwait through the effective conduct of Operation Desert Storm in winter 1991, the Bush administration shifted to what was essentially a policy of dual containment, through which it attempted to mitigate threats to the interests of the United States and its allies in the Persian Gulf region by using sanctions regimes against both Iraq and Iran, under the auspices of multilateral UN Security Council (UNSC) resolutions in Baghdad's case and largely unilateral economic restrictions in Tehran's case. It relied on the maintenance of a significant post-Gulf War U.S. military presence in Saudi Arabia to help enforce those sanctions and dissuade both Iraq and Iran from taking any provocative action against their neighbors.

Throughout Clinton's tenure in the White House, his administration emphasized the dual containment of Iraq and Iran, balancing one against the other, in an effort to minimize threats to United States and its allies posed by both states. The principal punitive measures Clinton employed in response to Iran's pursuit of the development of nuclear weapons and sponsorship of terrorist organizations, especially its connection to the June 1996 suicide bombing of the Khobar Towers U.S. military housing complex in Dhahran, Saudi Arabia, which killed nineteen American servicemen, were unilateral economic sanctions (Benjamin and Simon 2002). However, the administration also attempted to negotiate with the Iranian regime following the election of reform-minded President Mohammad Khatami in August 1997. Regrettably, that effort was quickly rebuffed by Iranian hardliners headed by Supreme Leader Ayatollah Ali Khamenei and U.S.–Iranian relations remained acrimonious over the balance of Clinton's second term in office. As then Secretary Madeleine K. Albright notes in her memoirs:

> We could have avoided the charge that we were too soft on Iran by ignoring the reform movement entirely, but that would have left us isolated internationally and provided no incentive for Iran to change further. . . . By offering an unconditional dialogue, we put the onus on Iran to explain why it was unwilling even to talk about our differences and laid the groundwork for formal discussions if and when they became possible. (Albright 2003: 325–326)

As was true of the Clinton administration, the George W. Bush administration also had a fleeting opportunity for cooperation with Iran, one that opened and closed quickly as the United States sought assistance in eliminating the Taliban regime and building a new Afghan state in the aftermath of al-Qaeda's terrorist attacks against the United States on September 11, 2001. An unwillingness for dialogue at upper levels in Washington and Tehran rendered cooperation vis-à-vis Afghanistan untenable in practice. Then, in his January 2002 State of the Union address, Bush himself described Iran as a member of an "Axis of Evil" threatening the peace of the world through the proliferation of weapons of mass destruction and sponsorship of terrorist groups. Later that year, the administration uncovered evidence of significant Iranian progress toward the development of nuclear weapons, which Tehran had achieved with Chinese and Russian assistance.

By spring 2003, when it launched Operation Iraqi Freedom, the Bush administration's focus was almost exclusively on eliminating the regime of President Saddam Hussein (Lansford and Pauly 2004). Saddam's removal resulted in a power vacuum that left the United States struggling to achieve progress in nation- and state-building efforts in Iraq over much of Bush's remaining 5.5 years in office. Given the challenges in Iraq and Afghanistan and requisite economic and military commitments to operations in those states, the Bush administration relied largely on multi-lateral diplomacy, with its European allies often taking the lead, to contain Iran's nuclear developmental efforts and support for terrorist organizations, as well as its meddling in Iraq from 2003 to 2009 (Pauly 2009).

After assuming office in January 2009, Obama spent the initial six months of his administration with the assumption that apologizing for what many around the world perceived as the misdeeds of his immediate predecessor, George W. Bush, would lead to constructive engagement with U.S. adversaries in general and Iran's theocracy specifically. In June 2009, the Iranian regime's violent quashing of a popular uprising that followed the disputed reelection of Mahmoud Ahmadinejad as president demonstrated to Obama that simply extending a hand would not change Tehran's behavior, whether with respect to its harsh treatment of domestic opponents of the regime who dared to call for political reform or, more significantly, regarding its sponsorship of terrorist groups or pursuit of the development of nuclear weapons. Consequently, the administration has since adopted a much stronger, more realist approach, toward containing Iran's threats to U.S. interests, one stressing the strengthening of economic and political sanctions against Tehran, including, most notably, the passage of UNSC Resolution 1929 in June 2010 and America's Iran Sanctions Act in July 2010. Both measures enhanced existing economic restrictions against the Iranian regime in an effort to constrain its freedom of action in each of the above three issue areas and came concurrent with ongoing diplomatic efforts to limit Chinese and Russian support for Iran's nuclear weapons developmental program and trade relationships with the Islamic state (Pollack 2010).

Assessment of the Obama Administration's Policies Toward Iran, 2009–2010

Obama set the rhetorical tone for his administration's foreign policy early and often in a manner designed to make a break from his predecessor by emphasizing both the importance of acting multilaterally with the imprimatur of international organizations such as the UN and a willingness to solve problems by engaging with America's adversaries as well as its allies. For example, in his inaugural address in January 2009, Obama pledged to U.S. adversaries such as Iran, "To those who cling to power through corruption and deceit and the silencing of dissent, know that you are on the wrong side of history, but that we will extend a hand if you are willing to unclench your fist" (Obama 2009a).

Furthermore, the administration emphasized a comparable diplomatic approach more formally in the context of its first National Security Strategy in May 2010, noting that, "Through engagement, we can create opportunities to resolve differences, strengthen the international community's support for our actions, learn about the intentions and nature of closed regimes, and plainly demonstrate to the publics within those nations that their governments are to blame for their isolation" (Obama 2010a: 11).

Although Obama's determination to set a multilateral tone in U.S. foreign policy once he took office was sensible given the historical utility of that approach over much, if not all, of the Cold War and initial decade of the post-Cold War era, his emphasis on apologizing repeatedly for instances of American unilateralism in the Bush administration's global war on terror was imprudent. It suggested to the Iranian leadership and other despotic regimes the potential for weakness emanating from Washington, leaving the impression that Obama might not act decisively should his administration be forced to respond to provocative action, whether regarding autocratic regimes' silencing of domestic dissent, support for terrorism or proliferation of WMD. Within days of Obama's address in Cairo, for instance, the Iranian regime's security forces were in the streets of Tehran cracking down violently on opposition supporters questioning the legitimacy of Ahmadinejad's electoral victory over runner-up Mir Hossein Musavi. White House responses to Iran's initial heavy-handed action against the opposition and subsequent repression of those demanding political reform fell short of unequivocal condemnation and have been ratcheted up to only a limited degree in the eighteen months since.

Political Measures

Politically, the Obama administration has used three sets of measures—one unilateral, one hybrid bilateral/trilateral, and one multilateral—to attempt to alter Tehran's behavior regarding the three issue areas Washington views as most significant to U.S. interests: 1) nuclear proliferation; 2) sponsorship of terrorism; and 3) Iranian domestic political reform. At the unilateral level, the administration worked with the U.S. Congress to pass the July 2010 Iran Sanctions Act, which used primarily economic means (see next the section on economic measures) to strengthen American diplomatic pressure demanding that Tehran come clean with respect to its nuclear ambitions and cease further efforts to acquire such weapons (Obama 2010b).

Bilaterally, once he took office, Obama sought to "re-set" the U.S.–Russian relationship in an effort to secure greater cooperation from Moscow vis-à-vis Iran's nuclear developmental efforts, a strategy that has had mixed results to date, but been marginally more effective than similar overtures regarding the Chinese–Iranian relationship. Additionally, Obama has had to strike a delicate balance in reassuring America's closest ally in the Middle East—Israel—that the United States takes seriously the threat a viable nuclear weapon in Tehran would present to Tel Aviv's security, while trying to give at least the appearance the Washington is not tilted too far in the Jewish state's direction in the Israeli–Palestinian peace process. Lastly, at the multilateral level, Obama marshaled the requisite support from Moscow and Beijing in particular to ensure passage of UNSC Resolution 1929, which strengthened existing and added new restrictions on the supply of materials central to Iran's nuclear weapons and missile developmental programs (UNSC 2010).

Economic Measures

Most, if not all, of the economic and political measures employed by the Obama administration to contain Iranian threats to the interests of the United States and its allies are interconnected and, as described above, have unilateral, hybrid bilateral/trilateral, and multilateral dimensions. Unilaterally, the Iran Sanctions Act strengthened existing American-based economic sanctions designed both to limit the transfer of technology and raw materials helpful to Tehran in acquiring a nuclear weapon and to deny members of the Iranian regime access to personal financial assets deposited in foreign banks (Obama 2009b). Bilaterally and trilaterally, the Obama administration has worked to increase the economic costs Tehran bears by continuing its nuclear weapons developmental program by exercising the limited pressure it can on Iran's trade public and private trade partners, most significantly China and Russia but also European Union (EU) and North Atlantic Treaty Organization member states and corporations therein (Pollack 2010). Multilaterally, UNSC Resolution 1929 is the strongest UN measure to date in terms of clamping down on Iranian finances, to reduce the regime's nuclear weapons development capacity and also exact a cost on members of the regime personally (UNSC 2010).

Collectively these measures have been effective in tightening the restrictions on Iran's freedom of action. However, the imposition of such restrictions also has the potential to backfire, in that some of their costs extend to the broader Iranian population (such as the reduction in the availability of gasoline, given the Islamic state's reliance on foreign refineries), which the regime can then blame on outside actors and deflect domestic political criticism in the process.

Military Measures

It is in the military context that the Obama administration, like the preceding George W. Bush administration, has the least freedom of action. After campaigning on a platform promising the expeditious withdrawal of American combat forces from Iraq, Obama followed through on that pledge, while increasing substantially the U.S. force presence in Afghanistan. The American military commitments in Afghanistan and Iraq, while leaving a significant footprint in the Middle East, also constrain its capacity for action against Iran and open a vulnerability for retaliatory action should Washington ever choose to use force to try to eliminate Tehran's nuclear weapons program. Not surprisingly, given his administration's affinity for diplomacy, Obama has de-emphasized military options, ranging from airstrikes to the use of ground forces, as options to strike at Iranian nuclear facilities, and it is unclear whether Israel would consider a military attack either. Nonetheless, a February 2011 International Institute for Strategic Studies report suggests Iran could still produce a nuclear weapon within 1–2 years (IISS 2011), which makes ruling out military action altogether imprudent.

Examination of U.S. Foreign Policy Options Toward Iran

With respect to the Obama administration's foreign policy approach toward Iran, there are four potential paths to follow moving forward:

1. The administration can seek engagement with the Khamenei-led regime in Tehran on Iranian terms, which essentially requires acknowledgment of Iran's right to develop nuclear weapons, repress its domestic political opponents, and continue to support terrorist groups without condemnation from Washington;

2. The administration can pursue diplomacy with Iran on American terms, which demands full Iranian compliance with United States, European, and UN demands regarding Tehran's nuclear developmental program and support for terrorism.

3. The administration can seek engagement with Iran on a combination of American, Iranian, and international terms, assuming partial Iranian compliance with United States, European, and UN demands on the aforementioned three issues; and

4. The administration can abstain from any attempts at further diplomacy with Tehran, which assumes that progress in mitigating any American concerns regarding Iran's behavior is simply not possible.

Political Measures

In the political context, the Obama administration's options in dealing with Iran are threefold:

1. It can accept the status and quo and maintain the present level of limited isolation of Iran in the international system, which equates to the avoidance of additional criticism of Iran's policies beyond the level of disapproval expressed to date.

2. The administration can work to achieve further isolation of Iran by ratcheting up U.S. rhetoric critical of Iran's nuclear weapons developmental program, its support for terrorist organizations such as Hamas and Hezbollah, and its repression of domestic opposition groups, which has continued all but unhindered since the June 2009 protests questioning the legitimacy of Ahmadinejad's reelection as president, and

pressing European allies, as well as China and Russia, to strengthen existing national and international sanctions on Iran.

3. The administration can enhance present assistance provided to domestic groups opposing the regime in Tehran by publicly encouraging democratic reform efforts in Iran and doing so consistently.

Economic Measures

As is the case at the political level, the Obama administration's economic options are threefold:

1. The administration can simply accept the status quo by maintaining the economic sanctions in place against the Iranian regime, at present, whether imposed unilaterally, bilaterally/trilaterally, or more multilaterally, as described in the previous section of the chapter.

2. The administration can work to further isolate Iran economically by strengthening present and adding new sanctions at one or more of the above levels, through collaboration with America's European allies, Russia, China, at the bilateral and multilateral levels, or via the UNSC.

3. The administration can enhance present assistance provided to domestic groups opposing the Iranian regime by funneling financial assistance to those actors.

Military Measures

Militarily, the Obama administration' has essentially six options:

1. The administration can rule out altogether the use of military force of any kind, direct or covert, to damage or destroy Iran's nuclear weapons developmental program or convince it that the costs of continuing to support terrorist organizations and repress its own population exceed the benefits.

2. The administration can threaten, publicly or privately, to use direct or covert military force to achieve one
   or more of the above three outcomes.

3. The administration can employ military air strikes in
   an attempt to damage or destroy outright one or more
   of Iran's nuclear weapons developmental facilities.

4. The administration can use covert action on the ground
   in Iran to encourage Iranian behavioral changes in
   one or more of the aforementioned trio of contexts.

5. The administration can prosecute a direct ground
   invasion of Iran to produce such changes in behavior
   by the regime in Tehran.

6. Should Iran acquire one or more viable nuclear weapons and the means to any such munitions to attack the
   United States or one of its allies directly, the administration could consider the use of its own nuclear weapons in response.

Options for Future U.S. Policies Toward Iran

Given the preceding discussion of the Obama administration's
available tools for use in containing Iran, there are multiple options
in terms of the overarching U.S. policy approach, as well as the
related political, economic, and military measures it possesses. Of
those options, the following are most prudent.

Underlying Policy Approach

The most prudent choices the Obama administration can and
should make regarding its overall policy approach toward Iran
are threefold:

1. The administration must emphasize unambiguously to
   Tehran, both publicly and privately, that the onus is on
   the regime to change its behavior regarding the development of nuclear weapons, sponsorship of terrorist organizations, and repression of domestic political opposition
   groups.

2. The administration must make it clear to the Iranians that the opening of any negotiations at any level has to come on American terms, while leaving open the possibility of a warmer U.S.–Iranian relationship should Tehran begin to alter its behavior as demanded by Washington on any of the above three central issues.

3. Absent any such changes, Obama and his national security team must continue to use all available means at its disposal to further isolate and thus reduce the freedom of action the Iranian regime possesses.

Political Measures

Politically, the Obama administration should focus on the second and third options outlined in the previous section. It must work to achieve further isolation of Iran by ratcheting up U.S. rhetoric critical of Iran's nuclear weapons program, its support for terrorist organizations, and its repression of domestic opposition groups and encouraging European allies, as well as China and Russia, to strengthen existing national and international sanctions on Iran. Given the economic leverage China holds over the United States by way of the substantial American national debt it has financed, Washington is much more likely to increase pressure on Tehran via Moscow, Berlin, Paris, and London than by way of Beijing. It is also much more probable that unilateral and hybrid bilateral/trilateral action will produce further isolation of Iran than can be achieved through the UNSC, in light of China's, as well as Russia's, veto power over that body's resolutions. The administration should also be more vociferous in its support of opposition groups calling on the regime to reform its autocratic political system. The potential for such an approach to work has only grown since the resignation of Egyptian President Hosni Mubarak as a result of massive public protests in Cairo in January and February 2011.

Economic Measures

Economically, the Obama administration should employ the second and third options described in the previous section. It must work to further isolate Iran economically by strengthening present and adding new sanctions unilaterally and bilaterally/trilaterally with its European allies, as well as the broader EU, and, to the extent possible, Russia and China. As denoted above, Washington has considerably less leverage with Beijing than any of these other actors. The administration should also enhance present assistance provided to domestic groups opposing Iranian regime by funneling financial and, perhaps, technological assistance to them to boost further the international media and popular attention on the protests that have erupted periodically in Tehran and other major cities since the June 2010 presidential election.

Military Measures

At the military level, the Obama administration should focus on the second, third, and fourth options outlined in the previous section. To that end, the administration must be willing to threaten, publicly and privately, the use of military force to cause Iran to discontinue its nuclear weapons developmental program, stop supporting entities identified by the United States and its allies as terrorist organizations, and allow its people a greater say in domestic politics. The administration must not rule out the use of military air strikes or covert action on the ground in Iran to achieve one or more of the above three objectives. However, within respect to Iran's nuclear program in particular, it should consider such action only as last resort if Tehran achieves an atomic weapons capacity that poses a direct, imminent threat to the United States or one or more of its allies, with an emphasis on Israel. One option the administration should rule out is a direct ground invasion of Iran. Such an operation would be extraordinarily difficult, if not impossible, to mount, given present U.S. force commitments in Afghanistan and Iraq. Moreover, such an undertaking might well lead the Iranian population, opposition groups included, to rally around the regime against an existential threat from Washington. Nor should it put the use of nuclear weapons on the table absent irrefutable evidence that Iran intends to strike either the United States or any of its allies, within or outside of, the Persian Gulf and broader Middle East regions.

Conclusions

This chapter was designed to examine and assess the extent of the validity of three central arguments. As such, since the end of the Cold War, variable strains of containment have been the policy options of choice for the United States to mitigate the threats Iran poses to the interests of the United States and its allies. All four U.S. presidents since the end of the Cold War—George H. W. Bush, Clinton, George W. Bush, and Obama—have relied in part, if not fully, on the same central strategy of containment employed by nearly all of their post-World II predecessors to deal with the Soviet Union in an attempt to minimize the threats posed to American and broader Western interests by Iran.

To date, the United States has used containment effectively to slow the pace of Iran's development of nuclear weapons. However, it has not been effective in either eliminating Tehran's nuclear weapons program or in convincing the regime to moderate its support for terrorist organizations or curb its repression of Iranian domestic opposition groups. The evidence presented here clearly demonstrates that containment has thus far and probably continues in the short term to limit the pace of Iran's nuclear weapons developmental program by increasing the costs associated with maintaining that program. However, it is also evident that the regime in Tehran has no intention of altering its behavior regarding nuclear weapons development, support for terrorist groups or minimizing the prospects for domestic political reform. If anything, the regime has only grown more resolute.

Finally, and moving forward, the United States must work to exert ever greater economic, political and, to the extent needed, military pressure on Iran in an attempt to mitigate the threats Tehran poses to the interests of the United States and its allies. The Obama administration should craft policies that target the regime in Tehran, while limiting the potential for the hardliners to engender more pronounced anti-Western sentiments within the Iranian population. The evidence confirms that the only means through which to lessen the threats Iran poses to the United States and its allies is to continually increase the economic, political, and security costs the Iranian regime will incur by developing nuclear weapons, supporting terrorist groups and repressing its domestic political opposition.

Ultimately, there are five basic possibilities for the future of the U.S.–Iranian relationship and the threats Tehran continues to pose:

1. The maintenance of the status quo with level of threats posed by Iran to the interests of the United States and its allies remaining the same.

2. The level of Iranian threats is gradually reduced.

3. There is a pronounced reduction in the level of such threats.

4. There is a gradual but manageable increase in the level of threats Iran presents.

5. There is a pronounced and unmanageable increase in the level of those Iranian threats.

Based on the existing evidence, the second and fourth of these possibilities are the most probable.

Works Cited

Albright, Madeleine with Bob Woodward. *Madame Secretary: A Memoir.* New York: Miramax Books, 2003.

Baker, James A. III and Thomas M. DeFrank. *The Politics of Diplomacy: Revolution, War & Peace, 1989–1992.* New York: G.P. Putnam's Sons, 1995.

Benjamin, Daniel and Steven Simon. *The Age of Sacred Terror.* New York: Random House, 2002: 224–225.

Bush, George H.W. and Brent Scowcroft. *A World Transformed: The Collapse of the Soviet Empire; The Unification of Germany; Tiananmen Square; The Gulf War.* New York: Alfred A. Knopf, 1998.

International Institute for Strategic Studies. "Iran's Nuclear, Chemical and Biological Capabilities: A Net Assessment." (3 Feb. 2011).

Lansford, Tom and Robert J. Pauly Jr. *Strategic Preemption: US Foreign Policy and the Second Iraq War.* Aldershot, UK: Ashgate Publishing, 2004.

Obama, Barack. "Inaugural Address." (21 Jan. 2009a). http://www.whitehouse.gov/blog/2009/01/21/president-barack-obamas-inaugural-address.

———. "Remarks by the President on a New Beginning." (4 June 2009b). http://www.whitehouse.gov/the-press-office/remarks-president-cairo-university-6-04-09.

———. The National Security Strategy of the United States (May 2010a).

———. "Remarks by the Preisdent at Signing of the Iran Sanctions Act." (1 July 2010b). http://www.whitehouse.gov/the-press-office/remarks-president-signing-iran-sanctions-act.

Pauly, Robert J. Jr. *US Foreign Policy and the Persian Gulf: Safeguarding US Interests through Selective Multilateralism.* Aldershot, UK: Ashgate Publishing, 2005.

————. "Identifying and Confronting the 'Axis of Evil': A Critical Retrospective." Eds. Tom Lansford, Robert P. Watson, and Jack Covarrubias. *America's War on Terror* 2nd ed. Aldershot, UK: Ashgate Publishing, 2009.

Pollack, Kenneth. "Pariahs in Tehran." *The National Interest.* Vol. 110 (Nov/Dec. 2010).

United Nations Security Council Resolution 1929 (9 June 2010) http:// daccess-dds-ny.un.org/doc/UNDOC/GEN/N10/396/79/pdf/n1039679. pdf?openelement.

Chapter 17

China Policy

De-Yuan Kao

Forty years ago, what was referred to as "Ping-Pong Diplomacy" opened the door for talks between the People's Republic of China and the United States. A few months later in 1971, a visit by Secretary of State Henry Kissinger to China helped pave the way for the historical handshake between President Richard Nixon and China's Chairman Mao. The next logical step in the relationship—formal diplomatic relations between the two great powers—was established in 1979 after series of bilateral talks during the presidency of Jimmy Carter. Subsequent years witnessed many high-profile visits between leaders of both countries and to both countries. Indeed, relations with China were very important to the United States during the Cold War and to this day remains one of the most critical relationships in the world. At the same time, recognition by the United States was significant to China's survival and development, and the two nations remain wedded by precarious but necessary ties as economic and military powers.

America's China policy was generally consistent and stable over the past forty years, despite turbulent international events and changes in leadership in both nations. After the end of the Cold War, both China and the United States realized the necessity of maintaining a healthy relationship. This is evident in the fact that some U.S. presidents adopted a harsher attitude toward China at the beginning of their presidencies, but eventually softened their positions after taking office. Economic and security situations during the 1990s and the early 2000s did not allow the United States to ignore China's growing influence. Under George W. Bush and through the Barack Obama presidency, this relationship has remained important owing to major global issues such as counter-terrorism, climate change, the global financial crisis, saber-rattling by North Korea, nuclear crises, and so on.

These issues are important to both the United States and China, and could not be solved or mitigated without their mutual collaboration. However, it is U.S. policy that often drives these issues, as the collaboration between the two powers is not always symmetrical. Under the presidencies of Bill Clinton and George W. Bush, the United States cultivated a relationship with China that was smoother than in the past, despite a set of challenges arising from imbalances in their respective interests and approaches to these various issues.

Unlike his predecessors' China policy, which was tough at first and more accommodating later,[1] Obama's attitude toward China seemed more obscure and softer in the first year of his presidency. This policy with a series of "soft gestures" toward China has incurred some public criticism (Krauthammer 2010). However, some changes have been seen since late 2009. Since then, the Obama administration has changed course somewhat and has adopted a much more conservative attitude toward China (Pomfret 2010d).

The Beginning: Economy First

The national security strategy of the United States has long emphasized economic issues core to the focal attention for the U.S. presidents. When Clinton and Bush took office in 1992 and 2000, respectively, they both confronted similar levels of economic recession. The severity of the problems had been accumulating over many years, ultimately culminating in such a massive global economic crisis that it could not but have been regarded as the top security threat to the United States when Obama came into power.

Unfortunately, some indicators tend to show that the Obama administration's efforts to solve such problems did not obtain their

---

1. Clinton once called for "an American that will not coddle tyrants, from Baghdad to Beijing." But in two years, he persuaded the Congress to offer China the PNTR status. Similarly, President Bush saw China as a "strategic competitor" during the campaign. But he soon developed strategic partnership with China after the terrorist attacks on September 11, 2001.

desired results. The U.S. gross domestic product dropped approximately 6 percent in the first quarter of 2009, and the unemployment rate even reached 10 percent in 2009, its highest since 1983 (Goodman 2009). In order to reverse these devastating trends, Washington needed assistance and cooperation from its partners.

Why the U.S. Needs China

Wayne M. Morrison, a specialist in Asian trade and finance, points out that China was the second largest U.S. trading partner, the third largest U.S. export market, and the largest source of U.S. imports in 2009 (Morrison 2010). In order to revive the domestic U.S. economy, Washington hoped that Beijing would adopt a more market-based currency policy, establish a more transparent investment environment, and act as a sincere member to implement its commitments in the World Trade Organization (WTO). Furthermore, in order to carry out its financial rescue and economic stimulus policies and programs, the U.S. government needed to borrow more money.

As expected, China became the most important lender. The fact that China's holding of U.S. securities exceeded $1.4 trillion at the end of June 2009, and its holdings of U.S. Treasury securities was almost $900 billion by the end of 2009, shows not only China's amazing purchasing power, it also proves how important China is to the U.S. economy (La Monica 2008). Although China's holding of U.S. Treasury securities dropped in 2010 under Obama, China has remained the largest creditor for the U.S. government. China, as one of America's most important trading partners, is an essential component for any efficacious prescription by Obama for an economic turnaround.

In addition to these critical economic issues, China could provide assistance in dealing with other global strategic problems as well. For example, the U.S. government has always expressed its concern about the tension in the Korean Peninsula. Several military engagements between the North and the South occurred in 2009 and 2010. Among them, two incidents were the most troubling since the Armistice Agreement was signed in 1953. The first was the Cheonan Incident that occurred in March 2010. An investigation report released in May 2010 by the Joint Civilian-Military Investigation Group concluded that North Korea should be held responsible for the sinking of South Korea's Cheonan naval vessel.

The U.S. government condemned the North and announced that there would be two joint military exercises with South Korea, which could be regarded as a direct military response to this incident (Barnes 2010). Compared with other countries' fierce denunciations of such blatantly illegal aggression, China, as North Korea's closest ally, only asked all relevant parties to remain calm without any further response (Young 2010). After South Korea submitted the official investigation report to the UN, the UN Security Council (2010) only condemned the attack but did not point out who the attacker was in its *President Statement*. Meanwhile, China refused to impose tougher sanctions on North Korea. It was obvious that there would not be any effective measures forthcoming out of the UN without China's close cooperation

The other incident was the artillery shelling of civilian residents on South Korea's Yeonpyeong Island in early November 2010. Just ten days before the shelling, Dr. Siegfried S. Hecker, former director of the Los Alamos National Laboratory, was invited by North Korean government to visit a reactivated nuclear plant. Dr. Hecker was "stunned" when he saw advanced technology installed in the plant (Sanger 2010a). Still, Washington expressed its firm support of South Korea and decided to hold joint military exercises with the South, knowing it still needs China to be a player in mitigating the actions of the North.

Other global issues, such as counterterrorism and climate change, also require strategic collaboration between China and the whole of international society. Taking both internal and external environment into consideration, China is of critical importance to the United States in a broad gamut of critical issues.

No Free Lunch

Obama came to power facing difficult domestic and foreign crises. China, with its increasing influence and power, could help the United States deal with many issues, from economic crises to security concerns. The largely asymmetric relations between China and the United States have given the former much more tactical leverage against the latter than it has ever enjoyed in the past. China is "now more willing to say *no* to the United States" (Cooper 2010a). Reflecting these changing circumstances is the fact that Obama has made a number of major concessions in several key issue areas for China in 2009. After all, there is no such as thing as free lunch, especially in a Chinese restaurant. China is aware of its special role in the situation facing the United States but would also like to see what might be offered in exchange for Chinese support.

A softer China policy can be seen in the tenor of what American officials do and say in response to this new and profoundly asymmetric relationship. For example, in the past several years, American officials have always mentioned the human rights situation in China before departing for China. Before becoming Obama's secretary of state, Hillary Clinton urged the then-President Bush to boycott the opening ceremony of the 2008 Olympics in China in response to both the bloody crackdown in Tibet and its failure to stop genocide in the Sudan (Holland and Zakaria 2008). Likewise, Nancy Pelosi, then the House Speaker and the most persistent voice on China's human rights performance, also asked the world to condemn China's suppression of the protests in Tibet (Hulse 2008). However, they both gave a low profile to these issues during their visits to China in 2009 (Sutter 2010: 262–263).

Additionally, the three meetings between China's President Hu Jintao and Obama in 2009 also revealed a softer U.S. attitude toward China. In order to ease tensions in the bilateral relationship, Obama not only postponed arms sales to Taiwan, which had been approved by the Bush administration in 2008, but he also cancelled a meeting with the Dalai Lama before his trip to China in November 2009 (Pomfret 2009). Obama did, however, meet with the Dalai Lama in early 2010. Furthermore, according to a report in *The Times of India* ("Obama Meets" 2009), Obama did not oppose President Hu's statement that "Tibet is part of China . . ." or correct Hu's assertion about "China's sovereignty over Taiwan."

Unfortunately, such amicable gestures did not earn China's support for the sanctions on Iran, more flexible Chinese mechanisms for the Renminbi, or assistance in solving the dispute between the two Koreas. China's stoic toughness has been a slap in the face for Obama, who behaved humbly during his visit to China.

Threat Perceptions and Policy Changes

Although Beijing and Washington have become closer due to their cooperation in several issues, neither one sees its counterpart as a "real friend." On the contrary, they are adopting a policy of "pretending to be friends" so as to deal with the ebbs and flows in the bilateral relationship (Yan 2010: 263–292). China's necessary role in the U.S. economic recovery plan, and its increasing influence on the world stage have gained itself more bargaining chips, which, also has been reflected in the changing balance in the Sino–U.S. relationship.

Through their course of interactions in 2009, Obama became more aware of these changes and realized that the balance shift would no doubt bring about some threats to U.S. national interests. For these reasons, Obama gradually adjusted his China policy, moving to a tougher posture. Since the beginning of 2010, the U.S. government has reaffirmed to its Asian allies that "we are here to stay" (Alford 2010). Secretary Clinton made a loud statement in Hawaii that America plans to continue playing the leading role in the regional architecture in Asia (Munakata 2010). To be more specific, changes in Obama's China policy can be seen in his attitude and policy toward several important issues.

Security

In the security field, the White House has made reengaging Asia a higher priority. The Obama administration also tried to rebuild key relations with its Asian allies. Several maritime incidents between China and the United States occurred in 2009 arousing the tensions between these two countries, especially regarding the South China Sea. To that end, in the 2010 Association of Southeast Asian Nations (ASEAN) Regional Forum, Clinton, with the support of other member states, made a public statement that "we oppose the use or threat of force by any claimant" (Pomfret 2010a), which was clearly designed to counter any Chinese unilateral proclamations of ownership of the South China Sea.

Regarding the relationship with Japan, Obama rekindled the major importance of its Japan relations. When Japan and China disputed fishing rights near the Senkaku (Diaoyutai) Islands in 2010, the United States expressed its commitment to support Japan and reaffirm Japan's vital relationship with the United States (Song 2010). The U.S.–Japan alliance is not only the "cornerstone" of peace in Asia and the Pacific, but also "one of the most important alliance partnership" in the entire world (Brower 2010).

South Korea, which faces serious challenges from the North, has always been a key U.S. concern. In fact, after the Cheonan Incident, the United States and South Korea held numerous joint military exercises to demonstrate their determination to deter North

Korean threats. Furthermore, in order to mitigate the nuclear crisis on the Korean Peninsula, Washington decided not to tolerate Beijing's passive attitude toward this issue and asked the Chinese government to respond firmly to Pyongyang's violation of promises undertaken during the nuclear negotiations.

The relations between China and Taiwan have improved dramatically since 2008, with the election of a pro-Chinese leader on Taiwan who had adopted a pragmatic *modus vivendi* for broadening ties with the mainland. Although Obama welcomed such improvements in cross-Strait relationship, whether the United States should feel concerned about these trends or not is still subject to a vigorous debate (Sutter 2010: 240–241). All advocates agree, however, that in order to maintain the strategic balance across the Taiwan Strait, it is necessary for the United States to continue arms sales to Taiwan (Sutter et al. 2009). And so, in January 2010, Obama approved an arms sales package to Taiwan despite China's opposition and retaliatory measures. This decision to sell more defensive weapons to Taiwan not only revealed practical U.S. support of Taiwan's democracy, but also was a move widely regarded as a sign that Obama wants Beijing to understand that the United States will not tolerate China's uncooperative attitude about counterterrorism and other key issues (Cooper 2010b).

Additionally, Washington has tried to cultivate better relations with other Asian countries, especially ASEAN member states naturally interested in countering China's increasing influence in the region. For example, the United States has resumed military ties with Indonesia (Cloud 2010), planned to hold talks with Myanmar after the release of Aung San Suu Kyi (Quinn 2010), built military relations with Vietnam (Mason 2010), and established better relations with Laos, Malaysia, and India (Pomfret 2010b).

Trade and Environment

With regard to trade and environmental issues, the Obama administration decided to impose greater pressure on China. Facing a widely unpopular economic recession at home, both the Congress and private enterprises have urged the Obama administration to "get tough" on China (Heilprin 2010). During his meeting with Premier Wen Jiabao, Obama strongly emphasized that China should correct its currency policy with a warning that "we have other means of protecting U.S. interests" (Sanger 2010b). Since the beginning of 2010, the United States not only imposed anti-dumping duties on products imported from China, it also requested the WTO to investigate China's trade practices. Trade disputes between China and the United States have become more contentious than ever.

During the 2009 Copenhagen Summit, Obama and Premier Wen were not able to reach a consensus regarding the necessity of international emission verification. Wen was furious and boycotted the meeting, but China's arrogant attitude backfired. Obama publicly mentioned that the United States has not tried to constrain China's laudable economic boom, but that the world needs China to take actions to curb its greenhouse gas emissions immediately (CBS News 2010). The view in China is that it is up to China whether they should prioritize environmental protection or spare no effort to develop its economy should not be decided by the United States. However, Obama is apparently eager to draw China into an international framework to offer more joint cooperation on climate change.

Human Rights

People doubted whether Obama would be firm on promoting human rights in the world, and many felt disappointed at his first-year performance (Roth 2010). During the first year of the Obama administration, both the U.S. president and his secretary of state failed to firmly request the Chinese government improve its human rights record (Applebaum 2009). However, Obama has become more active in discussing the human rights situation in China since 2010. According to the 2010 annual human rights report issued by the U.S. State Department, China's human rights record had degenerated even more over the past year (Knowlton and Faithi 2010). In the report, Washington condemned Beijing's censorship of the press, Internet, and alternative media. Furthermore, its performance was deemed as bad as that of North Korea, Iran, Iraq, and Sri Lanka. In the *International Religious Freedom Report* released in November 2010, China was included among those who demonstrated the least commitment to religious freedom and human rights (Addicott 2010). In addition to these reports, Obama resumed formal human rights talks with China in May 2010 to address bilateral concerns about the lack of progress through concrete results.

Obama tried to make clear its emphasis on human rights in action. Despite China's protest, Obama met with the Dalai Lama, the spiritual leader of Tibet, in February 2010 and reaffirmed his support of dialogue between China and Tibet (Spetalnick 2010). Furthermore, Obama requested Beijing release the newly selected Nobel Peace Prize winner, Professor Liu Xiaobo, who has been jailed many times since 1989. Additionally, the Obama administration has decided to fund a group operated by Falun Gong members, which is devoted to developing software to break China's Internet block (Pomfret 2010c). All these moves show that Obama became tougher on China regarding human rights issues.

Conclusion

As of 2011, the United States continues to face several critical problems. Domestically, the weak economy has become President Obama's biggest challenge. Doing business with China and entering China's market are undoubtedly prescriptions to improving the U.S. economy. Externally, the United States needs to seek China's assistance on a number of issues. Tensions on the Korean Peninsula might be lessened if the Chinese government could persuade North Korea to behave. Furthermore, China's support is necessary in the larger war against terrorism. Here, China could assist the United States in the UN, through its influence in the East, and bilaterally in terms of sharing intelligence.

China's attitude toward these problems is important to the United States, but it is more crucial to maintain a healthy and balanced relationship with China. Obama has recognized threats from China and seems to understand that a soft policy toward China could harm American interests. For that reason, the Obama administration has begun revising its policy. In the economic arena, the United States keeps urging China to adjust its currency policy so as to correct the gigantic deficit between both countries. In terms of security, the United States has asked for deeper and closer cooperation with its allies in Asia so as to preserve its influential status in this region.

After years of Washington conciliating Beijing, the necessity of bringing change in the U.S. policy is of great importance and urgency. A more muscular policy toward China could reassure America's allies and domestic constituents that the United States is still concerned about global issues. Although more friction might arise as the Obama administration adopts a hard-line policy, this shift also offers an opportunity for the United States to gain greater support.

Despite these changes, in the long term, the United States will maintain a stable attitude and policy toward China despite these fine adjustments. After all, a healthy and peaceful Sino–U.S. relationship is not only good for both countries; it is also beneficial to the world. So, the ebb and flow of China policy will not upset the balance or change the fundamental principles governing this discourse. It is reasonable to expect substantial continuity in the complex of the U.S.–China relations, with ever greater interdependence, growing mutual understanding and appreciation of the key interests, and a profound realization of the real gap that divides the two, leading to an urgent reevaluation of the primary importance of the seminal bridge between the stated interests of China and those often left unstated by the United States.

Works Cited

Addicott, A. "U.S. report: global religious freedom at risk." *The Washington Times* (22 Nov. 2010). http://communities.washingtontimes.com/neighborhood/flip-side-faith-politics-communication/2010/nov/22/us-report-global-religious-freedom-risj/ (accessed 25 Nov. 2010).

Alford, P. "US back in Asia and stay." *The Australian* (14 Jan. 2010). http://www.theaustralian.com.au/news/nation/us-back-in-asia-to-stay-hillary-clinton/story-e6frg6nf-1225819009663 (accessed 24 Nov. 2010).

Applebaum, A. "How to speak human rights." *The New York Times* (24 Feb. 2009). http://www.washingtonpost.com/wp-dyn/content/story/2009/02/23/ST2009022302443.html?sid=ST2009022302443 (accessed 25 Nov. 2010).

Barnes, J.E. "U.S. to hold military exercise with South Korea." *The Los Angeles Times* (24 May 2010). http://articles.latimes.com/2010/may/24/nation/la-na-korea-ship25-20100525 (accessed 25 Aug. 2010).

Brower, K.A. "Obama calls alliance with Japan critical to security." *BusinessWeek* (23 Sept. 2010). http://www.businessweek.com/news/2010-09-23/obama-calls-alliance-with-japan-critical-to-security.html (accessed 25 Nov. 2010).

CBS News. "U.S. vows tougher stance on China trade issues." (15 April 2010). http://www.cbsnews.com/stories/2010/04/15/world/main 6398251.shtml (accessed 25 Nov. 2010).

Cha, A.E. and G. Kessler. "Pelosi mum on rights before trip to China." *The Washington Post* (24 May 2009). http://www.washingtonpost.com/wp-dyn/content/article/2009/05/23/AR2009052301876.html (accessed 11 July 2010).

Clinton, H.R. "A conversation with U.S. Secretary of State Hillary Rodham Clinton." *Council on Foreign Relations* (8 Sept. 2010). http://www.cfr.

org/publication/22896/conversation_with_us_secretary_of_state_hill-ary_rodham_clinton.html (accessed 25 Nov. 2010).

Cloud, D.S. "U.S. to resume aid to Kopassus, Indonesia's controversial military forces." *The Los Angeles Times* (23 July 2010). http://articles.latimes.com/2010/jul/23/world/la-fg-0723-indonesia-obama-20100723 (accessed 25 Nov. 2010).

Cooper, H. "China holds firm on major issues in Obama's visit." *The New York Times* (17 Nov. 2010a). http://www.nytimes.com/2009/11/18/world/asia/18prexy.html (accessed 25 Nov. 2010).

———. "U.S. arms to Taiwan send Beijing a message." *The New York Times* (31 Jan. 2010b). http://www.nytimes.com/2010/02/01/world/asia/01china.html (accessed 7 Oct. 2010).

Goodman, P.S. "U.S. unemployment rate hits 10.2%, highest in 26 years." *The New York Times* (6 Nov. 2009). http://www.nytimes.com/2009/11/07/business/economy/07jobs.html?_r=1&adxnnl=1&adxnnlx=1289786404-K2/J8PbIlLdKcUkC9OFfUA (accessed 1 Sept. 2010).

Heilprin, J. "Obama urged to get tough on China." *The Washington Times* (17 Nov. 2010). http://www.washingtontimes.com/news/2010/nov/17/obama-urged-to-get-tough-on-china/ (accessed 25 Nov. 2010).

Holland, S. and T. Zakaria. "Clinton urges Bush to boycott Beijing Olympics." *Reuters* (7 April 2008). http://www.reuters.com/article/idUSN0642976020080407 (accessed 11 July 2010).

Hulse, C. "Pelosi suggests Bush boycott Olympics opening." *The New York Times* (2 April 2008). http://www.nytimes.com/2008/04/02/world/americas/02iht-boycott.1.11614705.html (accessed 11 July 2010).

The Joint Civilian-Military Investigation Group. *Investigation Result on the Sinking of ROK's "Cheonan."* (20 May 2010). http://news.bbc.co.uk/nol/shared/bsp/hi/pdfs/20_05_10jigreport.pdf (accessed 25 Sept. 2010).

Kirkland, J. "Steelworkers accuse China of unfair trade practices in clean technologies. *The New York Times* (10 Sept. 2010). http://www.nytimes.com/cwire/2010/09/10/10climatewire-steelworkers-accuse-china-of-unfair-trade-pr-10450.html (accessed 25 Nov. 2010).

Knowlton, B., and N. Fathi. "U.S. reports describes worsening human rights in Iran and China." *The New York Times* (11 March 2010). http://www.nytimes.com/2010/03/12/world/12rights.html (accessed 25 Nov. 2010).

Krauthammer, C. "The fruits of weakness." *The Washington Post* (21 May 2010). http://www.washingtonpost.com/wp-dyn/content/article/2010/05/20/AR2010052003885.html (accessed 15 Sept. 2010).

La Monica, P.R. "Why the U.S. needs China." *CNN* (21 Oct. 2008). http://money.cnn.com/2008/10/21/markets/thebuzz/index.htm (accessed 12 Nov. 2010).

Mason, M. "U.S. and Vietnam, once enemies, now military mates." *The Washington Times* (8 Aug. 2010). http://www.washingtontimes.com/news/2010/aug/8/us-and-vietnam-once-enemies-now-military-mates/ (accessed 25 Nov. 2010).

Morrison, W.M. "China–U.S. trade issues." *CRS Report for Congress* (29 July 2010). http://ncseonline.org/NLE/CRSreports/08Mar/RL33536. pdf (accessed 15 Sept. 2010).

Munakata, N. "The U.S., China and Japan in an integrating East Asia." *Brookings Northeast Asia Commentary.* Vol. 35. (13 Jan. 2010). http://www.brookings.edu/opinions/2010/0113_asia_trade_munakata. aspx (accessed 25 Nov. 2010).

Obama Meets Hu, Says Tibet Part of China. *The Times of India* (17 Nov. 2009). http://timesofindia.indiatimes.com/world/china/Obama-meets-Hu-says-Tibet-part-of-China/articleshow/5238752.cms (accessed 11 July 2010).

Pomfret, J. "Obama's meeting with Dalai Lama is delayed." *The Washington Post* (5 Oct. 2009). http://www.washingtonpost.com/wp-dyn/ content/article/2009/10/04/AR2009100403262.html (accessed 11 July 2010).

———. "Clinton wades into South China Sea territorial dispute." *The Washington Post* (23 July 2010a). http://voices.washingtonpost.com/ checkpoint-washington/2010/07/clinton_wades_into_south_china. html (accessed 15 Sept. 2010).

———. "U.S. continues effort to counter China's influence in Asia." (23 July 2010b). http://www.washingtonpost.com/wp-dyn/content/arti-cle/2010/07/22/AR2010072206037.html (accessed 15 Sept. 2010).

———. "U.S. risks China's ire with decision to fund software maker tied to Falun Gong." (12 May 2010c). http://www.washingtonpost.com/ wp-dyn/content/article/2010/07/22/AR2010072206037.html (accessed 15 Sept. 2010).

———. "U.S. takes a tougher tone with China." *The Washington Post* (30 July 2010d). http://www.washingtonpost.com/wp-dyn/content/ article/2010/07/29/AR2010072906416.html (accessed 15 Sept. 2010).

Quinn, A. "U.S. eyes talks with Myanmar after Suu Kyi release." *Reuters* (15 Nov. 2010). http://www.reuters.com/article/idUSTRE6AE 4IE20101115 (accessed 25 Nov. 2010).

Roth, K. "Obama's hesitant embrace of human rights." *The New York Times* (3 March 2010). http://www.nytimes.com/2010/03/04/opinion/04iht-edroth.html (accessed 25 Nov. 2010).

Sanger, D.E. "North Koreans unveil new plant for nuclear use." *The New York Times* (20 Nov. 2010a). http://www.nytimes.com/2010/11/21/ world/asia/21intel.html (accessed 24 Nov. 2010).

———. "With warning, Obama presses China on currency." (23 Sept. 2010b). http://www.nytimes.com/2010/09/24/world/24prexy.html (accessed 24 Nov. 2010).

Song, S. "Boat capitan freed." *Global Times* (25 Sept. 2010). http://china. globaltimes.cn/diplomacy/2010-09/576743.html (accessed 25 Nov. 2010).

Spetalnick, M. "Obama meets Dalai Lama, angering China." *Reuters* (18 Feb. 2010). http://www.reuters.com/article/idUSN1116932520100218 (accessed 25 Nov. 2010).

Sutter, R.G. *U.S.-Chinese Relations: Perilous Past, Pragmatic Present.* Maryland: Rowman & Littlefield Publishers, 2009.

Sutter, R.G., J. Wang, J.B. Jacobs, et al. "Roundtable: defining a healthy balance across the Taiwan Strait. *Asia Policy.* Vol. 6 (July 2009), 1–46.

There's No Free Lunch. *China Daily* (3 June 2009). http://www.china-daily.com.cn/cndy/2009-06/03/content_7965661.htm (accessed 11 Nov. 2010).

The United Nations Security Council. "Security Council condemns attack on Republic of Korea naval ship 'Cheonan.'" *President Statement,* S/PRST/2010/13 (9 July 2010). http://www.un.org/News/Press/docs/2010/sc9975.doc.htm (accessed 20 Aug. 2010).

Yan, X.T. "The instability of China–U.S. relations." *The Chinese Journal of International Politics,* Vol. 3, No. 3 (2010), 263–292.

Young, J.A. "China's premier avoids backing sanctions for N. Korea." *The Washington Times* (30 May 2010). http://www.washingtontimes.com/news/2010/may/29/china-offers-s-korea-condolences-ship-sinking/ (accessed 20 Aug. 2010).

Chapter 18

Counterterrorism Policy

Leonard Cutler

The record of the Bush administration in the aftermath of 9/11 includes the overthrow of the Taliban regime in Afghanistan, the disruption of al-Qaeda's power infrastructure, and the capture or killing of some of the terrorist organization's worst actors. However, it also included a violation of international as well as domestic legal standards related to torture, subjecting alleged terrorist prisoners to arbitrary indefinite detention and inhumane and degrading treatment, creating secret CIA-run prisons abroad, using unlawful rendition, and employing extensive international and domestic warrantless surveillance without court supervision. What are we to make of these conflicting results? On account of the latter actions, George W. Bush adversely affected our relationship with other nation-states, and compromised the goal of reducing anti-American sentiment in the global arena (Goldsmith 2007). Such outcomes are necessary to the successful prosecution of the country's counterterrorism policies and goals.

With the historic election of Barack Obama in 2008, it was expected that the American public would witness a significant departure from the Bush administration's policies, particularly related to national security and counterterrorism issues. Several hot button items including, but not limited to, the detention facility at Guantanamo Bay, the use of military commissions, indefinite detention of alleged terrorists, enhanced interrogation techniques, torture, extraordinary rendition, and the abuse of the state secrets privilege by the U.S. government were ripe for action by the new administration, which campaigned on the theme of changing course in counterterrorism policy to make it more consistent with constitutional principles and with international law.

What is evident is that midway through its first term, the Obama administration's policies are more consistent with the Bush administration's policies, yet there are substantial and notable distinctions between their approaches that could significantly impact counterterrorism policy for the foreseeable future. What is also noteworthy is that presidential candidates campaign in poetry, and once elected they govern in prose.

Closure of the Guantanamo Bay Prison Facility

Even prior to his inauguration, Obama said in an interview that he planned to issue an executive order during his first week in office closing the Guantanamo Bay detention facility. However, he added that the following:

> [C]losing Guantanamo . . . is a challenge. I think it's going to take some time and our legal teams are working in consultation with our national security apparatus as we speak to help design exactly what we need to do. We are going to close Guantanamo and we are going to make sure that the procedures we set up are ones that abide by our Constitution.[1]

The Bush administration publicly advocated for the closure of Guantanamo as early as 2006, however, as is demonstrated from the statement of Secretary of State Condoleezza Rice provided here, there were recognizable concerns to be addressed in attempts to do so and Bush never really made a serious public appeal to do so.

> . . . the United States doesn't desire to keep Guantanamo in being any longer than it's needed because we don't want to be the world's jailer. We must recognize, however, Guantanamo is there for a reason. There are some people who cannot either be safely released to their countries or certainly released at all. (Onikepe 2006)

---

1. See, http://jurist.law.pitt.edu/paperchase/2009/01/obama-orders-guantanamo-prison-closed.php.

In his second day in office, Obama did in fact issue two executive orders, the first directing that the Guantanamo Bay military prison be closed "as soon as practicable, and no later than one year from the date of the order."[2] The second order called for an immediate review of all the detainees held at the naval base to determine whether they should be transferred, released, or for that matter, prosecuted.[3] Approximately 240 detainees remained at Guantanamo when Obama issued his executive order calling for the closure of the prison facility. Of that group it was estimated that 150 individuals would be eligible for release or transfer to a foreign home or host nation. The balance would be subject to determinations relative to whether and where they were to be prosecuted.

On May 21, 2009, Obama delivered a major national security speech at the National Archives in which he focused on the closing of the Guantanamo Bay prison facility, and what to do about the remaining detainees still held there. He stated the following:

1. Some of the detainees would be tried in U.S. federal courts for violations of federal law.

2. A second category would be tried by reconstituted military commissions for violations of the laws of war.

3. A third category of detainees had been ordered released by the courts.

4. A fourth category included those who could be safely transferred to other nations.

5. The final group of detainees were those who could not be tried in the federal courts or by military commission, but the government believed were too dangerous for release or transfer.

The small group of detainees in the final category would be subject to what the president called prolonged detention accompanied by procedural safeguards and oversight by both the judicial and legislative branches of government.

---

2. *See,* Executive Order 13492. Review and Disposition of Individuals Detained at the Guantanamo Bay Naval Base and Closure of Detention Facilities, 74 Fed. Reg. 4897 (Jan. 22, 2009), Section 3.

3. *See,* Executive Order 13493, Section 4(c)(3).

One of the impediments to closing Guantanamo included the number of detainees held there who were from Yemen. In the early days of the Obama administration there were one-hundred Yemeni detainees who remained at Guantanamo, the largest representation of foreign nationals held there. Given al-Qaeda's extensive presence in that country, plans to provide transfers and returns to Yemen became problematic, at best. In January 2010, the Obama administration announced that detainees would no longer be sent home to Yemen, and the sixty Yemenis who had already been cleared to return home after extensive review, would be denied that opportunity.

About five weeks prior to the anticipated closing date for the Guantanamo prison, Obama ordered the federal government to acquire the Thomson Correctional Center, a near vacant super-max-security prison located in northwestern Illinois, as the site to send a limited number of detainees. The administration was hopeful that Congress would approve the requested funding as part of its military spending bill for the 2010 fiscal year, but Democratic leaders refused to do so. Given the 2010 midterm election results and the volatility concerning moving the detainees to American soil, considerable hostility to this proposal existed from marginal Democrats as well as Republicans, who have regained control of the House and picked up several seats in the Senate. Because of continued congressional resistance, Obama has not been able to transfer the detainees and his desired timetable for closing the Guantanamo facility has not been accomplished as originally anticipated in his executive order.

The Military Commissions Acts of 2006 and 2009

The Military Commissions Act (MCA) of 2006[4] established commissions that were lacking substantive evidentiary requirements as well as fair-trial guarantees. They were subject to considerable criticism and challenged by the legal community, which led to a Supreme Court decision, *Boumediene v. Bush*[5] in 2008. In that ruling, the court determined that the detainees held at the Guantanamo Bay facility in Cuba were entitled to the constitutional

---

4. Military Commissions Act of 2006, Public Law 109-366.

5. *Boumediene v. Bush*, 128 S. Ct. 2229 (2008).

protection of petition for *habeas corpus* relief despite the fact that they were not nationals of the United States, and despite the fact that the MCA specifically denied them such relief. The court's ruling was narrow but it led to several additional challenges by detainees held at other military sites who were seeking a determination that the *Boumediene* decision applied to them and that the entire law was unconstitutional.

Military commissions created post-9/11 produced only three case decisions, two by trial, and one by a plea deal (Cutler 2008). Their seven-year track record with respect to efficiency, effectiveness, and most importantly, equity, was questionable at best.

Hours after he took office on January 20, 2009, Obama made good on a campaign pledge by ordering prosecutors before the military commission tribunals to seek a 120-day delay in all pending cases. The president's intent was to determine what forum was most appropriate for future prosecution of charged prisoners. At that point it appeared the continuation of the military commission process as developed in the MCA was in serious doubt.

There were, after all, several flaws in the MCA that had to be addressed once the Obama administration decided to reinstitute the military commission process. The MCA made the standard on interrogation treatment retroactive to 1997 in order to exempt CIA and military personnel from prosecution for past treatment under standards the administration considered vague.[6] Hearsay evidence that would not be admissible in court martial or ordinary U.S. courts under the Federal Rules of Evidence could be admitted in trial by the military commission unless the party opposing its use, having been given a fair opportunity to challenge the evidence, "demonstrated that the evidence was unreliable or lacking in probative value."[7] The language also provided that classified evidence could be used against charged detainees in military commission trials, but that a summary of that evidence must be provided to defendants.[8] Any classified information "shall be protected and is privileged from disclosure if such disclosure would be detrimental to the national security."[9] This rule applied to "all stages of

---

6. MCA, § 950 p(a).

7. MCA, § 949 a(b)(2)(E).

8. MCA, § 949 d(f)(2)(A).

9. MCA, § 949 d(f)(1).

10. MCA, § 949 j(d)(1).

the proceedings of Military Commissions, including the discovery phase" (Gates 2007). Of overriding concern was the applicability of these provisions even to any classified evidence that "reasonably tends to exculpate the accused."[10] Therefore, the defendant could very well be denied access to some or all governmental evidence that would serve to prove his innocence, if such evidence was classified and the government, with the approval of a military judge, considered it impracticable to provide a summary version.

The right to a lawyer of one's choice was restricted under the MCA because the defendant must bear the cost unless the person offered his services *pro bono*. The civilian lawyer must be a U.S. citizen and have passed a highly restrictive security clearance of "secret or higher."[11] Even if the defendant retained a U.S. civilian lawyer with the necessary security clearance, he or she would still be represented by a U.S. military lawyer as associate counsel, even if that goes against the defendant's wishes.[12]

On May 15, 2009, the Obama administration announced five rule changes to the military commission system as a first step toward achieving more meaningful reforms to the MCA. The rule changes "prohibited the admission of statements obtained through cruel, inhuman, and degrading treatment; provided detainees greater latitude as to choice of counsel; afforded basic protections for those defendants who refused to testify; reformed the use of hearsay by putting the burden on the party trying to use the statement; and made clear that military judges could determine their own jurisdiction" (Wiegmann 2009: 3).

In late June, the Senate Armed Services Committee (SASC) reported the fiscal year 2010 Defense Authorization Bill to the full Senate (S.7390), which included section 1031 that replaced the MCA with a new and improved military commissions system. Principle components of the administration's reform were incorporated into the bill as well as several other necessary reforms. Noteworthy among the changes were the following:

- Whereas in the original MCA, the test for admission of testimony allegedly obtained through coercion was tied to the passage of the Detainee Treatment Act (DTA),[13]

---

11. MCA, § 949 c(b)(3)(D).

12. MCA, § 949 c(a)(5).

13. MCA, § 948.

the new MCA applied the post-DTA test to all statements regardless of when they were taken.

- The MCA and the Defense Authorization Bill allowed for the admission of hearsay evidence at trial, although the test in section 1031 provided that the military judge may admit hearsay evidence after taking into account all of the circumstances surrounding the taking of the statement, the degree to which the statement was corroborated, and the indicia of reliability within the statement itself. The test for admission allowed the judge to admit the evidence only if: 1) The statement was offered as evidence of a material fact; 2) the general proposer of the rule of evidence and the interests of justice were best served by the admission of the statement into evidence; and 3) either direct testimony of the witness was not available as a practical matter or the production of the witness would have an adverse impact on military or intelligence operations.[14]

- The Defense Authorization Bill provided accused al-Qaeda terrorists with the same rights with respect to access to classified information against them as U.S. service members subject to court martial. Section 1031 of the new MCA required that classified information be handled in accordance with rules of general courts-martial.

- The new MCA sought to provide the same procedures and rules of evidence applicable in trials by general courts-martial for trials by military commission.[15]

- The original MCA established a Court of Military Commission Review to serve as the appellate court for the military commission trial forum. Further appeals were then authorized through the D.C. Circuit and the Supreme Court.[16] The new MCA vested the appellate path directly from the trial commission to the U.S. Court of Appeals for the Armed Forces, which is the

14. MCA, § 949 a(b)(2)(E).
15. MCA, § 948 b(c).
16. MCA, § 950 f(a).

current appellate forum for the Uniform Code of Military Justice (UCMJ).

- The new MCA defined cruel or inhuman treatment for a person in their custody as a grave breach to Common Article 3 of the Geneva Conventions. The original MCA defined cruel or inhuman treatment as an act "intended to inflict severe or serious physical or mental pain or suffering, including serious physical abuse."[17]

- The principal purpose of the MCA was to create a system in which alien unlawful enemy combatants would be tried for violations of the law of war.[18] The new MCA changed the label to unprivileged enemy belligerent and defined this person as one who 1) engaged in hostilities against the United States or its coalition partners; or 2) purposefully and materially supported hostilities against the United States or its coalition partners.

The MCA of 2009 is a marked improvement over its predecessor. Most importantly it established the following:

1. It excludes any statements obtained through torture, coercion, or cruel, inhuman, and degrading treatment.

2. It permits the defendant to attend all sessions, to have the right to cross-examine witnesses, and to call his or her own witnesses in his defense.

3. It requires prosecutors to turn over any exculpatory evidence as well as any evidence that might impeach the credibility of a government witness

4. It permits the defendant the option of hiring his or her own civilian lawyers or relying on ones willing to work pro bono, and defense lawyers who need secret level security clearances are entitled to examine classified information.

5. It allows a defendant found guilty by a military commission to appeal his or her conviction to a three-judge

---

17. MCA, § 948 r(b), and MMC Rule of Evidence 304 (b)(3).
18. MCA, § 948 b(a).

military review panel and then to the U.S. Court of Appeals for the D.C. Circuit.

Although Article III courts using the UCMJ as the benchmark remain the ideal structure to prosecute the detainees, they are not necessarily the most practical solution in all cases. Military Commissions have played a consistent role in our constitutional and historic tradition, and their use, when properly authorized by Congress, has been upheld by the U.S. Supreme Court. Such Commissions have been constitutionally recognized agencies for meeting urgent governmental responsibilities relating to the laws of war without Congress formally declaring war (Cutler 2005).

In mid-November 2009, Attorney General Eric Holder announced that Khalid Shaikh Mohammed, the self-described mastermind of the September 11 attacks, and four others accused in the plot, would be tried in a federal court in the Southern District of New York. The five alleged terrorists were initially held by the CIA and subsequently transferred to Guantanamo in 2006 to face pending charges before a Military Commission. This decision by the Obama administration was a major policy reversal from the Bush administration and set the stage for one of the highest-profile and highest-security terrorism trials in American history. Despite the fact that Holder said that he would instruct prosecutors to seek the death penalty for all five of the accused, his announcement precipitated considerable criticism and concern from members of Congress, New York City leaders, and family members of the 9/11 victims. Many insisted that military tribunals were the more secure and appropriate venue for trying the terrorist suspects, and that utilizing federal civilian courts would turn the entire process into a circus atmosphere. The Obama administration subsequently reserved its decision as to where to hold the trial.

Prolonged Detention of Suspected Terrorists

Post 9/11, the Bush administration's war on terror strategy was to indefinitely hold alleged enemy combatants in American military facilities around the globe including the naval base at Guantanamo Bay, Cuba, and the air base at Bagram, Afghanistan. The intention was to employ "aggressive" interrogation techniques to gather valuable information from the prisoners that would be useful to our national security interests, and under the laws of war, to hold them without charge.

Since September 2004, the movement of prisoners to Guantanamo has virtually come to a halt, leaving Bagram as the preferred detention site. It is estimated that the population at Bagram increased seven-fold from the period between 2005 and 2010, with approximately 800 detainees being held there. Virtually all of the Bagram suspects were captured on the battlefield and were being held in a war zone, and could pose a serious threat to the United States if they were released. This group is distinct from the remaining Guantanamo detainees who were not captured on the battlefield and were not being held in a war zone. What they share in common is the fact that they have been imprisoned for over six years without the legal process providing them any relief.

Because Obama was committed to an expanded U.S. role in its combat operations against the Taliban in Afghanistan, the question arose early on as to how this administration would differ from the Bush administration in its policy of detention in Afghanistan. If Obama moved away from the Bush administration's highly aggressive detention policies, how would they be reconciled with his plans to increase the military surge in Afghanistan, an action that would most certainly lead to greater numbers of detainees being taken into custody from the battlefield theater of war, and how would that fit within a counterinsurgency strategy in that nation?

Obama initially maintained that the United States is not in Afghanistan to control that country or to dictate its future. U.S. forces are there to defeat al-Qaeda. However, the strategy for waging the war there bears striking similarities to the strategy employed by Bush in Iraq, including a surge in the number of troops in the theater and a shift toward counterinsurgency and nation-building as the core strategies for winning the war (Desch 2009). The Pentagon acknowledged that Afghanistan became the military's top priority in the war against al-Qaeda and the Taliban supporters to which they are linked, and over 100,000 troops and support personnel were committed there by Obama. Obama did, however, shift the strategy and command in Iraq in 2009 and withdraw over 90,000 combat troops from the operation in 2010, as promised during his campaign.

The Obama administration has reasserted the Bush administration policy that detainees held at Bagram, even those who were arrested in other countries and were subsequently transported to Afghanistan, are not entitled to challenge their unlimited or prolonged detention in U.S. courts. The Justice Department has argued that Bagram is unlike Guantanamo, and it is a traditional theater of war, therefore the courts have no jurisdiction over detainees held there. That view has been upheld by the D.C. Circuit in *Magaleh et. al. v. Gates*,[19] a May 2010 unanimous decision authored by Chief Circuit Judge David B. Sentelle. He wrote that foreign nationals held at the United States military prison at Bagram, do not have a right to challenge in U.S. courts their continued imprisonment. "Detainees held in an active theater of war in a territory under neither the *de facto* nor *de jure* sovereignty of the United States and within the territory of another *de jure* sovereign" are not entitled to *habeas corpus* (Guiora 2010).

Despite the Circuit Court's ruling, pursuing a policy of indefinite detention is not only ineffective to fighting the war on terror; it is contrary to rule of law, which is the basis of the American constitutional system and its regard for fundamental due process rights (Jones and Libicki 2008). Obama lacks such authority particularly as it applies to those individuals who have been apprehended in nation states far removed from the Afghan battlefield and were not directly participating in hostilities and were subsequently brought to the theater of war for incarceration. The authority to indefinitely detain totally lacks any credibility when it is extended to persons who are seized outside of the theater of armed conflict, who are not directly participating in combat, but may be in their homes, at work, on a street or in a field cultivating crops. Indefinite detention is the hallmark of repressive regimes such as Egypt, Libya, and Syria, which currently hold hundreds of individuals in prolonged detention without charge or trial. No other western democracy has resorted to long-term detention without charge.

The Obama administration has argued that pursuant to the implied authority extant in the AUMF, the President has the legal power to indefinitely, or for a prolonged period, detain alleged or suspected terrorists who are national security threats to the United States. This same argument was proffered by the Bush

---

19. *See*, 2010 U.S. App. LEXIS 10384 (D.C. Cir. May 21, 2010). This decision overturned a federal district court opinion written by District Judge John D. Bates, 620 F. Supp. 2d 51 (D.D.C. 2009) which stated that *Boumediene* extends to Bagram, at least for non-Afghan nationals captured outside of Afghanistan and taken there for detention.

administration from 2001–2008. Additionally, it is concluded, that under such circumstances, any legislative enactment from Congress is unnecessary and unwarranted. This decision not to seek and receive congressional support and explicit authorization to provide for prolonged detention of suspected terrorists creates an opportunity that such an action may not only be repeated, but expanded upon by presidents in the future on the basis of serving our nation's security. At some point it will be left to the U.S. Supreme Court to resolve this issue.

Rendition and the Use of State Secrets Doctrine

In his Senate confirmation hearing Leon Panetta, Director of the CIA, stated that the United States will continue to hand foreign detainees over to other countries for questioning, but only with assurances that they would not be tortured . . . "because the United States is committed to the rule of law, all prisoners of this country regardless of where they are moved will be treated humanely" (Hess 2009).

Although the practice of unlawful rendition did not begin with the Bush administration, it should have ended with it. Despite the remarks of Panetta insisting that he would require assurances when carrying out renditions that transferred individuals will not be tortured, there is no guarantee to protect people at risk of torture under such circumstances, despite promises of humane treatment from the receiving government. There is no failsafe system to monitor mistreatment and detainees, in many such situations, are too afraid of reprisal to report such abuses. The Obama administration has not ruled out extraordinary rendition, and it appears to have adopted the same criteria employed by the Bush administration to gauge the potential for another country to employ torture (Spillius 2010).

The extraordinary rendition case of Binyam Mohamed is particularly troubling. Born in Ethiopia, Mohamed was arrested in Pakistan in 2002 while trying to board a flight to London. He became the subject of rendition from Pakistan to Morocco between 2002 and 2004, where he was tortured by Moroccan officials at the behest of United States and British intelligence officials who participated in the harsh interrogation process. American officials claimed that he was recruited by al-Qaida and was involved in a conspiracy to launch attacks in the United States. Mohamed was later transferred to Guantanamo Bay where he was detained for an additional five years. In early 2009 he was released and returned to Britain.

In 2007, the American Civil Liberties Union (ACLU) brought a civil suit on behalf of Mohamed and others against a Boeing subsidiary, Jeppesen Dataplan, for knowingly aiding in the rendition and subsequent torture of the alleged terror suspects by the CIA. Before Jeppesen could file an answer to the original complaint, the Department of Justice (DOJ) intervened and asserted the state secrets privilege, arguing that fact finding in the case could jeopardize national security. The district court dismissed the case and a three-judge panel of the Ninth Circuit overturned the ruling on appeal.[20] The Obama administration then asked the Ninth Circuit to reconsider the case with a full panel, and was granted an *en banc* rehearing.[21]

This case represents the first time a federal circuit court weighed in on the Obama administration's use of the state secrets privilege to seek dismissal of civil claims arising from allegations of torture that occurred as part of the government's extraordinary rendition program. By a 6-5 vote, the U.S. Court of Appeals for the Ninth Circuit affirmed the district court's dismissal of the suit.[22]

Less than two months after the *Jeppesen* decision, the British government announced that there would be provided a compensation package of several million dollars to a group of former detainees, including Binyam Mohamed to settle all pending court suits initiated by them. Prime Minister David Cameron insisted that "we need to deal with the totally unsatisfactory situation where for the past few years the reputation of our security services has been overshadowed by allegations about their involvement in the treatment of detainees held by other countries" (Burns, Cowell 2010).

Obama told voters in 2008 that he opposed the government cult of secrecy, and once he became president, his administration developed improved policies and procedures governing the invocation of the state secrets privilege, but the Attorney General was provided the sole authority to assert it. The assertion of privilege

---

20. *See, Mohamed v. Jeppesen Dataplan, Inc.* 579 F. 3d 943 (9th Cir. 2009) (*Jeppesen I*).

21. *Rehearing en banc granted,* 586 F. 3d 1108 (9th Cir. 2009).

22. *Binyam Mohamed v. Jeppesen Dataplan, Inc.,* No. 08-15963 (9th Cir. 2010) (*Jeppesen II*).

in the *Jeppesen* case is certainly reminiscent of the Bush administration's position in earlier cases.

The Obama administration did develop enhanced internal oversight measures for the invocation of state secrets privilege, but they do not go far enough to secure proper checks and balances against potential abuse. Privilege concerns matters that are too critical and significant to leave to exclusive executive discretion. Congress has an institutional interest and a legitimate role in seeing that the President not use his state secrets claim effectively to withhold information from Congress itself. Congress should codify a state secrets privilege that insures both accountability and the protection of legitimate national security interests (Friedman and Hansen 2010).

Conclusion

Terrorism continues to pose a serious threat to the United States, and will most probably do so for years to come. The President and Congress, consistent with their constitutional duties and responsibilities, are the critical actors in the debate about how best to preserve constitutional values while protecting the nation's security.

When Bush stood before a joint session of Congress just days after the devastating terrorist attack of 11 September 2001, he declared that our war on terror may begin with al-Qaida but it does not end there. When he returned to Congress in January to deliver his State of the Union Address, he cited Hamas, Hezbollah, Islamic Jihad, North Korea, Iran, and Iraq in addition to al-Qaida as the principal sponsors of terrorism and emphasized the need for the president to assert his military powers. The United States was in a state of war against terror, terrorists, and terrorism which required the president to utilize such tools as indefinite detention, Military Commissions, enhanced interrogation techniques, and rendition to effectively combat this menace. The criminal justice system—including arrest, indictment, arraignment, extradition, and civilian trials—was inappropriate to address the terror threat. Bush also compared the war on terrorism to World War II and the Cold War, a global, generation-defining struggle against an enemy of extensive military and ideological power that would transform major portions of the globe. For over seven years the Bush administration linked al-Qaida and the Taliban together, as it did other terror groups and "enemies" of the United States.

They were the terrorists who committed the acts and those who harbored them.

Many of the policies pursued by Bush have extensive historical roots and precedence. For example, every wartime president asserted his right to indefinitely detain enemy forces without charge during the period of conflict. Military Commissions have been employed since the earliest days of the Republic for prosecution of war criminals. Rendition began under President Bill Clinton and possibly earlier. The responsibility of the executive office to protect national security interests led Bush to seek to use his full arsenal of tools to fight the war on terror.

The effect of the Bush administration's law of war strategy was to distort the legitimacy of practices that had been acceptable in prior wars. As Jack Goldsmith observed:

> The early Bush administration failed to grasp what Lincoln and Roosevelt understood well: The vital ongoing need to convince the citizenry that the president is using his extraordinary war powers for the public good and not for personal or institutional aggrandizement. By the time the Bush administration began to act on principle in the second term, it was too late; its credibility on these issues . . . severely damaged . . . was unrecoverable" (Goldsmith 2009).

Obama was a major critic of Bush's terrorism policies, including indefinite detention, the use of Military Commissions, enhanced interrogation techniques, rendition, and the abuse of the state secrets doctrine. As president, Obama has accepted the position that, legally, we are in a state of war with the organization that attacked the United States on 9/11, al-Qaida, and our aim is to defeat it, not the vague concept of terror or terrorism globally. Moreover, the Obama administration has essentially accepted the core legal position of the Bush strategy with respect to indefinite detention of alleged terrorists held at Guantanamo as well as other sites such as Afghanistan. A distinction in Obama's approach is that it has eliminated the use of the designation "enemy combatant," and narrowed the reach of those who can be detained from persons who "support" al-Qaida to individuals who "substantially support" them. Additionally, the administration has insisted that its authority is rooted in the AUMF and international laws of war. Obama vowed to work closely with Congress to maintain its support for his actions despite the fact that he believes additional legislative action is not required at this time. Bush relied upon his Article II authority as Commander-in-Chief to unilaterally detain suspected terrorists without congressional or judicial support, or for that matter international covenants or conventions. President Obama has yet to do so.

Both John Yoo and Jack Goldsmith have suggested that Obama has more in common with the ends of Bush's terrorism policies because he shares Bush's broad view of presidential power. However, it is also clear that there are discernable distinctions between the two presidents' approach to the legal framework employed in the war against terror. Obama emphasized respect for constitutional values and the need to observe the rule of law which led to his decision to close the Guantanamo Bay facility. Symbolically this detainee prison camp had developed a reputation as a legal black hole into which those who were captured in the war on terror were dumped. The President also: 1) established an aggressive timeline for its closure; 2) created a plan to transfer detainees housed there to a prison complex in northern Illinois; and 3) announced that the United States would try suspects being held at Guantanamo in Military Commissions or civilian courts depending on the suspect and allegations. Khalid Shaikh Moham- med and four other high profile terrorist suspects were selected by the Attorney General to be prosecuted in federal court.

The very recent acquittal in civilian court of the first Guan- tanamo detainee, Ahmed Ghailani, on all but one of more than 285 terrorism related charges, including all of the 224 murder counts for those killed in the 1998 embassy bombings in Nairobi Kenya, and Dar es Salaam in Tanzania, has escalated the attacks on the administration that civilian courts and juries cannot handle terror cases. The new chairman of the House Homeland Security Committee, Peter King (R-N.Y.), has maintained that Guantanamo detainees must be treated as wartime enemies and tried exclu- sively by Military Commissions.

This nation should remain on the offensive to protect the American people. The government should continue to bring the world's most dangerous terrorists to justice, and it should do so in the context of the rule of law. Arrest and detention without charge truly offends the Constitution and should never be permit- ted. Using humiliation and degrading abuse in interrogations is un-American, and seizing citizens of foreign nations and placing them beyond the reach of law is antithetical to the principles of justice that are held so dearly as core values of American society. Human rights guarantees provided in international treaties to which the United States is a signatory, such as the Geneva Conventions, as well as customary principles of international law to which we subscribe, must be upheld in word, deed, and spirit.

What may be the most difficult of the many issues raised by the Guantanamo detention experience, is the question of what to do with those detainees who cannot be released, transferred to other nations, or for that matter, prosecuted either by courts or Military Commissions. This category of detainee is deeply troubling because they are subject to prolonged if not indefinite detention. How is such a determination made and what criteria were used to determine that such individuals are too dangerous to be released? Certainly the fact that a person was tortured in detention or that he was detained on the basis of information extracted from torture cannot be a legitimate basis for prolonged detention, given that such evidence cannot be introduced for purposes of prosecution. How then could it be concluded that a person who could not be prosecuted because he was tortured, be detained indefinitely?

The decision by Obama not to seek explicit congressional approval for prolonged or indefinite detention of those held at Guantanamo, and for that matter others who may currently be in similar circumstances elsewhere, or those alleged terrorists who the United States may capture in the future, continues the unilateral decision making strategy that characterized Bush's failed counterterrorism policy. The lack of transparency in the Obama administration's decision making process concerning this group of detainees raises questions not only about the credibility of the process but as well the accuracy of the conclusion reached that these individuals pose a real threat to our national security interests. As Gabor Rona, international law director of Human Rights First, recently observed:

> . . . the Obama Administration has moved from an incorrect interpretation of presidential powers under the Bush administration to an incorrect interpretation of the laws of war, with the same result. The Bush administration said it didn't have to worry about international law and could arrange detention authority as it liked on the basis of executive authority. The Obama administration stakes but a narrower claim—it accepts that the laws of war matter, but it then develops a concept of detainable

persons which is essentially the same as Bush's, arguing that it is permitted under the laws of war. But the laws of war don't authorize detention so broadly—they do not permit the detention of anyone, anywhere, who has an association, even a substantial one, with an enemy, which is how the Obama team would have it. (Horton 2010)

It is of significance that post 9/11 neither the Republican nor Democrat President or Congress have been able to create a legally effective interrogation, detention, and trial system for detainees who are alleged to be unprivileged enemy belligerents. Obama (and future presidents) must work directly with Congress to address and respond to counterterrorism policy issues. To do so collaboratively will ensure that adherence for our constitutional values and heritage will not exclusively revolve around the personality of the Commander-in-Chief regardless of who occupies that office. Respect and observance of these constitutional values will preserve the rule of law in decision making consistent with American values of fairness and justice.

Works Cited

Burns, J.F. and Cowell, A. "Britain to compensate former Guantanamo detainees." *The New York Times* (17 Nov. 2010). www.nytimes.com/2010/11/17/world/europe/17britain.html.

Cutler, L. Development in National Security Policy Since 9/11: The Separate Roles of the President Congress and the United States Supreme Court. Edwin Mellen Press, 2008.

———. *The Rule of Law and the Law of War, Military Commissions and Enemy Combatants Post 9/11*. Edwin Mellen Press, 2005, 15. *See* "Counterterrorism and Human Rights," Number 1, January 2010, at 5.

Desch, M. "A necessary war taken to unnecessary extremes." *Peace Policy*. (1 Oct. 2009). http://peacepolicy.nd.edu/2009/10/01/necessary-war-unnecessary-extremes/

Friedman, L. and Hansen. "Jeppesen: A cry for congressional help on state secrets." *Jurist*—Forum (30 Sept. 2010]. http://jurist.org/forum/2010/09/jeppesen-a-cry-for-congressional-help-on-state-secrets.php.

Gates, R. *Manual for Military Commissions* (MMC) (18 Jan. 2007). http://www.defenselink.mil/news/commissionsmanual.html.

Goldsmith, J. *The Terror Presidency: Law and Judgment Inside the Bush Administration*. New York: W.W. Norton, 2007.

Goldsmith, J. "The Cheney fallacy." *New Republic* (18 May 2009). http://www.tnr.com/print/article/politics/the-cheney-fallacy.

Guiora, A. "The Bagram Habeas decision: Bad law, bad policy." *Jurist—Forum* (27 May 2010). http://jurist.org/forum/2010/05/the-bagram-habeas-ruling.php.

Hess, P. "Panetta takes back remarks on detainee rendition." *Associated Press* (6 Feb. 2009). http://timesunion.com/aspstories/storyprint.urp?storyID=767099.

Horton, S. "Rift in Obama counterterrorism policy?" *Harpers* (29 March 2010). http://www.harpers.org/archive/2010/03/hbc-90006793.

Jones, S.G. and Libicki, M.C. *How Terrorist Groups End: Lessons for countering Al Qaida.* RAND, Monograph Report MG-741-RC, 2008.

Onikepe, A. "United States dismisses UK call to close Guantanamo Bay." *Jurist* (11 May 2006). http://jurist.law.pitt.edu/paperchase/2006_05_11_indexarch.php.

Spillius, A. "Barack Obama to allow anti-terror rendition to continue." *The Telegraph* UK. (1 Feb. 2010). http://www.telegraph.co.uk/news/worldnews/northamerica/usa/barackobama/4425135/Barack-Obama-to-allow-anti-terror-rendition-to-continue.html.

Weiser, B. "Detainee acquitted on most counts in '98 bombings." *The New York Times* (17 Nov. 2010). www.nytimes.com/2010/11/18/nyregion/18ghailani.html.

Wiegmann, B. and M. Martins. Memorandum for the Attorney General, the Secretary of Defense, *Preliminary Report*, Detention Policy Task Force, 20 July 2009 (3).

Chapter 19

Obama, Libya, and War Powers

Louis Fisher

Three Wars

In 2011, President Barack Obama found himself involved in three wars, two inherited and one of his own making. Upon taking office, he decided to escalate the war in Afghanistan by sending in 30,000 additional troops. It was his expectation that he could begin withdrawing U.S. troops by fall 2011, but how quickly they could be withdrawn was uncertain, nor was it clear that Afghanistan had the capacity to independently defend itself against the Taliban. Obama had withdrawn troops from Iraq to a level of 50,000, with the plan of having few troops left by the end of his term. The likelihood of achieving that objective was complicated by continued terrorist attacks within the country. It was possible that Iraq might request that U.S. troops remain in the country to provide political stability.

President Obama achieved a military and political victory on May 1, 2011 by authorizing a military action in Pakistan that resulted in the death of Osama bin Laden, who was killed in a firefight in a compound in Abbottabad, Pakistan. The success of that operation did much to elevate Obama's standing in the polls as a decisive and effective leader, although the momentary bump in popularity was not likely to have a staying power, or certainly not into the 2012 presidential election. The raid on the compound, without the knowledge or approval of Pakistan, did much to deteriorate relations between the two allies battling international terrorism. Many factors contributed to this decline, including the continued use of armed drones by the United States into Pakistan, resulting in the deaths not just of terrorists but innocent civilians (DeYoung and Witte 2011: 1).

In March 2011, Obama opened a new war in Libya without seeking or obtaining authority from Congress. He sought legal and political support from two outside organizations, the UN Security Council (UNSC) and NATO allies. It was his expectation that the military operation would be limited and brief, taking a matter of days not weeks. Presidents frequently learn that they cannot anticipate or control the decision to use military force. What he announced on March 21, 2011 as a military engagement limited in its "nature, duration, and scope" turned out to be far more complicated, continuing month after month and departing from the initial objectives of the UNSC.

From No-Fly Zone to Regime Change

The decision to use military force against Libya began with Resolution 1973 passed by the UNSCon March 17, 2011. After expressing its earlier concern about the escalation of violence and heavy civilian casualties in Libya, the resolution established a ban on "all flights in the airspace of the Libyan Arab Jamahiriya in order to help protect civilians." The ban applied not to "all" flights but only those by the Libyan government. Military flights by coalition forces would be needed to enforce the ban. Passage of Resolution 1973 came only after the Arab League had agreed to support a no-fly zone over Libya (DeYoung and Lynch 2011: A1, A6). Once military action began and the Arab League watched the intensity and destructive force of the bombings, it "voiced concern about civilian deaths" from collateral damage (Fina and Jaffe 2011: A1).

On March 21, 2011, the president notified Congress that U.S. forces "at my direction" commenced military operations two days earlier against Libya "to assist an international effort authorized by the UN Security Council" (Obama 2011b). How can authority for a U.S. military action come from the UNSC rather than from Congress? Does the U.S. Constitution allow the transfer of congressional powers to outside bodies, including the UN and NATO? As explained below: No.

The March statement by President Obama offered several details on the scope of military operations. Acting under Resolution 1973, coalition partners began a series of strikes against Libya's air defense systems and military airfields "for the purposes of preparing a no-fly zone." The strikes "will be limited in their nature, duration, and scope." U.S. military efforts were designed to be "discrete and focused" on American capabilities "to set the conditions for our European allies and Arab partners to carry out the measures authorized by the U.N. Security Council Resolution."

Although Libya announced an immediate cease-fire, government forces continued attacks on Misurata and Benghazi, resulting in what Obama called the deaths of civilians, destabilization of the region, and "defiance of the Arab League." In response, he ordered U.S. forces to target Libya's air defense systems, command and control structures, "and other capabilities of Qadhafi's armed forces to attack civilians and civilian populated areas." Obama's March statement noted that U.S. ground forces were not deployed into Libya. He sought "a rapid, but responsible, transition of operations" to coalition and regional organizations, relying on NATO allies.

Expectations and plans about military action against Libya began to unravel week by week. On March 21, Obama announced at a news conference: "It is U.S. policy that Qaddafi needs to go" (Bumiller and Fahim 2011: A1, A11). The initial no-fly zone policy now added regime change. During this same period, Gen. Carter F. Ham, in charge of the coalition effort, stated that the United States was not working with the rebels: "Our mission is not to support any opposition forces" (Bumiller and Fahim 2011: A11). Allied bombing operations in Libya proceeded to do precisely that. On April 21, the Pentagon announced that the president had authorized the use of armed Predator drones against Qaddafi forces (Kirkpatrick and Shanker 2011: A1, A9). On April 25, NATO directed two bombs into a residential and military complex used by Qaddafi in central Tripoli (Denyer and Fadel 2011a: A9).

Newspaper reports on May 1 described a NATO air strike in Tripoli that killed one of Qaddafi's sons and three of his grand-children (Denyer and Fadel 2011b: A1; Fahim and Kirkpatrick 2011: 1). The children included a six-month-old granddaughter, a two-year-old grandson, and a two-year-old granddaughter (Denyer 2011: A8). On May 5, the Obama administration announced that it had begun efforts to release some of the more than $30 billion in assets it had seized from Libya and divert the money to Libyan rebels. Secretary of State Hillary Clinton announced that the administration would ask Congress for legislative authority to shift some of the frozen assets to help the Libyan people, including assistance to the rebels (Myers and Donadio 2011: A9; Sheridan 2011: A8).

Obama's Constitutional Position

In his March statement, President Obama explained that he directed the military actions against Libya not on congressional authority but "pursuant to my constitutional authority to conduct U.S. foreign relations and as Commander in Chief and Chief Executive." In a March 28, 2011 address to the nation, Obama described his Libyan actions in this manner: "The United States has done what we said we would do" (Obama 2011a: 2). His reference to "the United States" did not mean the executive and legislative branches working jointly. Obama alone made the military commitment. He did identify certain supporting institutions: "We had a unique ability to stop that violence: an international mandate for action, a broad coalition prepared to join us, the support of Arab countries, and a plea for help from the Libyan people themselves" (Obama 2011a: 3). Absent from this picture were Congress and the American people.

During his presidential campaign, *Boston Globe* reporter Charlie Savage asked Obama for his position on several constitutional questions. One question: "In what circumstances, if any, would the president have constitutional authority to bomb Iran without seeking a use-of-force authorization from Congress? (Specifically, what about the strategic bombing of suspected nuclear sites—a situation that does not involved stopping an IMMINENT threat?)" In a detailed response, Obama answered: "The President does not have power under the Constitution to unilaterally authorize a military attack in a situation that does not involve stopping an actual or imminent threat to the nation" (Obama 2008). He added that the president, as commander-in-chief:

> does have a duty to protect and defend the United States. In instances of self-defense, the President would be within his constitutional authority to act before advising Congress or seeking its consent. History has shown us time and again, however, that military action is most successful when it is authorized and supported by the Legislative branch. It is always preferable to have the informed consent of Congress prior to any military action.

Nothing that Libya did in 2011 amounted to "an actual or imminent threat" to the United States.

Taking the Country to War

Obama's analysis as a presidential candidate closely tracks the constitutional principles of the American Framers, who specifically and deliberately rejected the British political system that centered all of external affairs—including foreign affairs and the war power—in the executive. Their rejection is central to America's democratic and constitutional government. In his *Second Treatise on Civil Government* (1690), John Locke placed all of external affairs with the executive. Similarly, William Blackstone's *Commentaries on the Laws of England,* published in the 1760s, gave the whole of external powers to the executive: the power to declare war, make treaties, appoint ambassadors, issue letters of marque and reprisal, and raise and regulate fleets and armies.

The Framers denied the president the exclusive use of any of those powers, vesting them either exclusively in Congress or requiring the President to obtain Senate approval for treaties and appointments. This fundamental change in government reflected the Framers' intention to safeguard self-government and popular sovereignty. Statements at the Philadelphia Convention and the state ratification conventions repudiate the models of Locke and Blackstone. Alexander Hamilton, who looked to the British system with great admiration and affection, conceded at Philadelphia that the theories of Locke and Blackstone had no application to America and its commitment to republican government (Farrand 1937: 288–290). Pierce Butler stood alone in wanting to give the president the power to take the country to war against another nation. The president "will have all the requisite qualities, and will not make war but when the Nation will support it" (Farrand 1937: 318). Other delegates, denouncing his proposal, reserved to Congress the power to initiate war and permitted the President only defensive powers "to repel sudden attacks." Elbridge Gerry expressed shock at Butler's position. He "never expected to hear in a republic a motion to empower the Executive alone to declare war" (Farrand 1937: 318). Many policies adopted by the Framers do not deserve our support, including their acceptance of slavery and denying women the right to vote. But their opposition to executive wars remains on target for the twenty-first century. The United States has suffered greatly from such presidential wars as Korea under Harry Truman, Vietnam under Lyndon B. Johnson, and Iraq under George W. Bush.

The Korean War

Could President Obama receive "authorization" from the UNSC to use military force against another nation? Did the UN Charter somehow transfer the constitutional power of Congress to an international body? The answer to both questions: No. Authority under law and the Constitution must come from Congress. The UN Participation Act of 1945 speaks unambiguously about the procedure needed when presidents use American troops in a UN military operation: "The President is authorized to negotiate a special agreement or agreements with the Security Council which shall be subject to the approval of the Congress by appropriate Act or joint resolution" (22 U.S.C. § 287d; Fisher 2011).

Notwithstanding this law, President Harry Truman ignored it in 1950 when he went to war against North Korea. At no time did he seek or obtain authority from Congress. He chose to violate the Constitution, the 1945 statute, and his own public pledge to the Senate (Fisher 1995). During World War II, the United States and allied nations decided it was necessary to create an international body to act against aggression. The UN Charter provides that whenever member states agree to participate in a UN military operation, nations must act in accordance with their "constitutional processes." During Senate debate on the charter, President Truman from Potsdam wired this cable to Sen. Kenneth McKellar on July 27, 1945, pledging: "When any such agreement or agreements are negotiated it will be my purpose to ask the Congress for appropriate legislation to approve them" (U.S. Congress 1945).

To implement the charter, Congress was required to pass legislation that satisfied U.S. constitutional processes. The language in Section 6 of the UN Participation Act of 1945 did precisely that. Agreements "shall be subject to the approval of the Congress by appropriate Act or joint resolution" (59 Stat. 621, sec. 6). Statutory language could not be written more clearly. The legislative history of this provision, including hearings, committee reports, and floor debate, all point to the same result: the president must seek congressional approval in advance (Fisher 2004: 92–95).

With these safeguards in place to protect the Constitution and congressional powers, President Truman on June 26, 1950 announced that the UNSC had acted to order a withdrawal of North Korean forces to positions north of the 38th parallel, and that "in accordance with the resolutions of the UNSC, the United States will vigorously support the effort of the council to terminate this serious breach of the peace" (Truman 1950: 491). At that point he made no commitment of U.S. military forces. On the following day, he informed the nation that the UNSC had called on all UN members to provide assistance and that he had "ordered United States air and sea forces to give the [South] Korean Government troops cover and support." The military commitment deepened, eventually bringing China into the war on the side of North Korea. At no time did Truman seek authority from Congress.

Every administration that violates the War Power Clause of the Constitution understands the importance of avoiding the word "war" when unilaterally committing U.S. troops to hostilities. Truman's military initiative in Korea was the first time in 160 years that a president went to a major war without first receiving either a declaration or authorization from Congress. Other presidents have followed Truman's precedent. In November 1990, President George H. W. Bush obtained a UNSC resolution to act militarily against Iraq after its invasion of Kuwait, claiming that he did not need congressional authority. Nevertheless, Congress passed authorizing legislation in January 1991. In his signing statement, Bush said he asked for "congressional support," not authority, but the bill he signed into law provided express authorization (Bush 1990:40; 105 Stat. 3 [1991]).

President Bill Clinton relied on UNSC resolutions to act militarily against Haiti and Bosnia. At no time did he seek authority from Congress. When the UNSCrefused to support military action against Kosovo, Clinton turned to NATO allies for support. The NATO treaty may not give congressional authority to NATO countries any more than the UN Charter may vest congressional authority in the UNSC. Oddly (and unconstitutionally), Clinton sought approval from each NATO country for the Kosovo military operation but not from Congress (Fisher 1997, 2004: 198–201).

OLC Analysis

On April 1, 2011, the Office of Legal Counsel (OLC) of the Justice Department released a fourteen-page legal defense entitled "Authority to Use Military Force in Libya" (U.S. Justice Department 2011).

It begins by saying that in "mid-February 2011" there were "widespread popular demonstrations seeking government reform in the neighboring countries of Tunisia and Egypt, as well as elsewhere in the Middle East and North Africa," and "protests began in Libya against the autocratic government of Colonel Muammar Qadhafi." Therefore, there was sufficient time for President Obama to inform Congress of the developing problem and seek legislative authorization. Instead, the Obama administration devoted its energies to attracting support from allies, Arab nations, and the UNSC, not from the legislative branch.

The OLC looked to action by the UNSC as a source of authority for U.S. military action against Libya. Resolution 1973 "authorized member states, acting individually or through regional organizations, 'to take all necessary measure . . . to protect civilians and civilian populated areas under threat of attack in the Libyan Arab Jamahiriya, including Benghazi, while excluding a foreign occupation force of any form on any part of Libyan territory.'" The OLC interpreted Resolution 1973 not only as an initial authorizing instrument, but found supplemental justification for unilateral presidential military action.

To the OLC, Obama could "reasonably" determine that it was necessary to use military force to support "the UNSC's credibility and effectiveness." According to this logic, "[s]ince at least the Korean War, the United States government has recognized that 'the continued existence of the United Nations as an effective international organization is a paramount United States interest.'" The phrase "United States government" is very misleading. There was no collective judgment by the two elected branches in the form of public law. Instead, the OLC refers to two documents prepared by the executive branch: an OLC legal memo in 1992 and a State Department memo in 1950. Rather than looking outside the executive branch for legal authority, OLC looks inside for previous executive interpretations. Similarly, OLC cites itself in 1995 in a memo on Bosnia, which in turn relies on the OLC memo from 1992. Through this self-referential system, OLC concludes that "the UNSC's credibility and effectiveness as an instrument of global peace and stability were at stake in Libya once the UNSC took action to impose a no-fly zone and ensure the safety of civilians—particularly after Qadhafi's forces ignored the UNSC's call for a cease fire and for the cessation of attacks on civilians."

This is an extraordinary legal and constitutional argument. Barely any effort is made to analyze particular provisions of Articles I and II to determine the relative roles of Congress and the president in going to war. The OLC writes: "The Constitution, to be sure, divides authority over the military between the President and Congress, assigning to Congress the authority to 'declare War,' 'raise and support Armies,' and 'provide and maintain a Navy,' as well as general authority over the appropriations on which any military operation necessarily depends." After briefly reviewing this constitutional language, the OLC preferred to turn to what others have called "the historical gloss on the 'executive Power' vested in Article II of the Constitution," citing various broad concurrences and pronouncements by the Supreme Court on foreign policy and national security.

These multiple references have no connection to military action against Libya. For example, the OLC relies on this precedent: "as Attorney General (later Justice) Robert Jackson observed over half a century ago, 'the president's authority has long been recognized as extending to the dispatch of armed forces outside of the United States, either on missions of goodwill or rescue, or for the purpose of protecting American lives or property or American interests' (*Training of British Flying Students in the United States*, 40 Op. Att'y Gen. 58, 62 (1941)." There was no issue in Libya of missions of goodwill, rescue, or protecting American lives or property. Did Jackson mean that the president could dispatch armed forces against another country merely to satisfy "American interests"? There is no reason to think he intended such an unlimited doctrine.

According to the OLC, once the UNSC adopts a resolution and the country to which the resolution applies does not conform to the purpose of the resolution, a president may decide that the credibility and effectiveness of the UNSC are so threatened that it is necessary to use military force against the target country. Is this presidential action automatic? Not to the OLC, which advised: "the president is not required to direct the use of military force simply because the UNSC has authorized it." Therefore, the decision to use or not use military force, according to the OLC, is solely in the hands of the president, not Congress. In this case, citing an address by President Obama on March 28, 2011, the "writ of the United Nations Security Council would have been shown to be little more than empty words, crippling that institution's future credibility to uphold global peace and security."

The OLC relied in part on support from the Senate: "On March 1, 2011, the United States Senate passed by unanimous consent Senate Resolution 85. Among other things, the Resolution 'strongly condemn[ed] the gross and systematic violations of human rights in Libya, including violent attacks on protesters demanding democratic reforms,' 'call[ed] on Muammar Qaddafi to desist from further violence,' and 'urge[d] the United Nations Security Council to take such further action as may be necessary to protect civilians in Libya from attack, including the possible imposition of a no-fly zone over Libyan territory.'" Action by "unanimous consent" suggests strong Senate approval for the resolution, but the legislative record provides no support for that impression. Beyond the fact that passage of a resolution by a single chamber provides no statutory support, it is evident that Senate Resolution 85 had little support from individual senators.

The resolution begins with six "whereas" clauses. None provides convincing reasons for using military force in March 2011. For example, "Whereas 5" refers to the flight of Pan Am 103 over Lockerbie, Scotland, a tragedy that took the lives of 270 people in 1988. That terrible event cannot justify military action in March 2011. "Whereas 6" states that Libya's election to the UN Human Rights Council on May 13, 2010 sent a "demoralizing message of indifference to the families of the victims of Pan Am flight 103"— another statement that falls short of justifying military action in March 2011.

Senate Resolution 85 contains eleven resolutions. They applaud the courage of the Libyan people for standing up to Qaddafi, condemn violations of human rights in Libya, call on Qaddafi to desist from further violence, and appeal to the Qaddafi regime to immediately release persons arbitrarily detained. None of this supports military action against Libya. Resolution 7 urges the UNSC "to take such further action as may be necessary to protect civilians in Libya from attack, including the possible imposition of a no-fly zone over Libyan territory." When was this no-fly language added to Senate Resolution 85? Were senators adequately informed of this amendment? There is evidence that the sponsors of this resolution added the no-fly language without adequately alerting senators to this significant change.

Likewise, the legislative history of Senate Resolution 85 shows that there were no hearings and no committee report. It was not referred to a particular committee. Although the resolution passed by "unanimous consent" and implies bipartisan support, the sponsors of the resolution were ten Democrats (Bob Menendez, Frank Lautenberg, Dick Durbin, Kirsten Gillibrand, Bernie Sanders, Sheldon Whitehouse, Chuck Schumer, Bob Casey, Ron Wyden, and Benjamin Cardin) and one Republican (Mark Kirk). There was no debate on Senate Resolution 85. There is no evidence of any senator on the floor at that time other than Schumer and the presiding officer. Schumer asked for unanimous consent to take up the resolution. No one objected, possibly because there was no one present to object. Senate "deliberation" took less than one minute. When one watches Senate action on C-SPAN, consideration of the resolution began at 4:13:44 and ended at 4:14:19—or thirty-five seconds.

Congressional Action

President Obama hoped that his military initiative in Libya could be completed within a matter of days or a few weeks. As the operation continued for one month and then two, he began to run into problems with the timetable of the War Powers Resolution of 1973, which recognizes that Presidents might use military force without congressional action for up to sixty to ninety days. On June 3, 2011, the House passed a resolution (House Resolution 292) requiring Obama to clarify the objectives of U.S. policy in Libya and provide other information, including budgetary costs. The resolution, stipulating that Obama issue a report within fourteen days, stated that he "has not sought, and Congress has not provided, authorization for the introduction or continued involvement of the United States Armed Forces in Libya" (U.S. Congress 2011c). A resolution passed by a single chamber is not legally binding, but it would have been politically costly of Obama not to comply with the many reporting requirements.

Debate on this resolution and a separate resolution submitted by Rep. Dennis Kucinich (D-OH) offered lawmakers an opportunity to express their views on military action in Libya. A number of committee chairman rebuked Obama for failing to obtain authorization from Congress. Rep. Mike Rogers (R-NY), chair of the Intelligence Committee, stated that Obama "needs our approval to continue to move forward" (U.S. Congress 2011d). Rep. Ileana Ros-Lehtinen (R-FL), chair of the Foreign Affairs Committee, insisted that U.S. armed forces may only be used to defend and advance U.S. national security interests, "not to enforce, to quote the President, 'the writ of the international community,' nor because of the United Nations, nor because of the Arab League." She said that members of both parties were "outright angry about the disregard with which the President and his administration have treated Congress on the Libya military engagement." She referred to "the President's contempt for Congress" (U.S. Congress 2011e). Rep. "Buck" McKeon (R-CA), chair of the Armed Services Committee, fully agreed, "the administration has been disturbingly dismissive of Congress's role in the authorization of military force" (U.S. Congress 2011f).

House Resolution 294 passed by a vote of 268 to 145. The Kucinich resolution was turned down, 148 to 265. Both resolutions provoked a broad and vigorous discussion of Obama's intervention in Libya. In response to the House resolution, Obama submitted to Congress a report on June 15, 2011, providing details on political and military objectives, an assessment of the current situation, U.S. participation in the NATO operation, and current and projected military, humanitarian, and budgetary costs. A section on legal analysis determined that the word "hostilities" in the War Powers Resolution should be interpreted to mean that hostilities do not exist with the U.S. military effort in Libya: "U.S. operations do not involve sustained fighting or active exchanges of fire with hostile forces, not do they involve the presence of U.S. ground troops, U.S. casualties or a serious threat thereof, or any significant chance of escalation into a conflict characterized by those factors."

According to that reasoning, if the United States conducted military operations by bombing at 30,000 feet, launching Tomahawk missiles from ships in the Mediterranean, and using armed drones, there would be no "hostilities" in Libya under the terms of the War Powers Resolution, provided U.S. casualties are minimal or nonexistent. In short, a nation with superior military force could pulverize another country and there would be neither hostilities nor war. The administration advised Speaker John Boehner (R-OH) on June 15, that "the United States supports NATO military operations." At a minimum, the United States is supporting hostilities.

It is interesting that various administrations, eager to press the limits of presidential power, seem to understand that they may not—legally and politically—use the words "war" or "hostilities." Apparently they recognize that using words in their normal sense, particularly as understood by the general public, would acknowledge what the Framers believed. Other than repelling sudden attacks and protecting American lives overseas, presidents may not take the country from a state of peace to a state or war without seeking and obtaining congressional authority.

Also on June 15, 2011, ten members of the House filed a lawsuit in federal court. The names included Democrats (Dennis Kucinich, John Conyers, Michael Capuano) and Republicans (Walter Jones, Roscoe Bartlett, Dan Burton, Howard Coble, John Duncan, Timothy Johnson, and Ron Paul). They sought injunctive and declaratory relief to protect them and the country from "a stated policy of Defendant Barack Obama, President of the United States, whereby a president may unilaterally go to war in Libya and other countries without the declaration of war from Congress required by Article I, Section 8, Clause 11 of the U.S. Constitution." The lawsuit also sought injunctive and declaratory relief from "the violation of the War Powers Resolution resulting from the Obama administration's established policy that the President does not require congressional authorization to use military force in wars like the one in Libya." The lawmakers further sought relief from a policy "that a president may commit the United States to a war under the authority of the United Nations without authorization from Congress. The lawsuit challenged the administration's claim that a president "may commit the United States to a war under the authority of the North Atlantic Treaty Organization (NATO)." Finally, the case involves the freedom of the president to "use funds, previously appropriated by Congress, for unconstitutional and unauthorized wars in Libya or other countries."

Conclusions

Presidents have some discretion to use military force without advance congressional authorization, including repelling sudden attacks and rescuing American citizens. None of those justifications apply to Libya. America was not threatened or attacked by Libya. President Obama has called the military operation a humanitarian intervention that serves the national interest. Launching hundreds of Tomahawk missiles and ordering air strikes against Libyan ground forces, for the purpose of helping rebels overthrow Col. Qaddafi, constitutes war. Under the U.S. Constitution, there is only one source for authorizing war. It is not the UNSC or NATO. It is Congress.

To restore constitutional government, Congress and the public must confront presidents who commit troops to foreign wars without seeking legislative authority. No action by a president would more warrant impeachment and removal than usurping the war power from Congress and undermining representative government and the system of checks and balances. Members of Congress need to understand their institutional duties and discharge them. They take an oath to support and defend the Constitution, not the president.

Works Cited

Bumiller, Elizabeth and Kareen Fahim. "U.S.-led assaults hit Tripoli again: objective is near." *New York Times* (22 Mar. 2011) A1, A11.

Bush, George H. W. 1991. *Public Papers of the Presidents.* Washington, DC: U.S. Government Printing Office.

Denyer, Simon. "Mobs attack U.S., British, Italian embassies in Libya." *New York Times* (2 May 2011).

Denyer, Simon and Leila Fadel. "NATO bombards Gaddafi government complex in Tripoli." *Washington Post* (25 Apr. 2011a), A9.

———. "NATO strike kills son of Gaddafi." *Washington Post* (1 May 2011b), A1.

DeYoung, Karen and Colum Lynch. 2011. "U.N. Council opens door to strikes against Libya." *Washington Post* (18 Mar. 2011), A1, A6.

DeYoung, Karen and Griff Witte. "Pakistan relations reach a new low." *Washington Post* (16 June 2011), 1.

Fahim, Kareem and David D. Kirkpatrick. "Qaddafi survive NATO airstrike that kills son." *New York Times* (1 May 2011), 1.

Farrand, Max, ed. Records of the Federal Convention of 1787 (4 vols.), 1937.

Fina, Peter and Greg Jaffe. "U.S. jets strike Gaddafi's ground forces." *Washington Post* (21 Mar. 2011), A1.

Fisher, Louis. "The Korean War: On What Legal Basis Did Truman Act?," *American Journal of International Law*, 89:21 (1995) http://www.loufisher.org/docs/wp/425.pdf.

———. "Sidestepping Congress: Presidents Acting under the UN and NATO." *Case Western Reserve Law Review.* Vol. 47, No. 1237 (1997). http://www.loufisher.org/docs/wp/424.pdf.

———. *Presidential War Power.* Lawrence: University Press of Kansas, 2004.

———. "Obama's U.N. authority?" *National Law Journal* (18 Apr 2011). http://loufisher,org/docs/wp/authority.pdf.

Kirkpatrick, David D. and Thom Shanker. "Libyan rebels advance in west; U.S. will deploy armed drones." *New York Times* (22 April 2011), A1, A9.

Myers, Steven Lee and Rachel Donadio. "U.S. seeks to aid Libyan rebels with seized assets" 6 May 2011

Obama, Barack. "Barack Obama's Q&A," (2008). http://boston.com/news/politics/2008/specials/CandiateQA/ObamaQA.

————. 2011a. "Remarks by the President in Address to the Nation on Libya," March 28, http://www.whitehouse.gov/the-press-office/2011/03/28/remarks-president-addresss-nation-libya.

————. 2011b. Text of a letter to the Speaker of the House of Representatives and the President Pro Tempore of the Senate, March 21, 2011. http://www.whitehouse.gov/the-press-office/2011/03/21/letter-president-regarding-commencement-operations-libya.

Sheridan, Mary Beth. "U.S. to Free Up Frozen Libyan Assets for Humanitarian Assistance" (6 May 2011

Truman, Harry. *Public Papers of the Presidents*. Washington, D.C.: Government Printing Office, 1950.

U.S. Congress. The cable by President Truman as reprinted in the *Congressional Record*, 91:8185. 1945

————. *Congressional Record*, 157:S1952 (daily ed., 30 March 2011a).

————. *Congressional Record*, 157:S2010 (daily ed., 31 March 2011b).

————. *Congressional Record*, 157:H3999 (daily ed.,3 June 2011c).

————. *Congressional Record*, 157:H4013 (daily ed., 3 June 2011d).

————. *Congressional Record*, 157:H3999 (daily ed., 3 June 2011e).

————. *Congressional Record*, 157:H4005 (daily ed., 3 June 2011f).

U.S. Justice Department. Office of Legal Counsel, "Authority to Use Military Force in Libya" (1 Apr 2011). http://www.justice.gov/olc/2011/authority-military-use-in-libya.pdf.

VI

The Obama Administration

Chapter 20

The Policy Czar Debate

Justin S. Vaughn
José D. Villalobos

Obama's Controversial Embrace of Policy Czars

As has become the tradition during the first days of a new legislative session, dozens of bills and resolutions were filed in January
2011 as the newly installed Speaker of the House, John Boehner,
and his fellow Republicans ushered in the start of the 112th Congress. The legislation filed ran the gamut from proposed initiatives to repeal the comprehensive health care reform passed in
the previous session to attempts to permanently repeal the estate
tax. Among the 126 bills offered on January 5, 2011 was an effort
to restrain presidential personnel policy in one particular—and
recently controversial—way.

Submitted by Congressman Steve Scalise (R-LA), the Sunset
All Czars Act, known otherwise as House Resolution 59, aimed
to provide a legal and formal definition for the job of presidential advisors known as "czars." Resolution 59 sought to ban funding for salaries and administrative expenses associated with such
advisors. Terse and straightforward, the actual language of the
legislation devoted little attention to the controversial roots of the
governing problem it aimed to correct. Indeed, to read the two-
page document would give no indication to an otherwise unaware
reader of the debates surrounding or rationale for the use of czars.
Yet, the issue first came to the attention of the media and public
in the early days of the Obama administration, and latter led to

congressional hearings, breathless condemnation on conservative talk radio, and the resignation of at least one presidential appointee (see O'Brien 2011).

Controversy in the Administration's Early Days

Even before Obama's 2008 election victory, articles referencing the potential influence of would-be czars in the administration to come were published in outlets like the influential Website *Politico* (Lovely 2008). A month before Obama's inauguration, the *Wall Street Journal* also wrote about the ascendancy of czars in the administration-in-waiting (Meckler 2008). Within the Beltway, lawmakers and interest groups soon expressed concern that Obama might be "subverting the authority of Congress and concentrating too much power in the presidency" (Goler 2009; Hamburger and Parsons 2009).

Amid the turmoil, the White House began mounting defensive communication maneuvers, with Press Secretary Robert Gibbs even forced to defend the official title of pay czar (a.k.a. "Special Master for Compensation") with the media and the appointment of Kenneth Feinberg to that post. Communications Director Anita Dunn, following Gibbs' lead, also defended other White House personnel hired as czars, while White House Counsel Gregory Craig responded to multiple congressional inquiries, including those from fellow Democrats, but avoided invitations to appear before committee hearings into the czars. This was quite a lot of controversy for an institution that, by all accounts, has no set definition and is not a unique or even recent development.

What Exactly Are Czars?

The central challenge posed when attempting to analyze presidential use of policy czars is that of definition. Currently, a single universally accepted formal definition of the position does not exist (Pfiffner 2009). In recent years, as the use of czar-like personnel has become politically controversial, the imprecision of the term has grown; indeed, part of the task of the aforementioned Sunset All Czars Act initiative was to provide a formal and legal definition for the term. Generally, the term has been applied to presidential assistants given authority over a specific and important policy portfolio. They are paid and appointed by the president but they do not have broad administrative abilities, lack the ability to forward or implement policy, and their appointments do not require Senate confirmation—which is a good part of the controversy. Beyond this relatively amorphous definition, however, there is no clear consensus on what precisely constitutes a czar, be it from the perspective of the presidents who appoint them, the media who cover them, or the scholars who study them. For example, scholars have attempted to identify conditions such as lack of Senate confirmation or certain administrative hierarchical arrangements, only to have their efforts at clarity compromised by an actual president who refers to an advisor as a "czar" despite the lack of fit with scholarly dictates (e.g., see Pfiffner 2009; Schwemle et al. 2010; Villalobos and Vaughn 2010b).

To further complicate the definitional task, as Anita Dunn, Obama's former White House director of communications has pointed out, "Just to be clear, the job title 'czar' doesn't exist in the Obama administration," nor did it exist in any of the administrations that preceded Obama's (2009). Nevertheless, presidents and president-watchers alike have frequently used the term to describe positions occupied by individuals who have the president's trust as well as his ear, and thus the ability to affect significant change on the important policy task to which they have been assigned. As Patterson (2000: 264) notes, "[the czar] will be publicized as the super-person who will 'knock heads,' 'cut red tape,' 'ensure coordinated effort.'" Or, as conservative commentator Pat Buchanan has argued, "Czars are specialists, your go-to guy for this or that assignment. Naming a czar is a president's way of saying, 'This is so crucial an issue. I am assigning one of my best people to it, and he will report directly to me'" (Patten 2009: 58). It both views, the czars would seem to be indispensable to presidents dealing with complicated issues and wanted to have a single, trusted aide assigned to and responsible for the problem.

Given the gap between the relatively coherent idea behind the employment of czars and the ability to linguistically contain the concept within a neat definitional box, it helps to apply a basic categorization scheme that relies on practical distinctions for appraising czars in accordance with the origin and function of each appointment, while also considering usage of the term by certain parties. As such, an appointment may originate from the president himself (e.g., as an executive order) or may be appointed through Senate confirmation, with that latter considered less controversial.[1] For those appointments originating from the president, their function is most often geared toward an advisory role lacking direct control over policy. By comparison, Senate confirmed appointments are more likely to function with full legal authority over the policymaking process and have a more easily identifiable (i.e., traditional) position within the executive hierarchy. Table 20.1 provides a list of all Obama's czars, as well as information about their czar moniker, formal title and other relevant data.

In cases where appointees defy such expectations, scholarly debate often ensues over the appropriateness of their actions. From a legalistic perspective, some czars are simply glorified Cabinet members (often referred to as "PAS" personnel) in positions created by legislative statute. These personnel fall squarely within the constitutional construct set forth in Article 2, Section 2 of the Constitution and thus have full legal authority to make policy decisions. To date, 12 of President Obama's "czar" appointees have been confirmed by the Senate (see Table 20.2, page 329; Dunn 2009). Such positions with Senate confirmation are created by statute and have full legal authority to make policy decisions with the president's consent.

Others may be categorized as inferior officers or lower level employees of the White House, which are easier to appoint but more controversial due to the uncertainty and doubt they often generate concerning the extent to which they can influence or even communicate policy on the president's behalf (Pfiffner 2009; Schwemle et al. 2010). Higher-level officers report to a Senate confirmed officer "who Congress has given the power to prescribe duties for underlings" and "are housed within parts of the government that are subject to open records laws like the Freedom of Information Act" (Feingold 2009; see also *Edmond v. United States* 1997). Meanwhile, lower-level officers often are housed within the White House (and thus outside the purview of Congress) and answer directly to the president. Although lower-level czars can provide an immediate, upfront advantage in symbolically attending to an important issue, their limited capacity for being able to address policy problems in a substantive way can lead the public to develop false perceptions of their control over the policy process,

---

1. Indeed, some scholars argue that appointees with Senate confirmation are not "czars" at all (i.e., see Pfiffner 2009; Schwemle et al. 2010).

Table 20.1. Barack Obama's Presidential Policy "Czars"

"Czar" Title/ Label	Administration Title	Office Holder	Functional Categorization	Position Origin	New Position	Holdover Appointee	Tenure Length
"Afpak" Czar, Afghanistan and Pakistan Czar	Special Representative for Afghanistan and Pakistan	Richard C. Holbrooke	Secretary of State Appointed (Non-confirmed)	State Department	Yes	No	01/22/2009 to 12/13/2010 (died)
AIDS Czar	Director, Office of National AIDS Policy; Member, Domestic Policy Council President	Jeffrey Crowley	Presidential (Non-confirmed)	President	No	No	02/26/2009 to present
Asian Carp Czar	Asian Carp Director; Chair of the Asian Carp Regional Coordinating Committee; Director, Office of Economic Opportunity	John Goss	Council on Environment Quality Appointed (Non-confirmed)	Council on Environment Quality	Yes	No	09/08/2010 to present
Auto Czar, Car Czar	Treasury Advisor, Head of the Auto Task Force	Steve Rattner	Secretary of Treasury Appointed (Non-confirmed)	Treasury Department	Yes	No	02/23/2009 to 07/13/2009

continued on next page

Table 20.1. (Continued)

"Czar" Title/ Label	Administration Title	Office Holder	Functional Categorization	Position Origin	New Position	Holdover Appointee	Tenure Length
Auto Recovery Czar, Autoworker Czar	Member, Presidential Automotive Task Force; Director of the Recovery for Auto Communities and Workers	Ed Montgomery	Presidential (Non-confirmed)	President	Yes	No	03/30/2009 to present
Border Czar	Assistant Secretary for International Affairs, Special Representative for Border Affairs, Department of Homeland Security	Alan Bersin	Secretary of Homeland Security Appointed (Non-confirmed)	Department of Homeland Security	No	No	04/15/2009 to 03/27/2010
California Water Czar	Deputy Interior Secretary	David J. Hayes	Presidential Nomination, Senate Confirmed	Congress	No	No	05/22/2009 to present
Climate Czar	Special Envoy for Climate Change; President's Chief Climate Negotiator	Todd D. Stern	Secretary of State Appointed (Non-confirmed)	State Department	No	No	01/26/2009 to present

Title	Position	Name	Appointment Type	Appointed By			Dates
Climate Czar, Energy Czar, Global Warming Czar	Director, White House Office of Energy and Climate Policy; Assistant to the President for Energy and Climate Change	Carol Browner	Presidential (Non-confirmed)	President	No	No	01/22/2009 to present
Copyright Czar	Coordinator, Intellectual Property Enforcement	Victoria Espinel	Presidential Nomination, Senate Confirmed	Congress	Yes	No	09/25/2009 to present
Compensation Czar, Pay Czar, Gulf Claims Czar	Special Master for TARP Executive Compensation; Special Master for Pay Claims for the BP Oil Spill Fund	Kenneth Feinberg	Secretary of Treasury Appointed (Non-confirmed)	Treasury Department	No	No	06/10/2009 to present
Cyber Czar, Cyber Security Czar	Director, White House Office of Cybersecurity; Coordinator, Cybersecurity	Melissa Hathaway	Presidential (Non-confirmed)	President	No	No	2/09/2009 to 08/21/2009

continued on next page

Table 20.1. (*Continued*)

"Czar" Title/ Label	Administration Title	Office Holder	Functional Categorization	Position Origin	New Position	Holdover Appointee	Tenure Length
Cyber Czar, Cyber Security Czar	White House Cybersecurity Coordinator	Howard Schmidt	Presidential (Non-confirmed)	President	No	No	01/20/2009 to present
Domestic Violence Czar	Advisor to the President and the Vice President on Domestic Violence and Sexual Assault Issues	Lynn Rosenthal	Vice President Appointed (Non-confirmed)	Vice President	No	No	06/26/2009 to present
Drug Czar	Director, National Drug Control Policy (Cabinet Rank Removed)	R. Gil Kerlikowske	Presidential Nomination, Senate Confirmed	Congress	No	No	05/07/2009 to present
Economic Czar	Chairman, Economic Recovery Advisory Board	Paul A. Volcker	Presidential (Non-confirmed)	President	Yes	No	02/26/2009 to 02/06/2011
Ethics Czar, Transparency Czar	Special Counsel to the President for Ethics and Government Reform	Norm Eisen	Presidential (Non-confirmed)	President	Yes	No	01/21/2009 to 06/29/2010

Czar	Position	Appointment	Reports to	Senate Confirmed	Dates
Ethics Czar, Transparency Czar	White House Counsel	Presidential (Non-confirmed)	President	No	08/10/2010 to present
Faith-Based Czar	Director, White House Office of Faith-Based and Neighborhood Partnerships	Presidential (Non-confirmed)	President	No	02/06/2009 to present
Great Lakes Czar	Special Advisor to the EPA Administrator	Environmental Protection Agency Appointed (Non-confirmed)	Environmental Protection Agency	No	04/06/2009
Green Jobs Czar	Special Advisor to the President for Green Jobs, Enterprise, and Innovation; Member, White House Counsel on Environmental Quality	Presidential (Non-confirmed)	President	No	03/10/2009 to 09/05/2009
Guantanamo Base Closure Czar	U.S. Department of State Special Envoy	Secretary of State Appointed (Non-confirmed)	State Department	No	03/12/2009 to present

				Robert Bauer
				Joshua DuBois
				Cameron Davis
				Anthony K. "Van" Jones
				Daniel Fried

continued on next page

Table 20.1. (Continued)

"Czar" Title/ Label	Administration Title	Office Holder	Functional Categorization	Position Origin	New Position	Holdover Appointee	Tenure Length
Health Czar	Director, White House Office of Health Reform and Counselor to the President	Nancy-Ann DeParle	Presidential (Non-confirmed)	President Executive Order	No	No	04/08/2009 to 01/27/2011
Health IT Czar	National Coordinator for Health Information Technology, Department of Health and Human Services	David Blumenthal	Secretary of Health and Human Services Appointed (Non-confirmed)	President	No	No	03/20/2009 to 02/03/2011
Infotech Czar, Information Czar	Chief Information Officer at the White House	Vivek Kundra	Presidential (Non-confirmed)	Created by Statute	Yes	No	03/05/2009 to present
Intelligence Czar	Director, National Intelligence	Dennis Blair	Presidential Nomination, Senate Confirmed	Congress	No	No	01/28/2009 to 05/28/2010 (dismissed)
Iran Czar	Special Advisor for the Persian Gulf and Southwest Asia	Dennis Ross	Secretary of State Appointed (Non-confirmed)	State Department	No	No	11/31/2009 to present

Czar	Position	Name	Appointment Type	Reports To			Dates
Manufacturing Czar; Auto Czar, Car Czar	Senior Counselor for Manufacturing Policy; Senior Advisor, Presidential Automotive Task Force (took over for Steve Rattner on 07/13/2009)	Ron Bloom	Presidential (Non-confirmed)	President	No	No	09/072009 to present
Middle East Czar	Special Envoy for Middle East Peace	George Mitchell	Secretary of State Appointed (Non-confirmed)	State Department	No	No	01/22/2009 to present
NASA Czar	NASA Administrator	Charles F. Bolden	Presidential Nomination, Senate Confirmed	Congress	No	No	06/15/2009 to present
Performance Czar	U.S. Chief Performance Officer and Acting Director for Management, Office of Management and Budget	Jeffrey Zients	Presidential Nomination, Senate Confirmed	Congress	Yes	No	06/19/2009 to present
Regulatory Czar	Director, Office of Information and Regulatory Affairs, Office of Management and Budget	Cass Sunstein	Presidential Nomination, Senate Confirmed	Congress	No	No	09/10/2009 to present

continued on next page

Table 20.1. (*Continued*)

"Czar" Title/Label	Administration Title	Office Holder	Functional Categorization	Position Origin	New Position	Holdover Appointee	Tenure Length
Science Czar	Director, Office of Science and Technology Policy; Assistant to the President for Science and Technology; Co-Chair, President's Council of Advisors on Science and Technology	John Holdren	Presidential Nomination, Senate Confirmed	Congress	No	No	03/19/2009 to present
Stimulus Accountability Czar, Stimulus Oversight Czar	Chairman, Recovery Accountability and Transparency Board	Earl Devaney	Presidential (Non-confirmed)	Created by Statute	Yes	No	02/25/2009 to present
Sudan Czar	Special Envoy to Sudan	J. Scott Gration	Secretary of State Appointed (Non-confirmed)	State Department	No	No	03/18/2009 to present
TARP Czar	Assistant Secretary of the Treasury for Financial Stability	Herbert Allison	Presidential Nomination, Senate Confirmed	Congress	No	No	06/19/2009 to present

Technology Czar, Chief Technology Czar	Associate Director, Office of Science and Technology Policy, Chief Technology Officer, Assistant to the President	Aneesh Chopra	Presidential Nomination, Senate Confirmed	Congress	No	No	08/07/2009 to present
Terrorism Czar	Assistant to the President for Homeland Security and Counter-Terrorism	John O. Brennan	Presidential (Non-confirmed)	President	No	No	01/20/2009 to present
Urban Affairs Czar	Director, White House Office of Urban Affairs Policy	Adolfo Carrion	Presidential (Non-confirmed)	President, Executive Order	No	No	02/19/2009 to 05/03/201
War Czar	Assistant to the President and Deputy National Security Advisor for Iraq and Afghanistan	Douglas Lute	Presidential Nomination, Senate Confirmed	Congress	No	Yes	05/15/2007 to present
Weapons Czar	Under Secretary of Defense for Acquisition, Technology, and Logistics	Ashton Carter	Presidential Nomination, Senate Confirmed	Congress	No	No	04/27/2009 to present

continued on next page

Table 20.1. (*Continued*)

"Czar" Title/ Label	Administration Title	Office Holder	Functional Categorization	Position Origin	New Position	Holdover Appointee	Tenure Length
Weapons of Mass Destruction Czar, Nonproliferation czar	Special Assistant to the President and White House Coordinator for Arms Control and Weapons of Mass Destruction, Proliferation, and Terrorism	Gary Samore	Presidential (Non-confirmed)	President	No	No	01/29/2009 to present
Weatherization Czar	Senior Policy Advisor to the Assistant Secretary for the Office of Energy Efficiency and Renewable Energy in the Department of Energy	Gil Sperling	Career Incumbent	Department of Energy	No	Yes	09/01/2008 to present

Table 20.2. Barack Obama's Senate-confirmed "Czars"

Office Holder	"Czar" Title/Label	Administration Title
Herb Allison	TARP Czar	Treasury Assistant Secretary of the Treasury for Financial Stability
Dennis Blair	Intelligence Czar	Director of National Intelligence
Charles F. Bolden	NASA Czar	NASA Administrator
Ashton Carter	Weapons Czar	Under Secretary of Defense for Acquisition, Technology, and Logistics
Aneesh Chopra	Technology Czar	OSTP Associate Director, Chief Technology Officer
Victoria Espinel	Copyright Czar	Coordinator for Intellectual Property Enforcement
David J. Hayes	California Water Czar	Deputy Interior Secretary
John Holdren	Science Czar	OSTP Director and Assistant to the President for Science and Technology
Gil Kerlikowske	Drug Czar	Director of National Drug Control Policy
Douglas Lute[a]	War Czar	Assistant to the President, Deputy National Security Advisor for Iraq and Afghanistan
Cass Sunstein	Regulatory Czar	OMB Director of the Office of Information and Regulatory Affairs
Jeff Zients	Performance Czar	OMB Deputy Director and Chief Performance Officer

[a]Holdover from George W. Bush's administration.
OMB, Office of Management and Budget; **OSTP**, Office of Science and Technology Policy.

thereby setting relatively high (or even unattainable) standards of expectation concerning performance outcomes.

Concerning usage of the "czar" label, one can also distinguish between applications originating from media sources versus direct application by an administration's public relations outfit. Thus, in situations where the president refers to an appointee as a czar—whether that appointee is confirmed by the Senate or not—it is still possible to acknowledge the appointee as a "czar" in accordance with the aforementioned criteria and hold the president fully accountable for the actions of the appointee in that respect. However, when an ideological media figure declares a particular individual to be a czar even if the president has not, the appointee can also be acknowledged as a czar while also noting and taking full consideration of an administration's refusal to apply the term when appraising such personnel. This is an acceptable approach, particularly since presidents—as well as their White House spokespersons and other surrogates—very rarely negate the use of the term by media figures when responding to questions about them (but see Dunn 2009). Taken together, all three factors—origin, function, and term usage—can be considered and accounted for when determining allegations of czardom and are to be kept in mind when appraising and critiquing the president's employment of such personnel.

Obama's Use of Policy Czars in Historic Context

Although critics noting the significant increase in number of czars employed by the Obama administration are correct, it also should be noted that this president has not used his czars in a capacity any different from his predecessors. To better understand the way Obama has employed czars during the first few years of his term, a brief discussion of the evolving history of presidential policy czars can be useful.

Presidents have been using czars in a generally consistent manner since the Nixon administration, although the number has proliferated more recently. The practice, although less common, stretches back even further by way of similar advisory models in place in administrations in the early twentieth century, with roots of individual presidential advising—as distinguished from the Cabinet concept proffered in the U.S. Constitution—apparent since at least the 1829 inauguration of Andrew Jackson (see Relyea 2009).

Over time, presidents like Grover Cleveland, Warren G. Harding, and Herbert Hoover began assembling circles of informal advisers and confidants. Thereafter, with the post-Brownlow Commission growth of the Executive Branch in the forms of the Executive Office of the President and White House Office, the opportunity to institutionalize non-Cabinet advisory structures in a formal way presented itself for the first time during the administration of Franklin D. Roosevelt.

As the national government responded to severe predicaments like the Great Depression and World War II, FDR's independent advisors quickly became powerful. Gulick (1948: 13) refers to the incipient "czardoms" that populated the Roosevelt administration in these years, an institutional development that "did not disappear with the return of world peace." However, it was not until the Nixon administration that the use of policy czars became entrenched, as perennial institutions like energy and drug czars were first put in place. In the decades since, each successive administration has relied more on independent assistants to bring leadership, help prioritize policy problems, and cut through traditional interorganizational challenges. Since the Clinton administration, presidents have employed dozens of czars as a way of continuing existing administrative practices, responding to new problems, and signifying commitment to key issues and, thus, the constituencies that surround them.

Obama, in particular, has used czars as a way to manage policy issues and problems that span multiple bureaucratic entities. Three independent motivations for the way the president has determined which issue areas merit and demand czar-level attention can be identified: 1) The president has demonstrated a proclivity toward using czars to oversee agencies that relate directly to his policy agenda (e.g., Nonproliferation Czar Gary Samore, Regulatory Czar Cass Sunstein, Health Czar Nancy-Ann DeParle); 2) the president also has staffed out oversight and advisory authority to czars on hot-button issues, regardless of where those issues fall on his own agenda (e.g., TARP Czar Herbert Allison, Compensation Czar Kenneth Feinberg, War Czar Douglas Lute, Terrorism Czar John O. Brennan); and 3) the president has followed White House tradition by identifying czars to lead continuing, cross-administrative efforts on ongoing policy problems (e.g., Drug Czar R. Gil Kerlikowske, Middle East Czar George Mitchell, Faith-Based Czar Joshua DuBois).

Progress Report: Czar Performance in the Obama Administration (2009–2011)

The individual performance of Barack Obama's czars range as much as the reasons why the president chose to tap them for their leadership positions. Although some systemic factors such as issue salience, organizational structure, and proximity to the presidency have tended to determine individual czar's likelihood for leadership success (see Villalobos and Vaughn 2010a), other czars have seen more or less success because of personal factors like talent, skill, and luck. What follows is a brief progress reports on seven of Obama's most noteworthy czars—three Senate-confirmed appointees, two agency/department-appointed personnel, and two czars directly appointed by Obama himself.[2]

Cameron Davis (Great Lakes Czar)

Davis serves as the special to advisor Lisa Jackson, Environmental Protection Agency administrator, and is charged with overseeing and coordinating about a dozen federal agencies working on Obama's initiatives for cleaning up the Great Lakes (Flesher 2009). Under Jackson's discretion, Davis has only a moderate level of organizational authority and presidential access. His main priorities are working to solve issues related to "invasive species, polluted harbors, sewage overflows and degraded wildlife habitat" (Flesher 2009). Davis is also recognized as a longtime member of the Alliance for the Great Lakes (a.k.a. the Lake Michigan Federation). Jeff Skelding, director of the Healing Our Waters-Great Lakes Coalition previously praised Davis as a strong "coalition-builder" who "knows how to talk the languages of the different federal agencies . . . and the audiences that have a stake in protecting the lakes" (Flesher 2009).

Early on, Davis earned some immediate attention as an outspoken advocate working to streamline the administration's restoration efforts. In line with his promotion of the program, the Obama administration included $475 million in allocations for the 2010 budget to help with restoration efforts, with an additional $5 billion pledged over the next decade—a notable accomplishment

---

2. We also encourage interested readers to turn to Steve Stuglin's essay in Chapter 10 on "Team Auto's" efforts in the automotive bailout program, particularly with respect to the role played by Car Czar Steve Rattner.

(EPA 2010). Unfortunately, his work on the initiative has since received relatively little attention, which is not surprising given the low salience of the issue, but nevertheless reflects negatively on his ability to be a visible force for the administration.

Norman Eisen (Ethics Czar)

A well-known ethics advocate in Washington DC, best known for founding the watchdog organization Citizens for Responsibility and Ethics in Washington, Eisen is perhaps most famous as the man behind the Obama administration's controversial and ultimately inconsistently enforced policy of not allowing lobbyists to serve in the executive branch. More successful and lauded were his efforts (and those of the president) to bar lobbyists from serving on federal advisory boards and for engineering the unprecedented release of the names of those visiting the White House. Not surprisingly, Eisen's efforts earned him nicknames such as "Mr. No" and "The Fun Sponge" (Saslow 2009). Eisen served as the White House ethics czar from the time of Obama's inauguration until his installation via recess appointment by the president as ambassador to the Czech Republic in late 2010.

Kenneth Feinberg (Compensation Czar)

Feinberg has been assigned two of the most difficult tasks the Obama administration has had to handle: 1) Managing executive compensation for firms that received TARP bailout monies; and 2) administering the $20-billion dollar victim compensation fund established by BP following the Deepwater Horizon oil spill. Either of these tasks would be difficult to complete successfully; overseeing both in a celebrated manner would be near impossible, even without missteps, of which Feinberg has made a few. For example, during fall 2009, Feinberg imposed tough cuts on 175 employees from the top seven bailed-out companies on Wall Street, including AIG, Bank of America, Citigroup, General Motors, Chrysler, GMAC, and Chrysler Financial (Goldman 2009). Feinberg made it no secret that he had—without explicitly seeking the president's approval—decided who would be affected and by what amount (see Javers 2009; Reuters 2009). In fact, Feinberg stated at the time of his announcement that he had not recently spoken with Obama but had been in touch with Treasury Secretary Timothy Geithner as he exercised his authority to "claw back" executive compensation (Reuters, 2009). Critics questioned whether Feinberg had indeed acted within his legal authority, particularly since his appointment had been made without Senate confirmation. They also openly wondered why the president was so distant from all the action. Amid criticism from political opponents and some in the media (of both the policy and the manner in which the decision was made), Feinberg nevertheless went ahead with his plan, which the president publicly supported thereafter to quiet his critics.

Later, when dealing with managing the BP fund, Feinberg faced criticism that he was a "corporate shill" for BP, who paid his salary (Peterson 2010) and that his decision making on payouts was inconsistent and not fully transparent or neutral (Negrin 2011), all while proceeding at a glacial pace, a shortcoming President Obama himself was critical of (Leary 2010). In response, Feinberg's operation promised to speed up operations and developed a publicized methodology for subsequent payments (Clifford 2011). As the processes on each of these compensation programs winds down, it is equally likely that the roar of criticism concerning Feinberg will quiet and that, should another similar financial crisis emerge, another pay master will be given the nod.

John Holdren (Science Czar)

Holdren is the director of the Office of Science and Technology Policy. In his position, he serves as assistant to the president for science and technology and is co-chair of the President's Council of Advisors on Science and Technology. He was one of President Bill Clinton's top science advisors from 1994 until the end of the administration. Holdren is tasked with advising on the full range of science and technology policies that span across various policy spheres from environmental security to educational progress in enhancing the science and engineering workforce, as well as to broader issues such as national security and economic recovery. Perhaps most visibly, Holdren has been charged with promoting transparency and scientific integrity for policymaking across the various executive branch departments and agencies.

After Holdren's service under Clinton, the Bush administration initiated a pledge for the advancement of scientific information in the policymaking process but was instead subsequently criticized by watchdog groups such as the Union of Concerned Scientists (UCS) for allegedly undermining scientific integrity in the executive branch by having technical reports written or edited by unqualified political hacks (see Vaughn and Villalobos 2009). After just six weeks in office, Obama pledged to have new guidelines for restoring scientific integrity implemented within six months. Then, on March 9, 2009 (just ten days prior to Holdren's appointment), Obama released a presidential memorandum,[3] which laid out the framework for developing a multifaceted program for restoration and protection of scientific integrity within the executive branch (Vaughn and Villalobos 2009: 803). Holdren's subsequent unanimous confirmation and appointment to the executive branch as Obama's top science advisor brought new hope among scientists for improvements in restoring and protecting scientific integrity. However, progress on advancing scientific integrity in the Executive Branch has long since been delayed and many observers now view Holdren's efforts in promoting substantive changes as having been meager and largely ineffective. Indeed, the administration's new guidelines on scientific integrity arrived more than 15 months later than originally promised and the actual document has been panned by critics as little more than a vague, short memorandum of less than 1,500 words, which focuses on instituting minimum requirements (instead delegating such details to the lower federal agencies and departments) and otherwise lacks legally enforceable standards for protection against the violation of the administration's proposed principles (see Froomkin 2010).[4]

Holdren has demonstrated little progress elsewhere in attending to science and technology issues across the various policy spheres he attends to in serving the administration. Instead, most of the attention in the media has centered on the continued intrusion that politics has played in shaping scientific reports and information related to Executive Branch policy making. As Froomkin (2010) points out (and related to the criticism surrounding Browner's appraisal above), Obama's oil spill commission "revealed in October that the White House itself had squelched attempts by National Oceanic and Atmospheric Administration scientists to make public the agency's worst-case estimate of how much oil could spew from the blown-out BP well in the Gulf of Mexico," which "unlike the ones the White House were issuing—turned out to be about right."

---

3. See http://www.whitehouse.gov/the_press_office/Memorandum-for-the-Heads-of-Executive-Departmentsand-Agencies-3-9-09/ (accessed 9 March 2009).

4. See http://www.whitehouse.gov/sites/default/files/microsites/ostp/scientific-integrity-memo-12172010.pdf (accessed 17 December 2010).

Anthony K. "Van" Jones (Green Jobs Czar)

Van Jones worked for President Obama as special advisor for Green Jobs, Enterprise, and Innovation while serving as a member on the White House Council on Environmental Quality. Prior to his service, Jones was widely known as an environmentalist, civil rights activist, and attorney. During his service in the Obama administration, Jones fell prey to some of the most common criticisms promulgated by media critics upon so-called czar personnel. First, they charged that he lacked legal authority in a position that not only lacked Senate confirmation, but one that was also newly created by (and solely answerable to) the president. Additionally, his mission was broad and applicable across numerous policy spheres, which opponents considered threatening, particularly given the uncertainty concerning his organizational authority under his newly installed position. Soon after his appointment on March 10, 2009, opponents began criticizing his position and questioning his authority, as well as any implications his actions might have. More damaging to his performance, critics soon engulfed Jones with controversy regarding his past political activities, citing negative public commentary concerning congressional Republicans and other controversy alleging his connection to controversial petitions and radical political groups. By September, Jones found he was overwhelmed by controversy and unable to serve the president in an adequate manner, subsequently resigning from his post.

Interestingly, Jones rejected the "Green Jobs Czar" label that many in the media applied when referring to him during his tenure. The label drew attention from right-wing radio and television hosts who went after Jones concerning a number of his past endeavors. Trying to distance himself from the "czar" moniker, Jones insisted he was instead "the green jobs handyman. I'm there to serve. I'm there to help as a leader in the field of green jobs, which is a new field. I'm happy to come and serve and be helpful but there's no such thing as a 'Green Jobs Czar'" (Burnham 2009). These comments by Jones highlighted the administration's growing unease with the use of the czar term. What was once a title used to highlight a president's prerogative to attend to an issue (e.g., Nixon's employment of an energy czar) had suddenly become a means to derail key appointees from advising the president in positions considered to lack the legitimacy and authority afforded to other Senate confirmed personnel.

R. Gil Kerlikowske (Drug Czar)

The latest step up a long law enforcement career ladder, Kerlikowske is seemingly well equipped to serve as the Obama administration's official director of the Office of National Drug Control Policy and de facto drug czar, a powerful and visible position, although under the Obama administration no longer one that possesses Cabinet status. Known for taking a thorough and multipronged perspective toward reducing drug addiction in the United States, Kerlikowske openly espouses moving from the traditional criminal justice-centric perspective and toward a view that embraces norms of prevention and treatment, as well. These new values are echoed in the nation's new drug-control strategy and the president's request for nearly $340 million in additional funding for prevention and treatment programs (Aguilar 2011), along with Kerlikowske's announced decision to abandon the rhetoric of the "war on drugs" (Fields 2009). At the same time, concerns that Kerlikowske might lead a complete liberalization of national drug policy have proved unwarranted, as he has signaled strong opposition to legalization of marijuana (Shen 2009), including threatening the state of California with legal action should a related ballot initiative prove successful.

Cass Sunstein (Regulatory Czar)

Though one of the handful of Senate-confirmed czars in the Obama administration, Sunstein's tenure as administrator of the Office of Information and Regulatory Affairs (OIRA) in the Office of Management and Budget has not been spared from controversy. From a long-blocked nomination battle in the Senate—Democrats eventually had to force a cloture vote that passed with a mere three spare votes nine months into the administration—to his status as the first of Obama's czars to be called before a congressional hearing under the new Republican-dominated House of Representatives in the 112th Congress (Samuelsohn and Bravender 2011), Sunstein has proved a repeat target for the president's ideological opponents to attack. Moreover, the president's traditional ideological allies also express reservations about the regulatory czar. These concerns are based on Sunstein's demonstrated support for libertarian paternalism in his widely acclaimed academic writings, one where governments "nudge" citizens into better behavior with regulatory incentives rather than firmly mandating which options are available and which are not.

Most recently, Obama put Sunstein at the head of an admin-istration-wide effort to evaluate the economic impact of federal regulations with an eye toward minimizing those that harm job creation and economic growth (Samuelsohn and Bravender 2011); such an assignment will enable Sunstein to continue in the mis-sion *The New York Times* described as making regulations "more supple, not less robust" (Wallace-Wells 2010). The most significant months of Sunstein's work appear to be ahead of him, although in the fourteen months he worked for Obama prior to the new order, the famed academic had been credited with reversing the decline of OIRA, taking it from a place where "regulations went to die" to a more efficacious agency designed to determine whether the rules promulgated by bureaucrats to govern implementation of national policy are the best ones (Weigel 2011).

Conclusion

Clearly, czars have been an important and powerful component of Obama's approach to management and leadership in the first part of his time in office. By using czars, the president has been able to demonstrate the importance of policy issues, both to his own agenda and to the broader political system. Although the performance outcomes for these czars has been a mixed bag, with as many stories of success to report as tales of frustration and failure, it seems unlikely that the president would need to further employ (or at least expand on) such leadership strategies in the future. Regardless of the success of the aforementioned Republican anti-czar legislation, the rhetorical and institutional resistance to czars has increased to a point where it seems no longer pragmatic to use them, at least in the high-profile manner that this president and several of his predecessors have in recent decades.

Works Cited

Aguilar, J. "TT interview with Drug Czar Gil Kerlikowske." *Texas Tri-bune* (26 Jan. 2011). http://www.texastribune.org/texas-news-media/ tt-interview/tt-interview-with-drug-czar-gil-kerlikowske/ (accessed 2 Feb. 2011).

Burnham, M. "Obama's 'green jobs handyman' ready to serve." *New York Times* (10 March 2009). http://www.nytimes.com/gwire/2009/03/10/10

greenwire-obamas-green-jobs-handyman-ready-to-serve-10075.html (accessed 15 March 2009).

Clifford, C. "Gulf oil spill victims offered 3 years' damages." *CNN Money* (2 Feb. 2011). http://money.cnn.com/2011/02/02/smallbusiness/bp_claims_feinberg_final_payments/ (accessed 2 February 2011).

Dunn, A. "The truth about 'czars.'" *White House Blog* (16 Sept. 2009). http://www.whitehouse.gov/blog/The-Truth-About-Czars/ (accessed 1 Feb. 2011).

Edmond v. United States, 520 U.S. 651 (1997).

Environmental Protection Agency. "Great Lakes restoration initiative." *EPA* (3 Dec. 2010). http://www.epa.gov/greatlakes/glri/ (accessed 1 Feb. 2011).

Feingold, R. Statements from the judiciary subcommittee on the constitution. Hearing SD-226 on examining the history and legality of executive branch "czars," United States Senate Committee on the Judiciary. (6 Oct. 2009). http://judiciary.senate.gov/hearings/testimony.cfm?id=4098&wit_id=4083 (accessed 6 Oct. 2009).

Fields, G. "White House czar calls for end to 'war on drugs.'" *Wall Street Journal* (14 May 2009). http://online.wsj.com/article/SB124225891527617397.html (accessed 2 Feb. 2011).

Flesher, J. "Obama taps Cameron Davis as Great Lakes czar." *Huffington Post* (4 June 2009). http://www.huffingtonpost.com/2009/06/04/obama-taps-cameron-davis_n_211315.html (accessed 4 June 2009).

Froomkin, D. "New Obama scientific integrity memo is late and vague." *Huffington Post* (17 Dec. 2010). http://www.huffingtonpost.com/2010/12/17/new-obama-scientific-inte_n_798483.html (accessed 17 Dec. 2010).

Goldman, D. "Big pay cuts . . . What about Goldman?" *CNN Money* (22 Oct. 2009). http://money.cnn.com/2009/10/22/news/companies/executive_compensation_curbs/?postversion=2009102210%20 (accessed 22 Oct. 2009).

Goler, W. "Obama's czars draw criticism from both sides of the political aisle." *Fox News* (1 Aug. 2009). http://www.foxnews.com/politics/2009/07/15/obamas-czars-draw-criticism-sides-political-aisle/ (accessed 1 Aug. 2009).

Gulick, L. H. *Administrative Reflections from World War II*. Tuscaloosa: University of Alabama Press, 1948.

Hamburger, T., and C. Parsons. "President Obama's czar system concerns some." *Los Angeles Times* (5 March 2009). http://articles.latimes.com/2009/mar/05/nation/na-obama-czars5 (accessed 1 May 2009).

Javers, E. "White House: Pay czar decided on his own." *Politico* (22 Oct. 2009). http://www.politico.com/news/stories/1009/28596.html (accessed 22 Oct. 2009).

Leary, A. "Obama administration directs criticism to BP claims czar Kenneth Feinberg." St. *Petersburg Times* (25 Sept. 2010). http://

www.tampabay.com/news/politics/stateroundup/obama-administra-tion-directs-criticism-to-bp-claims-czar-kenneth-feinberg/1123951 (accessed 2 Feb. 2011).

Lovely, E. "Czar (n): An insult; a problem-solver." *Politico* (21 Oct. 2008). http://www.politico.com/news/stories/1008/14751.html (accessed 1 Feb. 2011).

Meckler, L. "'Czars' ascend at White House." *Wall Street Journal.* (15 Dec. 2008), A6.

Negrin, M. "Judge: Feinberg's fund isn't 'neutral.'" *Politico* (3 Feb. 2011). http://www.politico.com/politico44/perm/0211/part_of_bp_ad7e2361-52b2-4d45-88ba-50a4bcdec5f7.html (accessed 3 Feb. 2011).

O'Brien, M. "Republicans introduce bill to eliminate presidential 'czars.'" *The Hill* (1 Jan. 2011). http://thehill.com/blogs/blog-briefing-room/news/136487-republicans-introduce-bill-to-eliminate-presidential-czars (accessed 11 Jan. 2011).

Patten, D. A. "All the President's Czars." *Newsmax.* (Dec. 2009), 52–68.

Patterson, B. H. *The White House Staff: Inside the West Wing and Beyond.* Washington, DC: Brookings Institution Press, 2000.

Peterson, C. "Alabama official calls Feinberg a BP 'corporate shill,' WSJ says." *Bloomberg* (24 Aug. 2010). http://www.bloomberg.com/news/2010-08-24/alabama-official-calls-feinberg-a-bp-corporate-shill-wsj-says.html (accessed 2 Feb. 2011).

Pfiffner, J. P. "Presidential use of White House 'czars.'" Testimony before the Senate Committee on Homeland Security and Governmental Affairs. 22 Oct. 2009.

Relyea, H. C. "Presidential advice and senate consent: The past, present, and future of policy czars." Testimony before the Senate Committee on Homeland Security and Governmental Affairs. 22 Oct. 2009.

Reuters. "The Obama administration's pay czar Kenneth Feinberg says he can 'claw back' exec compensation." *Reuters* (17 Aug. 2009). http://www.nydailynews.com/money/2009/08/17/2009-08-17_us_pay_czar_says_he_can_claw_back_exec_compensation.html (accessed 17 Aug. 2009).

Samuelsohn, D. and R. Bravender. "Cass Sunstein summoned to Capitol Hill." *Politico* (20 Jan. 2011). http://www.politico.com/news/stories/0111/47901.html (accessed 1 Feb. 2011).

Saslow, E. "White House ethics? 'Mr. No' knows." *Washington Post* (13 March 2009). http://www.washingtonpost.com/wp-dyn/content/article/2009/03/12/AR2009031203748.html (accessed 2 Feb. 2011).

Schwemle, B. L., T. B. Tatelman, V. S. Chu, and H. B. Hogue. "The debate over selected presidential assistants and advisors: Appointment, accountability, and congressional oversight." *Congressional Research Service* (CRS). (22 July 2010), 1–81.

Shen, M. "Kerlikowske: Legal pot 'not in my vocabulary.'" *KOMO News* (7 Aug. 2009). http://www.komonews.com/news/local/52676987.html (accessed 2 Feb. 2011).

Vaughn, J. S., and J. D.Villalobos. "The Obama Administration's Challenges After the 'War on Science': Reforming Staffing Practices and Protecting Scientific Integrity in the Executive Branch." *Review of Policy Research*. Vol. 26, No. 6 (2009), 803–819.

Villalobos, J.D., and J. S. Vaughn. *Coping with Czars: Appraising the Leadership Role of Barack Obama's Science, Technology, and Health-Related Czars*. Paper presented at the 2010 Dupont Summit at the Carnegie Institution for Science, Washington DC, 2010a

———.*Obama's Czars in Historical and Legal Context*. Paper presented at the 2010 Annual Meeting of the American Political Science Association, Washington, DC, 2010b.

Wallace-Wells, B. "Cass Sunstein wants to nudge us." *New York Times Magazine* (13 May 2010). http://www.nytimes.com/2010/05/16/magazine/16Sunstein-t.html (accessed 2 Feb. 2011).

Weigel, D. "Nudge on trial." *Slate* (26 Jan. 2011). http://www.slate.com/id/2282619/ (accessed 26 Jan. 2011).

Chapter 21

Unilateral Directives

Graham G. Dodds

Barack Obama was elected president in part because of his promise to move beyond traditional political conflicts and to unite a divided country. He campaigned by assuring voters "Yes we can" bring about real change, in terms of both the substance and tone of politics. Yet, the president's many critics contend that he has not yet lived up to that promise. But that sort of political appeal remains at the core of the president's image and personality. Obama seems disinclined—both temperamentally and politically—to engage in confrontational actions or in sharply partisan politics. Even when he enjoyed large Democratic majorities in the House and Senate, the president eschewed the blunt imposition of his preferred policies and instead sought to constructively engage with his political adversaries, holding out the hope of reaching partial consensus with them. As Obama explained when he was a candidate for the presidency, "I am not a big believer in doing things unilaterally" (Easton 2008).

But for better or worse, unilateralism is a central feature of the contemporary presidency. In particular, presidents often turn to unilateral directives like executive orders to get things done, even when those actions meet with legislative resistance or judicial skepticism. Every single president has issued unilateral directives. To be sure, they have figured in many of the more important episodes in American political history and they are arguably a hallmark of the modern presidency (Greenstein 1978: 45–46).

There are more than two-dozen different types of unilateral presidential directives, but the most common are executive orders, proclamations, and memoranda (Relyea 1998). Executive orders and proclamations are the oldest and best-known types of unilateral presidential directives and are legally interchangeable, whereas memoranda are newer but increasingly popular.[1] There is no official definition of these directives, but they are generally written documents through which the president directs the operations of the Executive Branch of government. They are not explicitly mentioned in the Constitution, but their authority derives from Article II's vague grants of power and also from various statutory authorizations. And their limits are the same as their justifications: Unilateral presidential directives cannot go against the Constitution or existing law. But within those constraints, presidents can use unilateral directives for a great variety of purposes. Despite the importance of unilateral directives to the presidency and American politics, the existing literature on the topic is small, although scholars, journalists, and the public are increasingly aware of this major component of presidential power.[2]

In terms of Obama's use of unilateral directives, Table below 21.1 contains numerical comparisons of presidents' use of unilateral directives over the past thirty-four years, or the last eight full presidential terms plus the first twenty-three months of Obama's presidency. It lists only executive orders and proclamations, because there is currently no reliable catalogue of presidential memoranda and other directives.[3]

Table 21.1 indicates that, although there is considerable variation in the numbers of executive orders and proclamations issued by presidents, there is also a good amount of commonality across presidencies. The average number of executive orders issued per presidential term in this period is 190, and the average number of

---

1. In *Wolsey v. Chapman* (1879), the Supreme Court found no real distinction between executive orders and proclamations.

2. Beyond several articles in law reviews (e.g., Branum 2002), several articles in political science journals (e.g., Cooper 2001; Dodds 2008; Mayer 1999; Mayer and Price 2002; Moe and Howell 1999a, 1999b), and a few chapters in edited volumes (e.g., Dodds 2006; Howell and Kriner 2007), the last decade has seen five books on the general topic: Mayer (2001), Cooper (2002), Howell (2003), Warber (2006), and Rodrigues (2007).

3. The American Presidency Project at the University of California—Santa Barbara is currently trying to catalogue presidential memoranda.

Table 21.1. Presidential Executive Orders and Proclamations[a]

Presidential Administration	Number of Executive Orders	Number of Proclamations
B. Obama[b]	65	267
G. W. Bush (II)	118	478
G. W. Bush (I)	173	462
B. Clinton (II)	164	435
B. Clinton (I)	200	443
G. H. W. Bush	166	589
R. Reagan (II)	168	643
R. Reagan (I)	213	475
J. Carter	320	335

[a]Executive order counts are from *The Federal Register*, www.archives.gov/federal-register/executive-orders/disposition.html. Proclamation counts are from *The American Presidency Project*, http://www.presidency.ucsb.edu/proclamations.php
[b]As of December 13, 2010.

proclamations issued is 482.5. These numbers suggest that Obama is on track to meet or exceed the average number of executive orders and proclamations issued by his recent predecessors. And that suggests that this ostensibly consensual president has in fact embraced presidential unilateralism.

However, the real nature of Obama's use of unilateral presidential directives can best be understood not quantitatively but qualitatively. In part, this is because not all unilateral presidential directives are important. Some enact significant policies, but many are for minor administrative matters or serve only to make symbolic designations like National Leif Ericson Day or Fire Prevention Week (Leibovich 2009). Given the great variability in the significance of such directives, Phillip Cooper has concluded that "mere counting tells us nothing," in that it fails to distinguish between important and unimportant unilateral presidential directives (Cooper 2002: 13).[4]

---

4. In contrast, Mayer and Price (2002) have attempted to do quantitative analysis by first distinguishing significant and insignificant directives, by screening out directives not mentioned in multiple major mass media sources.

Therefore, it is necessary to examine some of Obama's more prominent and important unilateral presidential directives in some detail. The following eight brief case studies may help to indicate whether and how Obama's use of unilateral presidential directives comports with that of other presidents and also with his own political agenda.

Traditional Early Reversals

It has become tradition for presidents to issue at least several unilateral directives at the very start of their terms, in order to enact policies with significant political symbolism, to differentiate their presidency from that of their predecessor, and also to appease certain political constituencies. Presidential candidates often promise to sign such directives immediately upon taking office, and the media and the public has increasingly noticed this aspect of presidential political theater. For example, in October 2008, *Slate* magazine published a list of Bush-era executive orders that it said Obama should quickly reverse by issuing his own executive orders if he were elected (Bazelon and Wilson 2008).

Just days after Obama's election in November 2008, presidential transition team member John Podesta indicated that Obama would act quickly and unilaterally after his inauguration to make a break with some of his Bush's policies. Podesta said, "There's a lot that the president can do using his executive authority without waiting for congressional action, and I think we'll see the president do that" (Zeleny 2008). Podesta also indicated that Obama's team was systematically reviewing all of Bush's executive orders to see which should be kept, repealed, or amended (Ramsay 2008).

In January 2009, one day after the thirty-sixth anniversary of the landmark abortion case *Roe v. Wade*, Obama issued a memorandum to reverse Bush's "gag rule" or "Mexico City policy" of prohibiting the U.S. Agency for International Development (USAID) from providing funds to any international nongovernmental organization that either performs or promotes abortion as a method of family planning (Baker 2009). Ronald Reagan created the first such ban in 1984, Bill Clinton lifted it soon after taking office in 1993, then George W. Bush reinstated it in his first day in office, so this particular policy has seen a lot of unilateral reversals (Zeleny 2008). Obama's memo claimed that Bush's "excessively broad conditions on grants and assistance are unwarranted" and that "they have undermined efforts to promote safe and effective family planning programs in foreign nations."

In a policy area closely related to abortion, Obama issued an executive order in March 2009 to expand embryonic stem cell research, reversing Bush's policy on the issue. Obama's order was entitled "Removing Barriers to Responsible Scientific Research Involving Human Stem Cells," and it was a central part of his effort to ensure that ideology would not trump science, as arguably it had under Bush. However, in August 2010, a federal judge blocked Obama's directive, saying it violated a federal ban on destroying human embryos because its distinction between the destruction of an embryo and the results of that destruction was untenable (Harris 2010). The Obama administration subsequently appealed the decision and won a stay, such that stem cell research can continue until the judiciary reaches a final decision on the issue.

Organized labor was another policy area in which Obama issued several unilateral directives early in his presidency to reverse Bush orders. On January 30, Obama signed three separate executive orders to enact policies more friendly to labor unions. Executive Order 13494, entitled "Economy in Government Contracting," directed departments and agencies not to reimburse federal contractors for expenses incurred in discouraging employees from forming a union and engaging in collective bargaining. A second executive order concerned the "non-displacement of workers" and stipulated that when contracts for a portion of a large project expire, qualified employees who had worked there under the old contract must be given the chance to continue work at the same location under the new contract rather than be automatically terminated. The third executive order that Obama signed that day, entitled "Notification of Employee Rights Under Federal Labor Laws," required federal contractors to inform employees of their right to engage in collective bargaining under the National Labor Relations Act. Obama's order evoked a Bush executive order from 2001 that had required employers to notify employees of their rights not to join a union, not to pay for a union's political activities, and to decertify a union. Obama's order noted, "The attainment of industrial peace is most easily achieved and workers' productivity is enhanced when workers are well informed of their rights under Federal Labor laws."

A More Traditional "War on Terror"

Beyond using unilateral presidential directives to reverse his predecessor's policies about abortion and organized labor, Obama also
used them to alter the nature of Bush's controversial "War on Terror." On January 22, 2009 (his second full day in office), Obama
signed three executive orders to change Bush policies about the
detention of suspected terrorists. The first of these was Executive Order 13391, entitled "Ensuring Lawful Interrogations." Its
stated aim was "to improve the effectiveness of human intelligence
gathering, to promote the safe, lawful, and humane treatment of
individuals in United States custody," and it called for several
significant changes to Bush policies. The order reversed Bush's
Executive Order 13440 of 2007, which had limited the application
of the Geneva Conventions to suspected terrorists detained by the
United States. Obama's order also banned torture and humiliating
or degrading treatment of detainees, and it limited interrogation
techniques to those authorized by the U.S. Army *Field Manual*.
It mandated that the International Red Cross be given access to
detainees, and it established a task force on the interrogation
and transfer of detainees. The order also called for the closing of
secret prisons on CIA "black sites," saying, "The CIA shall close
as expeditiously as possible any detention facilities that it currently operates and shall not operate any such detention facility
in the future." Obama's order thus ended many of Bush's most
controversial counterterrorism policies. However, it did not explicitly ban the practice of extrajudicial rendition, whereby suspected
terrorists captured abroad may be sent to a third country to be
vigorously interrogated by a foreign government with few or no
limits on such practices.

In a second executive order issued that same day, Obama
declared that the detention facility at the U.S. naval base at Guantanamo Bay, Cuba "shall be closed as soon as practicable, and no
later than 1 year from the date of this order." The order suggested
that the indefinite detention of hundreds of suspected terrorists
served neither the interests of the United States nor justice, so
it called for a review of the 245 detainees then held there (Mazzetti and Glaberson 2009). The third executive order was entitled
"Review of Detention Policy Options," and it created a special task
force to identify options for dealing with people apprehended "in
connection with armed conflicts and counterterrorism operations."

Of the counterterrorism directives Obama signed that day, the executive order to close Guantanamo was the most controversial, particularly in Congress. In May 2009, the Senate voted 90 to 6 to block funding for the Guantanamo closure until it received a satisfactory plan of what would be done with the prisoners. Many members of Congress were nervous about closing the facility because they feared that civilian courts might let the detainees go, on the grounds that they were mistreated while in custody and thus any information obtained from their interrogations is tainted would be inadmissible (Johnson et al. 2010: 13). Seven months after the Senate vote, Obama issued a memorandum identifying a maximum security prison in Illinois as the facility to hold the remaining Guantanamo detainees and directing the secretary of defense and the attorney general to prepare for the relocation of the detainees. But Congress continued to resist such a change, and the administration seemed less and less inclined to press the issue. Even though the commander-in-chief's closure order seemed determinative, it clearly was not. As an anonymous administration official said, "The president can't just wave a magic wand to say that Gitmo will be closed" (Savage 2010).

In October 2009, Obama issued an executive order to reverse another Bush-era policy related to the intelligence community. In February 2008, Bush issued an executive order to weaken an oversight board whose task was to ensure that spy agencies obey the law. Before Bush's order, the Intelligence Oversight Board was obligated to notify the attorney general and the Department of Justice of any illegality engaged in by intelligence agencies. But Bush's order instructed the board to make a notification of illegality only if intelligence officials were not in the process of "adequately" addressing it themselves, and even then such notification would be forwarded to the attorney general for a criminal investigation only if the director of National Intelligence deemed it appropriate. Obama's order reversed Bush's order and thus reverted to the pre-Bush practice of mandatory notification. Former CIA deputy counsel Suzanne Spaulding said Obama's order restored the board's independence and credibility and would enhance public trust of secret intelligence activities (Savage 2009).

In November 2009, Obama issued another memorandum to alter Bush's policies regarding the War on Terror. Obama dictated a five-page memo that laid out the details of his Afghanistan troop surge, in order to be perfectly clear about the mission's goals, limits, and duration. It was highly unusual for a president to present such a detailed account of a major military undertaking, let alone to do so via a unilateral presidential directive, so Obama's memo marked a major change from the poorly defined and open-ended military campaigns of other presidents.[5]

Transparent, Open Government

Another controversial aspect of the Bush administration that Obama sought to reverse was its penchant for secrecy. Spurred by the 9/11 attacks and the prosecution of the War on Terror, Bush instituted a number of measures to enhance the secrecy of governmental actions and documents. In contrast, Obama has strived for greater transparency, and unilateral presidential directives have factored in this change.

Obama's very first executive order, which he signed in his first full day in office, reversed a Bush executive order from November 2001 that had limited public access to presidential records held by the National Archives and Records Administration. Bush's order rendered private many presidential records that had previously been publicly accessible, including some of his father's records. The Bush directive altered policies established by the Presidential Records Act of 1978, under which presidential papers become publicly available twelve years after the end of an administration, except for materials related to national security. Bush's order set forth additional reasons that documents could be kept secret, it stipulated that the current president can make a previous president's papers secret even if the previous president objects, and it raised the legal bar for individuals seeking to challenge the designation of presidential documents as secret.

Bush's directive was not the first to tighten public access to presidential documents (Reagan issued an executive order in 1989 to enact restrictions beyond those contained in the 1978 law), but it was very controversial. Former president, Bill Clinton, objected to it, and it was challenged by various academic groups, including the American Political Science Association, whose members often engage in archival research on presidential papers. And in 2007,

---

5. See Coll (2010), who reports on the memo as it is presented in Bob Woodward's book, *Obama's Wars*.

part of Bush's order was struck down by the DC District Court on the grounds that it went against the 1978 Act. Obama's action largely returned things to the post-Reagan, pre-Bush status quo.

Also on January 21, 2009, Obama issued a memorandum entitled "Transparency and Open Government," which directed the heads of executive departments and agencies to make government more transparent, participatory, and collaborative. The memo began by stating, "My Administration is committed to creating an unprecedented level of openness in Government." In a second memo issued that same day, Obama sought to enhance the public's ability to obtain governmental information via the Freedom of Information Act (FOIA). Obama's memo started by approvingly invoking Justice Louis Brandeis' famous quote about publicity, "Sunlight is said to be the best of disinfectants." It then indicated that "The Freedom of Information Act should be administered with a clear presumption: In the face of doubt, openness prevails." The memo also said, "All agencies should adopt a presumption in favor of disclosure, in order to renew their commitment to the principles embodied in FOIA, and to usher in a new era of open Government."

On December 29, 2009, Obama issued an executive order and also a memorandum relating to national security declassification.[6] The executive order was entitled "Classified National Security Information," and it loosened restrictions on public access to government documents. It revoked Bush's Executive Order 13292 of 2003, which had made it easier to keep many executive documents from public view and gave the vice president a significant say in the process of blocking declassification. Obama's order created a policy whereby no records can remain forever classified, and it established deadlines for declassifying materials that are exempted from the usual twenty-five-year declassification period. In an entry on the White House blog, William H. Leary, the National Security Council official responsible for declassification issues, wrote, "While the government must be able to prevent the public disclosure of information that would compromise the national security, a democratic government accountable to the people must be as transparent as possible and must not withhold information for self-serving reasons or simply to avoid embarrassment."

In addition to the above actions to enhance transparency and limit governmental secrecy, the Obama administration decided to

---

6. The memorandum sought to implement the executive order.

make its presidential memoranda publicly available. Unilateral presidential directives that are not labeled an executive order or proclamation are not legally required to be published in the *Federal Register*, but Obama's White House Website lists his presidential memoranda (as well as executive orders and proclamations), and most of the memoranda contain an instruction that they be published in the *Federal Register*.

Obama used a unilateral presidential directive to foster greater transparency in terms of the unseemly relationships between administration appointees and lobbyists. Obama's Executive Order 13490 of January 2009, entitled "Ethics Commitments by Executive Branch Personnel," sought to limit interactions between lobbyists and appointees in federal agencies. It prohibited appointees who had previously been lobbyists from engaging in governmental work related to their former positions for a period of two years, it banned appointees from accepting gifts from lobbyists, and it prohibited appointees from working as lobbyists until two years after the end of their governmental employment, so as to shut the "revolving door" between lobbyists and government.

Regulatory Review

On January 30, 2009, Obama issued a briefly worded executive order on regulatory review and planning to revoke Bush's orders such as 13258 (2002) and 13422 (2007), both of which had amended Executive Order 12886, signed by Clinton in 1993. Obama thus continued the practice of presidents unilaterally altering the nature of centralized regulatory review. Reagan was the first president to systematically involve the White House in regulatory planning, as he issued an executive order in 1980 that placed regulatory review in the Office of Regulatory Affairs (OIRA), within the Office of Management and Budget (OMB). Reagan's order also required that the benefits of any new regulation outweigh its costs. In 1993, Clinton issued an executive order to impose a less strict test on new regulations, by requiring that their benefits justify (but not necessarily outweigh) their costs.

In January 2007, shortly after the newly Democratic Congress began, Bush issued an executive order to alter the Clinton policy and give the White House even more say on regulatory policy, by having a political appointee in each agency supervise the development of new regulations. The order also stipulated that in deciding whether to make regulations, federal agencies had to identify a specific market failure that justified the regulation. And it required agencies to make an annual estimate of the total, combined costs and benefits of all of its regulations, not just for each individual rule. Obama's executive order revoked the Bush policy and returned to the Clinton policy.

Also on January 30, 2009, Obama issued a memorandum instructing the head of OMB to consult with agencies on a possible new directive on regulatory review. Obama's memo said, "centralized review is both legitimate and appropriate as a means producing regulatory goals," and it noted that such review had been carried out by OIRA for more than two decades.

Health Insurance Reform and Abortion

Health insurance reform was one of Obama's top domestic priorities and one of his chief legislative accomplishments in his first two years in office. But it became a reality only after an executive order ended more than a year of congressional wrangling. In order to gain the crucial support of a dozen pro-life House Democrats led by Rep. Bart Stupak (D-MI), Obama promised to sign an executive order on abortion funding immediately after signing the health care measure into law. The executive order may have been politically necessary, but as a matter of public policy it was largely unnecessary. The Senate bill, which the House reluctantly approved, already contained restrictive provisions about using federal funds for abortion. And restrictions of this sort had regularly been included in various other health care laws since 1976. Nevertheless, Obama's executive order explicitly reaffirmed existing restrictions on abortion funding and provided for their enforcement.

Gay Rights

The issue of gay rights has demonstrated both the power and the limits of unilateral presidential directives for Obama. In many areas of public policy in which homosexuals want changes for greater inclusion and equality, federal law limits what can be done short of passing further legislation. For example, the military's

"Don't Ask, Don't Tell" policy against homosexuals openly serving in the military is enshrined in law and therefore can be changed only by law (or by a court striking down the existing law), not by a unilateral presidential directive.[7] For this reason, Obama noted in October 2010 that "This is not a situation in which with a stroke of the pen I can simply end the policy" (Farole 2010). Nevertheless, he has issued unilateral directives to advance gay rights in some areas.

For example, in June 2009 Obama issued a memorandum to extend some benefits to same-sex partners of federal employees. The change enabled government employees to use sick leave to care for their domestic partners and to add them to their long-term care insurance, and it permitted domestic partners of Foreign Service personnel to use U.S. medical facilities abroad and to be included in housing provision. A year later, Obama added to this policy with another memorandum to extend benefits like employee assistance programs and child-care subsidies to the same-sex partners of federal workers. Federal laws preclude the extension of all federal employee benefits to same-sex couples via unilateral presidential directives, but these two memoranda added significant benefits (Chen 2010).

In April 2010, Obama issued a memorandum directing the Department of Health and Human Services (HSS) to prohibit discrimination in hospital visitation for same-sex partners. Many hospitals restrict visits by people not related to a patient by blood or marriage, which amounts to discrimination against many same-sex couples. Obama's memo applied to all hospitals that receive Medicare or Medicaid funds, which covers nearly all hospitals. The memo also directed HSS to develop rules that will enable patients to designate visitors and individuals who can make medical decisions on their behalf (Shear 2010).

Obama issued a more symbolic unilateral presidential directive for gay rights in May 2010, as he made a proclamation designating June 2010 as "Lesbian, Gay, Bisexual, and Transgender Pride Month." His proclamation invoked the nation's historical movement toward fulfilling the promise of equality and said, "An

---

7. The policy came about as an awkward compromise after Clinton sought to end the ban via an executive order in 1993 and members of the military and Congress resisted.

important chapter in our great, unfinished story is the movement for fairness and equality on behalf of the lesbian, gay, bisexual, and transgender (LGBT) community."

Economy

Due to the existence of extensive legislation about economic affairs, presidents generally have only limited opportunities to use unilateral directives for significant initiatives in that policy area. And unilateral presidential directives played a minor role in Obama's efforts to pull the country out of "the great recession," as those actions mostly focused on the administration of the 2008 Troubled Asset Relief Program, the $787 billion stimulus package of 2009, fiscal policy, and the role of the Federal Reserve. But Obama did issue a few unilateral directives to address some relatively minor or symbolic economic matters.

For example, at the outset of his presidency, Obama issued a memorandum to freeze the pay of senior White House staff. The memo noted that "Too many Americans have lost their jobs, their homes, their health insurance, or a substantial part of their retirement savings." It then said, "as a signal of our shared commitment to restoring the country's economic vitality and because of the serious economic conditions we are facing, I intend to freeze the salaries of senior members of the White House staff." The memo concluded by directing the chief of staff to report back to the president within thirty days on how to implement such a freeze. Obama's pay freeze was of limited economic significance but did entail some political symbolism.

In January 2010, Obama issued a memorandum ordering the Internal Revenue Service and other federal agencies to prevent private contractors that had not fully paid their taxes from doing business with the federal government (Stolberg 2010). These contractors reportedly owed more than $5 billion in unpaid taxes. Another effort addressed Congress's refusal to create a bipartisan budget commission on long-term fiscal problems; Obama did so via a unilateral presidential directive. Obama announced that he would use an executive order to unilaterally create the "Commission on Fiscal Responsibility and Reform" in his 2010 State of the Union Address. The commission's recommendations (which were released in late 2010 and endorsed by eleven of its eighteen members) are not binding on Congress, but the creation of the Commission arguably gave the president some political cover on an important issue.

Environment

Despite the Obama administration's actions on many different fronts, environmental issues have taken something of a back seat to other priorities, and this is reflected in the president's limited use of unilateral presidential directives in this area. He has, however, used unilateral presidential directives for environmental purposes on several occasions, often to reverse Bush-era policies, but none has really attracted much attention.

On January 26, 2009, Obama issued a memorandum about automobile emissions. It asked the head of the Environmental Protection Agency (EPA) to reconsider the 2008 denial of California's request for a Clean Air Act waiver in order to adopt emission standards that differed from those of the federal government, in particular by limiting greenhouse gas emissions. (The EPA approved the waiver five months later.) Also on January 26, 2009, Obama issued a memorandum to the secretary of transportation to move up the time table for issuing new, tougher fuel standards, such that they could be imposed on vehicles sold in 2011. The new rules would implement a 2007 law calling for significant improvements in gas mileage, a law that the Bush administration essentially did not enforce (Broder and Baker 2009).[8] Two weeks later, Obama issued a memorandum about energy efficiency standards for household appliances, requesting the Department of Energy to put forth new rules for energy efficiency for more than thirty categories of products, in order to save money and energy.

In March 2009, Obama issued a memorandum to suspend a late-term Bush rule that environmentalists claimed weakened the Endangered Species Act. Bush had permitted governmental agencies to determine for themselves if their planned actions posed a sufficiently significant environmental risk that the Fish and Wildlife Service or the National Marine Fisheries should be notified before those actions were undertaken (CNN 2009). Obama's

---

8. Obama issued another memorandum about fuel efficiency to the secretary of transportation and others in May 2010, requiring "that additional coordinated steps be taken to produce a new generation of clean vehicles."

directive decreased that degree of discretion and asked agencies to consult with those groups before taking any actions that might affect endangered or threatened species.

Another of Obama's unilateral presidential directives for environmental matters was significant both substantively and symbolically. In October 2009, Obama issued a lengthy executive order entitled "Federal Leadership in Environmental, Energy, and Economic Performance."[9] The order set environmental sustainability goals for federal agencies and mandated that they establish a 2020 greenhouse gas emissions target. It also called for greater efficiency, more conservation, less waste, and less consumption of petroleum. It sought to leverage the purchasing power of the federal government to promote green products and technologies.

In May 2010, Obama issued an executive order entitled "Chesapeake Bay Protection and Restoration," which created a federal committee to plan the coordinated restoration and protection of this endangered "national treasure." Similarly, in response to the BP-Deepwater Horizon oil spill in the Gulf of Mexico, Obama issued Executive Order 13543 in May 2010, to create a national commission to investigate the spill and offshore drilling in general. He also issued a thirty-day moratorium on new offshore drilling, during which time there would be a safety and environmental review (Shapiro 2010).

One aspect of environmental policy in which unilateral presidential directives have long played a major role is the creation and expansion of national monuments. Per the 1906 Antiquities Act, the president can unilaterally turn public land into a national monument, generally by issuing a proclamation. In the eleven decades since the act was passed, most presidents have used this power, and more than 2 million acres of environmentally or historically significant land have thus been preserved for posterity. Of the nineteen presidents who have served since 1906, only Richard Nixon, Reagan, George H. W. Bush, and Obama (thus far) have not designated national monuments. However, according to a document from the Department of the Interior that became public in February 2010, Obama is apparently considering creating fourteen new national monuments in nine western states at some point in the future (Johnson et al. 2010). National monument proclamations

---

9. Cf. Clinton's executive order 13,148 of 2000, entitled "Greening the Government Through Leadership in Environmental Management."

can be an excellent way for a president to create a lasting legacy, but they often are politically controversial. For example, Clinton's designation of the Grand Staircase-Escalante National Monument in Utah in 1996 played well with his liberal base, but it greatly angered western conservatives, who have long complained about what they perceive to be federal land grabs.

More to Come?

As the foregoing discussion demonstrates, Obama has made extensive use of unilateral presidential directives. By one count, he signed more unilateral presidential directives in his first 100 days "than any president since Franklin Roosevelt" (Talev 2009). And this chapter shows that since then, Obama has continued to use unilateral presidential directives to make his mark on several significant policy areas. He has used them to repudiate his predecessor's policies regarding abortion, stem cell research, labor, counterterrorism, transparency, regulatory review, and the environment. And he has used them to advance his own policies regarding health insurance reform and gay rights.[10] Thus, Obama's use of these directives largely fits with that of his predecessors, as they used unilateral presidential directives for similar purposes. It may also fit with Obama's own politics stylistically as well as substantively. For example, many of Obama's unilateral directives—especially his memoranda—are not just blandly worded bureaucratic documents but rather contain overtly political language and reflect the president's renowned rhetorical skills.

It may be the case that Obama will turn to unilateral presidential directives with greater frequency in the future, for a couple reasons. First, the Obama administration has signaled as much. After some of the president's legislative agenda stalled in Con-

---

10. It is worth noting that on the many occasions on which Obama used a unilateral directive to address a policy that Bush had instituted by a unilateral directive, he did not always reverse it. For example, in February 2009, Obama signed an executive order to create a new White House Office of Faith-Based and Neighborhood Partnerships, expanding the controversial program that Bush had originally created by executive order. After signing the order, Obama said, "the change that Americans are looking for will not come from government alone. There is a force for greater good than government. It is an expression of faith. . . ."

gress following the loss of the Democrats' sixty-vote filibuster-proof majority in the Senate in February 2010, the administration reportedly decided to be more open to unilateral action. On February 13, 2010, Rahm Emanuel (then-White House chief of staff) said, "We are reviewing a list of presidential executive orders and directives to get the job done across a front of issues" (Baker 2010). Obama was thus following in the footsteps of his predecessors, as "The use of executive authority during times of legislative inertia is hardly new" (Baker 2010).[11]

Second, insofar as Congressional intransigence can tempt presidents to rely more on unilateral directives, Obama will undoubtedly be subject to greater temptation during his second two years in office. Given the conservative, partisan character of the 112th Congress, it will be even harder for Obama to count on legislation for policy change, so unilateral alternatives will become more attractive. As Clinton noted two years after the historic 1994 Republican congressional victories and the ascendancy of Speaker Newt Gingrich, "One of the things that I have learned in the last two years is that the President can do an awful lot of things by executive orders" (Ragsdale and Rusk 1999: 126).

But useful although unilateral, presidential directives are, presidents cannot use them to do everything. There are constitutional, institutional, and political limits to their use. A unilateral presidential directive cannot go against a clear provision of the Constitution or a law, and although the former constraint is perhaps vague, the existence of extensive legislation in many policy areas significantly limits the possible use of unilateral presidential directives. For example, we have seen that law limits what Obama can do in terms of the economy and gay rights. Similarly, he will not be able to enact immigration reform or limit carbon emissions unilaterally, as those policies would require congressional action. Related to the constitutional constraints on unilateral presidential directives, presidents are bound by what the two other branches of government do, and they do not want to antagonize the other branches unnecessarily.

And last but certainly not least, there are political limits to what a president can do unilaterally. Extensive unilateralism can have a great political price. It can make a president look more like a tyrannical monarch than a representative of the people.

---

11. Cf. Jacobs and King (2010: 799).

Arguably, this is part of what contributed to George W. Bush's unpopularity (Dodds 2008). One of Obama's unilateral directives suggests that he is clearly aware of this downside of excessive unilateralism. In March 2009, he issued a memorandum on the controversial practice of presidents making signing statements to indicate their understanding of bills that they sign into law. Like unilateral presidential directives, presidential signing statements are not mentioned in the Constitution and pose certain constitutional worries, despite their long history of use. Indeed, Obama's memorandum noted that although presidents have long used such statements, they also have generated a lot of controversy. The memo then set forth a set of principles that would govern Obama's more reserved use of signing statements, and the president said he would issue them "with caution and restraint," but he reserved his right to issue them if Congress sent him bills with constitutionally problematic provisions. The memo also directed executive departments and agencies to seek the advice of the attorney general before relying on previous presidents' signing statements "as the basis for disregarding, or otherwise refusing to comply with, any provision of a statute." It was perhaps ironic that the president was using a unilateral presidential directive to indicate his reticence to use another controversial unilateral tool. But Obama's action was also unusual in that presidents seldom voluntarily declare that they will limit the use of one of the unilateral tools in their arsenal.

For Obama, the tension between unilateralism and democratic leadership is particularly acute. Greater use of unilateral presidential directives would go against Obama's politics of non-confrontation and being avowedly less unilateral than Bush.

Works Cited

Baker, Peter. "Obama reverses rules on U.S. abortion aid." *The New York Times* (24 Jan. 2009).
———. "Obama making plans to use executive power." *The New York Times* (13 Feb. 2010).
Bazelon, Emily and Chris Wilson. "Ten to toss." *Slate* (3 Oct. 2008). http://www.slate.com/id/2200774/.
Branum, Tara L. "President or King? The Use and Abuse of Executive Orders in Modern-Day America." *Journal of Legislature.* Vol. 28 (2002), 1.
Broder, John M. and Peter Baker. "Obama's order is likely to tighten auto standards." *The New York Times* (25 Jan. 2009).

Chen, Edwin. "Obama extends some U.S. benefits to same-sex couples." *Businessweek* (2 June 2010).

CNN. "Obama overturns Bush endangered species rule." (3 March 2009). http://edition.cnn.com/2009/POLITICS/03/03/endangered.species.act/index.html.

Coll, Steve. "Comment: Behind closed doors." *New Yorker Magazine* (11 Oct. 2010).

Cooney, John F. "Chief Executive Obama: An analysis of President Obama's use of his authority to manage the Executive Branch in his first month in office." (White Paper.) Venable, LLP. (March 2009).

Cooper, Phillip J. "The Law: Presidential Memoranda and Executive Orders: Of Patchwork Quilts, Trump Cards, and Shell Games." *Presidential Studies Quarterly.* Vol. 31 (2001), 1.

———. *By Order of the President.* Lawrence: University Press of Kansas, 2002.

Dodds, Graham G. "Executive orders since Nixon." Ed. Christopher S. Kelley. *Executing the Constitution.* Albany: SUNY P, 2006, 53–71.

———. "By order of George W. Bush: The Unilateral Directives of a Unilateralist President." *American Review of Politics.* Vol. 29 (2008), 197–213.

Easton, Nina. "Obama: NAFTA not so bad after all." *Fortune* (18 June 2008).

Farole, Jared A. "Obama: I can't unilaterally end 'Don't Ask, Don't Tell.'" *Wall Street Journal* (14 Oct. 2010).

Greenstien, Fred I. "Change and continuity in the modern presidency." Ed. Anthony King. *The New American Political System.* New York: AEI, 1978.

Harris, Gardiner. "U.S. judge rules against Obama's stem cell policy." *The New York Times* (23 Aug. 2010).

Howell, William G. *Power Without Persuasion.* Princeton, NJ: Princeton University Press, 2003.

Howell, W. and D. Kriner. "Power without persuasion: Identifying executive influence." Eds. B. Rockman and R. Waterman. *Presidential Leadership: The Vortex of Power.* New York: Oxford University Press, 2007.

Jacobs, Lawrence R. and Desmond S. King. "Varieties of Obamism: Structure, Agency, and the Obama Presidency." *Perspectives on Politics.* Vol. 8 (2010): 793–802.

Johnson, Alexandra, et al. "Rethinking unilateral powers in the Obama administration." *Presidency Research Group Report* (Spring 2010).

Leibovich, Mark. "Every dog (and norseman) has his day." *The New York Times* (11 Oct. 2009).

Mayer, Kenneth R. "Executive Orders and Presidential Power." *The Journal of Politics.* Vol. 61, No. 2 (1999), 445–466.

———. *With the Stroke of a Pen: Executive Orders and Presidential Power.* Princeton, NJ: Princeton University Press, 2001.

Mayer, Kenneth R. and Kevin Price. "Unilateral Presidential Powers: Significant Executive Orders, 1949-99." *Presidential Studies Quarterly.* Vol. 32, No. 2 (2002).

Mazzetti, Mark and William Glaberson. "Obama issues directive to shut down Guantanamo." *The New York Times* (22 Jan. 2009).

Moe, Terry M. and William G. Howell. "The Presidential Power of Unilateral Action." *Journal of Law, Economics, and Organization.* Vol. 15, No 1 (1999a), 132–179.

————. "Unilateral Action and Presidential Power: A Theory." *Presidential Studies Quarterly.* Vol. 29, No. 4 (1999b).

Ragsdale, Lyn and Jerrold G. Rusk. "Elections and Presidential Policymaking." Ed. Steven A. Shull. *Presidential Policymaking.* New York: M.E. Sharpe, 1999.

Ramsay, Kristi. "Obama team reviewing 'virtually every agency,' aide says." CNN. (9 Nov. 2008). http://politicalticker.blogs.cnn.com/2008/11/09/obama-team-reviewing-virtually-every-agency-aide-says/.

Relyea, Harold C. "Presidential Directives: Background and Review." Congressional Research Service. Washington, DC. (16 July 1998).

Rodrigues, Ricardo Jose Pereira. *The Preeminence of Politics: Executive Orders from Eisenhower to Clinton.* New York: LFB Scholarly Publishing LLC., 2007.

Savage, Charlie. "Obama strengthens espionage oversight." *The New York Times* (29 Oct. 2009).

————. "Closing Guantanamo fades as a priority." *The New York Times* (26 June 2010).

Shapiro, Ari. "Freeze On Offshore Drilling Was Verbal Order." NPR. (25 May 2010). http://www.npr.org/templates/story/story.php?storyId=127114044.

Shear, Michael D. "Obama extends hospital visitation rights to same-sex partners of gays." *Washington Post* (16 April 2010).

Stolberg, Sheryl Gay. "Obama aims at tax-evading contractors." *The New York Times* (21 Jan. 2010).

Talev, Margaret. "Obama's first 100 days in office haven't been quiet." *McClatchy Newspapers* (26 April 2009). http://www.mcclatchydc.com/2009/04/26/66673/obamas-first-100-days-in-office.html.

Warber, Adam. *Executive Orders and the Modern Presidency: Legislating from the Oval Office.* Boulder, CO: Lynne Rienner, 2006.

Zeleny, Jeff. "Obama weighs quick undoing of Bush policy." *The New York Times* (10 Nov. 2008).

Chapter 22

Vice President Joe Biden

Richard M. Yon

Perpetuating Influence or Restoring Historical Insignificance?

The vice presidency, which has historically been a rather peculiar office, has witnessed an increase in stature and prominence as well as influence in the past thirty years. The uniqueness of the vice presidency stems from the traversing authority and responsibility it has to two branches of government, as established by the Constitution. No other national office suffers from similar ambiguity. Nonetheless, this ambiguity partly explains the rather precipitous gains in influence and responsibility the vice presidency has witnessed over thirty years. Perhaps even more significant than the office's vagueness is the effect that individual vice presidents have had on the office and its ascendant influence. Although the ambiguity of the office creates an opportunity for exercising greater influence, vice presidential–presidential relationships dictate whether or not the vice president is indeed influential and, thus is rather case-specific.

This chapter explores Vice President Joe Biden's contributions to the vice presidency and the role he has played in the Obama administration. More specifically, Biden's vice presidency will be compared with other more recent vice presidents in order to determine whether Biden distinguishes himself from his predecessors by taking a more or less active role in the administration and whether he continued the precedents established by his predecessors.

Soon after Biden was elected vice president, a spokesperson for the vice president-elect commented, "He firmly believes in restoring the Office of the Vice President to its historical role" (Allen 2008). Although Biden routinely sought to distance himself in word from the Cheney model of the vice presidency, his desire to restore the historical role of the vice presidency does not suggest a return to the historical insignificance for the office or a desire to recede from influence in the administration. In fact, Biden perpetuated the growing influence by which the vice presidency has become characterized in recent decades. To understand this phenomenon, it is necessary to briefly examine Biden's Senate career and the circumstances surrounding his selection as Barack Obama's running mate.

Joe Biden: The Senator

Joe Biden's political career spans more than three decades. At the age of thirty, he was elected to the U.S. Senate from Delaware. During his senatorial career, he rose through the Democratic ranks to become chairman of the powerful Judiciary Committee and the Foreign Relations Committee. In this capacity he worked closely with presidential administrations and vice presidents from both parties and engaged in some of the most pressing domestic and international events (Biden 2007). According to then-Sen. Biden:

> As a United States senator I've watched (and played some small part in) history: the Vietnam War, Watergate, the Iran hostage crisis, the Bork nomination, the fall of the Berlin wall, the reunification of Germany, the disintegration of the Soviet Union, 9/11, two wars in Iraq, a presidential impeachment, a presidential resignation, and a presidential election decided by the Supreme Court. . . . I've seen Nixon, Ford, Carter, Reagan, Clinton and two Bushes wrestle with the presidency. (Biden 2007: xix)

Regardless of all of these momentous events, Biden's particular focus as senator pertained to crime and crime prevention, which harkened back to his early days in the Senate. Beginning in the 1970s, as a member of the Judiciary Committee, Biden worked on crime issues and developed both significant expertise and a national reputation on the subject. After decades of work on these important issues, Biden ushered through passage the Violence Against Women Act in 1994. Foreign affairs also made up a significant portion of his portfolio in the Senate. The break-up of Yugoslavia and the resulting genocide that occurred in the Balkans became an area of concern for Biden during his tenure as chair of the Subcommittee on European Affairs (of the Senate Foreign Relations Committee). Reflecting on his career in the Senate, Biden cites the termination of genocide in the Balkans and the passage of the Violence Against Women Act as his "proudest moments in public life" (Biden 2007: xix).

Due to his extensive political experience, Biden believed the presidency was within his grasp. He ran for the highest office in 1988 and again in 2008. It also should be noted that, during this time, he observed vice presidents begin to exercise greater authority and wield significantly more influence over the years. As chairman of the Senate Judiciary and Foreign Relations Committees, Biden acquired intimate knowledge of the inner workings of the presidency during times of crisis, war, and critical domestic and international events. This front-row seat enabled him to understand the new emerging and significant role played by vice presidents and the ability they had to usher in considerable changes and set precedents for future occupants of the office. As a result, he witnessed the emergence of the modern vice presidency. Therefore, Biden's experiences assisted him in defining a similar role as vice president to that of his recent predecessors, thus perpetuating the influence already attained by the office rather than restoring its historical insignificance.

Joe Biden for Vice President?

For the second time in his extensive political career, Biden announced his decision to run for president on January 7, 2007 and officially became a candidate on January 31, 2007 after filing his candidacy papers (Heilemann and Halperin 2010). The vision that encapsulated his quest for the presidency focused on seven key areas:

1. A stable Iraq—safety for its people, prosperity, border security, and a land free of terrorist training camps.

2. Development of renewable energy sources.

3. Health insurance for every American family.

4. Pension security.

5. Fully funded and solvent Social Security.

6. Affordable college education.

7. Fair share of taxes for the rich (Biden 2007: 363–364).

After a rather short-lived campaign, Biden went back to work in the Senate, however, he maintained frequent contact with candidates Hillary Clinton and Barack Obama by offering policy advice. As the nomination was still up for grabs, Biden became the focus of both campaigns for consideration as a possible running mate. For example, "when her [Hillary Clinton] aides asked who would be at the top of her VP short list, she mentioned [Evan] Bayh, [Joe] Biden, [Tom] Vilsack, and Ohio governor Ted Strickland" (Heilemann and Halperin 2010: 100). Furthermore, when speculating as to Obama's vice presidential pick, she thought there was a 50 percent chance that Biden would be chosen.

Sen. Biden resisted the idea of being considered for vice president. He enjoyed joking about the insignificance of the job even though he knew full well that significant potential existed in the office. Besides, given his experience in foreign affairs and his tenure as chair of the Senate Foreign Relations Committee, he had his eye on the position of secretary of state. He also doubted the prospects of his candidacy and began touting Hillary Clinton as the ideal vice presidential pick for Barack Obama. But as time progressed, Biden warmed to the idea of being considered for vice president.

After Obama won the Democratic nomination, Biden complained to Rahm Emanuel—who was advising his campaign—about not receiving any names for a possible running mate. Emanuel responded by stating that Obama had already made up his mind (to pick Biden) and that the campaign was just going through the process to make sure Obama's decision was right (Heilemann and Halperin 2010). This proved to be true, as Obama was becoming more and more convinced that Biden was the right choice for the job. For one thing, Biden appealed to the working class, was loved by the unions, and was respected by police officers as a result of his work on issues pertaining to crime. Also, Obama admired Biden's campaigning abilities, thus he began hinting to his advisors that he was leaning towards Biden as the vice presidential pick (Heilemann and Halperin 2010).

The relationship between Biden and Obama was, up to this point, cordial at best. "He'd [Biden] started out, like all the veterans in the field, thinking Obama was too big for his britches, not ready to be president . . ." (Heilemann and Halperin 2010: 337). In many ways, Biden's attitude toward Obama during their time together in the Senate was "condescending and patronizing to the point where it rankled [Obama]" (Heilemann and Halperin 2010: 338). James Traub of *The New York Times* contends that Obama's image irked Biden:

> As senators, Barack Obama and Joe Biden were far from close. Obama served on the Foreign Relations Committee, which Biden led; and Biden, who felt that he had earned his stars the old-fashioned way, bristled at Obama's status as an instant superstar . . . before Biden dropped out of the race [2008 presidential race] he criticized Obama as a foreign-policy neophyte who was copying his ideas. (Traub 2009)

Whereas most recent presidents and vice presidents had little to no preexisting personal or professional relationship prior to the nomination, Biden and Obama worked together in the Senate and served on the Senate Foreign Relations Committee together. Therefore, it is not surprising that there would be a bit of animosity between the two, especially given their differences. Biden was a thirty-plus year veteran of the Senate who was elected when Obama was in junior high school and also had extensive foreign policy credentials, whereas Obama only had three years of national office experience. Obama, at age forty-seven, was considered a novice who sought to change Washington, whereas Biden was a sixty-five-year-old Washington insider (Kenski, Hardy, and Jamieson 2010). Nonetheless, Biden's opinion of Obama began to change after Obama's race speech delivered in Philadelphia in March 2008. Indeed, "Biden had become an avid fan, telling aides it was the best oration he had heard since Dr. King" (Heilemann and Halperin 2010: 337). As both of their opinions of each other gradually improved, the likelihood of a Biden pick became more apparent.

By July 2008 the vice presidential short list shortened to just three names—Biden, Bayh, and Tim Kaine, the governor of Virginia. Throughout the process, Obama questioned whether Biden truly wanted to be vice president because he seemed hesitant during the vetting process (Heilemann and Halperin 2010). When questioned, Biden said his interest depended on what type of role Obama envisioned for his vice president, which harkens back to the debate and vagueness surrounding the office.

> The role he [Biden] could embrace was that of counselor in chief; weighing in on every important decision, foreign and domestic; contributing his expertise on congressional relations, legislative strategy, judicial appointments, all of it. The key, Biden said, was building a relationship based on candor. . . . (Heileimann and Halperin 2010: 340–341)

Biden understood the dynamic relationship of presidents and vice presidents and knew that it was imperative to come to an agreement with Obama in terms of his role in a presidential administration before accepting the position. Therefore, before accepting the offer, Biden solicited a promise from Obama that he would be included on "every critical decision" (Hornick and Levs 2008). In recalling their conversation, Biden stated in an interview on ABC's *This Week*:

> I said, I don't want to be picked unless you're picking me for my judgment. I don't want to be the guy that goes out and has a specific assignment. . . . I want a commitment from you that in every important decision you'll make, every critical decision, economic and political, as well as foreign policy, I'll get to be in the room. (Hornick and Levs 2008)

This statement reconciles with Biden's vision for the role of a vice president as discussed in the same interview with George Stephanopoulos on December 21, 2008. Biden stated that a vice president should give "the best, sagest, most accurate, most insightful advice and recommendations he or she can make to a president to help them make some of the very, very important decisions that have to be made." Biden thus saw his role as one of chief advisor or counselor to the president, one in which he can use his experience to assist the president by providing his best advice.

Both those inside and outside Obama's campaign lauded his pick of Biden for vice president. David Axelrod, chief Obama strategist, noted it "turned out to be a great pick for us. . . . Barack

Obama was more than enough change for people. They wanted to see him surround himself with some folks with a few gray hairs, and a long resume . . ." (Kenski et al. 2010: 127). Furthermore, polling results indicated that voters' positive opinion of Obama increased after Biden's selection (Kenski et al. 2010).

Despite newfound admiration for each other, Biden tested their relationship by making careless statements that questioned Obama's preparedness to assume the presidency. Additionally, Obama's political opponents made every effort to use Biden's own comments prior to his selection as the vice presidential nominee against Obama. For instance, during a primary debate when Biden was seeking the Democratic nomination for president he was questioned as to whether Obama was ready to be president. Biden stated, "I think he can be ready, but right now, I don't believe he is" (Kenski et al. 2010: 73). Surprisingly, Biden's comments also unintentionally questioned his own preparedness to be vice president. During the general election, Biden discussed Hillary Clinton's suitability for vice president: "Hillary Clinton is as qualified or more qualified than I am to be vice president of the United States of America. Quite frankly, it might have been a better pick than me." This not only questioned his abilities but also indirectly raised concerns about the quality of Obama's decision making. The first "presidential" decision a presidential nominee makes, after all, is to pick a running mate, and Biden was questioning the efficacy of that decision.

However, there is another side to the story. Other vice presidential picks, prior to being selected, also have questioned the suitability to be president of the person who nominated them. This includes George H. W. Bush's criticisms of Ronald Reagan's policies just prior to being picked in 1980 and Jack Kemp's frequent disagreements with Bob Dole prior to them running together in 1996. More, Biden's comment was a poor attempt at self-deprecating humor. Nevertheless, his unintentional gaffes were commonplace on the campaign trail and followed him to the White House.

Biden: The Vice President

Biden took office as vice president with an overall opinion rating (63 perccent) similar to that of his two most recent predecessors at the start of their vice presidencies—Dick Cheney and Al Gore (Pew Research Center 2009). However, disparities exist in terms of Biden's appeal to those identified as Republican voters. His favorability ratings among Republicans (36 percent) in 2009 was far lower than Cheney's appeal to Democratic voters (50 percent) in 2001 or Gore's appeal to Republican voters (42 percent) in 1993 (Pew Research Center 2009). In comparing Biden's favorability/ unfavorability ratings to that of Cheney and Gore, Gallup revealed through a poll conducted between July 8 and 11, 2010 that Biden falls somewhere in the middle with 43 percent favorable and 41 percent unfavorable compared with Gore (44 percent favorable and 49 percent unfavorable) and Cheney (36 percent and 52 percent, respectively) (Gallup 2010). Fortunately for Biden, the country held him in a more positive light than his counterparts according to this July 2010 Gallup poll.

In terms of his vision for the role of vice president and the types of responsibilities he would engage in, Biden took cues from many of his predecessors, even as far back as vice presidents Walter Mondale and Nelson Rockefeller. This is not surprising, given the nature of Biden's lengthy Senate career, in which he witnessed seven presidents and eight vice presidents navigate the political waters of the nation's capitol. Biden established himself as a chief counselor and advisor to the president, similar to what other vice presidents have done. Although, according to a *Larry King Live* interview given on December 22, 2008, Biden professed that his vice presidency would be very different from that of other vice presidents. Biden stated:

> Well, I think the Biden brand is going to be as different as all three [Mondale, Gore and Cheney] of those you suggested in the sense that, look Larry, I think that the role of the vice president is determined in large part by his relationship with the president and the circumstances that administration finds themselves in. (King 2008)

Biden's response illustrates a fundamental quality of the vice presidency—vice presidencies are unique. A vice president's role depends on the needs of a president given his or her own strengths and weaknesses. Context matters too! For example, Cheney's credentials as a White House chief of staff, congressman, and secretary of defense placed him in a unique position to assist the president with the War on Terror. Had Cheney's experiences been different so as to limit his knowledge of national security, defense issues, and foreign policy, or had the 9/11 attacks never occurred, it is very likely that his vice presidency would have been markedly different. Nonetheless, similar approaches and visions of the office in combination with precedents established by other vice presidents contribute to this trend of perpetuating influence.

Biden assumed the vice presidency with the same disdain for line assignments felt by other vice presidents. During the Carter–Reagan presidential transition, Mondale cautioned vice president-elect Bush about assuming line assignments because of the challenges other vice presidents encountered as a result of dispatching their responsibilities. Vice presidents that assume line assignments tend to focus most of their energy on those assignments, thus pigeonholing themselves. The result is a loss of influence in most other areas of the administration. However, Chase Untermeyer, executive assistant to Vice President Bush argued, "an ongoing vice-presidential assignment can be desirable if the subject is important to the president and a torment if it is not" (Untermeyer 1995). In examining recent vice presidencies, one finds that despite the misgivings line assignments engender among vice presidents numerous examples exist even among the country's most influential vice presidents.

Most vice presidents support line assignments within limits because of how important these assignments are to the president and his agenda. For instance, Vice President Bush led the Task Force on Regulatory Relief, which sought to deregulate parts of the U.S. economy (Untermeyer 1995). The marching orders for the task force clearly represented a significant component of not only President Reagan's economic vision and presidential agenda, but also one of his campaign promises. Similarly, Vice President Dan Quayle's responsibilities over the Council on Competitiveness is one in which he viewed as his most important contribution to the Bush administration. Similar to George H. W. Bush's own work with the economy in the Reagan administration, Quayle's work on the council sought to examine what the administration deemed to be excessive government regulations (Quayle 1997).

Perhaps Gore put up the most resistance to assuming line assignments. In following Mondale's lead, Gore outlined his role as vice president prior to assuming the office in a two-page memo. The memo particularly emphasized his interest in not assuming line assignments (Baumgartner 2006). Gore's aversion to line assignments led him to turn down the highly visible lead in chairing the task force to reform health care. Despite his reservations with line assignments, Gore did make an exception and chose to chair the Reinventing Government initiative, which studied the Executive Branch and made recommendations to modernize and consolidate some of its functions (Baumgartner 2006). Finally, Cheney assumed responsibility over line assignments in the Bush administration when he spearheaded the creation of the Office of Homeland Security, led efforts to review homeland security, and headed the energy task force in the early days of the administration (Hayes 2007).

In terms of line assignments, Biden stated during the campaign that he did not want to pursue specific duties and "would not cut as wide a swatch as Vice President Cheney" (Henry 2008). Furthermore, John Podesta stated, "[Biden] had a fairly clear sense in his own mind . . . that he didn't want to be the guy in charge of x portfolio" (Traub 2009). Regardless of his campaign statements, Biden began assuming responsibility over such assignments even prior to taking office. During the presidential transition, Biden chaired early economic meetings that consisted of the transition team's economic consultants in an attempt to develop a comprehensive economic recovery package to present to Congress. The mortgage crisis and economic recession that occurred in 2008 made this no ordinary line assignment. Instead, economic recovery became one of the most important items on the agenda. Therefore, as CNN senior White House correspondent Ed Henry stated, "The fact that Biden is leading the meeting suggests that the incoming Vice President will play a key role in helping to pass the stimulus package. That's significant because Biden's low profile in recent days has sparked speculation that he will be sidelined in the new administration" (Henry 2008). Given Biden's legislative experience it is not surprising that he would be tasked with handling legislative initiatives. And once the administration took office, Biden was deployed not only for the purposes of selling the economic stimulus package to Congress but also to the public. Biden stated during the vice presidential debate with Gov. Sarah Palin, "I would be the point person for the legislative initiatives in the United States Congress for our administration" (Henry 2008). Using his nearly forty-year experience in the Senate, the administration immediately considered the vice president to be the "senior ambassador to the Senate" and Biden even uses his regular workout schedules in the Senate gym to advance the administration's legislative initiatives (Henry 2008).

During the transition, Obama's team reported that Biden would chair the White House Task Force on Working Families.

Biden and the members of the task force, consisting of administration policymakers with input from business and labor groups, engaged with federal agencies in order to develop policy initiatives, identify reforms, and recommend new executive orders designed to help working middle-class families. Obama laid out several goals for the task force, which include the following: 1) The expansion of education opportunities; 2) reinstating labor standards; 3) income protection; and 4) ensuring retirement security (Hornick and Levs 2008; Lee 2008). This line assignment was the first major initiative led by Biden and it clearly segued with his involvement in the development of Obama's economic recovery plans.

Biden's participation in meetings exemplifies his agreement with Obama in terms of the vice president's role as chief counselor. Unlike his predecessor, Cheney, Biden is often an outspoken participant in meetings. "From the outset of his tenure as vice president, Biden has come to view himself as the one who asked the unpleasant and searching questions" (Traub 2009). Biden tends to speak at great lengths and is rather blunt in his assessments and advice, whereas other vice presidents were inclined to listen more and provide advice to the president in private. Biden attends all of the important foreign policy and national security meetings of the president and his involvement in policymaking is quite extensive. Furthermore, James Jones, former national security advisor to Obama, made clear to his staff at the beginning of the term that they work not only for the president but also for the vice president (Traub 2009).

The book, *Obama's Wars*, by Bob Woodward (2010) illustrates the fundamental role of the vice president in foreign policy decision making. In it, Woodward elaborates on Biden's involvement in the Afghanistan strategy by discussing a meeting of the National Security Council on March 12, 2009 in which Biden spoke for approximately twenty-one minutes to voice his opposition to a troop surge. Biden viewed the troop surge as "irresponsible" given the unreliability of the government in Afghanistan and also found the war to be unsustainable politically. Instead, Biden believed the best strategy to employ for Afghanistan was a plan he termed "counterinsurgency plus" in which they would target the real threat—al-Qaeda. Counterinsurgency plus would use fewer troops and could diminish concerns of some Middle East leaders that America's footprint in the region was widening (Woodward 2010: 309–310).

Nonetheless, Obama's choice of a troop surge in Afghanistan did not represent a lack of respect for the vice president's views and advice but instead the president valued Biden's input and demeanor in meetings and the counsel he offered. Biden's inability to sway the president to sign off on his proposal did not seem to diminish his influence either.

> I [Obama] said, Joe, I want you to say exactly what you think. And I want you to ask the toughest questions you can think of. And the reason is, is because I think the American people are best served and our troops are best served by a vigorous debate. . . . I wanted every argument on every side to be poked hard. And if we felt a little give there, we wanted to keep on pushing until finally you hit up against something that was incontrovertible and something that we could all agree to. And so in that sense I think Joe served an enormously useful function. (Woodward 2010: 160)

However, not all agreed with the president's assessments of Biden's contributions in meetings. The vice president received a great deal of opposition from members of the military, particularly Gen. David Petraeus and Stanley McChrystal, as well as Adm. Mike Mullen, regarding his views on Afghanistan strategy. For instance, after an October 7, 2009 meeting, Petraeus commented about Biden's contributions in meetings by stating that "the vice president tended to get lost in his own verbiage, erecting strawman arguments that he could then easily demolish" (Woodward 2010: 210). Regardless of these views, Biden was playing the exact role that Obama wanted him to fulfill—to be the skeptic and the interrogator.

The account of Biden's participation in Afghanistan strategy discussions illustrates several important facts about his vice presidency. First, Biden fulfills the role he envisioned for a vice president—one in which he is involved in all critical decisions of an administration. Second, Obama uses Biden's expertise and judgment, thus demonstrating the perpetuating influence exhibited by vice presidents in recent years. Finally, the vice president assists the president's decision-making style by fostering discussion, fleshing out options, unrelentingly questioning policy options, and being the administration's skeptic.

Just as Gore became the point person for science and technology issues in the Clinton administration and Cheney the point person for homeland security issues in the Bush administration, Biden quickly became an instrumental force on Iraq. Biden's involvement in Iraq began during the transition when president-elect Obama asked him to travel to Iraq, Afghanistan, and Pakistan in order to get a sense of the situation on the ground and meet with leaders to discuss Obama's thoughts in the region. By June 2009, Biden became the point person for the administration's efforts in Iraq, thus solidifying Biden's influence and using his foreign policy credentials, which Obama lacked.

In the midst of a calamitous political environment in fall 2010 in which Obama's agenda seemed stalled and Democrats were on the verge of losing their majority in Congress, Biden emerged as a significant force within the beltway despite rumors that he may not remain on the ticket in the 2012 presidential election. In fact, Biden's influence remained at an all-time high both inside the administration and beyond. Amid the talk of a possible running mate change in 2012, Obama reiterated his support of the vice president by stating, "The single best decision that I have made was selecting Joe Biden as my running mate" (Schwarz 2010). Biden's actions surrounding the 2010 midterm election only confirm Obama's view of him. Despite Democrats losing the majority in the House of Representatives during the election, the Vice President feverishly campaigned across the country in order to minimize losses and ensure control of the Senate remained in the hands of the Democrats, thus fulfilling a common function of the vice presidency. Despite great efforts, the Democrats took a massive hit in 2010 and 2011; however, this only underscores how indispensable Biden's talent will be in dealing with the 112th Congress.

Biden's dealings with the 111th lame-duck Congress serves as a prelude to Biden's indispensability and growing influence. With Senate Republicans adamantly opposed to Obama's New START Treaty (nuclear nonproliferation) and unwilling to move forward with other parts of Obama's agenda unless the Bush tax cuts for wealthy Americans were extended, the administration faced the prospects that nothing would get done and the Congress would live up to its moniker of a lame duck. Within the West Wing, Biden argued that waiting to take up the New START Treaty would make ratification of the treaty even more difficult after the New Year because the Democratic majority in the Senate would be down by five. Furthermore, Biden counseled the president for the need to negotiate with Republicans over the extension of the Bush tax cuts in order to make headway on the treaty before the new Congress took office (Cooper 2010).

> With the departure of Rahm Emanuel as chief of staff
> and Mr. Obama's need to negotiate with Congressional
> Republicans if he is to advance his agenda, the presi-
> dent is increasingly using Mr. Biden as a multipurpose
> emissary while continuing to seek his counsel behind
> the scenes. (Cooper 2010)

Therefore, Biden worked the phones and used connections he built
over his long Senate career to lobby Republicans to achieve the
two-thirds vote necessary to ratify the treaty. Moreover, the White
House and congressional Republicans reached consensus over the
fate of the Bush tax cuts, which enabled Congress to proceed with
ratification of the treaty and passage of a repeal of Don't Ask,
Don't Tell. This was a remarkable feat given the stalemate that
existed and the resulting productivity of a lame-duck Congress.

Since the departure of Obama's first chief of staff, Biden
began fulfilling the void in terms of serving as a liaison with Congress. ". . . The success of Obama's presidency hinges more and
more on the negotiating skills and political instincts of his No. 2"
(Nicholas 2010). Biden has proven adept at not only filling the
void left by Emanuel but also managing relations with both parties in Congress in order to make compromises and lobby hesitant
members of Congress. And it seems that both parties in Congress
embrace Biden's new role.

Biden's elevated stature and accomplishments in 2011 and
2011 seemed to have even quieted those critical of the gaffe-prone
vice president. "Not so long ago, White House aides seemed to want
Biden benched. They cringed at his repeated gaffes" (Nicholas
2010). However, aides once dismissive of Biden began embracing
his penchant for making gaffes. Aides seem to view it as "Biden-
speak"—being outspoken and candid; something they hope to use
to the administration's advantage in appealing to certain portions
of the electorate that value his candor. Regardless of his rhetoric, the political realities of Washington with the 112th Congress
appear to have ensured a place at the table and an influential
voice for the vice president in the West Wing and on Capitol Hill.

Conclusion

Biden's intent to restore the historical role of the vice presidency
does not signify a return to historical insignificance for the office.

Instead, Biden emulates many of his most recent predecessors in terms of his view of the proper role of a vice president, his responsibilities, and the influence he wields. Perhaps the one feature that separates Biden from other vice presidents is his proclivity for being outspoken in meetings and frequently embarking on long-winded monologues. Although this seemed to rankle some of the Obama insiders within the administration, he has since moderated himself and appears to have elevated his stature within the West Wing at the same time.

For the first two years of Biden's vice presidency, a disconnect developed between the role he sought as vice president and the role he actually assumed. However, with time Biden emerged as a true player who's skeptical and unrelenting questioning in meetings assisted Obama with his decision making; Biden also solidified his position as Obama's counselor. As the political context changed with the start of the 112th Congress, Obama realized he must rely more and more on the skills of his vice president, thus creating a more significant role for Biden on Capitol Hill and in the president's own inner circle. The vice president's activities in ushering Obama's agenda through a lame-duck Congress and successfully negotiating with Republicans in late 2010 ensured his perpetuating influence and the influence of the vice presidency.

Works Cited

Allen, Mike, "Biden to limit role of vice president." *Politico* (6 Dec. 2008). http://dyn.politico.com/printstory.cfm?uuid-0DB79A75-18FE-70B2-A83845D2E6029ED7 (accessed 11 Dec. 11, 2010).

Baumgartner, Jody C. *The American Vice Presidency Reconsidered.* Westport, CT: Praeger, 2006.

Biden, Joe. *Promises to Keep.* New York: Random House, 2007.

Cooper, Helene. "As the ground shifts, Biden plays a bigger role." *New York Times* (11 Dec. 2010). http://www.nytimes.com/2010/12/12/us/politics/12biden.html?_r=1 (accessed 2 Jan. 2011).

Gallup. "VP Favorable Ratings: Gore Down; Cheney, Biden Flat." (14 Jul 2010). http://www.gallup.com/poll/141269/favorable-ratings-gore-down-cheney-biden-flat.aspx (accessed 10 Nov. 2010).

Hayes, Stephen F. *Cheney.* New York: HarperCollins, 2007.

Heilemann, John and Mark Halperin. *Game Change: Obama and the Clintons, McCain and Palin, and the Race of a Lifetime.* New York: HarperCollins, 2010.

Henry, Ed. "Biden starting to raise profile." *CNN* (22 Dec. 2008). http://politicalticker.blogs.cnn.com/2008/12/22/biden-starting-to-raise-profile/ (accessed 10 Nov. 2010).

Hornick, Ed and Josh Levs. "What Obama promised Biden." *CNN* (21 Dec. 2008). http://articles.cnn.com/2008-12-21/politics/transition.wrap_1_joe-biden-middle-class-critical-decision/3?_s=PM:POLITICS (accessed 10 Dec. 2010).

Kenski, Kate, Bruce W. Hardy, and Kathleen Hall Jamieson. *The Obama Victory.* New York: Oxford University Press, 2010.

King, Larry. "Interview with Joe Biden." *Larry King Live* (12 Dec. 2008). http://articles.cnn.com/2008-12-22/politics/biden.lkl_1_joe-biden-brand-president-bush?_s=PM:POLITICS (accessed 28 Dec. 2010).

Lee, Carol E. "Biden to head new middle class task force." *Politico* (21 Dec. 2008). http://www.politico.com/news/stories/1208/16778.html (accessed 2 Jan. 2011).

Nicholas, Peter. "Biden is a linchpin of Obama's presidency." *Los Angeles Times* (31 Dec. 2010). http://articles.latimes.com/2010/dec/31/nation/la-na-joe-biden-20110101 (accessed 2 Jan. 2011).

The Pew Research Center for the People, the Press and the Poll. "Strong confidence in Obama—country seen as less politically divided." *Pew Research Center* (15 Jan. 2009). http://people-press.org/report/483/confidence-in-obama-country-less-politically-divided (accessed 10 Nov. 2010).

Quayle, Dan. "Standing firm." Ed. Timothy Walch. *At the President's Side: The Vice Presidency in the Twentieth Century.* Columbia: University of Missouri Press, 1997.

Schwarz, Gabriella. "Obama has praise for Biden." *CNN* (15 Oct. 2010). http://politicalticker.blogs.cnn.com/2010/10/15/obama-has-praise-for-biden/ (accessed 20 Oct. 2010).

Traub, James. "After Cheney." *New York Times* (24 Nov. 2009). http://www.nytimes.com/2009/11/29/magazine/29Biden-t.html?_r=1 (accessed 28 Dec. 2010).

Untermeyer, Chase. *At the President's Side: Historical Perspectives on the Vice Presidency.* Conference conducted at the Herbert Hoover Presidential Library, West Branch, IA, 1995.

Woodward, Bob. *Obama's War.* New York: Simon & Schuster, 2010.

Chapter 23

First Lady Michelle Obama

Robert P. Watson

Caricature and Character

Controversy is nothing new for *The New Yorker* magazine whose covers have featured Osama bin Laden riding on the subway in New York City and Barack Obama in bed with Hillary Clinton while the phone rings in the background (a clever reference to candidate Clinton's negative TV ad against her then-Senate colleague asking who Americans wanted answering the phone in the middle of the night in the White House). But that hardly seemed to matter when the July 21, 2008 issue of *The New Yorker* hit newsstands with a cover depicting then-presidential candidate Barack Obama as a Muslim and his wife, Michelle, as a Black Panther from the 1960s. The Obamas were depicted on the magazine's cover celebrating their election in the White House beneath a portrait of Osama bin Laden and with an American flag burning in the fireplace. Finally able to "let down their guard" after the campaign, Michelle sports an afro and revolutionary attire—including an automatic weapon—while Barack, in turban and Islamic tunic, gives his wife "dap"—the fist bump that Fox News once deemed to be a secret terrorist greeting (Lizza 2008).

Of course, the magazine sought to mock the perceptions of so many conspiracy theorists on the far Right of the American political landscape and explore the uncivil and paranoid tone that had recently pervaded the American body politic. The cover design was created by the artist, Barry Blitt, who defended his work, saying "it seemed to me that depicting the concept would show it as the fear-mongering ridiculousness that it is." Likewise, *The New Yorker's* editor, David Remnick, dismissed as misguided "absurdity" both the paranoia on the Right about the Obamas and the criticisms of his magazine (Sklar 2008).

However, the spoof was misunderstood by people on both sides of the political aisle and a brouhaha erupted over whether the magazine cover was brilliant satire or simply offensive. At the same time, ABC News reported that numerous high-level Democrats worried that readers would not grasp the satiric irony of the cover. Their concerns were justified. Eager for any morsel of "evidence" to support their belief that the Obamas were un-American radicals, many on the Right failed to read beyond the cover, seeing the magazine as vindication of their conspiracies. On the Left, a spokesperson for the Obama campaign labeled the cover "offensive" and "tasteless" (Tapper 2008b).

Ryan Lizza wrote the featured article in the same magazine. In it, Lizza explored Obama's career and politics and arrived at a completely different assessment of the candidate from that suggested by his critics and captured on the cover. Lizza states, "perhaps the greatest misconception about Barack Obama is that he is some sort of anti-establishment revolutionary. Rather, every stage of his political career has been marked by an eagerness to accommodate himself to existing institutions rather than tear them down or replace them . . . he has always played by the rules as they exist, not as he would like them to exist" (Lizza 2008). It was not the article, but the cover, however, that attracted attention and the entire incident ended up feeding the beast and playing into the conspiracies. To his credit, when asked by ABC's Sunlen Miller to comment on the cover, Obama simply shrugged and said, "I have no response to that" (Tapper 2008b). But the cover speaks to the image many on the Right held of Michelle Obama. Had there not been such perceptions of or worries about the Obamas, the magazine cover would not have resonated. As such, and despite Obama's public comment on the magazine, the Obama team sought to change Mrs. Obama's negative public image.

When Barack Obama announced his presidential campaign his wife was, arguably, the least well known of the spouses of those running in 2008. As such, the press struggled with how to present Mrs. Obama. Was she the anti-Laura, a new Hillary, or the second coming of Jackie O? Of course, the facts had little to do with the frame. Unlike Mrs. Kennedy, Mrs. Obama did not sail to Greece, ride horses, or winter in Palm Beach. Nor was she the subdued Laura Bush or scripted Hillary. In a way, Mrs. Obama is none of these previous first ladies, which has made it difficult for the media seeking a frame to use in discussing her. As the first black ever to serve in the office and having the misfortune of residing in the White House during a period of bitter political division and incivility as well as a new twenty-four-hour news cycle, hundreds of channels of talk radio, and the blogosphere, Mrs. Obama has received added scrutiny.

Both the press and Mrs. Obama's many critics resorted to using a few basic "frames" to portray her. A media frame is "a central organizing idea or story line that provides meaning to an unfolding strip of events" (Gamson and Modiglianin 1987). As such, reporters and journalists often employ simple anecdotes and stereotypes to portray individuals and events in a way that helps the consumers of news—the readers and viewers—understand them. The frames thus function as a system of interpretation and a filter for making sense of a complex world, and the public comes to rely on these narratives to understand the reports (Entman and Rujecki 1993). For example, the press has historically presented the first lady in dichotomous frames—first political partner or first housewife, co-president or hostess—depending on how "modern" or "traditional" the first lady appeared. First ladies such as Abigail Adams, Eleanor Roosevelt, and Hillary Clinton are portrayed one dimensionally as "modern," whereas Mamie Eisenhower, Bess Truman, and Laura Bush are presented as "traditional." Once that frame was used, the simple, dichotomous narrative not only continued throughout the first lady's time in the White House but became the dominant perspective used to report on nearly anything she did. Such simplistic frames led Mrs. Clinton to once admit, "Who I really am seems less important than what different groups want me to represent." It is through these powerful media frames that the public knows the first ladies (Anthony 2009).

What happened was that a few frames quickly emerged during the campaign that portrayed Mrs. Obama in a negative light. However, in part due to a rebranding of the first lady after the election, these frames have changed and are much more positive. As such, in an effort to identify the frames used to describe Mrs. Obama and compare her image during the campaign and after her husband's election, fifty articles about Michelle Obama—half from the campaign and half from her first ladyship—were examined. The articles were general biographical pieces about Mrs. Obama and came from three basic sources, each with roughly equal representation: Leading newspapers such as *The New York Times* and *Wall Street Journal*; reports from the five television networks; and widely read blogs and Websites.

Image, Criticism, and Media Frames

Throughout American history, first ladies have been criticized. Much of this criticism has been petty and frivolous and has come from the intense scrutiny of the president's wife. For instance, Nancy Reagan was criticized for being an extravagant spender, whereas Rosalynn Carter was derided for being too plain. Hillary Clinton was said to be too political, whereas Laura Bush could have been more political. Even Martha Washington was criticized for having too many horses pull her regal carriage and Eleanor Roosevelt, the standard by which all modern first ladies are measured, was subject to brutal and personal attacks (Watson 2000).

The spouses of presidential candidates have become fair game while on the stump in modern times as Lady Bird Johnson, Rosalynn Carter, Nancy Reagan, Hillary Clinton, and Teresa Heinz Kerry were all criticized in a way that attempted to undermine their husband's campaigns (Watson 2000). Not surprisingly then, as soon as the Obama campaign began to rise in the polls Mrs. Obama became a favorite punching bag of conservatives to the extent that the Rasmussen Report polls conducted during June 2008 revealed that Cindy McCain, wife of the Republican presidential nominee, enjoyed higher favorability ratings than her Democratic counterpart and that Mrs. Obama's favorability numbers were even below those of Laura Bush and Teresa Heinz Kerry during their husband's campaigns.

It has been an incredible journey for Michelle Obama, from an unknown politician's wife to one of the best-known first ladies in American history. But the journey has not come without challenges, including being presented in unflattering terms during the campaign to the extent that the independent fact-checking organization Politifact weighed in on the fallacies. Accordingly, Mrs. Obama emerged as a potential liability to her husband's presidential campaign, forcing the candidate to defend his wife, saying "There are dirt and lies that are circulated in emails, and they pump them out long enough until finally you, a mainstream reporter, asks me about it. . . . That gives legs to the story. If somebody has evidence that myself or Michelle or anybody has said something inappropriate, let them do it" (Brown 2008).

Indeed, Michelle Obama was hit hard during the campaign. Based on content analysis of fifty news pieces in major print, televised, and online sources that covered Mrs. Obama, it was possible to identify four basic, negative frames used to describe her during the campaign and, to a lesser extent, her first ladyship.

The "Angry Black Woman"

It might be said that Barack Obama's election in 2008 demonstrated that many Americans were ready to vote for a black candidate. But it also seemed that the public and press treated his wife less kindly. It is, of course, next to impossible to determine whether or not, or to what degree, the criticism of Mrs. Obama can be attributable to her race. As a successful, accomplished, and self-made African American woman and one of the few recognizable African American women on the national stage who is not an entertainer, there is always the question of whether or not there is resentment of Mrs. Obama by some whites or whether a latent version of racist anger with an "uppity negro" factored into the criticism (Black 2010). Indeed, as has been noted by one of Mrs. Obama's avid supporters, "There are so many white people who are not used to seeing a black woman in this position. She's the face of America, and they can't process it" (Hanan 2010).

Similarly, parts of the American public were uncomfortable with the rapid shift in racial dynamics and the long, ugly history of animosity was rekindled through incidents such as the ridiculous comments made by "Obama's preacher"—the Rev. Jeremiah Wright—during the campaign. As a result, "increasingly the racial animus (was) aimed not at Barack but at his wife, Michelle Obama" (Kaplan 2008). Mrs. Obama, dark-skinned and the daughter of an ethnic neighborhood, offered a contrast to her husband's biracial, international narrative. Not surprisingly, race was a key element used in frames for Mrs. Obama. The candidate's wife was depicted as an exception, as if there were no black women professionals in the middle or upper classes. The fact that, initially, Mrs. Obama did not try to "hide" her race only affirmed these frames and the narratives were reduced to commenting on her height, "athletic" arms, and even a faux shock over her sleeveless tops.

When Mrs. Obama discussed issues of race or appeared in the black community, her critics claimed she had "pro-black" leanings (whatever that meant), often portraying such activities as unprecedented and inappropriate. Yet, there is a long history of activism by first ladies on behalf of civil rights. This includes Mary Todd Lincoln, who raised funds for former slaves living in the capital city; Ellen Wilson, who promoted legislation to improve the slum-riddled living conditions for former slaves in Washington; Lou Hoover, who invited Jessie DePriest, who was black, to the White House; Eleanor Roosevelt, who opposed the practice of lynching in the military and championed the black contralto, Marian Anderson; and Lady Bird Johnson, who spoke throughout the South in support of the 1964 Civil Rights Act and her husband's reelection (Blake 2010; Watson 2000).

Similarly, American history has witnessed a number of negative stereotypes of black women. These pop-culture images include the maid or nanny, the single mother, and the "welfare queen." Fox News used one blatant example of such old and ugly stereotypes. When conservative columnist, Michelle Malkin, discussed whether the candidate's spouse was being unfairly criticized, Fox News featured the words "Outraged liberals: Stop picking on Obama's baby mama" across the bottom of the screen (Malkin 2008). Conservative commentators also described the Obama's "dap" as a "terrorist fist jab" and inaccurately portrayed Mrs. Obama's senior thesis at Princeton University—"Princeton-Educated Blacks and the Black Community"—as a "rant" against whites. The fact that she completed a degree in sociology with a minor in African American Studies was somehow misconstrued as further evidence of her "anti-white" views.

Among the negative images of Mrs. Obama that emerged was a crudely doctored image from the social media of her as a primate. At one point the image was the first one selected on Google's search engine under "Michelle Obama" (Amdurski-Matzaz 2009). The image was later removed but then reappeared under searches for "Hail to the Chimp" or "Michelle Obama ape" (Mays 2010).

"Un-American"

On February 18, 2008 at a campaign speech in Milwaukee, Wisconsin, Mrs. Obama uttered the infamous phrase: "For the first time in my adult life, I am proud of my country because it feels like hope is finally making a comeback." That evening, the candidate's wife altered her words to add context, stating: "For the first time in my adult lifetime, I'm *really* proud of my country, and not just because Barack has done well, but because I think people are hungry for change" (Tapper 2008a). The comment formed the basis of a blistering attack by conservative commentators and within the mainstream media about whether Mrs. Obama was "patriotic." Mrs. Obama and the Obama campaign were forced to defend the comment on grounds that it was taken out of context; that she was speaking about the political process and the issue of low voting turnout and the enthusiasm being generated by her husband's candidacy. The candidate complained that critics should "lay off my wife" and Mrs. Obama even made the point that she was "absolutely" always proud of her country. But the damage was done. The Republican Party of Tennessee posted the "proud" remark on its Website and conservative candidates all across the country used it to raise money. Former secretary of state, Lawrence Eagleburger, introduced Cindy McCain, the wife of Republican nominee John McCain, as someone who is "proud of her country, not just once but always" and Republican vice presidential nominee, Sarah Palin, referenced the comment repeatedly while on the campaign stump and to thunderous applause from her audiences, saying "You know, when I hear people say, or had said during the campaign that they've never been proud of America, haven't they met anybody in uniform yet? I get tears in my eyes when I see that young man, that young woman, walking through the airport in uniform . . ." (Brown 2008).

"Marie Antoinette"

From the beginning of the campaign, the Obamas were characterized by their critics as elitists, despite the fact that their backgrounds and life stories were anything but that. After much of the criticism of Mrs. Obama had subsided over the course of her first year in office, the same line of attack was reopened during her second year as first lady when she traveled to Spain with her daughter Sasha. While the President celebrated his forty-ninth birthday in Chicago, Mrs. Obama took what the White House described as a "private trip" with friends to Hotel Villa Padierna, one of the world's finest resorts.

The mistake the first lady made was taking a luxury vacation abroad while the American economy was struggling. Accordingly, the frame used by the media was that the first lady was "out of touch" and the blogosphere and conservative media outlets such as Fox News erupted with accusations that she was "tone deaf"

(Bailey 2010; Marr and Parnes 2010). A featured story in the *New York Daily News* described the first lady as a "modern Marie Antoinette" and the new buzz phrase was born (Tantaros 2010). The criticisms of the story far overshadowed the White House's rebuttal—that the Secret Service felt the hotel would be a safer venue, the first lady and her guests paid for their expenses, and Mrs. Obama met with the Spanish royal family during the visit.

The trip was insensitive but hardly unprecedented. Many first families have made similar trips, including Laura Bush who took her daughters Barbara and Jenna to Africa in 2007 for an exclusive safari and expensive private vacation without the president. Mrs. Bush also traveled to Paris while America was at war. Jacqueline Kennedy callously traveled on exotic international trips, even once returning from an Italian vacation to an angry crowd of picketers. Lou Hoover served elaborate dinners featuring foods that had to be trucked into Washington during the Great Depression and was soundly criticized, as was Nancy Reagan for her lavish lifestyle while her husband was cutting social programs, as was Mary Todd Lincoln for purchasing a pricey china service during the Civil War when so many other families were sacrificing (Watson 2000).

Another similar criticism that emerged during Mrs. Obama's first ladyship was that she employed the largest, most expensive staff of any presidential spouse in American history. After a journalist erroneously posted a blog suggesting Mrs. Obama demanded "an unprecedented number of staffers to cater to her every whim," commentators picked up on the story and suggested that no first lady ever had such an extravagantly large staff (Sweet 2009b). This criticism generated so much interest that a number of media organizations felt compelled to refute the numbers (Dykes 2009). In reality, Mrs. Obama employs roughly the same number of staffers as her two predecessors and less than both Lady Bird Johnson and Jacqueline Kennedy.

Mrs. Obama was even criticized by several prominent conservatives and commentators such as Glenn Beck, Rush Limbaugh, Sarah Palin, and Rep. Michelle Bachmann (R-MN) for promoting nutrition, exercise, and healthy lifestyles for children. The condemnation of Mrs. Obama's advocacy of children's health ran the gamut from the absurd to the hypocritical, including allegedly promoting "excess government" and intruding into the freedom to enjoy unhealthy foods and lifestyles. But the sniping even devolved to commenting on instances when Mrs. Obama, despite her rather disciplined personal nutrition and fitness regimen, ate anything that was not healthy. In early 2011, on his popular radio show, Limbaugh poked fun at first lady's waistline, commenting that she did not "project the image of women that you might see on the cover of the *Sports Illustrated* 'swimsuit issue,' or of a woman (professional baseball player) Alex Rodriguez might date every six months . . ." (Hartman 2011).

Another Hillary

Michelle Obama was presented as someone who wielded too much political influence. In short, she was "another Hillary." Even though the first lady maintained a lower political profile after her election, in 2010 another story broke that seemed to combine each of the frames used against Mrs. Obama. This time it was about a comment she was alleged to have made to Carla Bruni, wife of French president, Nicolas Zarkozy, during their visit to the White House in March 2010. When asked by France's first lady about life in the White House, the authors of a forthcoming "kiss-and-tell" book about Bruni—Michael Darmon and Yves Derai—claim Mrs. Obama responded, "Don't ask. It's hell. I can't stand it." Although the White House and Bruni have denied the statement was ever made, the rumor resonated with the existing negative frames of the first lady (Allen 2010; Dumitru-Steffens 2010). To elements of the American media and American public, Mrs. Obama, like Mrs. Clinton before her, could do nothing right and was the subject of intense criticism.

Image Management

One of the reasons for Mrs. Obama's image troubles initially was that she was unknown to most Americans. She had no brand. As a result, her critics were able to "introduce" her to the public on their terms and her early missteps both stuck and became defining frames. Michelle Obama was a political spouse that, early on, did not really like politics. She even once quipped after her husband's 2000 campaign for the U.S. House of Representatives that what she most enjoyed from the experience was because of visiting so many living rooms she now had ideas for redecorating! Mrs. Obama was hesitant about each of her husband's bids for office, expressing "ambivalence" about his U.S. Senate bid in 2004, and was not happy about him spending so much time away from home and away from their daughters (Remnick 2010). As such, politics caused some strain in the Obama marriage (Wolffe 2009). Reluctant on the campaign stump, in the initial months of the presidential campaign she limited her role by still working part-time in her executive position at the University of Chicago Medical School, traveling no more than two days a week, and campaigning overnight only when her daughters could join her. But, by 2008 Mrs. Obama was making in excess of thirty campaign appearances a month and began writing her own speeches, speaking without notes, and revealing her intelligent, eloquent, and passionate side. As such, she showed herself to be an astute student of politics and a quick study, skills that would serve her well as the Obama team sought to rebrand her.

. Another part of the challenge of rebranding Mrs. Obama was that she is a complex woman and none of the simple and dichoto-mous frames used for first ladies seemed to work. Nor were the early images of her as the new Hillary, the anti-Laura, or the second coming of Jackie helpful in understand the new first lady. She is both a self-made career woman and a doting mother, which challenged the antiquated and narrow orthodoxy of media frames for first ladies. As a young girl, Michelle Robinson skipped the second grade, was a member of the National Honor Society, and was raised in a working-class family on the tough South Side of Chicago. A vice president at the University of Chicago Hospital, former attorney with the prestigious firm of Sidley Austin, cum laude graduate of Princeton, and Harvard JD who speaks French and plays the piano, Mrs. Obama is also a humble woman, reluc-tant public figure, and doting mother. As such, no one single nar-rative proves comprehensive.

Mrs. Obama's image makeover began after criticisms of her "proud of my country for the first time" speech during the cam-paign. Shortly after the speech, in June 2008 Mrs. Obama appeared on the television show *The View*, where she talked casually about her children, marriage, and clothing choices, and appeared warm and at ease. Additional interviews were agreed to, continuing into her first ladyship; Michelle's wardrobe was softened, and the photogenic Obama family helped her morph from another Hill-ary to another Jackie. Her address during the first night of the Democratic National Convention in 2008 emphasized her humble roots and her family experiences, which she said were no differ-ent from those of any other mother. The speech, which presented

Mrs. Obama as the embodiment of the American Dream, was both well received and effective. Ezra Klein of *The American Prospect* said that it was "beautifully delivered, and smartly crafted," while conservative commentator and writer Andrew Sullivan raved that the address was "one of the best, most moving, intimate, rousing, humble, and beautiful speeches I've heard from a convention platform" (Ryan 2008).

After January 20, 2009, a different Michelle Obama was presented to the public. All recent White Houses have given considerable attention to the public image of the first lady and the Obama administration was no exception. It was not only the first lady's image that was at stake but the president's brand as well and the Obama administration employed photo opportunities, staffed the first lady's office with professional image handlers, and paid attention to Mrs. Obama's clothing, personal appearances, interviews, and pet projects. The new first lady's staff attended regular meetings with the president's staff to coordinate communications and messaging, her chief of staff began attending morning meetings with her counterpart in the Oval Office, and Mrs. Obama's policy director was in attendance at weekly policy briefings with the West Wing staff. The first lady realized that she needed to let the public decide how they felt about her rather than allow the filter of critics and media frames define her image. So, an able communications team was assembled, including Communication Director Camille Johnston and Press Secretary Katie McCormick Lelyveld. This team was quick to respond to any criticism of the first lady and lower her political profile (Caroli 2010). For example, although Mrs. Obama did speak with federal agencies about new executive orders and advocate her husband's stimulus, during the January 29, 2009 event to mark the signing of fair pay for women (Lilly Ledbetter) Mrs. Obama appeared but remained in the front row of the audience. Likewise, Mrs. Obama started sticking closely to her script when speaking, limiting the length of her remarks and appearances, and stopped discussing sensitive issues like race and policy (Swarns 2009).

Of course, the rebranding of Mrs. Obama was not without notice or criticism. Katherine Marsh of *The New Republic*, for instance, deemed her a "Stepford wife wannabe," trying to remake her "sassy self" (Marsh 2008). However, Mrs. Obama's public image improved markedly. Polls revealed that Mrs. Obama enjoyed the highest favorability of any new first lady since 1980 and was more popular than her husband through the first two years of their time in office. Her favorability numbers were at 76 percent in her first year, whereas Laura Bush was at 64 percent and Hillary Clinton at 60 percent at the same time in their first ladyships. The public described their new first lady with terms such as "warm," "classy," "nice," "elegant," "accessible," and "intelligent" (Silva 2009). At the same time, or perhaps as a result, the media used three new frames to discuss Mrs. Obama.

Michelle O or First Fashionista

Quite simply, Mrs. Obama methodically changed her fashion, and then made it a part of her new persona. Gone were top-of-the-line designer gowns and in their place were sundresses and "off-the-rack" clothing accessible to and worn by the everyday woman. The first lady was seen wearing such mall staples as Banana Republic and the White House Black Market and younger, ethnic, and American designers. The media soon began discussing the affordability of her clothing and the first lady was quoted admitting: "I stopped wearing pantyhose a long time ago because it was painful, and they always ripped" (Saul 2008).

The makeover included not just her attire but where and how she would be presented. For example, although other first ladies and celebrities who have graced the cover of *Vogue* were attired and posed by the magazine's staff, when Mrs. Obama sat for the cover shoot of *Vogue's* March 2009 issue she insisted on choosing her own dresses and used her own makeup artists and hairstylists. In place of Laura Bush's lavish blue silk gown and Hillary Clinton's sophisticated black velvet dress, Michelle Obama selected everyday clothing. The same control over her appearance occurred when Mrs. Obama sat for the covers of *People, Essence, "O"* and other popular magazines (Swarns 2009).

The makeover worked. The *Wall Street Journal's* fashion writer, Teri Agins, labeled the new first lady the "baby boomer pinup girl," while *Vanity Fair* applauded "haute couture likes her" (Halloran 2008). Tall, fit, and youthful, Mrs. Obama cut a very striking figure in everything she wore and both sent a message about her humility, practicality, and approachability while managing to find balance between the public and private spheres of the office and her image as mother and attorney (Hameiri 2009). In doing so, she has emerged as a fashion icon much as did Jackie Kennedy before her, even choosing many of the same classic and feminine styles. Whereas most previous first ladies had a grudging relationship with fashion and spouses such as Laura Bush and Hillary Clinton covered their femininity, Mrs. Obama has creatively embraced fashion and her image (Givhan 2010).

Mom-in-Chief

Through her image, calculated appearances, and frequent public remarks on the topic, Mrs. Obama has emerged as a role model for middle-class women struggling to find balance between work and family responsibilities. She is the very epitome of the modern woman—someone who has enjoyed and managed a successful career, maintained a healthy and faithful marriage, and raised two well-adjusted children. The first lady has carefully chosen women's magazines for interviews and her public remarks often include domestic topics such as the concerns of motherhood, which allowed her to approach more sensitive and political topics but always from the vantage point of a mother having a dialogue with other mothers around the country regarding shared concerns. She also has led by example, establishing a sense of normality in the White House for her daughters, emphasizing their homework and chores, and limiting her travel so as to not be away from "home." The first family's new puppy and swing set as well as the first lady's vegetable garden and "mall" clothing have reinforced the image.

First Volunteer

One of the main ways recent first ladies have managed their public image has been through their choice and manner of participating in social projects. Recent first ladies have become so identified with championing social causes—Lady Bird Johnson's "Beautification" program, Nancy Reagan's "Just Say No" campaign, Barbara Bush's advocacy of reading and literacy—that this has become an expected role of the first lady (Watson 2000). Mrs. Obama has pursued this role with tireless enthusiasm, planting her own garden and advocating gardening, becoming a spokesperson for health and fitness, and raising awareness about the dangers of childhood obesity. She also met with military spouses at bases around country and gave major addresses at Fort Bragg, Arlington National Cemetery, and other military sites to raise understanding about the sacrifices made by military families in terms of limited benefits, long deployments, and modest housing (Buckholtz 2009). The first family frequently volunteers their time in charitable pursuits, reused Christmas decorations in the White House and procured environmentally friendly holiday lights, and, unlike their predecessors, decided to pay with their own money the refurbishments to their private living quarters in the White House.

Mrs. Obama also has extended this role to international affairs, where she has promoted the causes of children around the world and international civic engagement during her visits abroad to Mexico, Haiti, and elsewhere (Sweet 2009a).

A Successful Transition

At the two-year mark of her first ladyship, Michelle Obama has transformed her image from an ugly caricature and liability during the campaign to one of the most popular and recognizable first ladies in history. She has been profiled in *Glamour*, *Ladies' Home Journal*, *People*, *Vogue*, and countless other magazines, and named to *Forbes'* most powerful women's list, *People's* most beautiful persons in the world list, *Time's* most influential list, *Essence's* list of "25 of the world's most inspiring women," *Vanity Fair's* list of "10 of the world's best dressed people," The Harvard 100—a list of influential Harvard alumni—and even *Maxim* magazine's list of the "hottest" women, which produced an embarrassed laugh from the first lady (Casserly 2010).

Perhaps most notably, Mrs. Obama has matured in her mastery of the nuances of politics over the course of the campaign and from the campaign to and through her first ladyship. During the campaign, Mrs. Obama appeared to be a politically engaged spouse. She was a guest on several talk shows such as *Larry King Live* and *The Daily Show With Jon Stewart* where she discussed politics, but during her first two years as first lady has largely avoided discussing politics, and even avoided serious news interviews. For instance, she did sit down with *The New York Times* but gave an in-depth interview on the topic of the White House vegetable garden. She has occasionally shared her support for her husband's agenda and admitted that getting the nation back on the right path was difficult (Celizic 2010). But, Mrs. Obama has worked to give the impression that she is disinterested in politics and wields little political influence. It is known, however, that she has lobbied members of Congress for such programs as AmeriCorps and support for military families, once prompting the chair of the

House Education Committee, George Miller (D-CA), to say "I didn't know she had this deep knowledge about what was happening on the Hill." She also reached out to senior Republicans, such as when she called the Senate minority leader, Mitch McConnell (R-KY) to thank him for voting for the Child Nutrition Act.

The first lady always stated that she was not a "political animal," but at the same time she often gave the impression that she was eager to be involved in politics. Such was the case toward the end of her first year in the White House when, despite several successful social projects and strong approval numbers, Mrs. Obama complained to friends and aides of feeling "marginalized" from policymaking. The first lady selected a new chief of staff and launched a comprehensive fitness and health initiative called "Let's Move!" (Caroli 2010). Similarly, during the 2010 midterm elections Mrs. Obama campaigned for Democrats, appearing on behalf of Democratic candidates across the country. As her new chief of staff, Susan Sher, noted, "From the beginning, she's wanted to hit the campaign trail. It was just a matter of figuring out what would work with her schedule and what would be most useful" (Benac 2010). So too did the first lady raise money, headlining fundraisers from New York City to Los Angeles for the Democratic National Committee and Democratic Women's Leadership Forum.

Perhaps the result of the growing partisanship and bitterness in American politics, but during her second year in office Mrs. Obama's approval numbers were in decline. Few Americans have been subjected to such vicious and persistent attacks as have the Obamas, and fewer still have responded to it with such grace and dignity. Prodded by Larry King on CNN to respond to aggressive criticism by conservatives including Sarah Palin, the former Republican vice presidential nominee, Michelle Obama said simply and calmly, "You know democracy is about critique." Of the constant criticism heaped on her husband, she observed, "Barack and I have been in the public eye for many years now, and we've developed a thick skin along the way. When you're out campaigning, there will always be criticism. I just take it in stride, and at the end of the day, I know that it comes with the territory" (Franke-Ruta 2010).

Whether or not the country will get a more political first lady during the remainder of Barack Obama's time in the White House or how her remarkable transformation continues remains to be seen. Mrs. Obama has earned the respect of the mainstream media, seems comfortable in her role, and has shown herself to be savvy enough to manage her positive image. Hers has been one of the most remarkable transitions of a political figure in American history. Still, as she has often said, "I still see myself as mo, the girl who grew up in the South Side of Chicago—Marian and Fraser's daughter. I've got this husband who does these interesting things—and I'm Malia and Sasha's mother."

Works Cited

Allen, P. "'She never said that': Angry White House denial after claims Michelle Obama told Carla Bruni that being first lady is 'hell.'" *Daily Mail* (17 Sept. 2010). http://www.dailymail.co.uk/news/world-news/article-1312777 (accessed 9 Nov. 2010).

Amdurski-Matzav, N. "Racist Obama image shines light on web searching." *Matzav* (2 Dec. 2009). (http://matzav.com/racist-obama-image-shines-light-on-web-searching accessed 9 Nov. 2010).

Anthony, Carl Sferrazza. "First ladies: Character to caricature." *Huffington Post* (22 Jan. 2009). http://www.huffingtonpost.com/carl-sferrazza-anthony/first-ladies-character-to_b_16008 (accessed 9 Nov. 2010).

Bailey, H. "First lady under fire for her glitzy Spanish vacation" *Yahoo News* (5 Aug. 2010). http://news.yahoo.com /s/yblog_upshot/20100805/pl_yblog_upshot/first-lady-under-fire-for (accessed 9 Nov. 2010).

Benac, N. "First lady jumping into midterm politics." *MSNBC* (11 Oct. 2010). http://www.msnbc.com/cleanprint/cleanprintproxy.aspx?12868 20250052 (accessed 9 Nov. 2010).

Black, R. "Michelle Obama under fire for mentioning daughter Malia's weight during obesity remarks." *New York Daily News* (5 Feb. 2010). http://www.nydailynews.com/fdcp?1287502078544 (accessed 5 Nov. 2010).

Blake, J. "What role does racial hostility play in the criticism of Michelle Obama?" *Los Angeles Wave* (18 Aug. 18, 2010). http://www.wave-newspapers.com/internal?st=print&id=101041124&path=/news (accessed 9 Nov. 2010).

Brown, C.B. "Michelle Obama becomes GOP target." *CBS News* (13 June 2008). http://www.cbsnews.com/stories/06/12/politics/politico/main4177755.shtml (accessed 5 Nov. 2010).

Buckholtz, A. "First lady Obama's attention can help the military child." *The Seattle Times* (30 April 2009). http://seattletimes.nwsource.com/cgi-bin/printstory.pl?document_id=2009105071&zsection (accessed 9 Nov. 2010).

Caroli, Betty Boyd. "Michelle Obama: Still struggling to define her role as first lady." *U.S. News and World Report* (6 Oct. 2010). http://politics.usnews.com/news/articles/2010/10/06/michelle-obama-still-struggling-to-define-her-role-as-first-lady.html (accessed 9 Nov. 2010).

Casserly, M. "The new *Forbes* power women." *Forbes* (6 Oct. 2010). http://www.forbes.com/2010/09/30/power-influence-michelle-obama-lady-gaga-power (accessed 9 Nov. 2010).

Celizic, M. "Michelle Obama: What you see is the real me." *Today Show* (3 Feb. 2010). //www.today.msnbc.com/id/35203291/ns/39628070#slice-2 (accessed 9 Nov. 2010).

Dumitru-Steffens, I. "Washington's PR machine deadline with Michelle Obama's hell." *Pamil-Visions* (16 Sept. 2010). http://www.pamil-visions.net/michelle-obamas-hell/218910/ (accessed 9 Nov. 2010).

Dykes, M.B. "Separating fact from fiction regarding the size of Michelle Obama's staff." *Yahoo News* (6 Oct. 2009). "A snapshot of some first ladies' staff." (6 Oct. 2009). (accessed 10 Nov. 2010). <www.snopes.com/politics/obama/firstlady.asp

Entman, R.M. and A. Rujecki. "Freezing Out the Public: Elite and Media Framing of the U.S. Anti-Nuclear Movement." *Political Communication*. Vol. 10 (1993), 155–173.

Franke-Ruta, G. "Asked about Sarah Palin, Michelle Obama praises 'strong female voices.'" *Washington Post* (10 Feb. 2010). http://voices.washingtonpost.com/44/2010/02/michelle-obama-declines-to-cri.html (accessed 9 Nov. 2010).

Gamson, W. and A. Modiglianin. "The changing course of Affirmative Action." Eds. R.G. Braungart and M.M. Braungart. *Research in Political Sociology*. Greenwich, CT: JAI Press, 1987, 137–177.

Givhan, R. "First lady Michelle Obama's travel attire is picture of fashionable tourist." *Washington Post* (5 Sept. 2010). http://www.washingtonpost.com/wp-dyn/content/article/2010/09/02/ar2010090205622 (accessed 9 Nov. 2010).

Halloran, L. "Like it or not, Michelle Obama is now a style icon." *NPR* (29 Dec. 2008). http://www.npr.org/templates/story/story.php?storyid=98610324 (accessed 9 Nov. 2010).

Hameiri, Y. "What does Michelle Obama's style say about the woman and the White House?" *Haaretz* (11 March 2009). http://www.haaretz.com/misc/article-print-page/what-does-michelle-obama-s-style-say-about (accessed 9 Nov. 2010).

Hanan, A. "Michelle Obama Watch." (accessed 9 Nov. 2010). http://www.michelleobamawatch.com

Hartman, Rachel Rose. "Rush Limbaugh says First Lady is no swimsuit model." *Yahoo News* (22 Feb. 2011). http://news.yahoo.com/s/yblog_theticket/20110222/ts_yblog_theticket/rush-limbaugh-says-first-lady-is-no-swimsuit-model (accessed 23 Feb. 2011).

Kaplan, E.A. "Who's afraid of Michelle Obama?" *Salon.com* (24 June 2008). http://www.salon.com/mwt/feature/2008/06/24/michelle_obama (accessed 9 Nov. 2010).

Lizza, Ryan. "Making it: How Chicago shaped Obama." *The New Yorker* (21 July 2008). http://www.newyorker.com/reporting/ 2008/07/21/080721fa_fact_lizza (accessed 5 Nov. 2010).

Malkin, M. "Outraged liberals: Leave Obama's baby mama alone." *Fox News* (11 June 2008). http://www.youtube.com/watch?v=tvezl2wna8 (accessed on 5 Nov. 2010).

Marr, K. and A. Parnes. "No vacation from attacks on Michelle." *Politico* (16 Aug. 2010). (http://www.politico.com/printstory.cfm? uuid= 7c30aecc18fe-70b20a8d8f40bf2153 accessed 9 Nov. 2010).

Marsh, Katherine. "Michelle Obama plays unique role in campaign." *New Republic* (25 August 2008). http://plugin-wordpress.spyderlinks.net/ michelle-obama-plays-unique-role-in-campaign.html (accessed 15 Nov. Nov. 2010).

Mays, J. "Michelle Obama chimp woman image returns." *Black Voices* (5 Jan. 2010). http://www.bvblackspin.com/2010/01/05/michelle-obama-chimp-women-image-returns/ (accessed 9 Nov. 2010).

Remnick, David. *The Bridge: The Life and Rise of Barack Obama.* New York: Vintage Books, 2010.

Ryan, E. "DNC: Rounding up the reaction to Michelle Obama." *Utne Reader* (27 Aug. 2008). http://www.utne.com/2008-08-27/politics/ dnc-rounding-up-the-reaction-to-michelle-obama.aspx see also http:// plugin-wordpress.spyderlinks.net/michelle-obama-plays-unique-role-in-campaign.html (accessed 9 Nov. 2010).

Saul, M. "With the help of off-the-rack dress, Michelle Obama eases harsh image." *New York Daily News* (19 June 2008). http://www.nydaily-news.com/fdcp?1287504090813 (accessed 9 Nov. 2010).

Silva, M. "Michelle Obama's popularity soars, topping recent first ladies, survey finds." *Chicago Tribune* (24 April 2009). <www.chicagotribune. com/news/nationworld/chi-talk-michelle-popularapr24,0,7472730. story (accessed 5 Nov. 2010).

Sklar, R. "David Remnick on that New Yorker cover: It's satire, meant to target 'distortions and misconceptions and prejudices' about Obama." *Huffington Post* (21 July 2008). http://www.huffington-post.com/2008/07/13/david-remnick-on-emnew-yo_n_112456..html (accessed 12 Nov. 2010).

Swarns, R. "First lady in control of building her image." *The New York Times* (25 April 2009). http://www.nytimes.com/2009/04/25/us/politics/ 25michelle.html (accessed 5 Nov, 2010).

Sweet, Lynn "Michelle Obama: Mexico, Haiti trips defining her image." *Politics Daily* (14 April 2009a). http://www.politicsdaily. com/2010/04/140michelle-obama-mexico-haiti-trips-defining-her-image.html (accessed 9 Nov. 2010).

———. "What Michelle Obama's staffers earn." *TheLastCrusade.org* (6 July 2009b). http://www.thelastcrusade.org (accessed 9 Nov, 2010).

Tantaros, A. "Material girl: Michelle Obama is a modern-day Marie Antoinette on a glitzy Spanish vacation." *New York Daily News* (5 Aug. 2010). http://www.nydailynews.com/opinions/2010/08/04/2010-08-04_ material_girl_michelle _obama_is_a_modern_day_marie_antoinette_ on_a_glitzy_spanish_vacation.html (accessed 9 Nov. 2010).

Tapper, J. "Michelle Obama: 'For the first time in my adult lifetime, I'm really proud of my country.'" *ABC News* (18 Feb. 2008a). (http://blogs.abcnews.com/politicalpunch/2008/02/michelle-obama-1.html accessed 9 November 2010).

———. "Obama camp hammers new 'ironic' New Yorker cover depicting conspiracists' nightmare of real Obamas." *ABC News* (13 July 2008b). http://blogs.abcnews.com/politicalpunch/2008/07/new-ironic-new.html (accessed 5 Nov. 2010).

Watson, Robert P. The Presidents' Wives: Reassessing the Office of First Lady. Boulder, CO: Lynne Rienner, 2000.

Wolffe, Richard. *Renegade: The Making of a President.* New York: Random House, 2009.

VII

Conclusion

Chapter 24

Making History

Douglas M. Brattebo
Robert P. Watson

A Final Word

This book is the byproduct of a conference ("The Obama Presidency: A Preliminary Assessment") convened at the University of Southern Mississippi's (USM) Gulf Coast campus in Long Beach, Mississippi on November 19–20, 2010. An assortment of scholars, academicians, policy analysts, and the like gathered to attempt that most challenging of tasks for presidency watchers: Characterizing the trajectory of a president's term around the time of its midpoint. As one eminent scholar of the modern presidency remarked when he politely turned down an invitation to give the keynote at the conference: "I try not to make pronouncements at that kind of conference. It's just too early to tell." Sage advice, that, but fortunately it did not deter the rest of us from stepping out on a limb regarding our effort to examine Barack Obama's presidency. The breadth and originality of the chapters of this edited volume testify to the rich analysis shared by all at the conclave and with the editors in the time since.

The conference concluded with all of the attendees taking part in a freewheeling roundtable discussion over lunch at USM's Fleming Education Center. The momentous nature of the midterm election results in November 2010 had significantly altered the political landscape, and this fact permeated the discussion. The conversation quickly settled on the central question those present

had touched on in so many contexts across two days together:
Was the Obama presidency destined for a Carter-like trajectory, as
some analysts had begun to suggest? Or, was the president capable
of righting the ship and navigating rough seas to win a second
term, much as was the case with Democrats Harry Truman in
1948 and Bill Clinton in 1996, presidents who also suffered defeat
in the first midterm elections of their administrations? A number
of participants wondered if Obama was politically astute enough
to pinpoint the new post-election center in American politics, and
whether he was ideologically nimble enough to stake a claim to it.
But, there was broad agreement about Obama's canniness, political agility, and prowess on the campaign trail. Still, most agreed
that his political future would be decided in large measure by the
degree to which the economy recovered, or failed to recover, over
the coming two years.

Highlights and Low Points at Midterm

Recent precedents suggested that it was at least possible for a
president with soft approval ratings and a bad economy to rebound
after a difficult midterm election cycle and achieve reelection. Ronald Reagan had come back to do so after 1982; likewise, Bill Clinton after 1994. But the historic magnitude and sharpness of the
economic collapse of 2008 seemed to set the current case apart
from those two examples. Perhaps only the Great Depression offers
a parallel example. The country's economic freefall was in process
when Obama took office on January 20, 2009, and it reached its
nadir in the second half of his first year in office. This left members of the conference doubting whether the high unemployment
numbers, serious structural problems with the American economy,
and record debts and deficits could be adequately addressed by the
time of the 2012 election. The problems the president inherited
are such that it will take years—and a lot of sacrifice, hard work,
and transformation—for the American economy to improve. Moreover, the seeming lack of patience apparent among both voters
and the wider American public for the pace of recovery along with
the extreme partisanship and venomous tone that define American politics in the second decade of the twenty-first century make
Obama's challenge even more daunting. Indeed, despite evidence
that the economic bleeding slowed to the point where the economy

stabilized and various indicators pointed to the recovery being well under way during the president's first two years, Obama received little to no tangible political benefit.

Still, with so much unknown and the dynamic nature of American politics around the time of Obama's midterm, few conferees expressed unalloyed confidence that the president's political future was either promising or grim. It was telling that the discussants' remarks were in accord with Lincoln's characterization in his second inaugural address of the pending outcome of the Civil War—"no prediction in regard to it is ventured."

Post-Election Session of Congress

The unpredictability of the course of events soon became tangible. During an unexpectedly productive, and politically significant, post-election session of Congress, Obama brokered a bargain with the Republican Party on extending the tax cuts of George W. Bush for taxpayers in all brackets for two additional years until the end of his term and gave Republicans the tax-free provisions in the inheritance tax they had so enthusiastically advocated. The Tax Relief, Unemployment Insurance Reauthorization, and Job Creation Act poured more stimulus, in the form of continuing income tax cuts, into the economy. It also reduced withholding taxes for Social Security from 6.2 to 4.2 percent for 2011. However, the deal also gave Democrats what they wanted—the reauthorization of an extension of federal unemployment benefits for more than one year. Just when it appeared Obama was at his lowest point, he succeeded in brokering a deal despite the fact that both political parties were at an impasse, standing in opposite end zones of the political football field.

Once again, however, the president did not seem to benefit in the eyes of the public, press, or his Republican opponents from the accomplishment, but he did parlay his efforts into securing a vote on other crucial pieces of business in Congress. On December 18, 2010, Congress repealed the "Don't Ask, Don't Tell" ban on open service by gays and lesbians in the U.S. Armed Forces. Obama thus delivered on a major promise to a key constituency of the Democratic Party base at a time when progressives were becoming particularly dissatisfied with his ability to bring "change" fast enough for their liking. Also, on December 22, the Senate approved the New START Treaty with Russia, providing a key foreign policy victory for the president during a period of reemerging rapprochement in the U.S.–Russia relationship. The post-midterm successes also included two other presidential priorities:

1. The Food Safety Modernization Act, which committed the FDA to a more rigorous policing of the nation's food supply and constituted the most significant food safety reform in decades; and

2. The James Zadogra 9/11 Heath and Compensation Act, which provided medical care to first responders whose health was compromised by toxins in the aftermath of the 9/11 attacks on the World Trade Center towers in New York City.

Questions regarding Obama's capacity to chart a course in response to the outcome of the 2010 midterm elections and to move rapidly to occupy the political center—and center stage—appeared to have been answered. Conservative political analyst Charles Krauthammer (2010) noted that "the great Republican ascendancy of 2010 lasted less than two *months*." As the president and his family flew to Hawaii to vacation over the holidays, he could take some solace in the appearance that he was back on his game. As 2011 commenced, his approval ratings had rebounded and hovered around 50 percent, his best standing with the public since early 2010. "Obama," concluded Krauthammer, "came back with a vengeance. His string of lame-duck successes is a singular political achievement. Because of it, the epic battles of the 112th Congress begin on what would have seemed impossible just one month ago—a level playing field" (Krauthammer 2010). In fact, it appeared that Obama had moved much more rapidly and purposefully to rejuvenate his presidency than either Reagan or Clinton had by the same points in their first terms. Clinton's political fortunes, it is worth recalling, had so dimmed by April 1995 that he had remarked in a press conference that "the president is still relevant here." Obama's relevance, apparent to his allies and adversaries alike, required no stating, despite massive and disciplined Republican opposition.

Reorganization of the White House Staff

Early in 2011, Obama moved to reorganize his advisory system for the second half of his term. William Daley was named as the president's new chief of staff, replacing Rahm Emanuel, who had fixed his sights on becoming mayor of Chicago; David Plouffe, co-mastermind with David Axelrod of the president's 2008 campaign, replaced Axelrod as senior adviser to the president; and Gene Sperling succeeded Lawrence Summers as director of the National Economic Council. In January 2011, Obama also signed an executive order to establish a new Council on Jobs and Competitiveness, and selected General Electric CEO Jeffrey Immelt to lead it. The significance of these moves, taken in tandem with a significant number of other staffing adjustments, was threefold:

1. The president was letting go of some members of his inner circle, from his days in Illinois politics, who had accompanied him to the presidency, a decision reflecting his willingness to trade familiar friends for proven veterans of other administrations and symbolizing his need to adjust the arc of his presidency and prepare for coming political battles.

2. The reconfiguration was designed to put in place an administrative team perceived as decidedly friendlier to business interests (Daley had served as secretary of commerce during the Clinton administration and Sperling was returning to the same job he had held in the same administration) that also indicated, along with the deal on tax cuts, that he had come to see the state of the economy, particularly growth and job creation, to be the key to his political future.

3. The 2012 primary and general election campaigns were very much on the president's mind and he was actively building his reelection apparatus in Chicago, where Axelrod relocated upon departing the White House.

Plouffe's arrival at the White House was the most notable exception to the outflow of Obama loyalists; with Axelrod in Chicago, it was no accident that the one other adviser equally responsible for Obama's rise to the presidency would be positioned inside the West Wing.

With some experts predicting that the presidential nominees of the two parties would need to raise approximately $1 billion each in 2012, it was not too early to lay the requisite groundwork.

At the same time, such changes within a White House are quite common at the midpoint of an administration.

The Events of Tucson

One of the great trials of Obama's first two years in office was the hyper-partisanship and mean-spirited incivility of American politics. America has always wrestled with anger in the form of fear- and blame-mongering, and her politics has often assumed the tone of a blood sport. The nation endured the Know-Nothing Party in the nineteenth century and has periodically suffered the antics of the Ku Klux Klan and other hate groups. At the same time, during the mid-twentieth century, such public figures as Father Charles Coughlin and Senator Joseph McCarthy (R-WI) wallowed in ugly xenophobia and jingoism. Although Obama campaigned on the theme of bringing the country together politically, a theme repeatedly discussed by him during his presidency, and the president regularly made public appeals to ratcheting down the anger in political discourse, the reality of the matter was that political discourse continued to degenerate, Republicans in Congress publicly announced their intention to oppose Obama on all fronts, and the political parties seemed incapable of agreeing on even the most basic of policy questions. Although the nation has long struggled with moments of excess passion, whereby fear replaces fact and paranoia replaces civility, the problem seemed to crystallize in January 2011.

As January progressed with the start of a new, more Republican, Congress, it seemed that the pieces were all in place for a titanic struggle between the White House and the new Republican leaders in Congress over the economic and political direction of the country. Fate then visited on the Republic a terrible reminder of the capriciousness of events. On January 8, 2011, a gunman in Tucson, Arizona, opened fire on Rep. Gabrielle Giffords (D-AZ) and several constituents who were attending a "Congress on Your Corner" meeting in a grocery store parking lot. Six citizens were killed, and Giffords, shot in the head, suffered severe brain injuries. Within forty-eight hours, the president and first lady Michelle Obama had led the country in observing a moment of silence for the victims. Two days later, the Obamas traveled to Tucson to visit hospitalized survivors of the attack and address a large crowd gathered for a memorial service at the University of Arizona. The mood in the arena was odd for a funereal occasion, with grief often taking the form of cheers and applause, in celebration of the worthy lives lost and also to let out several days of bottled-up stress from being at the epicenter of a national tragedy.

Uncertain at first in his delivery, Obama adapted quickly to the atmospherics, seeming to recapture the unifying themes that had drawn disparate voters to his banner in 2008. The president tackled the theme of civility directly:

> At a time when our discourse has become so sharply polarized—at a time when we are far too eager to lay the blame for all that ails the world at the feet of those who think differently than we do—it's important for us to pause for a moment and make sure that we are talking with each other in a way that heals, not a way that wounds.

Later in the speech, Obama added, "If this tragedy prompts reflection and debate, as it should, let's make sure it's worthy of those we have lost." Focusing near the end of his remarks on the youngest of the victims who died in the shooting, nine-year-old Christina Taylor Green, the president drove home his main point: "I want us to live up to her expectations. I want our democracy to be as good as she imagined it. All of us—we should do everything we can to make sure this country lives up to our children's expectations."

Obama clearly had risen to the occasion, providing succor and hope to a grieving nation. It was a performance some observers thought to be reminiscent of President Ronald Reagan's address to the country on January 28, 1986, when the space shuttle *Challenger* disaster took the lives of seven astronauts, and also of Reagan's remarks at a memorial service three days later. The other natural comparison was to President Bill Clinton's speech on April 23, 1995, at the memorial service for the bombing of the Alfred P. Murrah Federal Building in Oklahoma City that had killed 168 people four days earlier. Like both of those presidents, Obama reconnected with his fellow citizens and reminded them that there is within him a considerable residuum of leadership, humanity, and largeness of spirit without which it is scarcely possible to surmount the trials of the presidency. The fact that former Alaska governor Sarah Palin's remarks on the same day were widely panned as a display of vanity, petulance, and recrimination only helped to showcase Obama's exceptional grace under pressure.

The State of the Union

Obama's State of the Union speech, on January 25, 2011, took place in very different surroundings than the year before. During the 2010 address, the Democrats enjoyed robust majorities in both chambers of Congress. But, the president's remarks were overshadowed by hisses among Republican members, an exaggerated scowl from Supreme Court Justice Samuel Alito when Obama called out the high court for its decision in the case *Citizens United v. FEC* that weakened efforts to regulate campaign finance, and an outburst of "You lie!" by Rep. Joe Wilson (R-SC) while the president was explaining his agenda. However, in 2011, in a symbolic effort to showcase national unity and civility in the wake of the shooting of Rep. Giffords, many legislators from both parties volunteered to sit interspersed with one another, rather than sitting in two separate partisan groups. Obama thus told legislators near the outset, "What comes of this moment will be determined not by whether we can sit together tonight, but whether we can work together tomorrow."

The president stuck to big themes, rather than laying out a long list of bite-sized policy proposals, which had been the approach of his recent predecessors in their State of the Union addresses. Painting a picture of a U.S. economy gathering momentum, Obama framed a modest number of big proposals around the central theme of "winning the future." Saying, "This is our generation's Sputnik moment," the president beckoned Americans to focus on innovating, educating, building, reforming, and taking responsibility for the future. *Washington Post* political correspondent Dan Balz called the speech "a defense of the active use of government to prepare the country for the long-term challenge of global competitiveness, through spending on education, infrastructure, alternative energy and other projects" (Balz 2011). On the country's steadily worsening long-term fiscal imbalance and the need for deficit reduction, the president held his cards close to the vest, choosing to let his budget proposal for fiscal year 2012 provide details. All in all, it was a Reaganesque performance. The Republican Party, unable to unify its competing wings behind a single televised response, ended up offering two—the official one by Rep. Paul Ryan (R-WI) and a Tea Party response by Rep. Michele Bachman (R-MN).

A Preliminary Assessment

Obama's presidency is, in some ways, much like that of his predecessors. For instance, in a policy sense, he has continued many of the foreign policy initiatives of George W. Bush and employed both former Clinton aides and Clintonian approaches in his administration. Also, like most presidents in the modern era, Obama has "gone public" by reaching out to the American public through the media and his personal appearances and appeal, and he has continued to expand the powers of the office while relying less on his Cabinet and more on an inner circle of advisors. Such things are very much within the norm and reflect the trend in the modern era. In a macro sense, Obama has faced similar problems, relied on the same institutions, and emphasized the same ceremonial and symbolic facets of the office.

Where he has differed, however, is equally noteworthy. Obama is, of course, the first African American president. Indeed, there has been little diversity in the history of the American presidency. The presidents shared a similar demographic profile. Accordingly, like so many of his predecessors, Obama is taller than average, a Christian, and a trained lawyer who was educated at an elite university in the northeast, married "above himself" socially, and even owns a dog! But, unlike many of them, he is not of Scottish, Irish, English, or northeastern European descent and he grew up in modest means.

The Obama presidency has differed from his predecessors in the number of policy and issue czars being used. Although other presidents have designated czars as the symbolic heads of initiatives, Obama has appointed more than others to the extent that it has drawn criticism from conservatives. But, so does he face an array of challenges at home and abroad beyond what other presidents have faced.

In other appointments, Obama's presidency has differed a bit. The Obama administration is, like the administrations of Bill Clinton and George W. Bush, extremely diverse. Obama's Cabinet contained four women, four African Americans, three Asian Americans, and two Latinos. Accordingly, his may be the most diverse administration in American history. He also offered three Republicans positions in his Cabinet, but Sen. Judd Gregg (R-NH) declined the offer at the last minute, allegedly over opposition to the president's economic stimulus plan. In the transition period following his election, Obama made much progress in identifying and vetting possible appointments. Although he did get his Cabinet in place within three months, he encountered serious opposition by Republicans in trying to fill various diplomatic, judicial, and minor (boards, task forces, commissions) appointments. The Republican minority in the Senate used procedural mechanisms to prevent the president from filling many of these positions. At the midpoint of his presidency, a dismaying number of appointments remain vacant. Obama was, however, successful in getting both of his U.S. Supreme Court nominees confirmed. With the selection of Sonia Sotomayor and Elena Kagan to the bench, Obama enjoyed the distinction of appointing the first Latina to the Court and, for the first time, the Supreme Court contains three women. Moreover, both nominees were generally considered to be well-qualified, solid appointments to the Court.

Public Opinion

Like most presidents, Obama found his approval ratings dropping from the high numbers at the outset of his presidency. One unique aspect of Obama's approval is that the major polling organizations documented that the gap between the responses of Democrats and Republicans was at an all-time high, with an almost 70 percent differential between their perceptions of how Obama was doing his job. Although Democrats generally approved of the president's performance, for the first time in years a president received virtually no support from the opposition party. As a result of this bifurcation, by 2010, the president's numbers had dipped below 50 percent, where they remained for the entire year as is evident in Table 24.1.

Excessive attention was paid throughout 2010 to Obama's declining approval and the consecutive months he spent below the 50 percent mark. However, as observed in Table 24.2, when compared with other presidents in the modern era, Obama's approval numbers are relatively stable and relatively high. Only Kennedy and Eisenhower enjoyed average approval ratings higher than Obama, although Obama had only served two years at the time of this average.

Policy Record

Obama's presidency has been an active one, marked by the passage of more major pieces of legislation than any of his recent predeces-

Table 24.1. Obama's Approval Ratings

Date	Approval
May 2009	64%
Aug. 2009	56%
Oct. 2009	50%
Dec. 2009	52%
Feb. 2010	51%
April 2010	51%
June 2010	45%
Aug. 2010	46%
Oct. 2010	43%
Dec. 2010	47%
Feb. 2011	48%

Source: Gallup Poll ()

sors. Indeed, one needs to go back to the presidencies of Lyndon B. Johnson and Franklin D. Roosevelt to find a parallel. In just the first two years of his presidency, Obama could claim a number of significant successes: He signed into law a major economic stimulus; passed measures to rescue both the U.S. auto industry and financial institutions; changed the command structure and mission in the war in Afghanistan; withdrew more than 90,000

Table 24.2. Presidential Approval Ratings

President	Average	High	Low
Obama[a]	52%	69%	41%
G.W. Bush	49%	90%	25%
Clinton	55%	73%	37%
G. Bush	61%	89%	29%
Reagan	53%	68%	35%
Carter	45.5%	75%	28%
Ford	47%	71%	37%
Nixon	49%	67%	24%
Johnson	55%	79%	35%
Kennedy	70%	83%	56%
Eisenhower	65%	79%	49%
Truman	45.5%	87%	22%

[a]Obama's approval is through February 2011
Source: Gallup Poll (www.gallup.com/home.aspx)

combat troops from Iraq; developed a new Nuclear Posture Review and negotiated a nuclear nonproliferation treaty with Russia; reengaged in global climate-change talks with the international community; promoted a "Cash for Clunkers" initiative to increase auto sales; signed into law various consumer protections such as one limiting the predatory practices of credit card companies; ended restrictions on embryonic stem cell research and promoted federal support for stem cell research; passed a major health care reform act; repealed the Pentagon's "Don't Ask, Don't Tell" policy; and signed the first major food safety bill in years.

However, a number of Obama's initiatives stalled in Congress, where a very vocal, united, and committed Republican minority succeeded in delaying or defeating both the Democratic majority and president's agenda. At the same time, the president struggled to either build or retain public support for his agenda. Accordingly, although the Obama policy record can safely be said to have been historic in passing numerous major initiatives, the number of treaties, executive orders, and laws passed in his first two years are very much within the norm for recent administrations, and, in several cases, below that of his recent predecessors. This is evident in Tables 24.3 through 24.5.

President Obama used his veto power only twice in two years, which is a remarkably low figure and one that reflects both Obama's interest in working with Congress and the fact that his party was in control of both chambers of Congress. The two vetoes were of relatively minor acts. On December 30, 2009, the president used a "pocket veto" to stop an appropriations bill and in 2010 he used the same tactic to stop an interstate notarization bill, citing the need to protect consumers across state lines.

Dealing With the Anger and Misinformation

As the first president to serve during the rise of the social media as a powerful force in politics and society, Obama has both benefited from and suffered because of Facebook, YouTube, Twitter, blogging, and the Internet in general. For instance, Obama proved his mastery of the new communication technologies during the campaign, both raising record high donations online and remaining in contact with his supporters by having an active presence on multiple online platforms and sending regular text messages. The contrast between the tech-savvy Obama, with his ever-present Blackberry in hand, and John McCain who admitted that he nei-

Table 24.3. Total Public Laws Passed

President	Congress (Years)	# Bills
Obama[a]	112 (2011)	37
Obama	111 (2009–2011)	376
G.W. Bush	110 (2007–2009)	460
G.W. Bush	109 (2005–2007)	482
G.W. Bush	108 (2003–2005)	498
G.W. Bush	107 (2001–2003)	377
Clinton	106 (1999–2001)	580
Clinton	105 (1997–1999)	394
Clinton	104 (1995–1997)	333
Clinton	103 (1993–1995)	465
G. Bush	102 (1991–1993)	590
G. Bush	101 (1989–1991)	650
Reagan	100 (1987–1989)	713
Reagan	99 (1985–1987)	666
Reagan	98 (1983–1987)	623
Reagan	97 (1981–1983)	473
Carter	96 (1979–1981)	614
Carter	95 (1977–1979)	633
Ford	94 (1975–1977)	588
Nixon/Ford	93 (1973–1975)	650

[a]The number of bills in the 112th Congress is only for January and February of 2011

Source: THOMAS—U.S. Library of Congress (http://thomas.loc.gov/home/legislative data.php)

ther understood nor used "the email," could not have been sharper. Yet, ironically, the same social media as well as numerous radio programs and Fox News mounted a very successful effort to discredit the president and his policies from the moment he was sworn into office. As such, the president lost both the framing/marketing battle and control of his legislative agenda.

It is undeniable that the new social media communiqués and outlets have played a role in contributing to the hyper-partisanship and decline of civil discourse during Obama's presidency, building opposition to Obama and his agenda, and facilitating the rise of the Tea Party and other grassroots political movements. As of 2011, we are only beginning to understand and appreciate the

Table 24.4. Total Executive Orders Signed

President	Year	EOs
Obama	2011[a]	2
Obama	2010	35
Obama	2009	39
G.W. Bush	2008/2009	35
G.W. Bush	2007	32
G.W. Bush	2006	27
G.W. Bush	2005	26
G.W. Bush	2004	45
G.W. Bush	2003	41
G.W. Bush	2002	31
G.W. Bush	2001	54
Clinton	2000/2001	53
Clinton	1999	35
Clinton	1998	38
Clinton	1997	38
Clinton	1996	49
Clinton	1995	40
Clinton	1994	54
Clinton	1993	57
G. Bush	1992/1993	46
G. Bush	1991	46
G. Bush	1990	43
G. Bush	1989	31

[a]Obama's EOs in 2011 include only January and February

full magnitude of the power of the social media and the Tea Party movement remains very strong and vibrant across the country. However, one apparent result of these new political trends has been the distribution of political misinformation. In fact, entire Websites, publications, and even publishing companies have sprung up dedicated to opposing Obama and promoting viewpoints that he is a wildly dangerous and anti-American president.

For example, an alarming percentage of the American public believe that President Obama is not native born (the so-called "birther" movement) and therefore ineligible to be president, and a good deal of the political "chatter" online from 2009 to 2011 has promoted various perspectives on Obama, including that he is a Muslim; has ties to terrorists; is a socialist bent on eliminating

Table 24.5. Total Treaties Submitted to Senate

President	Congress (Years)	# Treaties
Obama	111 (2009–2011)	8
G.W. Bush	110 (2007–2009)	23
G.W. Bush	109 (2005–2007)	25
G.W. Bush	108 (2003–2005)	28
G.W. Bush	107 (2001–2003)	17
Clinton	106 (1999–2001)	49
Clinton	105 (1997–1999)	58
Clinton	104 (1995–1997)	36
Clinton	103 (1993–1995)	39
G. Bush	102 (1991–1993)	41
G. Bush	101 (1989–1991)	22
Reagan	100 (1987–1989)	22
Reagan	99 (1985–1987)	31
Reagan	98 (1983–1987)	32
Reagan	97 (1981–1983)	28
Carter	96 (1979–1981)	61
Carter	95 (1977–1979)	26
Ford	94 (1975–1977)	28
Nixon/Ford	93 (1973–1975)	37
Nixon	92 (1971–1973)	35
Nixon	91 (1969–1971)	25
Johnson	90 (1967–1969)	28

Source: THOMAS—U.S. Library of Congress (http://www.thomas.loc.gov/cgi-bin. thomas)

capitalism (and even democratic freedoms); is a secret member of the Black Panthers; is secretive in his approach to government; has accomplished little and spends an irresponsibly excessive amount of time on vacation; and that he is simply un-American (Corsi 2009, 2011; D'Souza 2010; Freddoso 2008; Goldberg 2009; Ingraham 2010; Klein 2010; Limbaugh 2010; Malkin 2010; Morris 2008; O'Leary 2008). The facts suggest otherwise.

All presidents face a bewildering array of criticisms, and not all of them are true, fair, or even within the realm of reason. Most politicians, and particularly presidents, are susceptible to charges that they are not as open and transparent as they should be or could be, and rightly so, as these are essential features of democracy. However, there is ample evidence that the Obama administration is among the most open and transparent in history. For instance, it has developed Websites listing all bills and posting all spending, including economic stimulus monies. The president also limited the number of lobbyists serving on commissions and in the White House, and posted information on the exceptions to this stated goal, promoted transparency through his electronic rule-making initiative and the Open Government Directive that released or made available record amounts of federal documents, ended the Bush-era "black-out" policy on any media coverage of war casualties, and, unlike his predecessor, listed both the full appropriations for the war in the budget and returned deceptive "off budget" programs to the annual federal budget.

A team of journalists with the *St. Petersburg Times* in Florida maintains a Pulitzer Prize-winning Website called Politifact, where they track on their "Obameter" all of Obama's campaign promises and whether or not he has kept them or broken them (PolitiFact 2011). Their research shows that, as of the end of February 2011, Obama had fulfilled 134 of his campaign promises, while another 220 campaign pledges were under way. The president attempted to forward another seventy-one initiatives promised during the campaign but they were either stalled in Congress or defeated by Republican opposition, and he compromised on forty-one of his promises, fulfilling at least part of the campaign pledge. Obama did, however, fail to keep thirty-eight campaign promises. It is always potentially problematic when politicians do not fulfill basic campaign pledges. The broken promises include some minor issues barely mentioned during the 2008 campaign such as doubling the size of the Peace Corps and organizing an international group to deal with Iraqi refugees, but also include major pledges such as repealing George W. Bush's tax cuts for the wealthiest Americans and increasing the capital gains tax. Yet, taken as a whole, these numbers are remarkably positive and very few presidents in history could claim such a record, especially at midpoint in their term.

Finally, this has also been a hard-working president, one engaged in the details of his presidency and conversant on the wide array of issues facing him. In his first year alone, the president gave a staggering 411 public speeches, comments, and remarks. In terms of openness, Obama gave 42 news conferences (twice the number of George W. Bush), 158 interviews (90 of which were televised), and 23 town hall meetings. Such numbers dwarf those of Obama's predecessors. The president visited 58 cities in 30 states, made 10 foreign trips to 21 countries, and had 74 meetings with world leaders. As such, Obama made more trips abroad and in his first year in office than any president in history. In terms of meeting with world leaders and traveling across the country, President George W. Bush tops the list, with Obama a close second. Obama also spent a record low number of days vacationing, just 26 days in his first year (in his first year in office, George W. Bush spent fully 69 days just at his Crawford ranch). He also made only 11 visits to Camp David, totaling 27 days, compared with 26 visits and 81 days by his predecessor (Knoller 2010).

Conclusion

Barack Obama may fail in his bid to win a second term, or he may secure one handily. At the end of February 2011, either outcome seemed entirely plausible. There was, however, a growing sense that all that had happened between the 2010 midterm elections and the president's 2011 State of the Union speech had set the stage for a major confrontation between Obama and the Republican leaders in Congress—and that this clash would determine the president's fortunes. Obama had been dealt a stinging defeat in the midterm elections, probably due in equal measure to the state of the economy, and the fact that large partisan majorities that undertake great initiatives (as the Democrats did on health care) inevitably provoke a backlash. So too did the president's own judgments about the sequencing of his agenda coupled with his own limits at and even inattention to forging a deeper bond with the citizenry factor into this equation. Yet, at crucial junctures, Obama accommodated himself quite quickly to new, painful realities and sought, insofar as possible, to set the scene in which the contest for a second term and his agenda would take place. That he was able to do so is far from a guarantee of success, but it is no small achievement and it speaks of a skill set superior to that of many presidents and presidential aspirants. Likewise, the president fulfilled promises to end combat operations in Iraq and, in 2011 began the end of the conflict in Afghanistan; and his shift from the Bush years to counter-terrorism and the hunt for al-Qaeda helped eliminate America's number one enemy, Osama bin-Laden.

The essence of presidential leadership may reside in determining precisely how, when, and how rapidly to respond to events. "I claim not to have controlled events," wrote Abraham Lincoln in his famous letter to Albert G. Hodges in the spring of 1864, when the outcome of the Civil War, like Lincoln's political future, was far from certain, "but confess plainly that events have controlled me." It is an elegant sentence that just a handful of people have come to understand fully—only after taking the presidential oath of office. Surely this notion has even greater meaning for Obama at the midpoint of his presidency than it did, just a few months ago, prior to a short span packed densely with events that no one could have foreseen altogether.

Works Cited

Balz, Dan. "Obama challenges the nation—and Republicans." *The Washington Post* (25 Jan. 2011).

Corsi, Jerome R. *The Obama Nation: Leftist Politics and the Cult of Personality*. New York: Pocket Star, 2009.

———. *Where's the Birth Certificate? The Case that Barack Obama is Not Eligible to be President*. WND Books (Online WNDbooks.com), 2011.

D'Souza, Dinesh. *The Roots of Obama's Rage*. Washington, DC: Regnery, 2010.

Freddoso, David. *The Case against Barack Obama: The Unlikely Rise and Unexamined Agenda of the Media's Favorite Candidate*. Washington, DC: Regnery, 2008.

Goldberg, Bernard. *A Slobbering Affair: The Love (and Pathetic) Story of the Torrid Romance between Barack Obama and the Mainstream Media*. Washington, DC: Regnery, 2009.

Ingraham, Laura. *The Obama Diaries*. New York: Threshold, 2010.

Klein, Aaron. *The Manchurian President: Barack Obama's Ties to Communists, Socialists, and other Anti-American Extremists*. WND Books (Online WNDbooks.com), 2010.

Knoller, Mark. "Obama's first year: By the numbers." *CBS News* (20 Jan. 2010). http://www.cbsnews.com/8301-503544_162-6119525-503 544.html.

Krauthammer, Charles. "Obama's new start." *The Washington Post* (23 Dec. 2010).

Limbaugh, David. *Crimes against Liberty: An Indictment of President Obama*. Washington, DC: Regnery, 2010.

Malkin, Michelle. *Culture of Corruption: Obama and His Team of Tax Cheats, Crooks, and Cronies*. Washington, DC: Regnery, 2010.

Morris. Dick. *Fleeced*. New York: Harper, 2008.

O'Leary, Brad. *The Audacity of Deceit: Barack Obama's War on American Values*. WND Books (Online WNDbooks.com), 2008.

PolitiFact. http://politifact.com.

Appendix A

Barack Obama Biography

Born: Honolulu, Hawaii (August 4, 1961)

Home: Chicago, Illinois

Marriage: To Michelle Robinson (October 3, 1992)

Children: Malia (b. 1998), Sasha (b. 2001)

Religion: United Church of Christ

Education: Attended Occidental College (1979–1981); BA, Political Science from Columbia University (1983); JD from Harvard Law School (1991)

Books: *Dreams from My Father: A Story of Race and Inheritance* (Times Books, 1995); *The Audacity of Hope: Thoughts on Reclaiming the American Dream* (Crown, 2006); *Of Thee I sing: A Letter to My Daughters* (Random House, 2010)

Career: Financial Consultant in New York City (1983–1985); Community Organizer in Chicago (1985–1988); Lawyer with Miner, Barnhill & Galland Law Firm in Chicago (1991–1995); Senior Lecturer, University of Chicago Law School (1992–1995)

Political Office: Illinois State Senate (1997–2005); U.S. Senate (2005–2008), member of the Health, Education, Labor and Pensions Committee; Foreign Relations Committee; Veterans Affairs Committee; and Environment and Public Works Committee

Appendix B

The Obama Administration

Cabinet

Attorney General—Eric H. Holder, Jr.

Secretary of Agriculture—Thomas J. Vilsack

Secretary of Commerce—Gary F. Locke; Rebecca M. Blank

Secretary of Defense—Robert M. Gates; Leon Panetta

Secretary of Education—Arne Duncan

Secretary of Energy—Steven Chu

Secretary of Health and Human Services—Kathleen Sebelius

Secretary of Homeland Security—Janet A. Napolitano

Secretary of Housing and Urban Development—Shaun L.S. Donovan

Secretary of Interior—Kenneth L. Salazar

Secretary of Labor—Hilda L. Solis

Secretary of State—Hillary Rodham Clinton

Secretary of Transportation—Ray LaHood

Secretary of Treasury—Timothy F. Geithner

Secretary of Veterans Affairs—Eric K. Shinseki

Executive Office of the President/Senior Staff

Chief of Central Intelligence—Leon Panetta; David Patraeus

Chief of Staff—Rahm Emanuel; Bill Daley

Council of Economic Advisors Chair—Christina D. Romer; Austan Goolsbee

Counsel—Greg Craig; Peter Rouse

Director of National Intelligence—Dennis Blair

Environmental Protection Agency Administrator—Lisa P. Jackson

National Economic Council Director—Lawrence H. Summers; Gene Sperling

National Security Advisor—James L. Jones; Thomas E, Donilon

Office of Management and Budget Director—Peter Orszag; Jacob J. Lew

Press Secretary—Robert Gibbs; Jay Carney

Senior Advisor—David Axelrod; David Plouffe

Senior Advisor—Valerie Jarrett

Solicitor General—Elena Kagan; Donald Verrilli Jr.

U.S. Ambassador to the United Nations—Susan Rice

U.S. Trade Representative—Ronald Kirk

Contributors

Douglas M. Brattebo *(PhD, University of Maryland; JD, George-town University)* is director of the Center for Engaged Ethics at Hiram College in Ohio. The center guides an across-the-college effort that brings the insights of a liberal education to bear on ethical concerns through awareness, reflection, and action. Brattebo teaches courses on ethics in foreign policy, Abraham Lincoln, the presidency, and citizenship. Brattebo's current research and teaching interests reside at the nexus of ethical leadership, civic education, globalization, and the preservation of the planet. He is currently working on the book *Presidential Ethics.*

Jack Covarrubias *(PhD, Old Dominion University)* is assistant professor of political science at the University of Southern Mississippi, Gulf Coast. He is also a member of the governing board of the National Social Science Association and co-editor of the journal *White House Studies,* and served previously in the U.S. Navy. His research interests include security studies, American foreign policy, and international development. He has published numerous books, chapters, and articles including, most recently *To Protect and Defend: Homeland Security Policy* (Ashgate), *Strategic Interests in the Middle East: Opposition and Support for U.S. Foreign Policy* (Ashgate), *America's War on Terrorism,* 2nd edition (Ashgate), and *Fostering Community Resilience: Homeland Security and Hurricane Katrina* (Ashgate).

Leonard Cutler *(PhD, New School of Social Research)* is professor of public law, chair of the Department of Political Science, and director of the Center for the Study of Government and Politics at Siena College in Loudonville, New York. Cutler also is on the board of the law school at the University of Albany. His areas of expertise include criminal law and procedure, constitutional law, and international law. His research has appeared in edited volumes and journals and he has authored several books including, most recently, *The Rule of Law and Law of War* (Edwin Mellen) and *Developments in National Security Policy of the United States—Post 9/11* (Edwin Mellen). Cutler has provided testimony to the Judiciary Committee of the U.S. Senate on "Restoring the Rule of Law" and the president's Interagency Task Force on Detainee Disposition on issues related to war powers, National Security Agency surveillance, and executive privilege.

Graham G. Dodds (*PhD, University of Pennsylvania*) is assistant professor of political science at Concordia University in Montreal, Canada. He previously served as research fellow at the Brookings Institution and as legislative assistant for the U.S. House of Representatives. Dodds teaches courses on American politics and political leadership and his main research interests include the presidency, American political development, and governmental apologies.

Byron W. Daynes (*PhD, University of Chicago*) is professor of political science at Brigham Young University and William J. Clinton Distinguished Fellow of the Clinton School of Public Service. His more than sixty articles and book reviews in the field of political science have appeared in such journals as *Women & Politics*, *Congress and the Presidency*, *Presidential Studies Quarterly*, and *The American Political Science Review*. He is also co-author and/or co-editor of fifteen books on American government, the presidency, and social policy, the latest of which are *White House Politics and the Environment: Franklin D. Roosevelt to George W. Bush* (Texas A&M University Press) (with Glen Sussman) and *Moral Controversies in American Politics* (M.E. Sharpe) (with Raymond Tatalovich).

Louis Fisher (*PhD, New School for Social Research*) was for four decades senior specialist with the Library of Congress, Congressional Research Service, and The Law Library. In 1987 he was research director for the House Iran-Contra Committee. Fisher has been invited to testify before Congress approximately fifty times on such topics as National Security Agency surveillance, executive spending discretion, the veto, executive privilege, whistle blowing, recess appointments, the budget process, and balanced budget amendment. He is the author of twenty books, including the forthcoming *Congress and the Constitution: A Staffer's Four Decades* (University Press of Kansas). Fisher is the recipient of the Aaron Wildavsky Award For Lifetime Scholarly Achievement from the Association for Budgeting and Financial Management and his 2006 book, *Military Tribunals and Presidential Power: American Revolution to the War on Terror* (University Press of Kansas), won the Neustadt Book Award from the American Political Science Association.

Matthew N. Green (*PhD, Yale University*) is assistant professor of politics at The Catholic University of America in Washington, DC. He served previously as research fellow at the Brookings Institution and legislative aide in the U.S. House of Representatives. He is author of *The Speaker of the House: A Study of Leadership* (Yale University Press) and has published articles in a number of journals, including *American Politics Research*, *Electoral Studies*, *Legislative Studies Quarterly*, and *Political Research Quarterly*.

Michael K. Gusmano (*PhD, University of Maryland*) is research scholar at The Hastings Center. Prior to joining The Hastings Center, Gusman was a postdoctoral fellow in the Robert Wood Johnson Foundation Scholars in Health Policy Program at Yale University and assistant professor of health policy and management at Columbia University. His research interests include the politics of health care reform, health and health care inequalities, and normative theories of policy analysis. His publications include the book *Healthy Voices / Unhealthy Silence: Advocating for Poor People's Health* (Georgetown University Press) and his most recent book (with Victor Rodwin and Daniel Weisz) is *Health Care in World Cities: New York, Paris, and London* (Johns Hopkins University Press).

R. Ward Holder (*PhD, Boston College*) is associate professor of theology at Saint Anselm College. He has authored the books *John Calvin and the Grounding of Biblical Interpretation: Calvin's First Commentaries* (Leiden University Press) and *Crisis and Revival: The Era of the Reformations* (University of Louisville Press), and edited the books *Reformation Readings of Romans* (Edinburgh University Press) (with Kathy Ehrensperger) and *A Companion to Paul in the Reformation* (Leiden University Press). His current research concentrates on the ways that theological doctrines and images inform both campaigns and governing.

De-Yuan Kao is a PhD candidate in the Department of Political Science at Boston University. He is also a visiting fellow in the Institute of European and American Studies at Academia Sinica in Taiwan. His research interests include U.S.–China–Taiwan relations, foreign policy, humanitarian intervention, and international regimes. His recent article "Change and Continuity in U.S. China Policy after the Cold War" was published in the book *Thirty Years of China–U.S. Relations: Analytical Approaches and Contemporary Issues.*

Tom Lansford (*PhD, Old Dominion University*) is academic dean of the Gulf Coast Campus and professor of political science at the University of Southern Mississippi. Lansford is a member of the governing board of the National Social Science Association and is co-editor of the journal *White House Studies.* He has articles in such journals as *Defense Analysis, The Journal of Conflict Studies, European Security, International Studies, Security Dialogue,* and *Strategic Studies.* He is also the author, co-author, or editor of thirty-one books and one-hundred essays, book chapters, and reviews.

Marie des Neiges Léonard (*PhD, Texas A & M University*) is assistant professor of sociology at The University of Southern Mississippi. She teaches courses on gender, race relations, family, and sociology. Her primary areas of research include social movements, transnational movements, and race relations. Léonard's recent research explores discourse on anti-globalization with a particular focus on French movement "ATTAC," as well as the more violent aspects of the anti-globalization protests, and ethnic riots and race relations in France.

Julie A. Lester (*PhD, Purdue University*) is assistant professor of political science at Macon State College. She teaches courses in American government, state and local government, and global issues. Her research interests include food and agricultural policymaking, the use of narratives in the policymaking process, and legislative behavior.

Casey Maugh (*PhD, Pennsylvania State University*) is assistant professor of communication studies at The University of Southern Mississippi (USM) and Director of the USM Gulf Coast Speaking and Writing Center. She served previously as a Peace Corps volunteer. Maugh's research interests include visual rhetoric, cultural studies, rhetorical theory and criticism, political communication, and public memory studies.

Robert J. Pauly (*PhD, Old Dominion University*) is associate professor of international policy and development at The University of Southern Mississippi. His research interests include U.S. foreign policy toward the states of Europe and the Greater Middle East, Islam in Europe, and the evolving relationships between the Islamic and Western worlds. He has authored five books including, most recently, *The Ashgate Research Companion to U.S. Foreign Policy* (Ashgate).

William D. Pederson (*PhD, University of Oregon*) is professor of political science, American Studies chair, and director of the International Lincoln Center at Louisiana State University in Shreveport. He is the author or editor of thirty books in American politics and the presidency, most recently, *James Madison: Philosopher, Founder, and Statesman* (Ohio University Press), *Lincoln Lessons* (Southern Illinois University Press), *Abraham Lincoln Without Borders: Lincoln's Legacy Outside the United States* (Pencraft International), and *Lincoln's Enduring Legacy: Perspectives from Great Leaders, Great Thinkers, and the American Experiment* (Lexington) (with Robert P. Watson and Frank J. Williams).

Brian Richard (*PhD, University of Southern Mississippi*) is assistant professor in the Department of Economic and Workforce Development at the University of Southern Mississippi. Richard's research and work in the community is in economics, fiscal policy, and public policy, including the casino industry, impact of economic development projects, and the economic impact of the Gulf oil spill. He studied finance at the University of Washington and earned a master's in economics from Clemson University, and taught economics at Millsaps College.

Sean J. Savage (*PhD, Boston College*) is professor of political science at Saint Mary's College in Notre Dame, Indiana. He was previously a Thomas P. "Tip" O'Neill Fellow and won the Emerging Scholar Award from the American Political Science Association. His main research interests are on political parties and the American presidency. Savage is the author of numerous articles and book reviews as well as the books *Roosevelt: The Party Leader,*

1932–1945 (University Press of Kentucky), *Truman and the Democratic Party* (University Press of Kentucky), and *JFK, LBJ, and the Democratic Party* (SUNY Press).

Max Skidmore (*PhD, University of Minnesota*) is University of Missouri Curators' professor of political science and Thomas Jefferson fellow at the University of Missouri-Kansas City. He has been Distinguished Fulbright Lecturer in India and Senior Fulbright Scholar at the University of Hong Kong. Skidmore has published extensively on a number of topics, including the presidency and is the editor of *Poverty and Public Policy: A Global Journal of Social Security, Income, Aid, and Welfare* (Policy Studies Organization). Among his numerous books are *Presidential Performance: A Comprehensive Review* (McFarland) and *After the White House: Former Presidents as Private Citizens* (Palgrave Macmillan). His most recent book is *Securing America's Future: A Bold Plan to Preserve and Expand Social Security* (Rowman & Littlefield).

Steven Stuglin is a PhD student in public communication at Georgia State University. His research focuses on the intersection of public policy, political rhetoric, and corporate management.

Glen Sussman (*PhD, Washington State University*) is university professor of political science at Old Dominion University. His primary research and teaching interests include environmental politics and policy, the American presidency, and political behavior. Sussman has published numerous articles, chapters, and books, including, most recently, *White House Politics and the Environment: Franklin D. Roosevelt to George W. Bush* (Texas A&M University Press) (with Byron W. Daynes) and is currently working on the book *The Politics of Global Climate Change in the United States* (Lynne Rienner).

Justin S. Vaughn (*PhD, Texas A & M University*) is assistant professor of political science at Cleveland State University. His areas of interest are the administrative presidency, presidential rhetoric, and the relations between popular culture and elite politics. He has authored several articles on the presidency that have been published in such journals as *Presidential Studies Quarterly, Political Research Quarterly, Administration & Society, The International Journal of Public Administration, White House Studies,* and *Review of Policy Research*. He is currently writing books on the rise of presidential policy czars (with José D. Villalobos) and the rhetoric of Barack Obama.

José D. Villalobos *(PhD, Texas A & M University)* is assistant professor of political science at the University of Texas at El Paso. His areas of interest are presidential management, presidential-bureaucratic policy making, and the public presidency. His publications include articles in *Presidential Studies Quarterly, Political Research Quarterly, Administration & Society, Race, Gender & Class, International Journal of Public Opinion Research, International Journal of Public Administration, International Journal of Conflict Management,* and *Review of Policy Research,* and he is working on a book on the rise of presidential policy czars (with Justin S. Vaughn).

Robert P. Watson *(PhD, Florida Atlantic University)* is professor and director of American Studies at Lynn University in Florida. He has published more than 150 articles, chapters, and essays on the presidency and topics in American politics and history, and authored, edited, or co-edited thirty-two books, including *The Presidents' Wives* (Lynne Rienner), *Public Administration* (Longman), *Anticipating Madam President* (Lynne Rienner), *The Roads to Congress* (Lexington), and *Life in the White House* (SUNY Press). A political commentator who has been interviewed by hundreds of print, radio, and television outlets around the country and internationally, Watson also serves as the analyst for NBC and PBS affiliates and two talk radio stations in Florida, and writes a column for the *Sun-Sentinel* newspaper. He regularly convenes community town halls, voter registration drives, and civic education programs, and cofounded two think tanks in Florida dedicated to civic education and political reform.

Matthew A. Williams *(MA, University of Southern Mississippi)* is research associate and adjunct instructor with the Center for Policy and Resilience at the University of Southern Mississippi. His research interests and grant work cover international security issues, the American presidency, and community resilience to natural and manmade disasters. Williams regularly presents at conferences and has several publication including, most recently, the chapter "Rebalancing America's War on Terror" in the book *America's War on Terror* (Ashgate), edited by Tom Lansford, Robert P. Watson, and Jack Covarrubias.

Richard M. Yon is a PhD candidate at the University of Florida and instructor of American Politics, Policy, and Strategy at the United States Military Academy at West Point. His areas of interest are the American presidency, vice presidency, Congress, and international relations. Yon has written or co-authored several book chapters, journal articles, and book reviews, and presented papers at several conferences. He is co-editor of the encyclopedia *American Presidents* (Salem Press) (with Robert P. Watson).

Index

431